PROMISELAND

PROMISELAND

A Century of Life in a Negro Community

Elizabeth Rauh Bethel

Temple University Press • Philadelphia

Temple University Press

© 1981 by Temple University. All rights reserved

✓Published 1981

Printed in the United States of America

Library of Congress Cataloging in Publication Data

Bethel, Elizabeth Rauh.
Promiseland, a century of life in a Negro community.

Bibliography: p.
Includes index.
1. Afro-Americans—South Carolina—Promised Land—
History.   2. Promised Land, S. C.—History. I. Title.
F279.P66B47   975.7'33   80-27732
ISBN 0-87722-211-8

What a fellowship
What a joy divine,
Leaning on the everlasting arms.

Contents

Tables

Preface

I first became aware of Promised Land in 1974, soon after I joined the faculty of Lander College in Greenwood, South Carolina, when Rev. Bernard White, then an eighteen-year-old college freshman, completed a standard assignment for all students enrolled in my Introduction to Sociology section, a comparison of his "home town" to the Twin Oaks commune in Louisa, Virginia. Bernard White lived at Promised Land. The essay was intriguing, but I was a new assistant professor with little time to pursue the tidbits White offered me in that paper. Over the next three years I met more young students from Promised Land as they passed through my classes. They were bright, diligent, serious, and conscientious—model students—and through them I gradually learned more about the community and its ethos.

During the Summer of 1977 I participated in a National Endowment for the Humanities Summer Seminar for College Teachers under the direction of Joan W. Scott, then at the University of North Carolina at Chapel Hill. The topic was the history of the family as social history. With no historical training but a sociologically oriented interest in the topic, I approached the summer with some trepidation. My fears and doubts were quickly dispelled by both Scott and my summer colleagues. They guided and coaxed me through the material, and I, in turn, found social history to be an exhilarating intellectual enterprise. Additionally, I realized that it provided both the theoretical and methodological frameworks for a study of Promised Land. I abandoned a tidily formulated research project and replaced it with a new task, the development of a research design for a social history of Promised Land. From the onset of that decision through completion of this manuscript, I have enjoyed Joan Scott's criticism, enthusiasm, wisdom, advice and friendship.

I returned to Lander College and my teaching responsibilities at the end of the summer, and between classes and on weekends I talked with anyone from Promised Land who was willing to talk. Those early interviews were relatively unstructured, designed primarily to establish the necessary rapport between a white researcher and a Negro community that would ground my work for the next two years. Peggy Evans, a former student and a lifetime resident of Promised Land, agreed to introduce me to a few of the older men and women in the community. Among the people I first met that fall was George L. Wilson, a man who would become a major contributor to this project. Wilson, the grandson of old Josh Wilson, the *ad hoc* sheriff of Promised Land in the 1880's, knows almost everyone who lives there or has lived there. He is an inveterate recordkeeper and during the course of my research attained the informal status of community archivist. As I won his trust George Wilson gradually shared many of his records with me and led me to other "old heads" at Promised Land, among them Lettie Richie Moragne, his first cousin, and Balus Glover, a childhood schoolmate. Through their memories I first came to know some of the original community settlers: the Moragne family, the most extensive kinship group at Promised Land; the Widemans; the Richies; the Redds; the Wilsons; and the Marshalls.

George Wilson sent me down the road from Promised Land to Verdery to talk with Joe T. Ligon, Jr., and his mother, Lucille Devlin Ligon, white people whose family had been involved with the community in various ways for as long as anybody at Promised Land could remember. The Ligons, in turn, introduced me to other community residents, and very quickly a network of relationships emerged. By October 1977 I was sitting in Elese Morton Smith's living room at Promised Land looking at old picture albums and scrapbooks, which she found in her garage. Mrs. Smith asked me that first day we met if I intended to write a book about Promised Land. I told her that, if I could gather enough information to warrant a book, I would certainly try to write it. From that moment Mrs. Smith committed herself to the project, and over the next two years she donated many hours of her time and energy to the research. Her style is epitomized in a conversation I taped in November 1977. The two of us were visiting with her sister, Benetta Morton Williams. By that time my interviews had become more focused; and our intention that day was to talk with her sister about Lizzie Chiles, the school teacher at Promised Land from 1898 to 1954. Mrs. Williams viewed me with some suspicion and asked rather bluntly, "What *exactly*, is you trying to do?" I hesitated, taken aback by the question and not yet willing to publicly admit that a book was in the making. Elese Smith was less timid than I and told her sister rather firmly that I was "trying to make a book" and had to have something to put in it. Emphatically, she issued an order: "Now you start talking!"

As my interviewing proceeded I was gradually included in various community activities, and eventually I was invited to church. Although I had taken the methodologically proper step for a community study such as this and established my credibility with the pastor of the A.M.E. church and even with the South Carolina African Methodist Episcopal (A.M.E.) bishop, those contacts did little to further my credibility at Promised Land. The extent of this failure was made painfully clear when my son Charlie and I dressed up one Sunday and attended services at Mt. Zion. Our blonde hair and fair skin set us well apart from everyone else in church, and our separateness was further emphasized as we sat alone in our pew. The experience was a galling encounter with Jim Crow in reverse. Week after week we attended church and occupied a pew by ourselves, even though the church was crowded and others would have been more comfortable had they taken a seat beside us. That period of research taught both of us a valuable lesson in humility rarely accorded white people by black people; without it I would never have understood the pride, the dignity, and the stubborn obstinance of the people at Promised Land.

Great progress is measured in small events. One Sunday people sat down beside us in the pew and the preacher stopped introducing us as guests. However tentatively, we were accepted; and that acceptance was the essential, but heretofore missing, ingredient of my research. Materials within the community magically appeared. Church records, family pictures, and even memories were recovered. Sunday School minutes, the records of the Little River Association, and membership lists and financial transactions of the community's burial aid society, lost for decades, were produced from dresser drawers and beneath beds. Some I took into town and xeroxed; others, the older and more valuable, I photographed one afternoon on George Wilson's porch while he held the pages for me. There had been some doubt as to whether or not I would be able to locate sufficient primary material to historically reconstitute Promised Land; but by Christmas my file cabinet, desk, and bookshelves were littered with Promised Land memorabelia.

The interviews continued; and in the spring 1978 one of my Promised Land students, Bettie Hill, needed a research project. I handed her a tape recorder and told her what I had learned about her home, beginning with the drama of its establishment in 1870. Armed with this new perspective on her home, Hill began a study of racism that led both of us to John and Cora Hall. Eventually I learned about cotton farming from Mr. Hall, as he explained patiently the all too common procedures by which "the white man robbed the nigger." From Mrs. Hall, who initially had no desire "to talk to no white school teacher" but who did so with great courtesy, I gleaned some of the most insightful information in this manuscript.

After Bettie Hill completed her class project she and I interviewed together for a time; and she, along with Elese Smith, opened doors in the community that probably would have been otherwise closed to me. The interviews assumed a more serious nature now, for the "old heads" were willing to tell me about the Klan, the beatings and the terror of being Negro in the rural South. Cora Hall was the first to take this risky step toward truth.

A grant from the South Carolina Committee for the Humanities funded a series of community meetings during the summer of 1978. Elestine Smith Norman and Peggy Evans worked with me on the project, as did my son Charlie, who served as my audio engineer. We taped the meetings, which were held at the churches, where I shared with everyone who came what I was learning about Promised Land. As I revealed my areas of knowledge, community residents told me new things, corrected misinformation and misinterpretations, and gave me more clues about the internal structure of their community. This was an important period methodologically because it established a precedent that has continued through the final draft of this manuscript. The community has monitored and reviewed my work at every stage. They have thoughtfully considered the manuscript, page by tiresome page and draft by draft. We have argued and debated points of interpretation along the way and have eventually resolved our disagreements. The college students read to the old heads, who left school while they were still children to work in the cotton fields; they will, I hope, read this same material one day to their grandchildren.

The culmination of the summer project was a community-wide program appropriately called a "turn-out" in the Promised Land tradition. One Sunday evening in late July hundreds of us packed into Mt. Zion and listened to speeches, essays, and orations on the topics that have occupied Promised Land residents for a century: the meaning of success, the importance of education, true womanhood, and true manhood. We sang some of the old songs and a lot of the new ones. Babies fell asleep on the pews, and a few of the old folks nodded a bit, but we were all still at Mt. Zion singing and enjoying a mutual exploration of the past until 10:30 that night.

The August homecomings and revivals began with a dizzying round of events. I met new people by the dozens as cars from New York and Philadelphia, Baltimore, Washington, and Chicago poured into Promised Land. I attended revival at Mt. Zion, Crossroads, and Jacob's Chapel and at every turn was introduced to more people home for revival week. I met Theresa and Isaac Moragne, who live in New York; Vernice Price Campbell and Elnora Marshall Williams, who live in Baltimore; and James Evert Turner, who lives in Chicago. More than a year later I would meet with them all again in their homes.

In the fall of 1978, supported by a Rockefeller Humanities Fellowship, I took a leave of absence from my teaching and began a new stage of research, combing the South Carolina Department of Archives and History and the Greenwood and Abbeville County courthouses. My mother, Esther Rauh, a recently retired office manager, came for a visit and found herself coopted into transcribing tax records. The janitorial staff at the Greenwood County Courthouse helped me salvage the old tax assessor's records destined for the county dump, provided a work space in the basement, and shared their morning pot of coffee with me. Land deeds, tax records, probate files, and school records all began to complete the picture of Promised Land shaped by the interviews. By winter I had extracted the bulk of the formal information that existed on the community and the people who created it. Still, Promised Land is an appealing place; and, although my data were gathered, I found myself sitting on George Wilson's front porch every few days, talking about the weather, the hogs, and anything else which would extend my stay. I had begun to feel that complex set of emotions which Isaac Moragne later described to me as "the mystique of Promised Land." It was time to leave or the book would not be written. In January 1979 I moved to Durham, North Carolina, and settled down to sort out the material and notes, which filled a file cabinet and several boxes. Elestine Norman became my community contact; we talked often by telephone, sometimes just to gossip and other times to conduct business. She asked this or that question for me to fill in missing pieces of information. I maintained a correspondence with Elese Smith and George Wilson, now my friends as well as my informants.

A research grant from The National Endowment for the Humanities extended the project for a second year and allowed me to travel north during the fall of 1979 and interview those who had left Promised Land to become the urban transplants and products of the Great Migration. I asked Elese Smith to go with me on these trips. Her interviewing skills were as well tuned as mine, and our team efforts had proven themselves during the previous year. She took her first airplane ride when we went to New York, and I have never been so impressed with the descent over Manhattan as I was the day I shared that experience with her. In New York Isaac and Theresa Moragne were our hosts, graciously escorting, introducing, and otherwise assisting us. I traveled alone to Chicago, armed with introductions by George Wilson to his kinsmen and assisted when I arrived by James Turner and Rosalie Wilson Williams. Elese Smith joined me for a third trip, this time to the Baltimore-Washington area; and there we renewed the acquaintance I had made the year before with Vernice Price Campbell and Elnora Marshall Williams, who in turn led us to the other Promised Landers.

As I worked through the winter of 1979 I realized that the most important data I had were, not the statistical and quantified descriptions of tax records, household structures, and demographic trends, but the interviews. I transcribed one tape after another and eventually realized that these were the core of Promised Land's history and that the collective story they told must stand forth in a bold relief, supported and supplemented by the other data.

Two methodological problems accompanied this concentrated use of the oral histories and interviews, validity and reliability. Unless both were firmly established, Promised Land's history would be little more than an interesting footnote. First I cross-referenced information from the individual interviews, establishing internal consistency among community residents on those points and issues that they, themselves, chose to emphasize. This procedure formed the equivalent of internal reliability and established a basic, community-wide perspective that described and interpreted strategic events and social processes from the vantage point of the people who lived at Promised Land. I then validated this perspective by comparing it to the more objective and empirical data extracted from the manuscript census tracts and tax, school, land transfer, and probate records. The convergence established the methodological equivalent of validity. Those portions of the interview-acquired data that did not meet tests for both reliability and validity were not used. It is to the credit of the many people who "talked to the tape recorder" that only three hours of interviews were rendered useless by the procedure.

These data taken alone do not lend themselves to generalization in an orthodox sense. Although sampling procedures followed the rules of random selection whenever possible, those who exploit historical material are rarely fortunate enough to sample from a complete universe. The early years of community life, the development of churches and schools, are described as idiosyncratic events, although there is little doubt that the conditions which led to the formation of the original institutional structures at Promised Land were representative of the nineteenth-century Afro-American experience in the rural South. When equivalent data were available for comparison to a larger population, I have so noted.

This manuscript has been read and critically evaluated by many people. Joan W. Scott and Herbert G. Gutman have constantly guided and criticized my efforts. Joan Scott recognized the potential of this study in its most embryonic form, and I have drawn on her vision often. Herbert Gutman's assistance came in many forms. His *Black Family in Slavery and in Freedom* heavily influenced my own work. His assistance has been sweeping, and I gratefully acknowledge its many facets. Ira Berlin posed a series of challenges as I formulated the research that vastly improved the questions and issues I pursued. Nell Irvin Painter helped me place the people of Promised Land within the broader context of Afro-American history. She was consistently generous with her scholarly expertise, and as we talked through many aspects of this book she became a close friend as well as a valued colleague. Donald M. Scott directed me to literature I would otherwise have neglected. Joel Williamson found time in his crowded end-of-term schedule to read and critique the completed manuscript. All of them were incredibly patient and gentle with my lack of formal training in the craft of history. My debt to the people of Promised Land is beyond measure. Only in retrospect do I fully recognize the effort they extended in opening their homes and their memories to my probes. Charlie Bethel grew from a child to a young man during the course of this research, and his involvement in my work has added to that growth valuable lessons in humanism. He was my principle research assistant, faithfully mapping cemeteries, helping with interviews, coding data, and verifying bibliography—the thankless tasks which too often go unnoted. Bessie Ruth Eaddy and Ellen Furlough, in quite different ways, provided the private and invisible encouragement essential to the writing of this book.

PROMISELAND

Introduction

At the Eastern edge of that part of the South known as the "Black Belt" or the "Cotton Belt" the land is exhausted from three centuries of intensive cotton cultivation. The region today is primarily a rural area, as it was a century ago, although the land now has little to offer people who live there. Pulpwood and textiles have replaced cotton as the region's major industry. The population, black and white alike, is rural working class. A generation ago their parents and grandparents were small farmers and sharecroppers. Here, in the South Carolina Piedmont, about mid-way between Charleston and Atlanta, lies Promised Land.

A state highway bisects the little community of about a thousand people. All of Promised Land that can be seen from this road is easily described. There is a church, a general store, and a building that was a few years ago the community school, closed when the county finally integrated its schools. White parents simply refused to send their children to the formerly all-Negro school in a Negro community. Today the building houses a Headstart program and serves the people at Promised Land as a community hall for family dinners, wedding receptions, and the meeting place for the volunteer fire department.

Houses are scattered along the highway for less than a mile. Some, close to a century old, are little more than shanties; others are respectable middle-class new brick homes. The contrast between old and new is vivid because the houses are frequently adjacent to each other, and neighbors also form extensive intergenerational kin groups. On weekend afternoons in good weather there is usually a baseball game in progress on the sandlot field beside the school. Attendance is high and not limited to local residents. For two generations the men at Promised Land have pitted their baseball team against other Negro teams in the region. Today competition blends easily with long-standing friendships.

At each end of the community there are redwood signs surrounded by tidy and well-tended flower beds advising drivers that they are entering and leaving the Promised Land community. Beyond the signs, back from the highway, and between the clusters of houses are huge gardens, some several acres in size. The cotton fields which dominated the community half a century ago are gone, replaced by stands of pine trees, which some landowners sell to the local pulp-wood yard. Further back from the road, not visible to the casual passer-by, are another church, more houses, and several small stores. The posted speed limit on the asphalt streets in these back areas is a modest thirty-five miles per hour, with good reason. Promised Land is a growing community, and there are many small children who play there.

With one notable exception white people rarely go to Promised Land. Only the county politicians occasionally appear in the two churches, soliciting support from a community known for a century for its bloc vote. They are received politely. Whites who stop at the general store for gas or a cold drink rarely feel welcome, and those native to the region know intuitively that whites do not go to Promised Land after sundown. Like the baseball games, this is a long-standing and cultivated community tradition. The people at Promised Land have good reasons to keep whites out of their community.

Promised Land residents have a great sense of community pride and not a little frustration at the obstacles they encounter in maintaining their community. Although they are only a mile or two from a municipal water main, they have no water other than that provided by two community wells, one on either side of the highway, and a few private wells. The community had no fire protection until the men organized and financed the Promised Land Volunteer Fire Department in 1978. A century of gerrymandering has made it difficult for the community to gain representation in the county government system. Their problems are those typical of second-class citizens. They cope collectively with this disability today in much the same way as they did in 1880, through ingenuity and self-sufficiency.

Originally Promised Land was a community of farmers, tenants, and sharecroppers. Today it is a community of laborers, clerical workers, and self-employed and blue-collar skilled workers. A century ago the community was established on the basis of landownership. It remains that today. The history of Promised Land is one of both continuity and change. These processes are not contradictions. Kinship, church, and politics were the building blocks that united a population of some ninety individual households during the 1870's.

Together these households forged a settlement based on economic security, held together by pressures from the world beyond the Promised Land boundaries as well as ties within the community. The same factors are the basis of community cohesion today. Residents are as politically astute as they were a century ago. Religion constitutes as potent a force in community life in 1980 as it did during the settlement years. Kinship is a major life theme, and the bonds are extensive and complex.

Promised Land is a microcosm of the many Negro communities where people have devised unique strategies for coping with their racially defined subordinate status. There are many such politically invisible but socially viable places scattered throughout the Black Belt and beyond—New Africa in Mississippi, New Rising Star in Alabama, Freetown in South Carolina, Peace in Arkansas. These communities lack the exotic quality of the Carolina and Georgia Sea Islands or the outlaw reputation and isolationist heritage of Coe Ridge, Kentucky/Tennessee and as a consequence have been bypassed by researchers armed with questionnaires, interview schedules, and Rorschach tests.[1]

The history of Promised Land is a study of race relations from a relatively unexplored perspective. It is not a restatement of the litany of racial oppression, although oppression forms an implicit theme within that history; nor is it a re-analysis of the self-hatred hypothesis. Rather, it is a case study of alternatives to self-hatred, retreat, and accommodation. By focusing on processes and events internal to community life, this study of Promised Land offers an understanding of the strategies one people devised out of a mutual desire to conduct their collective life with dignity and pride.[2]

The Promised Land community was born in 1870 in the midst of Reconstruction, a period of social, political, and economic chaos throughout the South. It was an unlikely time for the establishment of a community of freedmen whose descendants would still live there a century later. Despite the dislocations and confusion that marked the aftermath of war and the emancipation of four million Negroes, the families who originally settled at Promised Land needed no preparation for their freedom nor an introduction to emancipated ways of life. Fifty families began their individual liberation and their collective identity as self-sufficient and resourceful men and women eager to realize the promises of emancipation. The community these men and women established was in part an implementation of those promises. The presence and vitality of such a community in the 1870's attested to the initiative and pragmatic sense of economic and political imperatives Negroes held at the time of their emancipation. They did not have to be taught to live in freedom. They required only the opportunity to exercise those skills, to implement a social organization already established within the Negro culture prior to 1865 and to build from that foundation a viable and enduring community.

From the outset the Promised Land community was characterized by both material and symbolic dimensions of this cultural structure. The community was grounded in an identifiable and specific territorial setting that provided the principle material resource for community life. It was, as well, framed by a complex web of social relationships. It was a place where people lived, worked, and conducted their day-to-day routines. Like all communities, it was the product of an interplay between geography, social interactions, and the bonds which tie people to place. None of these dimensions are ever static or fixed in nature. The way in which a body of land is divided among community residents is shaped and reshaped by the biological facts of life and death, by the resources available to exploit and utilize that land, and by prevailing custom and tradition. The social interactions that take place within a communty setting are diverse and constantly changing. They are guided by bonds of kinship and friendship, by motives of power and economic gain, as much as by religious ideology. People are bound by the fabric of social life they find there, by the obligations and benefits of kinship that prevail within that setting, and by the opportunity for gain or perhaps just survival; and they leave their communities for new places for these same reasons. These fundamental assumptions about community guided this study of Promised Land, and from them three basic concerns shaped the research and ultimate analysis of this small but vigorous collective.[3]

First, what were the forces that attracted freedmen to and held them at Promised Land? In what ways were these attractions typical of the conditions surrounding freedmen in the years after 1865? In what way were they unique? The opportunity to acquire land was a potent attraction for a people just emerging from bondage, and one commonly pursued by freedmen throughout the South. Cooperative agrarian communities, instigated in some cases by the invading Union Army and in other cases by the freedmen themselves, were scattered across the plantation lands of the South as early as 1863. Collective land purchases and cooperative farming ventures developed in the Tidewater area of Virginia, the Sea Islands of South Carolina and

Georgia, and along the Mississippi River as refugees at the earliest contraband camps struggled to establish economic and social stability.[4]

These initial land tenure arrangements, always temporary, stimulated high levels of industrious labor among both those fortunate enough to obtain land and those whose expectations were raised by their neighbors' good fortunes. Although for most freedmen the initial promise of landownership was never realized, heightened expectations resulted in "entire families laboring together, improving their material conditions, laying aside money that might hopefully be used to purchase a farm or a few acres for a homestead of their own" during the final years of the war.[5]

The desire for a plot of land dominated public expressions among the freedmen as well as their day-to-day activities and behaviors. In 1864 Secretary of War Stanton met with Negro leaders in Savannah to discuss the problems of resettlement. During that meeting sixty-seven-year-old freedman Garrison Frazier responded to an inquiry regarding living arrangements by telling Stanton that "we would prefer to 'live by ourselves' rather than 'scattered among the whites.'"[6] These arrangements, he added, should include self-sufficiency established on Negro-owned lands. The sentiments Frazier expressed were not unusual. They were repeated by other freedmen across the South. Tunis Campbell, also recently emancipated, testified before the congressional committee investigating the Ku Klux Klan that "the great cry of our people is to have land." A delegate to the Tennessee Colored Citizens' Convention of 1866 stated that "what is needed for the colored people is land which they own."[7] A recently emancipated Negro representative to the 1868 South Carolina Constitutional Convention, speaking in support of that state's land redistribution program, which eventually gave birth to the Promised Land community, said of the relationship between landownership and the state's Negro population: "Night and day they dream" of owning their own land. "It is their all in all."[8]

At Davis Bend, Mississippi and Port Royal, South Carolina, as well as similar settlements in Louisiana, North Carolina, and Virginia, this dream was in fact realized for a time. Freedmen worked "with commendable zeal . . . out in the morning before it is light and at work 'til darkness drives them to their homes" whenever they farmed land which was their own.[9] John Eaton, who supervised the Davis Bend project, observed that the most successful land experiments among the freedmen were those in which plantations were subdivided into individually owned and farmed tracts. These small farms, rather than the larger cooperative ventures, "appeared to hold the greatest chance for success." The contraband camps and federally directed farm projects afforded newly emancipated freedmen an opportunity to "rediscover and redefine themselves, and to establish communities."[10] Within the various settlements a stability and social order developed that combined economic self-sufficiency with locally directed and controlled schools, churches, and mutual aid societies. In the years before the Freedmen's Bureau or the northern missionary societies penetrated the interior of the South, the freedmen, through their own resourcefulness, erected and supported such community institutions at every opportunity. In obscure settlements with names like Slabtown and Acreville, Hampton, Alexandria, Saxtonville, and Mitchelville, "status, experience, history, and ideology were potent forces operating toward cohesiveness and community."[11]

The drive for land among the freedmen was never matched by an equivalent availability of land, and after emancipation Negro land acquisitions resulted more often from planned development projects executed by Negro entrepreneurs than from private transactions between Negro and white farmers. This process, which doomed the majority of the freedmen to rental and sharecropping arrangements, was nowhere more evident than in the establishment of all-Negro towns in the West. Nicodemus, Kansas (1879), Mound Bayou, Mississippi (1887), and Boley, Oklahoma (1904) were typical cases of planned development of open lands by Negro entrepreneurs. All three communities initially prospered; their growth stimulated in each case by an influx of migrants drawn there by the promises of cheap, affordable land, economic self-sufficiency, and personal security. Each town, in turn, eventually withered into little more than a ghost town because none of the communities were able to withstand the crises and challenges inherent to Afro-American history, principally disfranchisement during the 1880's and 1890's, the boll weevil during the early years of the twentieth century, and the Great Migration.[12]

Economic factors combined with social and political conditions to seal the fate of these intentional community developments. Local Negro farmers were overly dependent on cotton as their single cash crop and fell victim first to the unpredictable cotton market of the late nineteenth and early twentieth centuries and then to the ravages of the boll weevil. But the failure of Mound Bayou, Nicodemus, and Boley was as much the product of local politics as economic problems. Negrophobia among white neighbors effectively isolated residents of the black towns. Local whites, fearing Negro political domination of their regions, blocked black efforts to establish viable local political machinery. The once optimistic local Negro leadership fled, and business failures compounded political impotence. Scarcity of capital, vastly unequal distributions of income, and an inability to provide residents with "the skills and industrial discipline necessary to re-enter the larger economy" eventually doomed the developments.[13]

At Promised Land and other small Negro residential enclaves in the South, the proximity of clustered Negro populations elicited less fear than it had in the West. White southerners were long accustomed to physical closeness between blacks and whites. The forms of discrimination that characterized southern culture were clearly insidious and designed to maintain rigid caste divisions through economic exploitation and political domination. Still, the Negro population was the backbone of the southern laboring class, and the white leadership structure sought control over that class rather than its eradication. The rhetoric of Pitchfork Ben Tillman, Tom Watson, and even Carter Glass stressed domination, not annihilation. These conditions distinguished southern Negro communities from those in the West, and places such as Promised Land provided living arrangements which were relatively peaceful in their isolation. There, in a world circumscribed by race and limited by poverty, Negroes had the opportunity "to walk the streets without encountering the thousand subtle reminders of membership in a subordinate class."[14] Community structures developed in an environment relatively free from white interference. This internal liberty, an unintended consequence of long-standing southern protocols in race relations, provided a clear advantage to the people at Promised Land not enjoyed by residents of the western towns.

The availability of land joined with established customs in black-white relations to form a framework conducive to community development at Promised Land. This set of conditions, peculiar to a specific historical and cultural setting, framed the second major concern. *How did landownership combine with other factors and resources to shape the nature of life at Promised Land? What were the common traditions and institutions that bound people together in a web of stable relationships which endured over a century?* Promised Land had fewer collective resources than many of the western towns at the time of its establishment. There was never a bank or a newspaper; and the small businesses at Promised Land, like Negro enterprises elsewhere, were always operated with the most minimal capital investment. The majority of the original settlers came to the community as impoverished freedmen, barely able to afford the ten-dollar down payment necessary to move onto one of the small farms. The assets these original settlers brought to Promised Land were largely nonmaterial.

The history of the community, as it unfolds, is clearly the history of a conventional people. The predictable routines and life events such as birth, death, and marriage were all managed within an orthodox framework remarkable for the absence of superstition and magical practices, rather than their presence. Promised Land has never celebrated such specifically Negro-centered events as Emancipation Day, a collective rite characteristic of Negro communities in the South Carolina and Georgia low country. Promised Land was shaped by three types of local institutions that fostered this conventionality: churches, schools, and mutual aid societies. All were active elements of community life from the earliest years of settlement, and all were typical of the foundations of southern Negro culture during the final quarter of the nineteenth century. Each provided a distinct contribution to the community.[15]

The economic security and independence established through landownership was supplemented by both the churches and mutual aid societies. Through these organizations the difficulties of old age, the crises of illness and death, or the catastrophe of a burned home were problems met and resolved through collective action. As the community attracted a body of nonlanded sharecroppers and laborers, people more susceptible to economic insecurity and white exploitation than the small landowners, the churches and mutual aid societies drew them into the web of local life. This integrative process offered the nonlanded an opportunity to share in at least a part of the benefits of community life. The schools, which operated under the indirect if not the direct guidance of the churches, taught a morality consistent with that the children learned at home and in Sunday School, a morality which mandated hard work, honesty, pragmatism, personal integrity, and self-sufficiency. These same values were reinforced for all the children by practically every adult in the community.

Traditional class divisions, whether forged by economic or social distinctions, were never rigidly delineated at Promised Land. Among the body of community professionals—for example, teachers, preachers, and small businessmen—there were both landowners and laborers, for Promised Land was too small and too poor to support a full-time professional class. The teacher was also a seamstress, the preacher a farmer. The storekeeper rented cotton land. The size of individual tracts of land quickly diversified as some laborers established permanent homes on small lots they bought from local farmers, and the landowning class soon included men and women who still farmed on rented and sharecropped land as well as most of the original owner-operators. Within the church and mutual aid society leadership was shared by landowners and nonlanded community residents. Positions of power and influence, at least as judged within the community setting, were held by both men and women.[16]

As the class structure of the community overlapped so too did the themes of community ideology. Children were taught independence and self-sufficiency and at the same time learned the obvious value of cooperation in the maintenance of community life. The presence of stable and inherently conservative local institutions in combination with an unusually open stratification system complemented the basic economic security of the land base.

This institutional framework formed the basis for most of the social life at Promised Land, a social life interfaced with kinship bonds families brought with them during the settlement of the original farms. As young teenagers matured and married during the early settlement years, the web of kinship further permeated and united the small population. Within twenty years few households remained untouched by this overlapping network of in-laws, cousins, and brother's-wife's-second-cousin. This inevitable process framed the nature of the third central concern, the bonds which tie people to place. That concern assumed a dynamic quality when cast within the context of Afro-American history. *Given the fact of the Great Migration, how were these ties of kinship resolved? In what ways were the obligations of kinship transplanted from a rural to an urban setting? How were the contradictions between the norms of earlier years and the conditions surrounding the Great Migration resolved by the families at Promised Land?*

The Great Migration marked a turning point for Afro-Americans. Prior to World War I the experience of Negroes in this country was largely one contained within the rural South. In 1920, two generations after emancipation, two-thirds of the Negro population still lived in the rural South, and not until the onset of World War II were the majority of the black population urban dwellers. The Great Migration and the years between the two world wars marked a time of rapid change for Negro Americans, a change which radically altered geographic as well as cultural identity. The people at Promised Land participated fully in this change; and the impact on community life, the local institutions, and the established kinship structures illustrates the flexibility of its social organization. Community outposts were established in most major cities that received large numbers of southern Negroes. In Chicago, Baltimore, New York, Washington, and Philadelphia, kinship groups relocated and maintained the continuity of their lives.[17]

At the same time, Promised Land did not wither into a dying town inhabited only by the elderly and social misfits. It retained vitality and became for the migrants a source of renewal. Homecoming and revival time each August drew the city dwellers home. The ubiquitous land prevailed and remained in the 1970's the source of attraction for yet a new wave of immigration into the community.

The South has been "the theater of the Negro's struggle" for economic self-sufficiency, political equality, and social autonomy for most of the century after emancipation. The majority of the Negro population was southern and rural throughout that century; and within the milieu of rural life the ownership of land afforded Negroes "a measure of independence, of security and dignity, and perhaps even power" in an existence otherwise restricted by the limitations of the caste system.[18] Promised Land and the people who have lived there during this century were actors within the southern theater, and their history reflects one aspect of a largely neglected drama.

Part I, The First Generation, traces the development of the community from its establishment in 1870 to the turn of the century. *Chapter 1* examines the factors which led to the transfer of 2,742 acres of land from white to Negro ownership and reconstructs the background and experiences of the original settlers. The interplay between whites and blacks and the fierce defense of their territorial integrity by community residents is clearly established during the first decade of the community's history, 1870 to 1880. *Chapter 2* examines the domestic and economic features of Promised Land during these early years, relying primarily on data extracted from the household and agricultural census manuscripts of 1880. *Chapter 3* focuses on land-use patterns from 1880 to 1900 and explores the earliest instances of intergenerational land transmission. *Chapter 4* details the establishment of churches and schools within the community, illustrating the importance of both institutions in the development of a cohesive social life and an inclusive collective consciousness.

Part II, The Second Generation, follows the residents of the community through a turbulent period of their history. *Chapter 5* establishes the major demographic and economic trends within which a series of crises occurred. Patterns of land transmission and subdivision, shaped now by the boll weevil invasion and World War I, in turn affected the community's occupational structure; and the first wave of migrants left Promised Land under the influence of these two events. *Chapter 6* explores the changing domestic and household patterns within the community and illustrates the ways in which these changes, prompted by economic factors, in turn influenced internal community dynamics. *Chapter 7* details the daily life and routines within the community, emphasizing the economic imperatives that act on all age groups and on both men and women. *Chapter 8* turns away from Promised Land and explores the process of migration, illustrating the balances ultimately established between economic and social forces for both those who left and those who stayed in the community.

Part III, The Third Generation, examines community life from the onset of the Great Depression to the modern civil rights movement. *Chapter 9* returns to the land and the impact of the New Deal on local farmers. The differential strategies for survival devised by landowner/farmers and nonfarmers forms the central focus for this chapter. *Chapter 10* follows the World War II experiences of three young men from Promised Land and relates the impact of those experiences to postwar conditions and community events. *Chapter 11*, like Chapter 8, turns away from the community and follows the migrants of the third generation, illustrating again the continuity of life most migrants established in urban environments.

The *Epilogue* summarizes the changes of a century as they are reflected in the contemporary land-use, church life, local politics, and education—the four institutional structures which established the initial stability within the community and provided a lifetime of continuity and security for three generations of Promised Land residents.

PART I

The First Generation
1870–1900

ONE

Settlement, 1870–1880

---

*For Sale: The homestead, grist mill, and 2742 acres of farmland
from the estate of Samuel Marshall, six miles from Abbeville.
Contact estate executors, S. S. Marshall and J. W. W. Marshall.*
Abbeville, South Carolina *Press*
12 November 1869

Dr. Marshall's Farm

Promised Land was from the outset an artifact of Reconstruction
politics. Its origins, as well, lie in the hopes, the dreams, and the
struggles of four million Negroes, for the meaning of freedom was
early defined in terms of land for most emancipated Negroes. In
South Carolina, perhaps more intensely than any of the other southern states, the thirst for land was acute. It was a possibility sparked
first by General William T. Sherman's military actions along the Sea
Islands, then dashed as quickly as it was born in the distant arena of
Washington politics. Still, the desire for land remained a goal not
readily abandoned by the state's freedpeople, and they implemented
a plan to achieve that goal at the first opportunity. Their chance came
at the 1868 South Carolina Constitutional Convention.

South Carolina was among the southern states which refused to
ratify the Fourteenth Amendment to the Constitution, the amendment which established the citizenship of the freedmen. Like her
recalcitrant neighbors, the state was then placed under military
government, as outlined by the Military Reconstruction Act of 1867.
Among the mandates of that federal legislation was a requirement
that each of the states in question draft a new state constitution
which incorporated the principles of the Fourteenth Amendment.
Only after such new constitutions were completed and implemented
were the separate states of the defeated Confederacy eligible for
readmission to the Union.

The representatives to these constitutional conventions were selected by a revolutionary electorate, one which included all adult male Negroes. Registration for the elections was handled by the Army with some informal assistance by "that God-forsaken institution, the Freedman's Bureau."[1] Only South Carolina among the ten states of the former Confederacy elected a Negro majority to its convention. The instrument those representatives drafted called for four major social and political reforms in state government: a statewide system of free common schools; universal manhood suffrage; a jury law which included the Negro electorate in county pools of qualified jurors; and a land redistribution system designed to benefit the state's landless population, primarily the freedmen.

White response to the new constitution and the social reforms which it outlined was predictably vitriolic. It was condemned by one white newspaper as "the work of sixty-odd Negroes, many of them ignorant and depraved." The authors were publicly ridiculed as representing "the maddest, most unscrupulous, and infamous revolution in history."[2] Despite this and similar vilification, the constitution was ratified in the 1868 referendum, an election boycotted by many white voters and dominated by South Carolina's 81,000 newly enfranchised Negroes, who cast their votes overwhelmingly with the Republicans and for the new constitution.

That same election selected representatives to the state legislature charged with implementing the constitutional reforms. That body, like the constitutional convention, was constituted with a Negro majority; and it moved immediately to establish a common school system and land redistribution program. The freedmen were already registered, and the new jury pools remained the prerogative of the individual counties. The 1868 election also was notable for the numerous attacks and "outrages" which occurred against the more politically active freedmen. Among those Negroes assaulted, beaten, shot, and lynched during the pre-election campaign months were four men who subsequently bought small farms from the Land Commission and settled at Promised Land. Like other freedmen in South Carolina, their open involvement in the state's Republican political machinery led to personal violence.

Wilson Nash was the first of the future Promised Land residents to encounter white brutality and retaliation for his political activities.[3] Nash was nominated by the Republicans as their candidate for Abbeville County's seat in the state legislature at the August 1868 county convention. In October of that year, less than two weeks before the general election, Nash was attacked and shot in the leg by two unidentified white assailants. The "outrage" took place in the barn on his rented farm, not far from Dr. Marshall's farm on Curltail Creek. Wilson Nash was thirty-three years old in 1868, married, and the father of three small children. He had moved from "up around Cokesbury" within Abbeville County, shortly after emancipation to the rented land further west. Within months after the Nash family was settled on their farm, Wilson Nash joined the many Negroes who affiliated with the Republicans, an alliance probably instigated and encouraged by Republican promises of land to the freedmen. The extent of Nash's involvement with local politics was apparent in his nomination for public office; and this same nomination brought him to the forefront of county Negro leadership and to the attention of local whites.

After the attack Nash sent his wife and young children to a neighbor's home, where he probably believed they would be safe. He then mounted his mule and fled his farm, leaving behind thirty bushels of recently harvested corn. Whether Nash also left behind a cotton crop is unknown. It was the unprotected corn crop that worried him as much as his concern for his own safety. He rode his mule into Abbeville and there sought refuge at the local Freedman's Bureau office where he reported the attack to the local bureau agent and requested military protection for his family and his corn crop. Captain W. F. DeKnight was sympathetic to Nash's plight but was powerless to assist or protect him. DeKnight had no authority in civil matters such as this, and the men who held that power generally ignored such assaults on Negroes.[4] The Nash incident was typical and followed a familiar pattern. The assailants remained unidentified, unapprehended, and unpunished. The attack achieved the desired end, however, for Nash withdrew his name from the slate of legislative candidates. For him there were other considerations which took priority over politics.

Violence against the freedmen of Abbeville County, as elsewhere in the state, continued that fall and escalated as the 1868 election day neared. The victims had in common an involvement with the Republicans, and there was little distinction made between direct and indirect partisan activity. Politically visible Negroes were open targets. Shortly after the Nash shooting young Willis Smith was assaulted, yet another victim of Reconstruction violence. Smith was still a teenager and too young to vote in the elections, but his age afforded him no immunity. He was a known member of the Union League, the most radical and secret of the political organizations which attracted freedmen. While attending a dance one evening,

Smith and four other League members were dragged outside the dance hall and brutally beaten by four white men whose identities were hidden by hoods.[5] This attack, too, was an act of political vengeance. It was, as well, one of the earliest Ku Klux Klan appearances in Abbeville. Like other crimes committed against politically active Negroes, this one remained unsolved.

On election day freedmen Washington Green and Allen Goode were precinct managers at the White Hall polling place, near the southern edge of the Marshall land. Their position was a political appointment of some prestige, their reward for affiliation with and loyalty to the Republican cause. The appointment brought them, like Wilson Nash and Willis Smith, to the attention of local whites. On election day the voting proceeded without incident until midday, when two white men attempted to block Negroes from entering the polling site. A scuffle ensued as Green and Goode, acting in their capacity as voting officials, tried to bring the matter to a halt and were shot by the white men.[6] One freedman was killed, two others injured, in the incident which also went unsolved. In none of the attacks were the assailants ever apprehended. Within twenty-four months all four men—Wilson Nash, Willis Smith, Washington Green, and Allen Goode—bought farms at Promised Land.

Despite the violence which surrounded the 1868 elections, the Republicans carried the whole of the state. White Democrats refused to support an election they deemed illegal, and they intimidated the newly enfranchised Negro electorate at every opportunity. The freedmen, nevertheless, flocked to the polls in an unprecedented exercise of their new franchise and sent a body of legislative representatives to the state capitol of Columbia who were wholly committed to the mandates and reforms of the new constitution. Among the first legislative acts was one which formalized the land redistribution program through the creation of the South Carolina Land Commission.[7]

The Land Commission program, as designed by the legislature, was financed through the public sale of state bonds. The capital generated from the bond sales was used to purchase privately owned plantation tracts which were then subdivided and resold to freedmen through long-term (ten years), low-interest (7 percent per annum) loans. The bulk of the commission's transactions occurred along the coastal areas of the state where land was readily available. The labor and financial problems of the rice planters of the low-country were generally more acute than those of the up-country cotton planters. As a result, they were more eager to dispose of a portion of the landholdings at a reasonable price, and their motives for their dealings with the Land Commission were primarily pecuniary.

Piedmont planters were not so motivated. Many were able to salvage their production by negotiating sharecropping and tenant arrangements. Most operated on a smaller scale than the low-country planters and were less dependent on gang labor arrangements. As a consequence, few were as financially pressed as their low-country counterparts, and land was less available for purchase by the Land Commission in the Piedmont region. With only 9 percent of the commission purchases lying in the up-country, the Marshall lands were the exception rather than the rule.

The Marshall sons first advertised the land for sale in 1865. These lands, like others at the eastern edge of the Cotton Belt, were exhausted from generations of cultivation and attendant soil erosion; and for such worn out land the price was greatly inflated. Additionally, two successive years of crop failures, low cotton prices, and a general lack of capital discouraged serious planters from purchasing the lands. The sons then advertised the tract for rent, but the land stood idle. The family wanted to dispose of the land in a single transaction rather than subdivide it, and Dr. Marshall's farm was no competition for the less expensive and more fertile land to the west that was opened for settlement after the war. In 1869 the two sons once again advertised the land for sale, but conditions in Abbeville County were not improved for farmers, and no private buyer came forth.[8]

Having exhausted the possibilities for negotiating a private sale, the family considered alternative prospects for the disposition of a farm that was of little use to them. James L. Orr, a moderate Democrat, former governor (1865 to 1868), and family son-in-law, served as negotiator when the tract was offered to the Land Commission at the grossly inflated price of ten dollars an acre. Equivalent land in Abbeville County was selling for as little as two dollars an acre, and the commission rejected the offer. Political promises took precedence over financial considerations when the commission's regional agent wrote the Land Commission's Advisory Board that "if the land is not bought the (Republican) party is lost in this district."[9] Upon receipt of his advice the commission immediately met the Marshall family's ten dollar an acre price. By January 1870 the land was subdivided into fifty small farms, averaging slightly less than fifty acres each, which were publicly offered for sale to Negro as well as white buyers.

The Marshall Tract was located in the central sector of old Abbe-

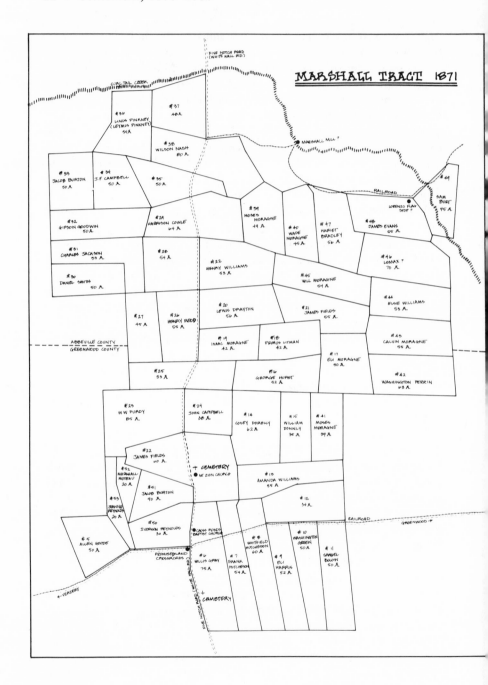

MARSHALL TRACT 1871

ville County and was easily accessible to most of the freedmen who were to make the lands their home.[10] Situated in the western portion of the state, the tract was approximately sixty miles northwest of Augusta, Georgia, one hundred and fifty miles northeast of Atlanta, and the same distance northwest of Charleston. It would attract few freedmen from the urban areas. Two roads intersected within the lands. One, running north to south, linked those who soon settled there with the county seat of Abbeville to the north and the Phoenix community, a tiny settlement composed primarily of white small-scale farmers approximately eighteen miles to the south. Called New Cut Road, Five Notch Road, and later White Hall Road, the dirt wagon route was used primarily for travel to Abbeville. The east-west road, which would much later be converted to a state highway, was the more heavily traveled of the two and linked the cluster of farms to the village of Greenwood, six miles to the east, and the small settlement of Verdery, three miles to the west. Beyond Verdery, which served for a time as a stagecoach stop on the long trip between Greenville and Augusta, lay the Savannah River. The road was used regularly by a variety of peddlers and salesmen who included the Negro farmers on their routes as soon as families began to move onto the farms. Despite the decidedly rural setting, the families who bought land there were not isolated. A regular stream of travelers brought them news of events from well beyond their limited geography and helped them maintain touch with a broader scope of activities and ideas than their environment might have predicted.

The Marshall Tract had only one natural boundary to delineate the perimeter of Negro-owned farms, Curltail Creek on the north. Other less distinctive markers were devised as the farms were settled, to distinguish the area from surrounding white-owned lands. Extending south from White Hall Road, "below the cemetery, south of the railroad about a mile" a small lane intersected the larger road. This was Rabbit Track Road, and it marked the southern edge of Negro-owned lands. To the east the boundary was marked by another dirt lane called Lorenzo Road, little more than a trail which led to the Seaboard Railroad flag stop. Between the crossroads and Verdery to the west, "the edge of the old Darraugh place" established the western perimeter. In all, the tract encompassed slightly more than four square miles of earth.[11]

The farms on the Marshall Tract were no bargain for the Negroes who bought them. The land was only partially cleared and ready for cultivation, and that which was free of pine trees and underbrush was badly eroded. There was little to recommend the land to cotton

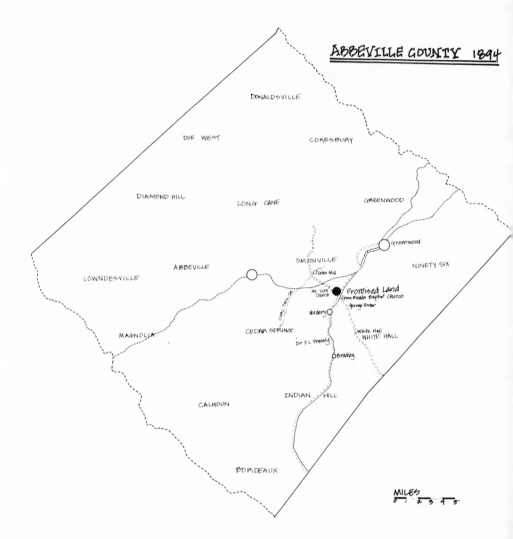

ABBEVILLE COUNTY 1894

farming. Crop failures in 1868 and 1869 severely limited the local economy, which further reduced the possibilities for small farmers working on badly depleted soil. There was little credit available to Abbeville farmers, white or black; and farming lacked not only an unqualified promise of financial gain but even the possibility of breaking even at harvest. Still, it was not the fertility of the soil or the possibility of economic profit that attracted the freedmen to those farms. The single opportunity for landownership, a status which for most Negroes in 1870 symbolized the essence of their freedom, was the prime attraction for the freedmen who bought farms from the subdivided Marshall Tract.

Most of the Negroes who settled the farms knew the area and local conditions well. Many were native to Abbeville County. In addition to Wilson Nash, the Moragne family and their in-laws, the Turners, the Pinckneys, the Letmans, and the Williamses were also natives of Abbeville, from "down over by Bordeaux" in the southwestern rim of the county which borders Georgia. Others came to their new farms from "Dark Corner, over by McCormick," and another nearby Negro settlement, Pettigrew Station—both in Abbeville County. The Redd family lived in Newberry, South Carolina before they bought their farm; and James and Hannah Fields came to Promised Land from the state capitol, Columbia, eighty miles to the east.

Many of the settlers from Abbeville County shared their names with prominent white families—Moragne, Burt, Marshall, Pressley, Frazier, and Pinckney. Their claims to heritage were diverse. One recalled "my grandaddy was a white man from England," and others remembered slavery times to their children in terms of white fathers who "didn't allow nobody to mess with the colored boys of his." Others dismissed the past and told their grandchildren that "some things is best forgot." A few were so fair skinned that "they could have passed for white it they wanted to," while others who bought farms from the Land Commission "was so black there wasn't no doubt about who their daddy was."[12]

After emancipation many of these former bondsmen stayed in their old neighborhoods, farming in much the same way as they had during slavery times. Some "worked for the marsters at daytime and for theyselves at night" in an early Piedmont version of sharecropping. Old Samuel Marshall was one former slave owner who retained many of his bondsmen as laborers by assuring them that they would receive some land of their own—promising them that "if you clean two acres you get two acres; if you clean ten acres you get ten acres" of farmland. It was this promise which kept some freedmen on the Marshall land until it was sold to the Land Commission. They cut and cleared part of the tract of the native pines and readied it for planting in anticipation of ownership. But the promise proved empty, and Marshall's death and the subsequent sale of his lands to the state deprived many of those who labored day and night on the land of the free farms they hoped would be theirs. "After they had cleaned it up they still had to pay for it." Other freedmen in the county "moved off after slavery ended but couldn't get no place" of their own to farm.[13] Unable to negotiate labor or lease arrangements, they faced a time of homelessness with few resources and limited options until the farms became available to them. A few entered into labor contracts supervised by the Freedman's Bureau or settled on rented farms in the county for a time.

The details of the various postemancipation economic arrangements made by the freedmen who settled on the small tracts at Dr. Marshall's farm, whatever the form they assumed, were dominated by three conscious choices all had in common. The first was their decision to stay in Abbeville County following emancipation. For most of the people who eventually settled in Promised Land, Abbeville was their home as well as the site of their enslavement. There they were surrounded by friends, family and a familiar environment. The second choice this group of freedmen shared was occupational. They had been Piedmont farmers throughout their enslavement, and they chose to remain farmers in their freedom.

Local Negroes made a third conscious decision that for many had long-range importance in their lives and those of their descendents. Through the influence of the Union League, the Freedman's Bureau, the African Methodist Church, and each other, many of the Negroes in Abbeville aligned politically with the Republicans between 1865 and 1870. In Abbeville as elsewhere in the state, this alliance was established enthusiastically. The Republicans promised land as well as suffrage to those who supported them. If their political activities became public knowledge, the freedmen "were safe nowhere"; and men like Wilson Nash, Willis Smith, Washington Green, and Allen Goode who were highly visible Negro politicians took great risks in this exercise of freedom. Those risks were not without justification. It was probably not a coincidence that loyalty to the Republican cause was followed by a chance to own land.

Land for Sale to the Colored People

I have 700 acres of land to sell in lots of from 50 to 100 acres or more situated six miles from Abbeville. Terms: A liberal cash payment; balance to be made in three annual payments from date of purchase.

J. Hollinshead, Agent

(Advertisement placed by the Land Commission in Abbeville *Press*, 2 July 1873)

The Land Commission first advertised the farms on the Marshall Tract in January and February 1870. Eleven freedmen and their families established conditional ownership of their farms before spring planting that year. They were among a vanguard of some 14,000 Negro families who acquired small farms in South Carolina through the Land Commission program between 1868 and 1879. With a ten-dollar down payment they acquired the right to settle on and till the thin soil. They were also obliged to place at least half of their land under cultivation within three years and to pay all taxes due annually in order to retain their ownership rights.[14]

Among the earliest settlers to the newly created farms was Allen Goode, the precinct manager at White Hall, who bought land in January 1870, almost immediately after it was put on the market. Two brothers-in-law, J. H. Turner and Primus Letman, also bought farms in the early spring that year. Turner was married to LeAnna Moragne and Letman to LeAnna's sister Francis. Elias Harris, a widower with six young children to raise, also came to his lands that spring, as did George Hearst, his son Robert, and their families. Another father-son partnership, Carson and Will Donnelly, settled on adjacent tracts. Willis Smith's father Daniel also bought a farm in 1870.

Allen Goode was the wealthiest of these early settlers. He owned a horse, two oxen, four milk cows, and six hogs. For the other families, both material resources and farm production were modest. Few of the homesteaders produced more than a single bale of cotton on their new farms that first year; but all, like Wilson Nash two years earlier, had respectable corn harvests, a crop essential to "both us and the animals."[15] Most households also had sizable pea, bean, and sweet potato crops and produced their own butter. All but the cotton crops were destined for household consumption, as these earliest settlers established a pattern of subsistence farming that would prevail as a community economic strategy in the coming decades.

This decision by the Promised Land farmers to intensify food production and minimize cotton cultivation, whether intentional or the result of other conditions, was an important initial step toward their attainment of economic self-sufficiency. Small scale cotton farmers in the Black Belt were rarely free agents. Most were quickly trapped in a web of chronic indebtedness and marketing restrictions. Diversification of cash crops was inhibited during the 1870's and 1880's not only by custom and these economic entanglements but also by an absence of local markets, adequate roads, and methods of transportation to move crops other than cotton to larger markets. The Promised Land farmers, generally unwilling to incur debts with the local lien men if they could avoid it, turned to a modified form of subsistence farming as their only realistic land-use option. Through this strategy many of them avoided the "economic nightmare" which fixed the status of other small-scale cotton growers at a level of permanent peonage well into the twentieth century.[16]

The following year, 1871, twenty-five more families scratched up their ten-dollar down payment; and upon presenting it to Hollinshead obtained conditional titles to farms on the Marshall Tract. The Williams family, Amanda and her four adult sons—William, Henry, James, and Moses—purchased farms together that year, probably withdrawing their money from their accounts at the Freedman's Savings and Trust Company Augusta Branch for their separate down payments. Three of the Moragne brothers—Eli, Calvin, and Moses—joined the Turners and the Letmans, their sisters and brothers-in-law, making five households in that corner of the tract soon designated "Moragne Town." John Valentine, whose family was involved in A.M.E. organizational work in Abbeville County, also obtained a conditional title to a farm, although he did not settle there permanently. Henry Redd, like the Williamses, withdrew his savings from the Freedman's Bank and moved to his farm from Newberry, a small town about thirty miles to the east. Moses Wideman, Wells Gray, Frank Hutchison, Samuel Bulow, and Samuel Burt also settled on their farms before spring planting.[17]

As the cluster of Negro-owned farms grew more densely populated, it gradually assumed a unique identity; and this identity, in turn, gave rise to a name, Promised Land. Some remember their grandparents telling them that "the Governor in Columbia [South Carolina] named this place when he sold it to the Negroes." Others contend that the governor had no part in the naming. They argue that these earliest settlers derived the name Promised Land from the conditions of their purchase. "They only promised to pay for it, but they never did!" Indeed, there is some truth in that statement. For although the initial buyers agreed to pay between nine and ten dollars per acre for their land in the original promissory notes, few fulfilled the conditions of those contracts. Final purchase prices were greatly reduced, from ten dollars to $3.25 per acre, a price more in line with prevailing land prices in the Piedmont.[18]

By the end of 1873 forty-four of the fifty farms on the Marshall Tract had been sold. The remaining land, less than seven hundred acres, was the poorest in the tract, badly eroded and at the perimeter of the community. Some of those farms remained unsold until the early 1880's, but even so the land did not go unused. Families too poor to consider buying the farms lived on the state-owned property throughout the 1870's. They were squatters, living there illegally and rent-free, perhaps working a small cotton patch, always a garden. Their condition contrasted sharply with that of the landowners who, like other Negroes who purchased farmland during the 1870's, were considered the most prosperous of the rural freedmen. The freeholders in the community were among the pioneers in a movement to acquire land, a movement that stretched across geographical and temporal limits. Even in the absence of state or federal assistance in other regions, and despite the difficulties Negroes faced in negotiating land purchases directly from white landowners during Reconstruction, by 1875 Negroes across the South owned five million acres of farmland. The promises of emancipation were fulfilled for a few, among them the families at Promised Land.

Settlement of the community coincided with the establishment of a public school, another of the revolutionary social reforms mandated by the 1868 constitution. It was the first of several public facilities to serve community residents and was built on land still described officially as "Dr. Marshall's farm." J. H. Turner, Larkin Reynolds, Iverson Reynolds, and Hutson Lomax, all Negroes, were the first school trustees.[19] The families established on their new farms sent more than ninety children to the one-room school. Everyone who could be spared from the fields was in the classroom for the short 1870 school term. Although few of the children in the landless families attended school regularly, the landowning families early established a tradition of school attendance for their children consonant with their new status. With limited resources the school began the task of educating local children.

The violence and terror experienced by some of the men of Promised Land during 1868 recurred three years later when Eli and Wade Moragne were attacked and viciously beaten with a wagon whip by a band of Klansmen.[20] Wade was twenty-three that year, Eli two years older. Both were married and had small children. It was rumored that the Moragne brothers were among the most prominent and influential of the Negro Republicans in Abbeville County. Their political activity, compounded by an unusual degree of self-assurance, pride, and dignity, infuriated local whites. Like Wilson Nash, Willis Smith, Washington Green, and Allen Goode, the Moragne brothers were victims of insidious political reprisals. Involvement in Reconstruction politics for Negroes was a dangerous enterprise and one which addressed the past as well as the future. It was an activity suited to young men and those who faced the future bravely. It was not for the timid.

The Republican influence on the freedmen at Promised Land was unmistakable, and there was no evidence that the "outrages" and terrorizations against them slowed their participation in local partisan activities. In addition to the risks, there were benefits to be accrued from their alliance with the Republicans. They enjoyed appointments as precinct managers and school trustees. As candidates for various public offices, they experienced a degree of prestige and public recognition which offset the element of danger they faced. These men, born slaves, rose to positions of prominence as landowners, as political figures, and as makers of a community. Few probably had dared to dream of such possibilities a decade earlier.

During the violent years of Reconstruction there was at least one official attempt to end the anarchy in Abbeville County. The representative to the state legislature, J. Hollinshead—the former regional agent for the Land Commission—stated publicly what many local Negroes already knew privately, that "numerous outrages occur in the county and the laws cannot be enforced by civil authorities." From the floor of the General Assembly of South Carolina Hollinshead called for martial law in Abbeville, a request which did not pass unnoticed locally. The Editor of the *Press* commented on Hollinshead's request for martial law by declaring that such outrages against the freedmen "exist only in the imagination of the legislator."[21] His response was probably typical of the cavalier attitude of southern whites toward the problems of their former bondsmen. Indeed, there were no further reports of violence and attacks against freedmen carried by the *Press*, which failed to note the murder of County Commissioner Henry Nash in February 1871. Like other victims of white terrorists, Nash was a Negro.[22]

While settlement of Dr. Marshall's Farm by the freedmen proceeded, three community residents were arrested for the theft of "some oxen from Dr. H. Drennan who lives near the 'Promiseland.'"[23] Authorities found the heads, tails, and feet of the slaughtered animals near the homes of Ezekiel and Moses Williams and Colbert Jordan. The circumstantial evidence against them seemed convincing; and the three were arrested and then released without bond, pending trial. Colonel Cothran, a former Confederate officer and respected barrister in Abbeville, represented the trio at their trial. Although freedmen in Abbeville courts were generally convicted of whatever crime they were charged with, the Williamses and Jordan were acquitted. Justice for Negroes was always a tenuous affair; but it was especially so before black, as well as white, qualified electors were included in the jury pool. The trial of the Williams brothers and Jordan signaled a temporary truce in the racial war, a truce which at least applied to those Negroes settling the farms at Promised Land.

In 1872, the third year of settlement, Promised Land gained nine more households as families moved to land that they "bought for a dollar an acre." There they "plow old oxen, build log cabin houses" as they settled the land they bought "from the Governor in Columbia." Colbert Jordan and Ezekiel Williams, cleared of the oxen stealing charges, both purchased farms that year. Family and kinship ties drew some of the new migrants to the community. Joshuway Wilson, married to Moses Wideman's sister Delphia, bought a farm near his brother-in-law. Two more Moragne brothers, William and Wade, settled near the other family members in "Moragne Town." Whitfield Hutchison, a jack-leg preacher, bought the farm adjacent to his brother Frank. "Old Whit Hutchison could sing about let's go down to the water and be baptized. He didn't have no education, and he didn't know exactly how to put his words, but when he got to singing he could make your hair rise up. He was a number one preacher."[24] Hutchison was not the only preacher among those first settlers. Isaac Y. Moragne, who moved to Promised Land the following year, and several men in the Turner family all combined preaching and farming.

Not all of the settlers came to their new farms as members of such extensive kinship networks as the Moragnes, who counted nine brothers, four sisters, and an assortment of spouses and children among the first Promised Land residents. Even those who joined the community in relative isolation, however, were seldom long in establishing kinship alliances with their neighbors. One such couple was James and Hannah Fields who lived in Columbia before emancipation, While still a slave, James Fields owned property in the state capitol, which was held in trust for him by his master. After emancipation Fields worked for a time as a porter on the Columbia and Greenville Railroad and heard about the up-country land for sale to Negroes as he carried carpet bags and listened to political gossip on the train. Fields went to Abbeville County to inspect the land before he purchased a farm there. While he was visiting, he "run up on Mr. Nathan Redd," old Henry Redd's son. The Fieldses' granddaughter Emily and Nathan were about the same age, and Fields proposed a match to young Redd. "You marry my granddaughter, and I'll will all this land to you and her." The marriage was arranged before the farm was purchased, and eventually the land was transferred to the young couple.[25]

By the conclusion of 1872 forty-eight families were settled on farms in Promised Land. Most of the land was under cultivation, as required by law; but the farmers were also busy with other activities. In addition to the houses and barns which had to be raised as each new family arrived with their few possessions, the men continued their political activities. Iverson Reynolds, J. H. Turner, John and Elias Tolbert, Judson Reynolds, Oscar Pressley, and Washington Green, all community residents, were delegates to the county Republican convention in August 1872. Three of the group were landowners. Their political activities were still not received with much enthusiasm by local whites, but reaction to Negro involvement in politics was lessening in hostility. The *Press* mildly observed that the fall cotton crop was being gathered with good speed and "the farmers have generally been making good use of their time." Cotton picking and politics were both seasonal, and the newspaper chided local Negroes for their priorities. "The blacks have been indulging a little too much in politics but are getting right again." Iverson Reynolds and Washington Green, always among the community's Republican leadership during the 1870's, served as local election managers again for the 1872 fall elections.[26] The men from Promised Land voted without incident that year.

Civic participation among the Promised Land residents extended beyond partisan politics when the county implemented the new jury law in 1872. There had been no Negro jurors for the trial of the Williams brothers and Colbert Jordan the previous year. Although the inclusion of Negroes in the jury pools was a reform mandated in 1868, four years passed before Abbeville authorities drew up new jury lists from the revised voter registration rolls. The jury law was as repugnant to the whites as Negro suffrage, termed "a wretched attempt at legislation, which surpasses anything which has yet been achieved by the Salons in Columbia." When the new lists were finally completed in 1872 the *Press,* ever the reflection of local white public opinion, predicted that "many of [the freedmen] probably have moved away; and the chances are that not many of them will be forthcoming" in the call to jury duty. Neither the initial condemnation of the law nor the optimistic undertones of the *Press* prediction stopped Pope Moragne and Iverson Reynolds from responding to their notices from the Abbeville Courthouse. Both landowners rode their mules up Five Notch Road from Promised Land to Abbeville and served on the county's first integrated jury in the fall of 1872. Moragne and Reynolds were soon followed by others from the community—Allen Goode, Robert Wideman, William Moragne, James Richie, and Luther (Shack) Moragne. By 1874, less than five years after settlement of Dr. Marshall's farm by the new Negro landowners began, the residents of Promised Land remained actively involved in Abbeville County politics. They were undaunted by the *Press* warning that "just so soon as the colored people lose the confidence and support of the North their doom is fixed. The fate of the red man will be theirs."[27] They were voters, jurors, taxpayers, and trustees of the school their children attended. Their collective identity as an exclusively Negro community was well established.

Only Colored Down in This Old Promised Land

Abbeville County, South Carolina
Mr. John Lomax passed through the Promised Land yesterday,
and he thinks the crops there almost a failure. The corn will not
average two bushels to the acre, and the cotton about 300 pounds
[less than one bale] to the acre. A large quantity of sorghum cane
was planted. It was almost worthless. The land appeared as if it
had been very well cultivated.
Abbeville *Press*
30 September 1874

The forty-eight men and women who established conditional ownership of the farms at Promised Land between 1870 and 1872 were required by law to place at least half of their land under cultivation within three years of their purchase. There was, however, no requirement about the crops to be planted. The men who established that cultivation standard probably assumed that cotton would be the major cash crop, as it was throughout the Piedmont. At Promised Land cotton was indeed planted on every one of the farms, but not in overwhelming amounts. The relatively small cotton fields were overshadowed by fields of corn, peas, and sorghum cane; and the sense of permanence among the settlers was clearly evident when "they planted peach trees and pear trees and had grape vines all over" the land, which only a few years before was either uncleared of native pine forests or part of the up-country plantation system. Cotton, the antebellum crop of the slaves, became the cash crop of freedom. It would never dominate the lives of the farmers at Promised Land.[28]

The 1870's were economically critical years for the new landowners. They had mortgage payments to meet and taxes to pay, but they also had families to feed. In 1870, when the price of cotton reached twenty-two cents a pound, all this was possible. In the following years, however, cotton prices declined dramatically. This, combined with generally low cotton yields, resulted in economic hardship for many of the farmers. Poverty was their constant neighbor, and their struggle for survival drew them into a cycle of indebtedness to white "lien men."

In those depression years there was little credit in the Piedmont. "The poor people wasn't able to buy their fertilize. That's what makes your cotton."[29] Storekeepers and merchants reserved their resources for the local white planters, and the Negro farmers were forced to find credit from other sources. They turned to their white landowning neighbors and in some cases their former masters, the Devlin family in Verdery; the Tuck family, nearby farmers; and the Hendersons, Verdery merchants. To them the Promised Land farmers paid usurious interest rates for the fertilizer they needed "to make a bale of cotton" and the other supplies and foodstuffs they required to survive the growing season.

It was during this decade that the community farmers learned to maintain a skillful balance between a small cotton cash crop and their subsistence fields. Careful in the management of debt, most landowners probably used their cotton crop to meet their mortgage payment to the Land Commission and their tax bill to the county. There was never any surplus on the small farms, and a crop failure had immediate and personal consequences. At best a family would go hungry. At worst they would lose their farm.

Times were hard; and, despite generally shrewd land and debt management, twenty of the original settlers lost title to their land during the early 1870's. All migrated from Promised Land before the 1875 growing season. An advertisement in the *Press* attracted some new purchasers to the vacated farms, but most buyers learned of the land through friends and relatives. New families once again moved on to the land.[30] Wilson Nash bought the farm originally purchased by John Valentine; both men were church leaders and probably discussed the transaction in some detail before the agreement was finalized.

Allen Goode, Wells Gray, and James Fields added to their holdings, buying additional farms from discouraged families who were leaving. Moses Wideman's younger brothers, William and Richmond, together bought an eighty-five–acre farm and then divided it, creating two more homesteads in the community. J. H. Turner, who secured a teaching position in an Edgefield County public school, sold his farm to his brother-in-law Isaac Y. Moragne. Each of the landowners had a brother, a cousin, or a friend who was eager to assume the financial burden of landownership; and none of the twenty vacated farms remained unoccupied for long. Promised Land quickly regained its population. The new arrivals strengthened and expanded the kinship bonds, which already crisscrossed and united individual households in the community.

Marriage provided the most common alliance between kinship groups. The Wilson and Wideman families and the Fields and Redds were both so related. The use of land as dowry, first employed by James Fields to arrange his granddaughter's marriage to Nathan Redd, provided a convenient and viable bargaining tool. When Iverson Reynolds bought his thirty-acre farm he also purchased a second, twenty-acre tract in his daughter's name, looking forward to the time of her marriage. "When Oscar Pressley married Iverson Reynolds' daughter, Janie, Iverson Reynolds give him that land or sold it to him. But he got that farm from old Iverson Reynolds when he got married." The Moragnes, Turners, Pinckneys, and Letmans were also united through land-based dowry arrangements. "The Moragne women is the ones that had the land. All them, the Turners, the Pinckneys, and the Letmans—all them got into the Moragnes when the women married these men."

Marriage did not always accompany kinship bonds, for at Promised Land, like every place else, "some folks have childrens when they not married. Things get all mixed up sometimes." Still, the community was a small and intimate place, woven together as early as the 1880's by a complex and interlocking series of kin ties, which were supplemented by many other kinds of personal relationships. The separation of public and private spheres blurred; and, married or not, "when the gals get a baby" everyone was aware of the heritage and family ties of new babies. "Andrew Moragne supposed to been his daddy, but his momma was a Bradley so he took the name Bradley." Even so, promiscuity and illegitimacy were not casually accepted facts of life. Both were sinful and disgraceful not just to the couple but to their families as well. For women a pregnancy without marriage was particularly painful. "Some might be mean to you then," and many refused to even speak publicly to an unmarried women who became pregnant. "All that stop when the baby is born. Don't want to punish an innocent baby."[31] Legitimate or not, babies were welcomed into families and the community, and the sins of the parents were set aside. Ultimately, the bonds of kinship proved more powerful than collective morality, and these bonds left few residents of the community excluded from an encompassing network of cousins, aunts, uncles, and half-brothers and sisters.

As the landowning population of Promised Land stabilized, local resources emerged to meet day-to-day needs. A molasses mill, where the farmers had their sorghum cane ground into molasses by Joshuway Wilson's oldest son Fortune, opened in the community. Two corn and wheat grist mills opened on Curltail Creek. One, the old Marshall Mill, was operated by Harrison Cole, a Negro who subsequently purchased a vacant farm in the community. The other, the former Donalds Mill, was owned and operated by James Evans, an Irish immigrant whose thirst for land equaled that of his Negro neighbors.[32] North Carter, the youngest son of landowner Marion Carter, opened a small general store at the east-west crossroads, where he sold candy, kerosene, salt, and other staples to his neighbors, extending credit when necessary, knowing that they would pay when they could. Long before the final land purchase was completed, the freedmen at Promised Land had established a framework for economic and social self-sufficiency.

The farms, through hard work, decent weather, and an eight-month growing season, soon yielded food for the households. A pattern of subsistence agriculture provided each Promised Land family a degree of independence and self-reliance unknown to most other Negro families in the area. Cows produced milk and butter for the tables, and chickens eggs and fresh poultry. Draft animals and cash money were both scarce commodities, but "in them days nobody ever went hungry." Hogs provided the major source of meat in the community's subsistence economy. "My mother and them used to kill hogs and put them down in salt in wood boxes and cover them so flies couldn't get to them for about five or six weeks. Take it out and wash it, put on red pepper and such, hang it up to dry, and that meat be *good*."[33] The absence of an abundant cotton crop was not a sign of lack of industry. Prosperity, as well as productivity, was measured against hunger; and, in the never-ending farm cycle, fields were planted according to the number of people in each household, the number of mouths to be fed.

Community and household autonomy were firmly grounded in the economic independence of the land. Both were strengthened with the establishment of a church in Promised Land. In 1875, fully a decade before the final farms were settled, James Fields sold one acre of his land to the Trustees of Mt. Zion A.M.E. Church.[34] It was a sign of the times. At Promised Land, as elsewhere in the South, freedmen withdrew from white churches as quickly as possible. Membership in the Baptist and Methodist denominations increased tenfold between 1860–1870 as the new Negro churches in the South took form. Mt. Zion was relatively late in emerging as a part of that movement for independence from white domination, but the residents of Promised Land were preoccupied for a time with more basic concerns. The fields had to be established as productive before community residents turned their energies to other aspects of community development.

The Field's land, located squarely in the geographical center of Promised Land, was within a two-mile walk of all the houses in the community. On this thinly wooded tract the men carved out a brush arbor, a remnant of slavery days; and Isaac Y. Moragne led everybody in the young settlement in prayers and songs. From the beginning of their emancipation schools and churches were central components of Negro social life; and at Promised Land religion, like education, was established as a permanent part of community life while the land was still being cleared.

Newcomers and Community Growth

Most families survived those first settlement years, the droughts and crop failures, Ku Klux Klan attacks, and the violent years of Reconstruction. They met their mortgage payments and their taxes, and the years after 1875 were relatively prosperous ones. Promised Land was well established before the Compromise of 1877, the withdrawal of federal troops from the state, and the election of Wade Hampton as governor. The political squabbles among the white Democrats during the years after Hampton's redemption of South Carolina touched the folks at Promised Land only indirectly. The community was, for the most part, preoccupied with internal events.

By 1880 the community had expanded from forty-nine to eighty-nine households, an average growth of four new families each year for the previous decade. Fifty of those families were landless, attracted to Promised Land for a combination of reasons. Probably at least some of them hoped to acquire land there. Promised Land was the only place in the area where Negroes had even minimal hope of buying land after 1877. Local farmers and planters, never eager to sell land to Negroes, now grew even more recalcitrant as Democratic white rule was re-established. Sharecropping dominated farming arrangements between whites and Negroes throughout the Cotton Belt. The landowners at Promised Land, "well, they was wheels. They *owned* their farms."[35] And the respect and prestige they commanded within the county's landless Negro population were another kind of attraction for landless families.

The violence of Reconstruction was moderated only slightly, and a concern for personal safety was surely another reason Negroes moved to Promised Land. Few of the early settlers, those who came before the mid-1880's, could have escaped that violence, even if their contact was indirect. Wilson Nash, Willis Smith, Allen Goode, Washington Green, Wade and Eli Moragne all headed landowning households. For any who might forget, those men were constant reminders of the dangers which lay just beyond the community's perimeter.

The men at Promised Land still exercised their franchise, fully aware of both the dangers and the benefits which they knew accompanied political activity. Together they walked the three miles to Verdery and collectively cast their ballots at the post office "where Locket Frazier held the box for the niggers and Red Tolbert for the whites." Perhaps they walked together as a symbolic expression of their solidarity, but much more likely it was because of a practical concern for their own safety. They were less vulnerable to attack in a group. As it had in the past, however, this simple exercise of citizenship enraged the local whites; and, once again, in the early 1880's the men at Promised Land faced the threat of violence for their partisan political activities.

Them old Phoenix rats, the Ku Klux, come up here to beat up the niggers 'cause they went to Verdery and voted. Them old dogs from Phoenix put on red shirts and come up here to beat the poor niggers up. Old George Foster, the white man, he told them "Don't go down in that Promiseland. Josh Wilson and Colbert Jordan and them got some boys up there, and they got shotguns and Winchesters and old guns. Any white man come in to Promiseland to beat the niggers up, some body going to die. They'll fight 'til hell freezes over. You Phoenix rats go back to Phoenix." So they went on down to Verdery, and they told them the same thing.[36]

Their reputation, their readiness, and their willingness to defend their land were clearly well-known facts about the people at Promised Land. The "Red Shirts" heeded the warning, and white terrorists never again attempted to violate Promised Land. This, too, must have been a part of the community's attraction to landless families who moved there.

Promised Land in 1880 was a community which teemed with activity. Most of the newcomers joined in the brush arbor worship services and sent their children to the community schools. Liberty Hill School and the white schoolmaster were replaced by "schools scattered all around the woods" taught by Negro men and women who lived at Promised Land. Abbeville County maintained a public school. Crossroads School for Colored was taught by H. L. Latimer. The Mill School, maintained by the extensive Moragne family for their children, was held in James Evans' mill on Curltail Creek and was taught by J. H. Turner, Moragne brother-in-law. The Hester School, located near the southern edge of the community, was so named because it met in the Hester family's home. All three private schools supplemented the meager public support of education for Negro children; and all were filled to capacity, because "folks had big families then—ten and twelve childrens—and them schools was crowded."[37]

The representatives to the 1868 South Carolina Constitutional Convention who formulated the state's land redistribution hoped to establish an economically independent Negro yeomanry in South Carolina. The Land Commission intended the purchase and resale of Dr. Marshall's farm to solidify the interests of radical Republicanism in Abbeville County, at least for a time. Both of these designs were realized. A third and unintended consequence also resulted. The land fostered a socially autonomous, identifiable community. Drawing on resources and social structures well established within an extant Negro culture, the men and women who settled Promised Land established churches and schools and a viable economic system based on landownership. They maintained that economic autonomy by subsistence farming and supported many of their routine needs by patronizing the locally owned and operated grist mills and general store. The men were actively involved in Reconstruction politics as well as other aspects of civil life, serving regularly on county juries and paying their taxes. Attracted by the security and prestige Promised Land afforded and the possible hope of eventual landownership, fifty additional landless households moved into the community during the 1870's, expanding the 1880 population to almost twice its original size. Together the eighty-nine households laid claim to slightly more than four square miles of land, and within that small territory they "carved out their own little piece of the world."[38]

TWO

On Land and Liens

The white man was glad to give you a crop lien 'cause he want that money to build mansion houses. You can travel from here to Philadelphia and see houses built that way, falling down now. White man done robbed the poor nigger out of the cotton money to build them mansion houses, and the nigger don't know. The white man believe in give you clothes to wear, food to eat, and take your cotton. He think that pretty white cotton too good for the nigger.
Cora Frazier Hall
Promised Land, South Carolina

Farming dominated life at Promised Land during the 1880's and 1890's. It was the foundation of economic autonomy for almost every family in the community. Not a single 1880 household was without at least one agricultural worker, and in most households everyone over the age of twelve or thirteen labored for at least part of the year in the fields. Everyone was a vital part of the household economy. Children were put to work as soon as they were able to "pull out the grass and chop the cotton." Those too young to go to the fields and work helped out at home by tending baby brothers and sisters. By the age of eight boys and girls alike could "chop cordwood and cook like a growed women." Old people, too, maintained active roles in their households even after they "left the cotton picking to the younger ones." There were still meals to cook and babies to tend. In those days "the womens worked as hard as the mens."[1]

On Crop Liens and Renting Land

Within this world dominated by farming there were, nevertheless, dramatic differences between farmers who worked their own land and those who worked the lands of others. The most immediately apparent of those differences lay in the average value of farm production. Among landowners farm production in 1879 averaged $216.41, twice that of sharecroppers and tenants. The basis for this difference lay in the prevailing patterns of financial arrangements and credit extensions inherent in the crop lien system.

Farmers who either rented or sharecropped land were usually dependent upon their landlords for a variety of commodities and supplies—flour, molasses, and other food staples, as well as items directly necessary to agricultural production such as seed and fertilizer. They obtained these items through their landlords rather than directly from merchants and pledged a portion of their crop as repayment for the advances and "furnishings." The landlord's primary goal was the production of a profitable cash crop, and landlords universally required that tenants and sharecroppers concentrate their fields in cotton as a condition of these arrangements. As a result, landless farmers could not produce those commodities most directly beneficial to their households—"corn for us, and the mules too"—because they lacked control of the land they farmed.[2]

The crop lien system operated in such a way that it imposed a second type of restriction on those indebted to landlords. In addition to control of the land, the men who held crop liens also controlled marketing procedures. While landowners at Promised Land loaded their cotton onto wagons and drove into Greenwood where they sold their crop directly to the local mills, tenants and sharecroppers were forced by their indebtedness to market their crops in a more circuitous manner. Crop liens were paid off at the end of the season in cotton bales, not cash; and the value of the cotton was invariably discounted in this exchange between creditor and debtor. The arrangement entailed a three-way loss for the Negro tenants and sharecroppers. First, they paid usurious interest rates for the credit they received in March. Second, the prices they paid for commodities obtained as "furnishings" from the lien man were much higher than cash prices; and this mark-up continued throughout the growing season. And third, at the end of the cotton harvest in October, they received credit for their crop which was well below fair market value. Indebtedness accumulated from year to year, and the tenants and sharecroppers were soon trapped in a never-ending routine of debt and obligation to white landlords. Landowners, because they produced their own "furnishings" and sold their cotton on the competitive market, realized twice the farm production of the landless.[3]

Folks Was Farming and Needed Lots of Childrens

At Promised Land there were few mules, and plows too were old and scarce. Like poor people everywhere, the folk in the community worked their land by human labor; and every hand at the plow or on a hoe increased the food and cotton yielded up by the land in the fall. Economic exigencies shaped family life as they did other activities. Although landowners, tenants, sharecroppers, and wage laborers alike lived primarily in nuclear families headed conjointly by a husband and a wife, the details of their household composition were shaped by their relationship to the land. The differences between owners and tenants, between laborers and sharecroppers reflected the economic strategies families devised in their struggles for survival, struggles based in large part on their separate economic conditions and options.

Families with many young children, not yet old enough to be economically productive, generally farmed less land than those with older children who could work the fields. These younger families, probably because of their already limited labor resources, did not often bring aging parents or other nonproductive relatives into their households. Those people went where they could best be cared for or were the most needed themselves. Grandma Fannie Moragne, the aging matriarch of the Moragne clan, lived with her oldest son Bill and his wife Lucy in her old age. Crippled and barely able to walk, Grandma Fannie lived in a house where there were no small children and where she, instead, was the focus of attention. There, from her bed in a relatively peaceful and quiet setting, the old woman "would talk and laugh just like she used to" with her grandchildren and great grandchildren who stopped by every day or two for a visit.[4]

Nieces and nephews in need of a home, grandchildren whose parents were "away," and unmarried adult sisters and brothers, all found places in family life and household structures guided by the needs of the farms and the abilities of households to absorb another person. It was unusual for anyone to live alone at Promised Land. Individual needs were generally met through collective solutions, and the ways in which households were constituted were governed by two considerations: practical labor requirements and the affective bonds of kinship. The balance between them linked family life to the economic strategies and land tenure arrangements among the community residents.

Table 1.

*1880 Household Structure by Land Tenure Groupings**

Variable	Land-owners	Tenants and Sharecroppers	Wage Laborers
Percent of Total Population	44	26	30
Percent Married†	86	87	68§
X̄ Age for Head of Household†	49	46	36§
Percent of multigeneration Households†	7	14§	8
Percent with Nonkin in Household†	3	21§	2
X̄ Size of Household‡	6.24§	4.79	4.65
X̄ Household Laborers Over 13‡	3.44§	2.38	2.00

*U.S. Bureau of Census, 1880 Household MSS, Smithville and White Hall Townships, Abbeville County, S.C.

†Using the landowning group as the theoretic statistical model, binomial tests yielded significant differences, $z > 1.96$, $p < .05$.

‡ANOVA and subsequent t-tests yielded $F > 4.79$ df $= 2, 80$; $t > 2.87$, df $= 21, 44$; $p < .01$. Average size of households nationwide in 1880 was 5.04 persons. U.S. Department of Commerce, *Bicentennial Statistics*, p. 378.

§Statistically greater/smaller.

All small farmers in the Piedmont labored under a common set of disadvantages. The soil was everywhere exhausted; and the success of even a small cotton crop depended upon intensive use of feritilizer, expensive to buy but essential to make a crop. Negro farmers were further circumscribed. In addition to the disadvantages they faced from the worn out soil, they also labored under the restraints of race. For them even more so than for the small white farmers, the credit essential to planting and fertilizing their crops was extended only with exorbitant interest rates. They avoided indebtedness as much as possible and minimized cotton crops, concentrating their efforts on consumable production.

The farm equipment and draft animals that would have enhanced their production capabilities were expensive technological luxuries and were usually replaced by human effort on the small farms. The "lien man" was avoided as much as possible because repayment of that debt was commonly made with raw cotton. Those farmers who were best able to avoid entrapment in the crop lien system, mortgaging a future crop at planting time in the spring to obtain seed and fertilizer and even the other "furnishings" like food and clothing which a family needed to live, were the men and women who owned their own land.

Ironically, farming on a white man's land held little hope of profit because the lien men and the landlords took the cotton to pay for the supplies they advanced and the land they provided. But those who farmed their own land had little hope of profit either. They avoided the indebtedness which plagued tenants and those who "farmed on halvers" (sharecroppers who pledged half their future crop to the landlord for the opportunity to work the land); but they lacked the resources, supplies, and machinery to grow a cotton crop of any substance.

Still, landownership was the only hedge against chronic poverty. The economic stability it afforded was apparent in three aspects of social life. First, landowning households differed markedly from those of their nonlanded neighbors. Second, farm production, even though limited by lack of capital and primitive technology, was greater among the landowners than the landless. And third, land management strategies reflected the greater economic flexibility enjoyed by the owners.

The landowning farmers were all either married or widowed in 1880, and they lived predominantly in nuclear families. Although owners were similar in age to the tenants and sharecroppers (see Table 1), their households were a third larger than those of the landless families; and within those larger households there were significantly more people to work the land. The principle source of field hands was older children, and there were more children between the ages of sixteen and twenty in landowning households than in those of tenants and sharecroppers.

These young adult children married somewhat later than children of the landless families. Landowning parents apparently exercised some control over the timing of their children's marriages and probably over their choice of mates as well. The source of their control in both matters was the land, which was also the source of their children's compliance to parental wishes. Farming parents had some practical labor needs. Without mules or machinery it was essential that families keep their older children at work in the fields as long as possible in order to maximize the land's potential. Among landowners a parental promise of land proved an effective device to gain this

Table 2.
Women's Work and Household Composition, 1800*

Variables	Housekeepers	Farm Laborers
Percent Landowners	34	66
Percent Nonlanded	25	75
$\bar{X}$ Dependent Children†		
Landowners	2.55	2.50
Nonlanded	2.00	1.95
$\bar{X}$ Additional Child Laborers†		
Landowners	2.09	0.81
Nonlanded	2.20	0.36

*U.S. Bureau of Census, Household MSS, Smithville and White Hall Townships, Abbeville County, S.C.
†X^2 = NSD

end; and a number of landowning parents either gave or sold portions of their farms to their children for nominal sums when they did finally marry, perhaps as a reward for their obedience. The children, in turn, were influenced by an artificial land scarcity and were apparently willing to delay marriage in order to eventually own even a small piece of land. It was one of the few foundations of economic security for Negroes attaining maturity in the last two decades of the nineteenth century. Thus, a double set of motives—labor needs on the part of an older generation, and a desire for secure land tenure on the part of the younger generation—operated in complement at Promised Land. Landless families lacked this lever for control, and for their children economic independence in their own adulthood was attained in other ways.

This single aspect of domestic life held specific consequences for the adult women in landowning households. Women generally worked in the fields with the other family members and were described occupationally as "farm laborers" by the census taker when they did so or as "housekeeping" when they did not. (In 1880 none of the women at Promised Land did "day work," domestic service.) Among the landowners 34 percent of the adult women were housekeeping exclusively, as compared to 25 percent of the women in the landless households. The difference between the two groups was directly related to the differences in their household labor arrangements and the greater availability of children to work the fields in landowning households.

Housekeeping as a full-time woman's role was only possible if she had labor replacements in the fields. The presence of young children in a household (see Table 2) did not affect adult women's labor among either the landowning or the landless families. In all households women worked in the fields, shifting to housework exclusively only when their children matured and replaced their labors as farm hands. Because the children in landowning families remained in their parents' homes for a longer time than the children of tenants and sharecroppers, proportionately greater numbers of women in landowning families retired from field work.

The full implications of this process on domestic life among landowners can only be surmised, but there were probably certain advantages those families had over households in which the adult women spent the majority of their time and energy in field work. Housekeeping women assumed greater control over the family garden than did women already working the fields. In those families the children were generally responsible for the garden. Housekeeping women, with their years of farm experience and the skill and knowledge which derived from that, were doubtless more effective gardeners than the children. A Piedmont garden will, with care and skill, yield almost year round; and the housekeeping women's gardens probably did so with great frequency.

In addition to their contributions to food production, housekeeping women were also able to spend a greater amount of time in food preparation than women preoccupied with field work. Those women who worked exclusively or primarily at home canned and pickled their garden produce in greater proportions than the field laboring women. As a result, family diets were more nutritious and well balanced in those families. Housekeeping women had the time to cook more elaborately. Fresh fruit pies during the summer months and preserved vegetables in the winter months were delicacies found more often on the table of families with a "housekeeping" woman among the adults, generally a wife and mother but occasionally a grandmother or unmarried sister. Better fed, the members of those families were capable of more work themselves. They were healthier.

There were other aspects of family life perhaps also affected in a positive way by the presence of a "housekeeping" parent. Those women, with greater leisure time, could have given greater attention to some of the cosmetic aspects of life. They had the time to sew and mend, to launder, and to plant flower beds. They could also tend to their smallest children personally rather than leave that responsibility to surrogates. Each of these possibilities created an atmosphere which fostered family stability and continuity, two more of the indirect benefits of landownership.[5]

Farm production was another aspect of the general advantages landowning community residents enjoyed, and one which was closely tied to household structure. Without human labor, farming was impossible; and as the number of field hands increased, so too did a family's agricultural production.[6] The increase (see Table 3) was a function of both labor arrangements and prevailing patterns of agricultural economics. Landowners were less dependent on crop liens than tenants and sharecroppers and as a result were able to plant their fields more in harmony with their families' unique needs or on the basis of opportunities for trade within the community. Farmers with crop liens had an obligation to plant in cotton, the common medium for repayment of agricultural debt. Primus Letman, a landowning farmer, and Cyrus Lites, a sharecropper, both lived at Promised Land in 1880. Both farmed there, Letman on his own forty-two–acre farm and Lites probably on a fifteen-acre tract at the western edge of the community, most likely owned by Negro Daniel Smith. The circumstances under which they farmed and their clearly different resources and arrangements illustrate the extent to which landowning farmers had an economic advantage over their landless neighbors.[7]

Primus Letman, Landowner

Primus Letman was fifty-one years old in 1880. He headed a family which included his wife Francis, one of the four Moragne sisters who lived at Promised Land, and thirteen children, ranging in age from eight months to sixteen years. The two oldest children, sons of thirteen and sixteen, worked the fields alongside their parents. Together the family cultivated thirty-five acres of land, eighteen of them planted in cotton. Letman's planting patterns were typical of the landowning farmers. Like his neighbors, he diversified and planted a good portion of his tilled acreage in consumable crops, four acres in corn, three in oats, six in wheat, and one in sorghum cane. In addition to the five bales of cotton they harvested that fall, slightly more than one hundred and thirty pounds of lint cotton to the acre, the Letman family also harvested forty bushels of corn, twenty of oats, and sixty-one of wheat. The single acre of cane produced thirty gallons of molasses. Measured against the harvest John Lomax observed when

Table 3.
*Summary of Cultivation Variables by Tenancy**

Variables	Landowners	Tenants and Sharecroppers
X̄ Acres Planted in Corn	8.11	6.92
X̄ Acres planted in Oats/ Wheat	7.69	8.41
X̄ Acres Planted in Cotton	15.87	14.38
X̄ Cotton Production (in bales)	2.94	2.46
X̄ Value of Machinery	$6.23	$9.30
X̄ Value of Animals†	$38.98	$26.54
X̄ Farm Production†	$216.41	$108.39
Percent of Population Owning Draft Animals‡	85	54
Percent Owning Milk Cows	74	62
Percent Owning Hogs	57	62

*U.S. Bureau of Census, 1880 Agricultural Census MSS, Smithville and White Hall Enumeration Districts, Abbeville County, S.C.
†t > 2.58, df = infinity, p< .01.
‡Using a binomial test, z > 2.71, p < .01.

he passed through Promised Land six years earlier, cotton production had declined and grains had increased for Letman and the other landowners. The family supplemented these food crops with the fruit from their six-acre orchard, which contained thirty peach and two apple trees.

The family apparently worked the farm under the most primitive conditions. Letman had an old plow worth only four dollars, and his single draft animal was an ox. The Letmans were too poor to purchase a mule "from the man in Abbeville who brought them down from Tennessee," or they did without the mule and avoided the forty dollar debt that purchase would have meant.[8] The animals they kept, like the fields they planted, were to feed the family, not to aid in growing cotton. There were two milk cows on the farm which provided the family with dairy products. One calved during the year, and Letman purchased another from a neighbor. Both were butchered for fresh meat. Ten laying chickens made their contribution to the family's diet, remarkably well balanced for a family in otherwise impoverished circumstances.

Primus Letman's resources were the most minimal. His livestock were valued at forty dollars, a figure which included the ox, the two milk cows, the calf, and the laying hens. His farm yielded $395 worth of commodities during the 1879 growing season and was the single source of income for the household of fifteen. The family's per capita income was twenty-six dollars that year. Even though the family was relatively prosperous by community standards, this well being was tempered by the number of children in the family, "more children than the Lord should allow;" and family resources were stretched to the limit.[9]

Cyrus Lites, Sharecropper

Landowners like Primus Letman lived in relatively stable, if impoverished, conditions. The plight of tenants and sharecroppers contrasted sharply with that of the owners, for these landless families were dependent upon landlords, white and Negro, for most of their daily, routine needs. They were bound to a specific tract of land for only a single growing season, and they moved from landlord to landlord with great regularity, "We farmed down here below Verdery. We farmed at Cedar Springs. We farmed all around" in an unending and usually futile search for slightly more advantageous arrangements. The lives of tenants and sharecroppers were fraught with insecurities. Agreements were rarely made in writing, and the landless had no protection against unscrupulous landlords. As a group they were less literate than the landowners and more vulnerable to being cheated. When unfairly treated their only recourse was to change landlords, and as a result they formed a less stable part of the community population.

The landless, particularly tenants and sharecroppers more so than the wage laborers in the community, were trapped in an endless cycle of nineteenth-century rural poverty. Tenants and sharecroppers "could rent a farm and take a lien from the lien man in them days. You could have five farms, take a lien for each farm," but the land still had to be worked by hand, and the debt repaid in cotton. The landless farmers rarely operated on a cash basis, either at the beginning of the planting season or at harvest. Without money there could be no land. Without control of land, there would never be any money: "the white man done robbed the poor nigger. Took all his cotton to pay for them liens."[10]

Men like Cyrus Lites scratched an existence from the Piedmont clay within this milieu of poverty and exploitation. Lites, aged sixty-one, was a widower and headed a household of himself and his two teenaged children, a son and a daughter. None of them could read or write. The three worked fifteen acres of land and maintained a two-acre permanent pasturage. From their six-acre cotton patch they harvested a single bale, eighty pounds of lint cotton to the acre. The family cotton production was only two-thirds that of the Letman family's. Their pitifully small cash crop probably did little to ameliorate the family's poverty. At least half the cotton paid the landlord, and the rest the lien man for seed, fertilizer, and other "furnishings."

The Lites family did plant two small grain crops in addition to the cotton patch. Four acres in corn yielded thirty-five bushels, and two acres in oats yielded thirty bushels. Their grain production was roughly equivalent to the Letmans'.[11] The Lites family planted neither wheat nor sorghum cane, which supplied by-products more suitable to human consumption than the corn and oats, which were destined for the mule. Flour, molasses, meat, and fresh fruits and vegetables were rare luxuries at the Lites table.

Like the Letmans, the Lites family farmed with the most limited resources, one plow worth only two dollars and a mule so poor that the census taker valued it at nothing. Lites estimated his 1879 farm production at sixty dollars, or twenty dollars per household member. Their income was below average even for the poverty-bound yeomen at Promised Land. The differences between the Letman and the Lites households affected not only their farming styles but also the basic quality of their lives. The Letmans were better fed, more economically secure, and better educated on the whole than the Liteses. The Letman family cultivated eight acres per worker, whereas the Lites family cultivated only five acres per worker. The difference was probably related, at least in part, to the nature of the diets in the two families. The Letman table reflected the family's own resources, high in protein and relatively well balanced. The Liteses existed on cornbread, greens, fatback, and molasses, food high in calories but low in nutritional value and not able to support the physical demands of labor-intensive farming. The Lites family, like twenty-five percent of the other families at Promised Land, lived a precarious existence, their survival balanced between the honesty of their landlord, the fairness of the lien man, good weather, high cotton prices, and no illness or injury in the family. When all occurred in the same year, then a tenant family like the Liteses might "break even."

I Worked for Mr. Bulow. He Was a Colored Man.

Twenty-nine percent of the 1880 Promised Land population worked for wages. These agricultural laborers, usually among the most impoverished nineteenth-century rural Negroes, were unusual in their situation at Promised Land.[12] They were the youngest of the land tenure groups in the community, and they were also less often married than any of the others (see Table 1). When married, their families, like the tenants' and sharecroppers', were smaller than those of the landowners; but in their case size was a function of youth. They were still in the early years of their childbearing cycles. Rarely were their children old enough to work in the fields, and because of this the young families lack a primary resource for farming, household workers. Wage laboring families rarely lived in extended family units, households which incorporated exceptionally young or old dependent relatives at Promised Land; and most were, in an economic sense, husband-wife work teams.

Probably many of these couples expected to establish secure land tenure at some point in their lives. The majority were related to landowning farmers, and two-thirds of the laborers subsequently inherited land in the community, usually before they reached their forties. Many lived on their parents' land and worked for them. Others found work with friends and neighbors, landowners like Samuel Bulow, Isaac Moragne, and James Fields. All three hired nonkin as extra hands on their farms. During the 1880's probably only a few of the wage laborers were required to seek work outside Promised Land. Despite their youth and family obligations, the absence of secure land tenure was not a serious economic or social disadvantage for these young couples. Theirs was not a permanent status nor a permanent occupation.

The domestic arrangements of tenants and sharecroppers reflected the marginality of their economic conditions. Like the landowners, they were men and women in middle age. Their households, in contrast to those of the owners and the wage laborers, often included more than two generations, cousins and in-laws and, with even greater frequency, nonkin (see Table 1). Additional relatives rarely posed an economic advantage for these families. Generally they were either elderly women—grandmothers and mothers-in-law—or young children—frequently nieces and nephews. These additions meant more mouths to feed and bodies to clothe, but because of their age these additional members of the landless households made little contribution to a family's farm production.

Typical of such families were John and Lucy Chiles, a young couple in their twenties with three small children to support. They share-cropped fifteen acres of John Campbell's farm, barely enough land to raise a single bale of cotton and maintain a small garden. In addition to their children, the Chileses also supported John's seventy-two year old mother. She contributed little more to the family economy than minimal child care while John and Lucy worked their rented fields. The Chileses were among the most destitute of the families at Promised Land. They supported six people on their fifteen-acre patch.[13]

Lucius and Millie Means, about the same age as the Chileses, also sharecropped fifteen acres in the community. Unlike the Chileses, their landlord was Negro landowner Samuel Bulow. The Chileses' landlord, John Campbell, was white, the nephew of James Evans, owner of the Evans Mill. Both Evans and Campbell invested in land around Promised Land and worked their investments with Negro sharecroppers. Bulow, however, was an established and respected member of the community. He was seventy years old when he employed the Meanses as sharecroppers and may have been motivated as much by neighborliness as pecuniary interests in the arrangement he derived with them. Lucius was the son of Bulow's landowning neighbor David Means. The elder Means was middle aged, and Lucius was his oldest son. There were other children still living in the Means household, and Lucius could not look to his father for work. Bulow was elderly, and the relationship between them met mutual economic needs, but it contained a subtle element of amity as well.

The young Means couple was an exception to the general pattern of sharecropping or tenancy. Most families who farmed this way lacked either sufficient resources or family connections to rise above the most meager level of subsistence existence. Those who established a secure tenancy within the community were rare. Landless families were commonly forced to look beyond Promised Land for a satisfactory landlord. Abner Goode, Allen Goode's older brother, was one such local sharecropper. He rented a fifty-acre farm near the community, which he cultivated with the help of his wife, his oldest daughter, and a niece who lived with his mother, Mary Goode. Both mother and son, Mary and Abner, maintained independent households at Promised Land, living in small cabins at the edge of Allen Goode's land. Mary's household was the most impoverished, for she supported four young granddaughters. Only twenty-year-old Becky worked for her Uncle Abner. The other three girls were still too young to be sent to the fields and were wholly dependent upon their grandmother, and probably their uncles as well. Other than providing living space for his kin, Allen Goode apparently felt no obligation to either his aged mother or to his older brother, for he farmed independent of their efforts, using only his wife and one child as field hands.

In a few cases households at Promised Land were, not family units, but were two or three young men living together, renting or share-cropping cooperatively. (Generally the oldest man in these house-holds was listed as the "head" by the census taker, and the others were described as either "partners" or "boarders.") The youths who farmed under this arrangement were demographically similar to the wage laborers rather than other sharecroppers and tenants, with whom they shared only a common land tenure status. The nonkin cooperative farming arrangements served a very practical purpose. This was a strategy whereby young men established economic and social independence from their families while still unmarried. Such independence was otherwise not possible, for during the 1880's solitary farming was impractical. The level of poverty in the community and the labor intensive demands of cotton cultivation made some form of cooperative work partnership essential for those who chose to stay. Work partnerships coincided with domestic arrangements among these farmers; and, although such partnerships were general-ly based on marriage, the alternatives of kinship and friendship also provided foundations for such pragmatic economic alliances. Inde-pendence and adulthood for the youth of Promised Land during the final quarter of the nineteenth century were defined, not in terms of age or marital status, but through economic productivity. Adulthood was attained only with economic self-sufficiency.

Negro Farmers, Negro Landlords, and Negro Tenants

Land-use within the Promised Land community was not cast within clearly defined modes. Even among the landowning households, only 42 percent (N = 16) cultivated their own holdings exclusively, nei-ther renting additional acres to supplement their small farms nor renting out additional land in an effort to bypass the poverty inher-ent among owner-operators. Forty percent of the landowners (N = 15) rented out all or part of their farms; and 18 percent (N = 7) rented additional acreage themselves, often from neighbors and kin. Tenancy, in one form or another, dominated the agricultural patterns at Promised Land; and for this reason the Lites family was more typical of the local farmers than were the Letmans.[14] The arrangements derived in these tenancies were dictated to a great extent by individual household circumstance and particularly by available laborers within specific households.

Old age was one aspect of household composition that often affected land management strategies, as illustrated by Samuel Bulow's situation. Bulow, who owned a fifty-acre farm at Promised Land, cultivated none of the farm himself. He utilized both sharecropping and tenancy to exploit his lands. Fifteen acres were sharecropped by his neighbor's son Lucius Means; and the remaining thirty-five acres were rented to his daughter Adeline and her husband, James Burt. His motives were probably mixed, for Bulow was advanced in age and not capable of the sustained physical efforts required for field work; yet, he was apparently unwilling to relinquish control of his farm. As a consequence, tenancy by members of the younger generation was a logical solution to his dilemma. All three households benefited in the arrangement. The Meanses lived close to their parents and at the same time established a degree of economic independence on their small patch of land. The Burts, who like most young couples lacked the resources to purchase land of their own, enjoyed a secure tenancy on the Bulow farm and probably looked forward to the time when they would be able to purchase the farm from Bulow. In this case both kinship and friendship stimulated a solution to the problem of land distribution and allocation.

Old age was not the only factor which prompted a landowner to rent out his farm. Isaac Moragne, who was only twenty-seven years old in 1880, also leased part of his farm to his landless brother Andrew. Isaac, a preacher and a teacher, apparently had little interest in farming. Like Adeline and James Burt, Andrew Moragne lacked the resources to purchase land of his own. For these two brothers tenancy was a solution to separate economic realities, although the details of the situation differed radically from those faced by Sam Bulow, the Burts, and the Meanses. Isaac, like most landowners, was reluctant to relinquish ownership of the farm, even though he did not cultivate the land himself. As was the case with the Bulow farm, kinship established a framework for an economic exchange of benefit to both men.

Reciprocity and mutual benefit characterized other rental arrangements in the community; and kinship frequently proved the basis for these patterns, which were repeated in both the Hutchison and the Reynolds families. Whitfield Hutchison, the jack-leg preacher, also had little interest in his farm and rented it to his brother Frank. Frank cultivated the entire thirty-acre tract in addition to his own twenty-four–acre farm. In the Reynolds family Iverson and Clayborn were the family farmers. Both owned farms of their own, and both rented additional land. Iverson cultivated his brother Irwin's thirty-acre farm and also his daughter Janie's twenty acres until that tract was transferred to Oscar Pressley when he married Janie. Clayborn rented all of Wells Gray's seventy-five–acre tract, which he farmed in addition to his own thirty-two–acre farm. Gray and Clayborn Reynolds had been neighbors for five years when this agreement was reached, and their relationship certainly extended beyond the formal landlord-tenant one which generally governed such situations.

In other cases land rental agreements between neighbors and kin had a note of benevolence. This motive was apparent in the arrangements derived within the Williams family, which were unlike the land rentals which occurred between Moragne, Hutchison, and Reynolds family members. In those cases the landlord-tenant relationships were between brothers and instigated by practical matters of convenience. One brother owned land but lacked an interest in farming. Another brother, in need of land, rented from him. Both benefited in the exchange. The Williams family distributed their holdings in a somewhat different way. The effect of this distribution was an equalization of available farmland among all adults in the family. The extent to which the Williams family strategy contrasted with that of the other kinship groups may stem from the fact that the two landowning members of the family were women, Elsie Williams and her daughter Amanda. In the other families all the arrangements took place between men and were stimulated by alternative occupational choices available to the landowners.

Both Elsie and Amanda cultivated farms purchased during the original Land Commission sales. A second child, Elsie's youngest son Henry, was landless. Mother and daughter each rented fifteen acres of land from their own farms to Henry during his young adulthood. At the same time both women continued to farm their own reduced acreage. It was in this way that the Williams family diverged from the land rental patterns in other families. Both landowners were farmers themselves and partitioned their land for reasons other than those which motivated Isaac Moragne or Whitfield Hutchison. The arrangement the family made was probably more a compromise of desires than a rational economic exchange, but such a compromise was wholly within the spirit of reciprocity which united kinship groups into cooperative economic units. Henry obtained a degree of independence and self-reliance generally not possible in renting or sharecropping from a white landlord and maintained his status as a member of a landowning family. The two women retained ownership of their farms, as had Isaac Moragne, Whit Hutchison, and Wells Gray. The outcome in the Williams family was the same as it had been for the others. All participants in the arrangement were able to assert themselves as economically self-sufficient individuals.

Tenancy arrangements within Promised Land were not limited to agreements between kin, although kinship was the most prominent factor in many of the situations. Samuel Bulow rented to his neighbor's son, and Wells Gray rented an entire farm to his friend and neighbor Clayborn Reynolds. These situations still contained an element of affective bonds which probably ameliorated the more utilitarian aspects of tenancy. There were other rentals in the community which were less likely to have been based on personal relationships, however. Typical of these were the farming patterns of the five Chiles brothers, long-time landless residents of Promised Land. The five men were scattered throughout the various farms, each making his own independent tenancy arrangements. Henderson Chiles rented thirty-five acres of land from Negro landowner Charles Jackson. Iverson Chiles rented thirty acres from Willis Smith. Jordan and Harris Chiles both sharecropped on James Evans' land up by the flour mill, and John Chiles sharecropped on John Campbell's land.

Although Campbell was white, his land lay within the borders of the original Marshall Tract; and he exploited his holdings through community residents. In addition to the acreage farmed by John Chiles, there were two other Negro sharecropping families living on the farm; and two additional tracts were rented directly to Negro landowners Jacob Burton and Gipson Goodwin. Campbell maintained a residence near his uncle, James Evans, up on Curltail Creek. This was the only case of white landownership within the original boundaries of the Marshall lands. Yet the integrity of the community's racial homogeneity was maintained, probably inadvertently, through Campbell's tenancy arrangements.

Two Negro landowners, Harriet Bradley and Jacob Burton, also cultivated their lands exclusively through the use of sharecroppers. Both were elderly, and their choice of method was probably less motivated by pecuniary interests than was Campbell's. They, like Isaac Moragne, Samuel Bulow, Elsie and Amanda Williams, and the other landowners who rented out portions of their farms, were tied to their land by symbolic forces. Despite their age neither chose to sell their farms; the value of land was measured by these former slaves as much in terms of the security and the prestige of ownership as by the small income it provided.

The strategy James Fields used in the management of his land holdings combined the rather altruistic motives of the Williams family with the more practical approach taken by other nonfarming landowners in the community. Fields purchased two separate tracts of land from the Land Commission, although at the time of his purchase he, like Samuel Bulow, Elsie Williams, Harriet Bradley, and Will Donnelly, was advanced in years. He employed Mose and Martha Wideman as farm laborers in the cultivation of one of the tracts and James and Millie Kennedy as laborers on the second. In addition to these two couples, both of whom were still in their twenties and were typical of the wage laborers, Fields provided living space and a small garden plot to another elderly couple, Isaac and Clarissa Stephan. The Stephans were in their eighties and had no relatives at Promised Land. Perhaps separated from their families during slavery, perhaps not able to locate children sold away from them, this old couple lived a marginal existence. Without Fields' kindness their lives after emancipation would have been much different. The Widemans and the Kennedys both had landowning relatives, and their relationship with Fields was based on characteristically reciprocal economic needs. The Stephans, however, offered no economic advantage to Fields; and their residence on his land can be explained only in terms of a prevailing mood of philanthropy.

These three separate land management strategies emerged at Promised Land between 1875 and 1880: family farming, a cultivation style limited to operator-owned land; owner-renter farming, an agriculturally and economically expansive technique that involved renting lands to farm in addition to your own; and landlord farming, a farming style based on tenancy and/or employing persons outside the household as wage laborers. Each of these strategies was associated with specific age groups and domestic situations, and each served the needs of the families who owned the small farms.

Those landowners who engaged in family farming owned neither more nor less land than those in the other two groups, nor was there any difference in the overall size of their households or their domestic labor forces. That is, it was not a shortage of either land or labor that motivated some landowners to rent additional land or prompted them to lease out portions of their farms. The only apparent difference between the family farmers and the other owners was their age.

Family farmers were middle age, an average of forty-five. Owners who rented additional lands were significantly older, averaging fifty-five at the time they were engaged in their tenancy. Those who rented out their lands were either exceptionally young or very old. Although the average age of the third group was thirty-five, the figure is deceptive. These entrepreneurs lay at both ends of the age spectrum, and the motivations for the young were probably quite different from those of the elderly.

The family farmers elected the most conservative of the farming strategies. They were thirty years old at the time of emancipation and acquired their land during mid-life. All had young, but maturing, families at the time of their purchases. For this group, those who saw and directly experienced much of the violence of Reconstruction, aspirations and expectations were fixed on their land. For the older group, those who expanded their farming operations to include rented property as well as their own holdings, emancipation came somewhat later in life, at about the age of forty. For many of these landowners, emancipation from slavery coincided with the maturation of their children; and they entered an era of economic independence and landownership with quite different household labor forces. Few in this group failed to take advantage of their young adult children. They were quick to expand their farming operations, putting every available hand to work. These patterns, which initially were established on the basis of household composition, persisted into the 1880's. In addition to the economic benefits these owner-renters derived from their expanded farming operations, they also accrued an added bonus—their families remained intact for a much longer period of time than those of farmers who owned no land or who did not farm land other than that which they owned, for their adult sons and daughters realized an economic advantage of their own by remaining at home.

Landlords, the third distinctive group of community landowners, were divided in age. The older men and women in this group were motivated by a desire to retain ownership of their land, even though they were unable to farm it themselves. The symbolic power of landownership was strong, and this was no better illustrated than by this group of aging freedmen. Through rental and sharecrop arrangements older landlords were able to remain economically independent and enjoy the higher status their ownership afforded long after they lost the physical ability to farm. At the same time, it was this group who provided an unusual entrance into the community life for the younger generation, those who were babies or small children at emancipation. As they created tenancies at Promised Land, their own children and the sons and daughters of their neighbors were able to establish a degree of economic independence and retain residence in the commuinty, a feat which would have been impossible had they been forced to establish tenure with white landlords. The aging landowners thus played a subtle, but vital, role at Promised Land, for it was their flexibility in land management and their ability to adapt an otherwise exploitive land management strategy to good purposes which benefited the whole of the community.

The younger landlords, who were in their mid-twenties at the time of emancipation, were still physically capable of cultivating their own land. Few were married or encumbered by the responsibilities of a family when their enslavement ended. At the same time, few were able to maintain a farm either, for they lacked the domestic labor force necessary to do so. Their initial land management strategy was quite utilitarian and in many ways paralleled the approach of the older owners. In order to retain the status of landowners they rented or sharecropped the farms acquired from the Land Commission. Like the family farmers and those who expanded their farming, the patterns of these entrepreneurs persisted into the 1880's long after the earlier situations which first stimulated the adaptions had changed.

THREE

Buying and Selling,
Building and Willing

Only colored here in this old Promise land. Won't no whites stay
on here. Had their own gin. Had their own store. Had a Mason
Hall. The old people told us this. We keep the land now. We got all
the land down in here willed to our grandchildren.
Cora Frazier Hall
Promised Land, South Carolina

Although farming was the central focus of life in Promised Land
during the 1880's, it was not the only way in which the community
lands were exploited. Before the final deeds to farms were issued by
the Land Commission, community residents began a lively series of
land exchanges.[1] The earliest of these established churches and
schools, and the creation of these vital institutions was soon followed
by other forms of land transfers. Kinsmen and neighbors bought and
sold pieces of land regularly. New residences were created on lots far
too small for farming, and a new class of landowners emerged during
the 1890's—men and women who lived in Promised Land but worked
beyond boundaries of the community. Old men transferred their land
to their wives and sons and daughters, some before their death and
some through inheritance. Gradually the shape of the community
shifted from fifty small farms to more than one hundred tracts of land
of varying sizes, and this shift prompted adaptions in work as well as
living arrangements.

Buying and Selling

In 1875 James Fields sold one acre of his land to the Mt. Zion African
Methodist Episcopal Trustees for forty dollars. In 1882 Wells Gray
sold two acres of his land to the Crossroads Baptist Church Board of

Deacons for thirty-two dollars. The prices charged by both Fields and Gray were high when compared to land prices in other parts of the county, which still hovered around ten dollars an acre for similar land. They were even greater when cast within the impoverished conditions of the Promised Land farmers. Yet the churches were central to community life; and the prices paid for the church lands were solid investments, for the benefits returned to the community residents were reaped many times over. The churches fostered an immediate sense of community cohesion and order in Promised Land, which might otherwise never have developed.

Both James Fields and Wells Gray were community benefactors, although this may have been the unintended consequence of their land-use strategies rather than conscious and intentional behavior. In addition to the lands they made available for the churches, they also partitioned small lots from their farms for the establishment of two schools in 1887. There was a hint of competition between the two men and the religious factions within Promised Land which they apparently represented in these transactions. Fields sold three acres of his land to the Abbeville School District Association for eighty-four dollars, or twenty-eight dollars an acre; and Gray sold a single acre of his land to the Baptist Educational Society and Union for twenty dollars only months later.[2] As the institutional frameworks within the community were established, the denominational lines were also drawn among community residents. The Baptist children attended the school Gray established, and the Methodist children went to the public school. While the source of this division was probably doctrinal, it did not have longstanding effects on internal community dynamics; and before the end of the nineteenth century all the children in the community were attending the public school.

In addition to the establishment of these basic religious and educational institutions which served the entire community, there were three other types of land sales which began during the 1880's: transactions between kin; transactions between nonkin; and transactions between Negroes and whites.[3] Each type was distinguishable from the others, shaped by a different purpose. Some were designed to redistribute a given tract of land within a kin group, most often intergenerationally. Others were motivated by individual economic situations, particularly those which involved the sale of small home lots; and still distinct from these were sales which were apparently instigated by friendship and benevolent considerations.

During the 1881 to 1890 decade transactions between kinsmen were typically sales between parents and their adult children in which original homesteads were partitioned into smaller tracts of land. Of the six instances three occurred within a single family, as Beverly White partitioned his farm between three of his four sons. At the age of sixty-one White and his wife, Ann, who was twenty-five years his junior, lived alone on their farm. Their four sons, Nimrod, William, Samuel, and Paris, maintained independent households in Promised Land. Nimrod and Paris, the eldest and the youngest, lived on their parents' land and were employed by their father as farm laborers. Samuel and his wife worked for Isaac Moragne on his farm, and William and his wife worked on Osburn Aiken's rented farm. The Aikens, like the Beverly Whites, were an elderly couple; and William probably served the same function on their farm that his brothers fulfilled on their father's.

In 1881 White subdivided his farm, selling portions of it to Nimrod, William, and Samuel. Nimrod was thirty-six when he acquired 3.75 acres, his portion of the family land. Samuel, then twenty-nine, and William, thirty-one, both purchased 9.75-acre tracts. All three paid their father the same amount for their land, thirty-two dollars. There was no adjustment in Nimrod's price to compensate for his smaller portion. Paris, the youngest son, received no land. At the age of twenty-three he lived next to his father and continued to work for him. Beverly White retained ownership and control of 9.25 acres of the original farm and in so doing also maintained a degree of control over his youngest son. Despite his landless situation, Paris remained at Promised Land for a time, working his father's diminished farm and probably expecting to either inherit or purchase the remaining tract. The land was not to be his, however; for when Beverly White died in 1895, he willed the remaining property to Nimrod and William in equal portions. When his brothers took title to the lands he expected to receive, Paris migrated from Promised Land.

Wells Gray, like Beverly White, also sold portions of his land to two of his children during the 1880's. His daughters, Amy Gray Wright and Janie Gray Morris, both acquired twenty-acre farms from him, paying only nominal amounts for the land—"one dollar, love, and affection." His sons, Benjamin and Willis, received no land until shortly before their father's death in 1895.[4]

Gray followed a pattern established by James Fields and Iverson Reynolds when he used a portion of his land as dowries for his daughters. It was a pattern repeated by other landowning fathers, although the size of the gifts varied according to the amount of land a man owned and the number of daughters in a family. Primus Letman, who owned forty-two acres, but who had thirteen children, gave his oldest daughters, Millie and Liza, "places to build their homes when they got married, two acres each"; but he was not able to provide his younger children with land.[5] Regardless of the size of the dowry, the gifts served two purposes. Land enhanced a woman's marriageability and thus enabled her to attract a more desirable husband. The dowries of land served their intended purpose, for they assisted young women in establishing stable and independent households. There was a second and more subtle effect which these gifts had on daughters of landowners. They bound the young women and their husbands to the community.

Women generally achieved symbolic as well as factual independence from their parents at marriage, marked by the establishment of separate households. Autonomy for young men was not so easily obtained, for their adulthood was measured in terms of economic self-sufficiency. Landowners generally retained control of their farms until well into their own old age; and, therefore, their sons faced quite different problems than their daughters in achieving their own independence. Older sons were generally middle age before family land was available to them, and by that time most had established other land tenure arrangements. Fathers were trapped by their own desire for landownership and the desire to assist their children. As a result the older sons frequently moved away from the community; and "the babies got the land."[6] Seldom did sons, if they stayed at Promised Land, achieve independence before their fathers' deaths, because only then were family lands finally transmitted to male heirs.

Although the majority of the land sales between kinsmen that took place during the decade of the 1880's were intergenerational, two transactions within the Moragne family occurred between brothers. Both were probably instigated by Beverly White's sale of land to his son. Isaac Moragne sold two parcels of his farm to his brothers Andrew and Eli. Andrew, who was landless at the time, purchased nine acres; and Eli, already a landowner, bought a fourteen-acre tract. As was the case with the White family, both men paid Isaac fifty-six dollars for their parcels, even though Eli's was almost twice the size of Andrew's. The two sales took place only weeks after William White purchased land from his father and left Isaac's employ. Isaac, preoccupied with his twin professions of teaching and preaching, was probably not able to manage all of his forty-two–acre farm alone; and, with the loss of White, he faced spring planting with a labor shortage. The sales took place just before planting time, and it was also possible that Isaac intended the cash realized from the sales to meet the expenses of spring planting. Apparently he sold land rather than incur a crop lien. Whatever the specific motives which prompted the sales, Isaac Moragne's work was not on the farm. Although he retained ownership of nineteen acres of his original farm, actual responsibility for cultivation was delegated to his wife, Anna; and from that time on no wage laborers were employed by the Moragne family to assist with the farming. Anna and the children worked the fields alone.

In addition to these subdivisions of farms which occurred between kin, four of the original farms from the Marshall Tract exchanged hands intact. New landowners settled in the community, and in several cases original landowners expanded their initial holdings. Samuel Burt and the Wideman brothers, William and Richmond, all acquired their farms during the 1881 to 1890 decade from original settlers. Joshuway Wilson bought thirty-eight acres of land from John Campbell, who had perhaps tired of the supervision of share-croppers. The purchase expanded Wilson's holdings to seventy-two acres. Allen Goode also increased his landholdings by forty-two acres through the purchase of additional land, one tract acquired from a Negro neighbor, the other from a white man. William Moragne also bought thirty-five acres from a white neighbor. Both Moragne and Goode bought land which lay at the edge of the original Promised Land perimeter and in this way slightly expanded the borders of the community. Harriet Means settled at Promised Land with the purchase of a fifty-four–acre farm, the final tract in Dr. Marshall's farm to be sold by the Land Commission. All of these sales involved tracts of at least twenty acres, sufficiently large to be considered working farmland rather than home lots. Many of the settlers were obviously intent upon farming as their occupation and were quick to buy up whatever land was available.

A second type of land sale between nonkin involved much smaller parcels of land, lots far too small for farming but quite adequate as permanent residential sites for otherwise landless community residents. Two of these purchases were contracted with white landowners. Jefferson Floyd, a local surveyor, sold a small home lot to his Negro assistant, White Chappell; and James Evans, the miller, sold a small lot to his assistant, Bevy Miller. Notably, both sales between white sellers and Negro buyers occurred within the context of employer-employee relationships. Although social conditions usually precluded such land sales from white to Negroes, the additional relationship between Floyd and Chappell and Evans and Miller was apparently sufficiently strong to transcend those prevailing norms.

Neither sale was typical of a marketplace exchange, for both were of such small parcels of land that there was little economic benefit for the sellers. Neither buyer was a farmer, and the only attraction which their purchases held for either was that they provided secure home sites within the boundries of an established Negro community. Chappell and Miller were among the first community residents whose work was not directly agricultural, and their obviously intentional residence in Promised Land was an early indication of the attraction the community held for Negroes in the neighborhood.

Land sales between nonkin residents within Promised Land added to the population of young Negroes who intentionally chose the community as their permanent residence, for most of these sales entailed the establishment of new home sites. Wells Gray sold two small parcels of his land during the 1880's, one to William W. Frazier and the other to Adeline Crawford. Both sales were based on interpersonal alliances. Frazier subsequently married Gray's daughter, Amy; and there can be little doubt that his purchase was a variation on the dowry arrangements fathers commonly made for their daughters. Crawford was the daughter of Gray's neighbor, Elias Harris. She was newly married when she purchased her land from Gray; and the tract enabled her to establish a permanent home at Promised Land, close to her father's household but also independent of it. Whether or not Harris assisted his daughter and her husband directly in their purchase, either financially or by intervention with Gray, the prevailing expectations of neighborly assistance were probably potent forces behind the sale.

Many of the eighty men and women who became landowners through the purchase of small home lots were already tied to other community residents through bonds of kinship. After their land purchases they were attached to Promised Land in a more concrete way, and the dual bonds of land and family were powerful ones.[7] Most of these new landowners established and maintained permanent homes and remained at Promised Land to raise their families. Some rented or sharecropped on nearby farms. Others were preachers and teachers, carpenters, or laborers on the pulpwood and railroad industries, all common occupational alternatives for Negroes in the Piedmont during the final years of the nineteenth century. These same occupations were also supplementary forms of work for local farmers during the slack months of the agricultural cycle.

During the 1891 to 1900 decade the land exchanges within the community intensified. There were proportionately fewer sales between kin than in the 1881 to 1890 decade, but there was a dramatic

increase in the size of the tracts kinsmen exchanged. During the 1881
to 1890 decade kinship sales averaged 9.70 acres. In the following
decade, 1891 to 1900, this increased to an average tract size of 73.50
acres, an increase which signaled a shift in local land management
strategies. Wilson Nash typified the conditions which accompanied
this shift. At the age of sixty-one Nash sold all of his holdings, one
hundred and sixteen acres of farmland, to his wife, Moriah, for the
nominal sum of one hundred dollars. Other elderly men disposed of
their farms in a similar manner. Wells Gray sold twenty-two acres of
land to his son Benjamin for three hundred dollars only months
before his death. Lymus Pinckney sold his fifty-four–acre farm to his
fourteen-year-old son, Andrew A. (A. A.), for three hundred dollars.
All three of these sales were probably substitutes for the transmission of land through inheritance, but the farms were sold intact
rather than being subdivided as Beverly White had done ten years
earlier. Although motives are never stated in deeds of sale, these
landowners had witnessed the dissolution of their neighbor Beverly
White's farm and the dispersal of his children. They had also seen the
heirs in other families lose title to their inheritances when Negro
estates were probated through white-controlled courts. Perhaps they
chose sale before their death as a strategy to avoid the problems
inherent in other tactics.

As the average size of tracts exchanged between kinsmen increased between 1881 and 1900, there was a concomitant decline in
the average size of tracts Promised Land residents sold to nonkin
during the same period. Between 1881 and 1890 the average size
tract of land sold to nonkin was 29.92 acres. This figure declined by
more than half during the 1891 to 1900 decade, to 10.85 acres.
Although the general trend in these sales was toward more small
home lots, there were also several instances of intact farms being
sold. Hannah Fields, James Fields' widow, sold a fifty-five–acre farm
to Samuel Burt, a young member of Mt. Zion church, the church
Fields established twenty years earlier. Burt's father had been a
community resident since 1871, and Burt married the daughter of a
local farmer. His brother James was already established on Samuel
Bulow's farm and would inherit the land at Bulow's death. Burt's
network of family relationships and his own good reputation were
probably both instrumental in the purchase he negotiated with Hannah Fields.

Iverson Reynolds, then sixty, divested himself of his farm, selling
to nonkin under circumstances similar to those which characterized
the Fields-Burt transaction. Reynolds sold his twenty-seven–acre

farm to Sarah Devlin and her two daughters, Ellen Frazier and Lou Ellen Goode. Both daughters were married to sons of other landowning families, but the three women farmed the Reynolds place collectively for more than fifteen years. Although the sale price was nominal—ten dollars—there were no apparent kinship bonds between Reynolds and the three women. Reynolds was not yet ready to retire from farming, however; for six years later, at the age of sixty-six, he bought a ninety-acre farm from George H. Harrison, a white neighbor, paying market value of ten dollars an acre for the land.

Both the Fields and Reynolds sales, although they were made to nonkin, followed the trend in land management established twenty years earlier. There was a high priority placed on assisting established community residents, and this assistance was often defined through landownership. The larger, farmable tracts of land in the community were consistently sold to men and women who were both known and respected by local residents. Family connections provided a valuable advantage is establishing this necessary respect.

The sale of small home lots proliferated during the 1891 to 1900 decade. Wells Gray, one of the largest landowners in the community, continued his pattern of selling off small parcels of land to various community residents. A. A. Moore, the preacher at Crossroads Baptist Church, the church Gray helped establish; Henry Latimer, the teacher at Crossroads School for Colored; and Jesse Ray, a sixty-two-year-old long-time sharecropping resident of Promised Land, all purchased lots from Gray during the final decade of the nineteenth century. Moore paid twenty dollars an acre; Latimer eighteen; and Ray one hundred. There was still little consistency in land prices at Promised Land. Each transaction was probably based on a complex balance among need, desirability of the purchaser, the seller's economic situation, and the location of the land. The personal factors that influenced the decision to sell land doubtless influenced the selling price.

The sale of land by white farmers to Promised Land residents increased during the 1890's, both in size of tracts and in numbers of transactions. W. L. Bradley was one Negro purchaser who was probably typical. Like White Chappell and Bevy Miller during the 1880's, Bradley bought his land from his employer, the Wilkerson family, for whom he worked as a farm laborer for fifty cents a day. In Bradley's case, however, the purchase was not a small lot. Instead, it was a sizable, fifty-four–acre farm at the eastern edge of the community near Moragne Town. The site was a prime one. There were two springs on the land and a number of natural berry patches. His great grandchildren later remembered Bradley's farm for another attraction, "the biggest pine tree in South Carolina, with limbs bigger than a man's waist." Still, Bradley came to his land through the generosity of his white employer, a special relationship within which the usual protocols and restrictions of race were often suspended.[8]

Despite the extensive land trade within Promised Land during the final quarter of the nineteenth century, the community did not assume the spatial organization of a "town." Unlike the land development patterns which characterized other Negro settlements—Cass County, Michigan; Boley, Oklahoma; Mound Mayou, Mississippi; and Nicodemus, Kansas—or early colonial settlements such as Andover, Massachusetts, the newly established households at Promised Land were scattered throughout the four square miles of community farmland rather than clustered around a common focal point such as the churches or schools.

The reason for this development pattern was related in part to the original plans for the Marshall Tract devised by the Land Commission. Promised Land, like the other plantations the commission purchased during the 1870's, was never intended to be a town or even a scattered settlement but, rather, a set of contiguous farms. All acreage was privately owned from the onset of the settlement period, and no land was ever set aside as "common" or collective. In addition to this initial condition, the freedpeople who came to Promised Land had lived as slaves in clustered housing. The spatial distribution of their houses now, most rather squarely located in the center of their own farms, was a symbol of their freedom. They lived on their own land. As new families moved into the community, they favored locations near one of the roads. The creation of a "town" was never of primary importance to either the original landowners or those who moved into Promised Land during the final quarter of the nineteenth century.[9]

Building a Community

The foundations of the Promised Land community were vested in the land; and the shape which the community assumed, both materially and symbolically, derived from the ways in which that land was exploited. By the 1890's Promised Land was no longer a collection of small farms but clearly a Negro settlement incorporating more than two hundred and fifty-households. The men and women who first established homes within the community boundaries were quick to establish the building blocks of their community: schools; churches; and as great a degree as possible of economic self-sufficiency. The land afforded the basis for all three.[10]

Land-use patterns led to an elaboration of these local institutions which furthered the community's identity and solidified the self-sufficiency of local residents. The lands of the Marshall Tract were never used exclusively for farming after the 1870's, and the area around the crossroads proved valuable for the establishment of local business. First, North Carter opened a small store there, where he sold kerosene and other supplies to his neighbors. During the 1890's Frank Hutchison, whose land was also situated on the crossroads, sold a small lot to John L. Turner, a second generation member of the Moragne clan. There young Turner established a home, asserting his adulthood and independence; and he also went into business, opening a second store. Competition was probably not particularly intense between the two men. Carter was a Methodist; Turner a Baptist; and the denominational divisions likely defined their separate customers in much the same way as they dictated school attendance for the local children. Further, Carter was an old man near the age of retirement by the time Turner opened his store; and, finally, the community had grown large enough to support both enterprises. All three conditions in combination probably moderated the potential for rivalry between the two stores.

The Carter and Turner stores were not the only local businesses at Promised Land. When Joshuway Wilson died his land was subdivided among his children, each receiving a small tract of the farm. His oldest son Fortune opened a molasses mill on his inheritance. With sorghum cane stacked all over his yard during the fall, Fortune Wilson operated a lively local business. He ground the cane in a simple mill powered by two mules, then boiled the juice in great cast iron pots over open fires. Wilson's pay from his neighbors was not money but a percentage of the syrup. "If they had ten gallons, maybe he would get one-fourth of that." Wilson converted his barter within Promised Land to cash by bottling the molasses in corked jugs, loading it onto his wagon, selling it through the countryside to both white and Negro customers.[11]

Despite the preponderance of farmers in the community, there were those who found work beyond the cotton fields. Promised Land was on the mail route for the Verdery Post Office; and, when it first opened "Wes Fisher and John Reynolds, they run the post office. Two Negroes, the first to open up that post office in Verdery. They run it for twenty years," until the whites regained control of local patronage positions and installed their own Democratic representatives in local civil service jobs. Even after that, though, "Locket Frazier, he rode the mail." The reputation the community established as fiercely protective of its integrity necessitated a Negro route man, for "won't no white deliver the mail to Promiseland" during the nineteenth century.[12]

Between 1880 and 1890 the Seaboard Air Line Railroad purchased rights-of-way through Promised Land, one instance of the "penetration of the South by northeastern capital . . . to take charge of the region's railroad, mines, furnaces, and financial corporations."[13] Some of the landless and small landowners found work laying track for the route which passed through their community. This railroad line became a vital link between Promised Land and distant cities, a link facilitated by the establishment of Lorenzo Station, actually only a flag stop on the long route of the Seaboard across the Black Belt. Lorenzo was up by the Nash place at the northeastern rim of Promised Land; and, although it was little more than a flag stop, it became a point of embarkment for local residents. There they boarded the train for Saturday rides into Greenwood. The train ran from New Orleans to New York, and it offered the possibility of a variety of jobs to some of the men long after the track was laid. Among the first local youth to seize this opportunity was Joshuway Richie, old Josh Wilson's grandson. Young Richie, like many other southern Negroes, discovered that the railroad was "a path of emigration" when he secured a job as a porter on the train and began a life which, to those he left behind, seemed filled with travel and adventure, "like a sailor going from port to port."[14]

While Richie rode the rails, others stayed put in Promised Land. The community was filled with preachers, teachers, and craftsmen. J. L. Turner operated his store during the week and stood in Baptist pulpits on Sundays. Isaac Moragne and A. A. Moore also preached at the local churches, and Henry Latimer taught in the Baptist-sponsored school. Amanda Pressley taught in the public school; and her father, Oscar Pressley, was a carpenter. He "used to make all the coffins for the people who died. Didn't have no funeral home back then. Somebody die that morning, they bury them that evening. You could hear him hammer and nail for a mile." Wade Moragne was a mechanic; and he repaired wagons, plows, and almost anything else which broke at Promised Land. Elijah Turner was an old man, but he used his skills from slavery days to make his living. Turner wove baskets from hickory strips and sold them to his neighbors. Those baskets carried laundry down to the spring on wash day, stood at the end of cotton patches to hold picked cotton, and found their way into almost every home in the community.[15] Local industry emerged in response to local needs. The stores and the mills, Oscar Pressley's carpentry, Wade Moragne's mechanical and Elijah Turner's basketry skills were all parts of an independent economy which freed the people at Promised Land from unnecessary dependence on services managed and controlled by whites.

Community autonomy was further evident in the social and self-help organizations which developed. Although "the Baptists didn't believe in no secret societies," the Methodists had no such restrictions; and the men from Mt. Zion established a Masonic Lodge in the community, directly across the road from their church. The Redds, the Widemans, the Richies and the Jordan brothers built the Mason Hall, which quickly assumed an important role in community life. The Masons had their secret meetings there, but other organizations also used the hall. The Promised Land Union Burrial Aid Society, a mutual aid organization whose membership overlapped that of the Masons but expanded to include women, also met in the hall; and, when the one-room schools needed additional space, the teachers moved some of their scholars over to the hall.

The people at Promised Land lived always at the brink of economic chaos. Their ability to avoid indebtedness to lien men, to establish self-sufficiency on subsistence-oriented farms, and to utilize talents within the community for many of their daily needs were important strategies in forestalling routine economic crises; but these measures were of little help when a family experienced troubles of a more disastrous nature. Wooden houses heated with fireplaces and wood stoves regularly burned to the ground, leaving families homeless. Death always brought a family crisis, as did sickness. During these times community resources were mobilized through either the churches or the mutual aid societies—the Masons, the Ladies' Aid Society of Mt. Zion, and the Union Burrial Aid Society. "Back then it was the Masons what buried you, or the society," which also provided sick benefits to its membership in addition to death benefits and funeral arrangements. The families at Promised Land "didn't need no insurance men back then, not when you got the Masons. Keep them white insurance men out." Houses were rebuilt through the same processes, with collective efforts by the Masons and the Union Burrial Aid Society.[16]

Social activities were an important part of community life; and the Masons assumed responsibility for one of the major annual events at Promised Land, the Fourth of July picnic. "The mens would get together and bar-b-que a pig," and the women baked pies and brought baskets of food to the all-day affair. The atmosphere was festive and drew "folks from all over, not just from Promised Land." The Price family came from Verdery; and others came from White Hall, Bradley, and Long Cane. Luther Moragne had moved to Ninety-Six, and he loaded his family into the wagon for a three-hour ride back to Promised Land. The ladies sold the food; the children "bought candy with their little one penny"; and everybody waited for the baseball game in the church yard. Social activities brought most of the community residents together on a regular basis and were probably helpful in moderating some of the denominational divisions which separated the Baptist and Methodist congregations. They served other purposes as well, however; for they provided regular opportunities for play and recreation within the community, activities which were almost completely unavailable to Negroes as Jim Crow became more and more a guiding principle of life during the 1890's.[17]

FOUR

Does God Divinely Bless
the Education?

*Used to be schoolhouses sitting everywhere in the woods around
here. Teacher used to walk by here every day, that lady did. Oh
Lord, people had ten and twelve children then. Folks was farming
at that time, you know, and needed to have lots of children.
Schools would be full, churches would be full, and everything like
that. Now there's a lot of houses, but not so many children.*
George L. Wilson
Promised Land, South Carolina

Public education in South Carolina was implemented by the same
constitution which established the Land Commission. Prior to this
1868 social innovation there were attempts by various northern
benevolent societies, in cooperation with the Freedman's Bureau, to
initiate educational systems for Negro children in the South; but
throughout the Piedmont the efforts were haphazard and taught
under conditions so primitive as to neutralize those educational
efforts that did occur.[1] There was no evidence that any of the early
ventures reached the children living with their parents on Dr. Marshall's farm.

After 1868 the state common school system was plagued by chronic
underfinancing and mismanagement. The three-mill property tax
and one-dollar per adult male poll tax designated to finance the
public schools quickly proved inadequate. In 1871 the Abbeville
school commissioner reported deficits in the county's school funds of
$1,500, and that same year teachers complained to the state superin-
tendent that they were not paid for their work of the previous term.[2]
Despite the problems eleven public schools were in operation in the
county that year. Five of them educated three hundred and fifty-three
Negro scholars. One was Liberty Hill School on Dr. Marshall's farm.[3]

The teacher at Liberty Hill was white. After him the teachers in Promised Land were Negroes, and they were always permanent members of the community. These two facts set the children in the community apart from many other Negro children in the Piedmont. Their circumstances were unusual, because more typically Negroes did not live in isolated, racially homogeneous settlements such as Promised Land. They were more likely to be scattered among white families, living on the small plots of land which they sharecropped. Such separation was a necessity which accompanied land tenure arrangements. The children in these families walked many miles to attend school. In contrast, the schools in Promised Land were centrally located; and the children walked only short distances to attend them. The teachers there were the children's neighbors, often their uncle, aunt, or cousin. Community schools suffered from the same financial problems that limited the education of Negro children elsewhere in the state, but the Promised Land schools were enriched by the personal bonds that prevailed between scholars and teacher. The power of those bonds was most evident in the rate of school attendance. Forty-five percent of the children between the ages of six and twelve attended school for the brief two month term in 1880, the overwhelming majority of them from landowning families.[4]

During the 1880's and 1890's there were "schoolhouses sitting everywhere in the woods around here." Before the public school building was erected, Promised Land children attended classes in the Baptist church and in private homes, for parents and community supported education as wholeheartedly as they did the local church and the Fourth of July picnic. "There was one school down at the crossroads; one over towards the Bell place, I think they called it Mt. Moriah School. And there was the Mill School," so called because classes were held in James Evans' flour mill on Curltail Creek. There were so many schools because "people had ten and twelve childrens then. Schools would be full, churches would be full, and everything like that."[5]

In 1887 Henry Latimer opened the Crossroads School for Colored, sponsored by the Crossroads Baptist Church. Few children under Latimer's instruction advanced beyond the third or fourth grade because "when March come we go to the cotton fields, knock [down] cotton stalks, and pick cracked cotton." Farm labor frequently intervened in the educational process at Promised Land, as it did for other Negro children; but family demands also took precedence over school for local children. "I only went to the fourth grade. Had to stop then. My mother couldn't buy no more books after that. School didn't have books for the children then." Despite the poverty and the family need for child labor, however, instruction proceeded; and work was mixed with play during the children's school days. "We had spelling first lesson, reading second lesson, then arithmetic." Games were interfaced with lessons; and between reading and arithmetic "we jumped rope, played marbles, this and that, every day."[6]

Haphazard and casual education for Negro children continued even after Greenwood County built a public school in the community in 1897, for the children were still limited by economic exigencies and political realities. "Highest I got was the third grade. Them old crackers with the government, they didn't have the school but one month before Christmas and two months after."[7] Yet the teachers were drawn from within the community, and they taught as best they could under the limiting circumstances. Sarah Wideman, daughter of landowner William Wideman, and J. L. Turner both held classes in the public Promised Land School. Bristoe Turner, Primus Letman's son-in-law, took over Latimer's position at Crossroads School for Colored, where he compensated for a lack of books by "writing out our lessons on little cards. First we learn A, B, C. Then, when we learn that good, he give us our numbers on more little cards."[8]

Crossroads School was privately financed, with Latimer and Turner paid through the Sunday collections. Promised Land School was financed by public funds. The first year that it opened the county school district provided twenty-five dollars for desks and fuel, ten dollars for charts and maps, and twenty-five dollars for repairs. It was the only money "them old crackers from the government" ever invested in the education of Promised Land's children aside from the teacher's salary of twenty-five dollars per month for the three month school term.[9] Repairs, upkeep, textbooks, and school supplies were provided by the parents, if they could.

The Promised Land public school was a simple, one-room log cabin. It was heated by a wood stove, which sat in a sandbox in the center of the room; "but we didn't have no wood for the stove. Boys had to go out and break off limbs. Sometimes when school be over we almost froze to death it so cold. We had a time then."[10] What few books there were passed from child to child within families. The desk money appropriated by the county bought lumber, and the benches, which lined the room, were built by the men whose children sat on them.

Childhood was brief in Promised Land, and education was a luxury for youth. The leisure of sitting in a classroom and studying lessons was an adjunct to other needs. Cotton fields, poverty, and family obligations drew the scholars away from their reading, writing and arithmetic; and for most of the local youth the schoolhouse was little more than a brief interlude between infancy and adulthood. By the age of eight most children could read and also cook a meal. By thirteen their education was finished; courtship had begun; and they were thoroughly familiar with the most efficient ways to knock down cotton stalks before plowing, chop and thin the new cotton plants, and pick cracked cotton in October, after the fields were stripped of the best cotton by the adults. The lessons the Promised Land children learned were taught as much in Sunday School as they were in the schoolhouse.

> *. . . whereas it is been about one fourth of a Century since this Sunday School was planted here as a Mustard Seed by the hands of Bro. H. Watson, G. W. Green and Sister Amanda Reynolds. . . . Be it resolve that We do here by make and appropriation sufficient to cover the apenses of having each of there picture taking at present on tin type . . . and handsomly fraimed with a historical speech of their work on the Sunday School. And be hung upon the walls of our church that unborn generation may not only read of their Work but will also have their likeness to look upon.*[11]
>
> The comite—
> Bro. R. H. J. Marshall
> Bro. B. L. Wims
> Bro. W. A. Turner
> W. L. Bradley, Sect. 10 June 1893

Religion provided for Promised Land a deep and enduring sense of community and a collective solidarity complemented by social responsibility. It was not unusual that the first manifestations of this spirituality took the form of African Methodism. Before James Fields migrated eighty miles from Columbia and "retired to his farm in Abbeville County" and provided the land for the first church, African Methodism was already organized and active in the region.[12] Its ministers freely interjected their opinions and positions into local and state politics.[13] Active involvement in the church afforded an entrance into other aspects of the social world. From the Valentine family in Abbeville one man worked as the local A.M.E. organizer, another held a conditional title to a farm at Promised Land for a brief time, and still a third established himself as a Union soldier during the war.[14] These were typical of the effects which the ideology of African Methodism had on its membership. Stressing social activism, it was a stimulating and vibrant denomination grounded in the joint principles of democracy and self-reliance. The patterns and ideology of the church were wholly consistent with the rhythm of life at Promised Land.

Mt. Zion thrived in its environment. It had the early advantage of a solid alliance with the local Republican interests in the county, and it was securely planted among a body of landowning Negroes. A century-old tradition of independence from white interference and domination were compatible with the possibilities for life within the community. Whether by design or accident, Mt. Zion also enjoyed the ecological advantage of centrality.[15] The lot which James Fields sold to the church trustees was no more than two miles from the most distant cabin at Promised Land, less than a thirty-minute walk for most.

Initially all the residents of Promised Land worshiped together, meeting biweekly to sing, pray, and occasionally listen to a traveling preacher. "First they had a brush arbor, but a storm knocked it down." This remnant from slavery times, used then as a clandestine setting for religious meetings, was adapted now to the needs of freedom. The first Mt. Zion was built in 1882 after the big storm. "My uncle and granddaddy went into the woods and cut fat pine to make pins" for the log structure. The men worked together to erect the church; and the women brought them their meals, which they ate together in the church yard. "That old Mt. Zion stood for eighty years" and elicited a great deal of pride among community residents. "It had a steeple so high you could see from Abbeville to here up in the top." The spire towered far above the cabins in the little settlement; and a great, seven-hundred-pound bell hung in its peak. "They ordered that bell from Atlanta, Georgia. Paid so much by the month for it—they was just poor people back then." The bell was shipped by train from Atlanta to Abbeville, then brought by wagon to Promised Land. A team of men and mules working together were required to hoist it into the steeple, and there it remained for three quarters of a century. "They ring that bell to tell somebody's a'coming, somebody's a'dying."[16]

Religion was an integral part of community life, not limited to formal prayer services and Sunday School lessons. Old men sat by their hearths on winter nights and on their porches during summer evenings, where together they read and discussed the meaning of the Word of God. School books may have been scarce, but there was always a Bible present, and it was well read in every house in the community. Discussion evolved into debate, and the debates led ultimately to a deep schism among Mt. Zion's membership. The church divided over the doctrinal issue of baptism.

African Methodism followed the Anglican tradition of baptism by sprinkling in infancy. There were those who derived a more literal interpretation of this basic rite of salvation. Eli, William, and Calvin Moragne, together with their brothers-in-law Jonathan Turner and Primus Letman, supported adult baptism by immersion. The Pinckney, Burton, and Nash families also endorsed adult baptism, as did Willis Smith's son William. In 1882, the same year that old Mt. Zion was erected, Wells Gray sold two acres of land to Moses, Eli, and William Moragne and Jacob Burton, deacons of the newly formed Crossroads Baptist Church. Then "some folks left Mt. Zion and went over to the Baptists. Other folks never went to church at all until they was Baptists."[17]

The two churches were established on lots less than one hundred yards apart, separated only by a thinly wooded meadow. That in itself was evidence of the intimacy and friendship that prevailed between the two congregations. The ties were extensive, for the memberships of Crossroads and Mt. Zion frequently intersected family groups. Isaac Moragne remained an active Methodist, as did his sons and daughters, although all his brothers and sisters affiliated with the Baptists. Henry Redd's daughter Mary Ellen married George Martin, a Baptist preacher, and shifted her membership from Mt. Zion to Crossroads. His son Nathan Redd married James Fields' granddaughter and remained active in Mt. Zion. Fortune Wilson's son George married Primus Letman's daughter Ada; and "he come over to my church, 'cause I sure wasn't going to be no Methodist."[18]

There were no apparent status differences between the two congregations, and the fact that the church memberships were intertwined by kinship and friendship mollified any tendency toward competition which may have been present. The two groups soon supported each other's church-related activities in much the same way they supported their neighbors' secular activities. "In them days the Baptists and the Methodists didn't have nothing at the same time"; and, when one church sponsored a special program or singing convention, the event was attended by members of both congregations.[19] A pattern of mutual respect and interdenominational support pervaded Promised Land's religious activities long before it was popularized in more urban settings.

The leaders of the two churches had much in common. Most were landowners, primarily men who were original settlers in the community. The Moragne, Turner, Pinckney, and Nash families dominated Crossroads; and their counterparts—James Fields, Henry Redd, the Wilsons, the Widemans, the Marshalls, and the Reynoldses—controlled Mt. Zion. All of the men who were earlier visible participants in local Republican politics were now equally visible in the leadership structures of the churches. Before the first generation concluded its tenure at Promised Land a pattern of local leadership was established that incorporated three central facets of community life—land, politics, and church. This elitist, unified leadership structure proved a functional one for Promised Land.

Self-Government and Social Responsibility

The Sunday School Board, not the deacons, stewards, or trustees, was the major de facto body of church government at Mt. Zion during the nineteenth century. Both officers and Sunday School teachers were elected to the board by popular vote. (Later persons were placed in these offices by the appointment of the pastor.) The Sunday School superintendent, Oscar Pressley, chaired board meetings, directed regular church services, and was responsible for the basic organizational matters of church business. The board secretary, John J. Reynolds, kept minutes of all official meetings and maintained church records. This prestigious position, also filled at other times by North Carter and R. H. Marshall, required a literate person, one able to maintain accurate written records of all church business and events. Although in fact the jobs of superintendent and secretary often overlapped, in theory they were separate and always filled by different people. In the absence of the secretary, however, Oscar Pressley occasionally recorded the minutes; in Pressley's absence meetings were conducted by either the assistant superintendent or the secretary. The other officers of the Sunday School Board—assistant superintendent, W. A. Turner; treasurer, C. H. Watson; and librarian, T. M. Goode—were support positions. The duties of these offices were primarily administrative, and the officeholders rarely initiated discussion of issues. Neither did they generally become involved in issue-related debates.

Sunday School teachers, like board members, were elected to their positions by popular vote. Thus, for them as well as for the board officers, their positions were a reflection of their prestige and status within the church congregation. The teachers met regularly with the board; generally the purpose of these weekly meetings was "to swap thoughts on the lessons" for the coming Sunday. The board did not function as an oligarchy in these meetings. Positions were aired, issues debated, and in the end solutions and decisions were reached through consensus. The method was an effective one and probably prevented the emergence of any serious divisons within the leadership structure. These meetings were not without humor, particularly when the topics addressed certain sinful pleasures. On one occasion "the Temperance lesson was read and in a jovial manner the necessity of being temperate in all things" was discussed by the teachers.[20] Even the Negroes at Promised Land did not escape the prudery of the Gilded Age. (In fact, it touched them deeply. In later years the women of the community, angered with their men's whiskey stills and drinking in the woods, occasionally reported the location of the stills to the sheriff in order to control the problem.)[21]

The Sunday School Board wrote its own set of by-laws, set the time of Sunday School, regularized board meetings, regulated teacher absences, specified the role of assistant teachers (who taught their classes one Sunday of each month), provided for public readings of the quarterly church financial reports, and reserved the right to "chastise" any teacher found in neglect of duty. Weekly meetings skillfully incorporated elements of participatory democracy, parliamentary procedure, and religious ritual. In a thoroughly bureaucratized manner the superintendent chaired all board meetings and Sunday School sessions and played a major role in the conduct of special church services. Meetings of all kinds—worship, business, or social—opened with a hymn and prayer and closed with a traditional benediction. God was an omnipotent and imposing presence in Promised Land.

The Sunday School Board also functioned as an *ad hoc* adjudication body, for it exercised a great deal of control over the Sunday School teachers' behavior. That control was occasionally informal, as in the meeting called for the purpose of "a general talk with each other on the part of negegent [negligent] Teachers." The board implored, threatened, and reasoned with various teachers to be "more interested to thear duty." Neither church, Sunday School, nor board meetings ever began at the regularly scheduled time; and the board officers repeatedly deliberated the problem of chronic tardiness. Their efforts were effective on at least one occasion, when Miss A. Perrin "arose and stated that she would try with all her soul to be on time each Sunday morning." She was not alone in the neglect, for her pledge elicited a collective response: "All teachers voted themselves with the same pledge on motion of Miss Lizzie Rykard." Teacher problems more serious than tardiness were also a board concern, as noted in one abrupt entry. "Miss Annie Wilson has varied from the pledge she made the Board on May 25, 1890. [She] Was no longer a teacher therefore." The board was serious in the discipline of Sunday School teachers, and the fact that the teachers submitted themselves to interrogation and even to expulsion from their offices was an index of the board's disciplinary power within church and community.[22]

General administration of church affairs also fell within the board's prerogatives, and this was most concretely expressed in the management of church finances. The board was careful, judicious, and quite precise in its use of church funds. The financial records of Mt. Zion attest to two facts of life in Promised Land. The first was the level of poverty in the community, for the church treasury seldom collected more than fifty dollars during any given year throughout the nineteenth century. Weekly collections were counted in pennies and nickels. The second aspect of community life reflected by the records was the overriding sense of social responsibility which dominated church and community. Money was never used carelessly. The financial records were maintained over a quarter of a century without error. Every penny collected was precisely accounted for in the quarterly financial report. Typical of the period was the financial record which spanned May 1895 to April 1896:

Promised Land SC
April 19, 1896

Money Received from May 26, 95 to Dec 29, 95	
Total Amt Received	$19.30
Paid out for Home purposes (Lititure)	8.15
Cause of Mission	3.18
To the Poor	2.35
Contengent deligate	1.50
To District Sups & other purposes	1.25
Total Amt expended	$16.43
To Balance carried over to 96	2.87
Money Received from January 5, 96 to April 19, 96	6.46
To Balance from 95	2.87
Paid out for Home purposes	$5.17
Cause of Mission	1.80
	7.51
Money in Treasure	1.82

Money Collected for Sunday School purposes from Jan 5, 1896 to
April 19, 96

Tot amount received	$6.46
Tot amount brought forward from 1895	2.87
Total	9.33
Total amt Expended for all purposes	7.51
Balance on hand	$1.82

Mt. Zion collected a grand total of $25.76 during this twelve-month
period. Over half the collections were used to maintain the church
and purchase supplies such as books, pens, paper, and the like.
Twenty-eight percent of the church funds ($7.33) were expended for
charitable purposes, and the balance of the money was paid to the
district supervisor and presiding elder. There were no funds allocated
for a pastor's salary; and Isaac Y. Moragne received his pay in food,
clothing, and other consumable goods from the community and the
congregation.

A portion of the church funds was used for routine purposes.
Teachers and representatives from Mt. Zion were sent to institutes
and meetings with two or three dollars in expense money. Educational expenditures dot the financial pages of the records. On one occasion
the board was shown a "class book" and immediately moved to order a
number of books sufficient to provide "one for each Sunday School
Scholar." The books, at the price of five cents each, amounted to a
total expenditure of $4.50, a large sum for a church with an annual
income ranging between twenty and fifty dollars.

The single greatest expense acted upon by the board was the
construction of benches for the church. Plans for the benches began
early in 1890 when, at one of its meetings, the board "Empowered R.
H. Marshall to draw up the plans of building the benches and give
over to Sect the next [meeting] in order [to determine] who will build
the benches." The project proved expensive, and from October 1889
until mid-1890 all church collections were earmarked to finance the
benches. The board's involvement in the project did not end with the
financial arrangements. A debate over construction, design, and
style ensued; and various points were argued at board meetings for
several months. The most troublesome issue was whether the new
benches would have slat or solid backs. When the building specifications were finally set forth in the minutes of a board meeting, the
matter had been resolved without a vote.

The Sunday School had on hand the sum of 53 65 cent. that the Sunday School approate the same and ord(er) a set of Benches made & present to the Trustes of Mount Zion A.M.E. Church.

The Plain or order by which Benches or to be mad 1. Plain finish 2. Toggle in stead of mates 3. the seat is to ProJect 2 or 3 (inches) foreard so as to give about 16 inches frount 4. Slat Back Put on with Post-nails.

Mt. Zion's Sunday School Board was a governing body thoroughly familiar with carpentry and the details of construction. The extent of their skill and their concern that the work they contracted for produce goods of maximum quality was evident in the building specifications. Their involvement in and concern for the project was further apparent when, in a later meeting, the board allocated additional funds for the purchase of kiln-dried wood. Green wood would warp in time, and the Sunday School Board intended that these benches serve the needs of the little congregation for as long as possible.[23]

The Sunday School Board was not limited to the conduct of Sunday School lessons and control of Mt. Zion's finances. Its scope was far-ranging and at times visionary. At one board meeting Professor T. J. Walker presented a proposal for a Teacher's Institute, to be established in Promised Land and sponsored by Mt. Zion. Members of the board seized on Walker's proposal, which they viewed as an opportunity to raise money within the bounds of religious activity. In a formal action they voted that the church "go into business" with Walker. The scheme was never realized, and Walker soon disappeared from Promised Land. Nevertheless, the board's receptivity and positive action on the proposal signaled a willingness, even an eagerness to expand the services of the church and to do so in a way financially advantageous to both church and community. Such an institute, if realized, would have drawn men and women into Promised Land from throughout the Piedmont and greatly increased the community's geographical area of influence.

The Sunday School Board, through its leadership capacity, served as the conscience of the Mt. Zion congregation, assuming responsibility for a variety of nonadministrative obligations. On one occasion the board received a gift of Bibles and other religious literature, material sorely needed in the church. Their gratitude was apparent in the formal resolution recorded in the minutes:

Wher as we have received through the agency of our pastor Rev. N. Chiles Such a beautiful lot of Bibles, Testemons & other perodical

*to the amt of Twenty five ($25.00) wish, for the small sum of $3
25/100 to cover the cost of packing & Transportation*

*And whereas the School wer greatly in need of said Bibles etc,
And is herby greatly benefitted by the reception of them.*

*Resolved 1st That we do herby tender to Rev. N. Chiles for those
most highly appreciated from a rising vote of thanks.*

> *Signed Respectfully for the fishers of men*
> *R. H. Marshall, Teacher*

Gifts rarely came to the Promised Land community, for its residents
were considered relatively prosperous. Most owned their land. Their
family and community lives were stable. Few were hungry. Yet their
well-being was relative. There was little money in the community for
books, even Bibles; and, although most of the residents placed great
value on education and literacy, many lacked the resources necessary
to nurture "book learning." Their struggles in this regard were apparent through their gratitude to Rev. Chiles more than in their
overt behaviors.

Mt. Zion leaders always viewed the Promised Land community as
their primary missionary and charitable responsibility. This commitment was formalized in a set of resolutions set forth by the
Sunday School Board "on Behalf of the Poor and Needy." In this
formal statement of church policy, the board recognized that there
were in the community those "in a Suffering condition for want of
proper Attention" as well as elderly men and women, "those who
heads are White by the pass of many winters." These two groups, the
aged and the indigent, were the responsibility of the church body as a
whole. To meet this obligation the collections from one Sunday each
month were set aside for "purposes of charity," to be used exclusively
for "relief to the poor and suffering." It was the duty of each member
of the board to be aware of the special needs of persons in the Mt. Zion
congregation and to bring those needs to the attention of the board as
a whole. The guidelines for contributions to this special charity fund
were explicit: "Let such help be given to each according as their need
and according to our means."[24] The policy was implemented immediately and brought Mt. Zion to a central position in community
life.

Worship and Social Concerns

Within this context of self-government and social responsibility the Mt. Zion congregation conducted its religious routines. Sundays began formally at 9:30 when the great bell rang out the beginning of Sunday School. The day was given over to worship, for preaching began when Sunday School ended, with very little concern for the specific timing of the two separate activities. Preaching continued into mid-afternoon; and there was often an evening service, which reconvened the congregation after dinner. The community church has traditionally attended to the moral education of its congregation, and Mt. Zion was not an exception to this pattern. When Rev. H. E. Lewis delivered an exceptionally effective sermon one Sunday, the secretary noted in the church minutes that "the discourse was pregnant with Biblical Truth and was a feast for hungry souls."

Education and enlightenment within the context of church services were not limited to sacred matters. To the contrary, the secular world was of equal concern at Mt. Zion; and this concern was particularly evident in the church services held on "Children's Day," an annual spring event marked by special services. Then—suspending the regular routine of preaching—essays, talks, and orations by various members of the congregation freely mixed the sacred and secular worlds. Laymen called upon the principles of Christianity to interpret earthly matters, and the day was not so much a celebration for the children of the congregation as it was a day devoted to their education on matters of immediate contemporary concern.

The subjects addressed on Children's Day were diverse, and often pondered metaphysical as well as concrete issues:

> *What has the niggro done to envelop America?*
> *Labor degsegaten*
> *True womanhood*
> *What advantage is ed(ucation) to a people of a community re-*
>   *ligioully?*
> *Does God divinely bless the education?*
> *We must be industrus*
> *How to be Successful in Life*
> *Our educational Money*
> *Young men, can we better our condition? If so, in what way?*[25]

The orations were planned in advance and were not extemporaneous speeches. They addressed a wide variety of topics; for the one hundred and ninety young scholars who sat quietly and listened to them, these talks were lessons in practical Christianity. They emphasized self-improvement, material as well as moral prosperity, and upward mobility. Hard work, self-discipline, and race pride were all promulgated on Children's Day, for the education of the children was as much a collective responsibility as care of the sick and elderly. This obligation, too, was met within the context of church structure.

I Found The Lord!

Whether church services celebrated special occasions, such as Children's Day and Easter—the most common of the unique church services—or were regular Sunday routines, they, like the board meeting, followed an orderly and predictable sequence. There was seldom any deviation from that order which marks a rational, bureaucratized ecclesia. Services opened with singing and a prayer, which were followed by Bible readings, preaching, and collections of money, and closed with a traditional benediction. Only under rare and unusual circumstances did the church body give way to more ecstatic expressions of spirituality. When this did occur the entire congregation shifted focus, often in order to accommodate the needs or desires of a specific individual. The Sunday "J. O. Pressley came in—full of the holy gost" was one such example of the Mt. Zion congregation's ability to make this shift. As R. H. Marshall began the traditional closing exercises that afternoon, Brother Pressley entered from the rear door, and "the school wer silent for a few moments" as he expressed the joy of his personal encounter with the Lord. Sunday school closed that day, not in its usually orderly ritual, but with a song requested by Brother Pressley, "Thou Didst Leave Thy Throne." His request was no doubt honored out of a deep and intrinsic respect for this most personal religious experience.[26]

Personal encounters with the Lord were not particularly unusual events and occurred with regularity among all age groups and both sexes. Equally common to Oscar Pressley's experience, which he shared with the entire church congregation that Sunday afternoon, was a solitary encounter. Young Ada Letman, Primus and Francis Letman's daughter, was left alone at home one afternoon to finish up the washing and "put me on some dinner" while her mother went to revival at Crossroads. As she went about her work she could hear the people singing and praying, and as she washed and cooked she prayed along with them. Sitting on the front steps, she "felt the spirit lift me up and I just went flying, throwing up my arms and hollering." Her uncle Wade Moragne heard her from his house and "come running to see what was wrong with me." Young Ada, at the age of fourteen, told her uncle that she had "found Jesus. He's in my heart and I'm just so happy."[27]

For Oscar Pressley, for Ada Wilson, and for all the others who "found Jesus," religion held very personal meanings. They rejoiced together in their individual discoveries and "went back to God" again and again in order "to be sure" that their experiences were not illusory. For others a confession of faith did not come easily. When "the preacher begged some men to come to the Mourner's Bench one afternoon" during church, he couched the call to a confession of faith within a warning: "You may not get in here again." It was a recurrent concern among the community population; for despite the relative security which came with living at Promised Land, there was always the possibility that "you can be killed when you walk home from church" or be abducted by the Ku Klux Klan with no warning at all. Life in this Negro community held an element of uncertainty and danger, and behind every religious experience there was the possibility that "you might not get home tonight." This subtle, but enduring, aspect of life made it unwise to "turn your back on the Lord"; and when there was a call to a confession of faith, most responded.[28]

There were no recreational facilities in Promised Land aside from the activities sponsored by the Masons, and there were certainly few public settings in Abbeville County where Negroes were welcomed or felt comfortable. Because of this isolation and exclusion, community church activities contained an element of sociability as well as spirituality. That it drew into its congregation Negroes living well beyond Promised Land—in Verdery, Bradley, Troy, and Long Cane—probably added to the social life within the church; but equally important was the location. At Promised Land "we didn't have to mess with no white folks," and this temporary release from racial tension enhanced the church's popularity among the county Negroes.

On weekends Promised Land opened its doors, and "folks come from all over to go to old Mt. Zion." The distances were great for many of the visitors, some of whom came "all the way from Atlanta and Greenville" to share in the August revivals and other special occasions. "They come in two-horse wagons, spend the night, spend the weekend," enjoying chicken dinners and ice cream from churns turned in the church yard. The Board of Stewards, the church trustees, and the Ladies' Aid Society alternated sponsorship of "turnouts" every two weeks during good weather; and these well-attended events were highlights in an otherwise exhausting routine of farm life.[29]

The Old Ones Passed On

As the nineteenth century drew to a close and the people of Promised Land looked back over their first generation of community life, there were already many visible changes which had occurred. James Fields, Wells Gray, Beverly White, Elias Harris, and Calvin Moragne were gone, buried in the cemetery of the community they helped establish. Two churches, a number of schools, the Carter and Turner stores, Fortune Wilson's molasses gin, and two hundred and ninety-seven Negro families stood now where less than half a century before there was a plantation big house and a row of slave cabins. As the old folks passed the heritage of slavery died with them, for in this community of freeholders that was a past best forgotten. Parents looked to the future and raised children to know and value freedom.

This freedom was defined in many ways. The ability to own and to buy and to sell land, to incur debts and meet financial obligations, to support churches and schools and the right to learn were all aspects of this freedom. Equally important was the freedom to travel about, to board the train at Lorenzo Station and ride to Greenwood on Saturday afternoon; and for some travel and distance assumed even greater dimensions. Among the first Promised Land residents to realize the full potential of these expanded horizons was young Joshuway Richie, who made his way to Atlanta. There he roomed alone. Others in the family would soon follow, finding work as unskilled laborers, dishwashers, and domestics. The backbreaking manual labor required to generate "one little nickle, one little dollar" in the city was still an improvement for these men and women. Since the age of twelve most had labored over cotton plants under the hot Carolina sun. Neither hard work, long hours, nor self-discipline were strangers to them.

The coming to power of the Redeemer Democrats in the South in 1877 marked the beginning of a struggle between various white political factions for control of local and state political machinery. It was a struggle in which Negroes were reduced to mere pawns. The fate of the Negroes was fixed by the 1875 Mississippi plan for disfranchisement; and various coalitions of political expedience among Populists, lily-white Republicans, and Redeemer Democrats during the final quarter of the nineteenth century never posed any realistic hope for a reversal of the disfranchisement movement. One by one the southern states followed Mississippi, devising and implementing various legal strategies to disfranchise and otherwise set apart their Negro populations. South Carolina began this process in 1882 with the Eight Box Law, a "Chinese puzzle" designed solely to confuse illiterate Negro (and white) voters and invalidate their ballots. The 1895 constitution and various Jim Crow laws completed the scheme and ended for a generation any possibility of an alliance between the Populists and the Negroes.[30]

Conditions were no different in the South Carolina Piedmont, or in the Promised Land community, than elsewhere in the state. Those Negroes who established secure land tenure, either as owners or as tenants, within Promised Land had little hope or opportunity for economic mobility. The community entrepreneurs, whether they sold land, operated small businesses, or marketed molasses and baskets, did so primarily within a Negro world. Preachers and teachers exercised their professional skills in churches and classrooms filled exclusively with dark faces. For all of them status outside the community was fixed by the customs of southern racism.

The strategies for survival devised, individually and collectively, to cope with the conditions of Negro existence constituted the core of community life at Promised Land. Even within the apparently static position of a subordinate caste, there were still opportunities for the exercise of initiative and creativity; and the men and women of the community regularly extended themselves in this way. Excluded from participation in the white world except as laborers and servants, they established an independent and self-sufficient community woven together by kinship and friendship and anchored in the land that they owned. Promised Land was a community which teemed with a sense of self-contained business acumen a decade after emancipation. In the brief span of twenty-five years the lessons of slavery were forgotten and, despite the political, economic, and social obstacles imposed on them by whites, the residents of Promised Land forged an active definition of their freedom.

The two hundred and eighty families in the community began a new generation and a new century under a regime dominated by Tillmanism and a racist ideology which for all practical purposes limited every aspect of their activity and behavior outside the community. In a more realistic sense, however, Tillmanism deprived them of very little. Although the white men who were their neighbors, their landlords, and their former masters never wanted them to be free, the 1895 constitution only circumscribed voting and established racially segregated schools. Community residents could still take the train from Lorenzo, going east to Greenwood or west to Atlanta. Their children attended "segregated" schools which were never integrated because there were never any white children at Promised Land. Most of the men still voted, for Promised Land was a community of literate preachers, teachers, carpenters, and subsistence farmers who paid their poll tax regularly and kept their receipts. Their choices at the ballot box narrowed, but after the "'Publicans went back North" in 1877 there were few options for them at the polls anyway. As early as 1877 and certainly by 1895, well-being rested on the ability to band together for protection and to rely on a few trusted white men who intervened in their affairs only under particularly stressful conditions. As they entered the twentieth century, "only colored here in this old Promiseland. Won't no whites stay on here."[31]

PART II

THE SECOND GENERATION
1900–1930

FIVE

They Owned Their Own Place

When I was growing up Oscar Pressley was an important man at Promiseland. He was a preacher, and he owned his own place. That was important—to own your own place. And he had a little money. Daymon Marshall, Nathan Redd, Dolphus Frazier and Celia Frazier—all those people owned their own place. That's what made them important.
Benetta Morton Williams
Promised Land, South Carolina

There's Lots of Places Like Promised Land

At Promised Land as elsewhere in the rural southern corners of Negro culture, life at the turn of the century was dominated by the conventions of Jim Crow. The racial division separated Negroes from whites in almost all aspects of their lives and established a clearly defined color line that set apart the two worlds. The techniques that enforced racial separation and white domination of Negroes included both legal strategies and informal, extralegal practices.[1] The power of the law, white defined and white enforced, was supplemented by violence, fear, and intimidation.

Segregated schools, railroad cars, water fountains, eating places, and residential areas were as much a part of life for the residents of Promised Land as they were for Negroes in Chicago's Black Belt or Atlanta. Social convention restricted personal movement, work opportunities, and living arrangements irrespective of geography. Limited education and low wages perpetuated established patterns of economic exclusion as effectively as Ku Klux Klan attacks and the poll tax. On the Negro side of the color line a cultural system developed, fostered by an isolation which made it invisible to and protected from the white world. This parallel body of institutions, as vital in Promised Land as it was among other Negro enclaves, served to both avoid and surmount the inescapable disadvantages of race.

Central to Negro social environment and its separate cultural milieu was a relatively independent economic system. Despite limited capital, fraternal, mutual aid, and self-help societies proliferated in Negro culture and formed a stable equity base for that economy. Most of the organizations supplemented the work of local churches in some way. They provided various forms of burial insurance, sick pay, unemployment insurance, and at times outright charity to a people cut off from other types of societal resources. These organizations were among the most widely supported sectors of the Negro economy.

Most of the organizations were similar to the Promised Land Union Burrial Aid Society, small, underfinanced, and hard pressed to adequately meet the needs of their impoverished memberships. Many, particularly those in rural areas, became insolvent and collapsed during the 1920's and 1930's. In cities, where capital was greater and management skills were more sophisticated, some prospered during even the most difficult times. One Washington, D.C. mutual aid society amassed such capital that it established the National Benefit Life Insurance Company. In Atlanta, the Atlanta Life Insurance Company was chartered by a prosperous fraternal organization; and in Durham, North Carolina the North Carolina Mutual Life Insurance Company was established by the Grand Order of the True Reformers in much the same way.[2] After the Promised Land Union Burrial Aid Society failed during the 1930's, North Carolina Mutual sent an agent from Durham to Promised Land; and the company wrote burial insurance policies for many community residents. Even as one part of the cultural system collapsed, another emerged to mediate the effects of exclusion and discrimination Negroes confronted as routines of their daily life.[3]

Landownership was a second, somewhat smaller building block in the equity base of the Negro economy. The five million acres of land Negroes owned in 1875 expanded to ten million at the turn of the century, then to fifteen million acres by 1910. This steady, if unspectacular, growth in landownership was apparent at Promised Land, where landowners dominated almost all aspects of community life by their numbers as well as their influence. As among other freeholders, life was organized around this slim but vital economic resource. Families were fed from the bounty of the land; friendships were formed on the basis of common land tenure and shared membership in churches and fraternal organizations. The leaders in these groups were the wealthiest among the poor, the landowners.[4]

At Promised Land the benefits the community reaped from the stability of the landowners were clear. The community and its residents endured and survived the boll weevil, the crop failures, and the capricious cotton market that plagued local farmers throughout the years of the second generation. Although some of the population was pulled away during the Great Migration, few of those who went north then ever completely severed their bonds with the community. The continued relationship between those who stayed and those who left added yet another element to community life, one which extended the stability already well established at the turn of the century.[5]

Promised Land's institutional structures were somewhat eroded but still intact when the Great Migration peaked with the onset of World War I. During their tenure at Promised Land, the second generation's expectations were raised and then dashed to despair. Interracial violence declined, then once again escalated as economic conditions worsened for whites as well as Negroes. Businesses, even the small ones at Promised Land, prospered and then failed. Jobs were plentiful, then nonexistent. Across the South a similar decline was evident for other Negroes as mutual aid societies and fraternal organizations disappeared and the fifteen million acres of farmland Negroes owned in 1910 dwindled back to ten million in 1930.[6] The community fortress against this deterioration rested on three factors: an ideology of self-help and mutual aid; churches and schools maintained and controlled by community residents; and an economy grounded in subsistence farming.

In 1880, 42 percent of the Promised Land families "owned their own place." Less than a generation later half the community residents were freeholders; and by the conclusion of the "Number One War," more than a generation after Promised Land was established, two-thirds of the residents lived on land which they owned.[7] Despite an overall decrease in community population during the early years of the twentieth century, the proportion and the number of landowners steadily increased. It was important to own your own place. Land was the major source of status, prestige, power, and security at Promised Land. The mass of Negro-owned land provided the basis for a community identity that set residents apart from and above other Negro farmers in the neighborhood.

The patterns of land acquisition that emerged during the early years of the twentieth century reflected the power of kinship bonds in the community, for the majority of those persons who became new landowners were tied by birth or marriage to first generation landowners. The gradual increase in landowners did not, however, involve an expansion of Promised Land's territorial boundaries. After

Table 4.
Promised Land Population by Land Tenure, 1880–1942*

Year	Total Population in Households†	% Landed	% Nonlanded
1880	89	41	59
1897	283	42	58
1909	199	57	43
1915	172	66	34
1922	210	68	32
1932	144	66	34
1942	176	73	27

*Based on a random sample by year, 1897 to 1942, of Tax Auditor's Duplicate Books, Smithville and White Hall Townships, Greenwood County, S.C.

†These population figures are for Greenwood County only. After the creation of Greenwood County in 1897 approximately 10 percent of the original Promised Land acreage remained in Abbeville County. These figures are, therefore, slightly deflated, but accurate, representations of general population growth and decrease trends.

the original land sales concluded in the 1880's, there was little additional land in Abbeville County available to Negro purchasers. With one or two exceptions, white planters and farmers generally refused to sell their lands to Negroes. As a result even those black yeomen financially able to negotiate a land purchase were restricted to sharecropping or tenancy by prevailing customs and patterns of discrimination.

From 1889, the date which officially marked the conclusion of the Land Commission program, until the 1950's there was an artificially induced land scarcity among Negro farmers. Forces beyond the control of the community, prevailing racism and attempts to limit the economic alternatives of Negroes in the South, operated in tandem to produce this scarcity. These conditions directly influenced landowning and land transfer patterns in the Promised Land community in much the same way as they did among other Negro landowners throughout the rural South. Those lands already in Negro hands were continually subdivided as they were transmitted from one generation to the next. The strategies by which the farms at Promised Land were transferred from the first to the second generation paralleled social and affective relationships in the community. Both were governed and dominated by established bonds of kinship.[8]

Prior to 1900 only 18 percent of the land exchanges in Promised Land occurred between kinsmen. The first generation landowners were relatively generous in providing home sites for community newcomers, and the frequency with which small lots were created from larger farms was concrete evidence of the prevailing mood of generosity among the local farmers. It was a generosity, however, that depended upon a relatively abundant supply of land. After 1900 the pattern shifted dramatically as land grew increasingly scarce. Adding new acreage to the original community territory was virtually impossible and land transfers between kin dominated the community's internal land trade. Seventy-five percent of all new landowners who established tenure between 1900 and 1915 were children of original settlers. Few of the aging farmers offered even small home lots for sale to persons outside their own families. They chose, instead, a variety of strategies which preserved family-based landownership and solidified control of the community territory within the same families who dominated landownership during the first generation. Cut off from any possibility of physical expansion, Promised Land became a rural ghetto. It was farmland, but it was as tightly circumscribed as contemporary Chicago. Ghettoization established an internal restraint on community development which further

Table 5.
Summary of Landownership, 1880–1942*

Year	X̄ Acres in Tracts†	Percent of Adult Population Owning Land
1880	47.7	41
1897	34.8	42
1909	32.5	57
1915	21.2	66
1922	19.1	68
1932	18.2	66
1942	21.7	73

*Based on a random sample by year, 1897 to 1942, of Tax Auditor's Duplicate Books, Smithville and White Hall Townships, Greenwood County, S.C.

†Correlation of size of holdings with number of landowners yielded a coefficient of $r = -.90$, $p < .01$.

emphasized community isolation. Promised Land was no longer open to any Negro family in need of a home as it had been during the nineteenth century. Now a closed community turned to a maturing generation of its own children, and they inherited the static land base.

At Promised Land technology was primitive by contemporary standards. Life and work still centered on farming; and, in addition to their subsistence fields, most folk had a small cotton patch, their only source of cash income. Rarely did more than one-third of the farmers own mules—contrary, short-lived, and expensive creatures. The bulk of the farming was accomplished by back-breaking, labor-intensive stoop work. Any household with children in it had a ready supply of free labor. "My momma, she hitched me up to the plow when I was twelve and said 'Now just pull good and straight John.' And I pulled that plow as good as any mule. When my brother got big enough he pulled that old plow too."[9]

These same children who pulled the plows, chopped the cordwood, and tended the babies eventually grew to adulthood and established independent, autonomous households. At marriage a young couple was expected to sever residence with both sets of in-laws. Except under the most extraordinary circumstances, they did so with regularity. Usually landless at the time of their marriage, few newly-weds were so fortunate as to immediately acquire land. More often, they established their first home on their parents' land, if possible, and turned to sharecropping or tenancy in their struggle for economic independence.

Among the rural families at Promised Land, where five to ten children matured sequentially from a single household, not all could inherit the few acres which made up the family farm. Established farmers, owners or tenants, were reluctant to give up any of their land while cotton prices remained relatively stable, around 12¢ a pound. Per acre crop yields increased during the decade for farmers, owners, tenants, and sharecroppers alike, reflecting some technological modernization within the cotton industry. For those with land this was a time of relative prosperity, and as a result maturing children were often displaced. There was little land available to them and economic survival was often possible only by leaving the land.

Even those children who did inherit land now received only an acre or two. In contrast to their parents, for whom land had been an economic asset, heirs of these minute remnants of the family farm experienced landownership as an economic liability. Year after year, regardless of the size of their holdings or the lack of productivity, taxes on the tiny parcels came due; and they always had be paid, or "the government take the land back."[10]

Unable to establish secure tenancy near their homes, many youth in the second generation faced a critical juncture in their lives. If they remained at Promised Land, on the small patch of land which was their portion of an already meager inheritance, they were unable to make a living. Without some sort of employment they faced the loss of their land to the sheriff's hammer in the annual county tax sales. Their life decisions were complicated by the fact that they were the first generation of Negroes born free, and their expectations and aspirations were doubtless shaped by this condition. They did not know the strictures and restraints of the slavery regime; yet they were not unaware of the dangers which followed dark skin, for they grew to maturity during the violence of Reconstruction. Few of these youths had any realistic choices when they emigrated from Promised Land. It was unlikely that they moved to other farms in the Cotton Cotton Belt. Land was no more available there than at Promised Land. Their destiny probably lay in the southern cities and the open and more readily available lands to the West.[11]

These departing youth left behind evidence of the growing disadvantage posed by ownership of diminished parcels of land. In 1880, when the average size farm was 47.7 acres, all the owners lived at Promised Land. By 1909, when the average size of individual holdings decreased to 32.5 acres, only half the landowners still lived in the community. A pattern of absentee ownership followed the internal redistribution of the original farms; and, as the size of the tracts further dwindled, there was an ever increasing proportion of landholders living outside Promised Land.[12] The majority of the owners who migrated from the community prior to the 1920's owned, not the smallest home lots, but the middle sized tracts, generally portions of land acquired through inheritance rather than outright purchase that were useless to men and women who expected to live their adulthood as farmers.

My Father's Farm

Between 1897 and 1915 half of the new landowners in Promised Land acquired their land through inheritance. This was a predictable shift from the patterns of land transmission established during the nineteenth century, when most land was exchanged through sales and the buyer and seller were seldom kinsmen. Many of the original settlers, in their thirties and forties when they moved to Promised Land after emancipation, were now aging grandfathers. At their deaths their farms were transmitted to the second generation. The mechanics of these conveyances varied, but most resulted in a common outcome. Family farms were altered as the land moved through the generations; and the details of the transformations were central factors in the shape of life within the community. Despite the changing details, land continued to be the major focus of life and livelihood for the residents of this agricultural community.

Washington Perrin, Calvin Moragne, Willis Smith, Jacob Burton, and Joshuway Wilson all "passed" intestate as the second generation matured. In each case their farms were divided among many heirs.[13] This division of original farms provided a small amount of land to each of their children, which enabled those young adults to establish permanent and stable homesteads on their fathers' land.

For most, the inheritance of a divided farm failed to meet the expectations held privately for their personal futures. These young men and women grew to adulthood in privileged positions at Promised Land. Their fathers were community leaders who were respected landowners. Their families had been wealthier than their nonlanded friends and neighbors. The inheritance of a pitifully small tract of land was for most a reduction in status; and, although these heirs had secure homes on family lands, many were then forced to continue their own farming activities as tenants or sharecroppers.[14]

The downward mobility they experienced was acute, especially in contrast to the ideology of success and progress they learned as children. The sermons, talks, and orations they heard annually on Children's Day at Mt. Zion taught one set of values; but the conditions of their adult lives made the expectations they held unrealistic. Under such circumstances entire families of original settlers frequently "either moved away or died out."[15] To remain at Promised Land under these conditions entailed a loss of status, prestige, and economic security.

The disposition of Joshuway Wilson's farm and the fate of his children following his death was typical of the direction many children of landowners followed during the transitional period around 1900. Wilson and his wife Delphia "passed" unnoticed in official records. Neither of them left a will, nor were they in debt at the time of their deaths. There were, therefore, no pressing claims against the Wilson estate; and the probate followed common law. The thirty-seven–acre farm was equally divided among the eight surviving children, each receiving slightly more than four acres of land. Three of the Wilson children were women, and they settled on their small inheritances and built permanent homes on the family land. The Wilson sons responded differently from their sisters. They, too, initially established homes on their four-acre tracts; and for a time they stayed at Promised Land, renting or sharecropping. Only the oldest son, Fortune, who opened a molasses mill on his inherited land, devised a local alternative to farming. One by one, his younger brothers moved away to Atlanta and Chicago. Taxes on their small parcels of land were paid annually with the money they sent home to Fortune or their sisters. But the Wilson family farm, now partitioned, lay idle during the second generation.[16]

Not all cases of intestate inheritances concluded in such a manner, for it was common that landowners be in debt at the time of their death. When this was the case and claims were pressed against the estate, land and personal property were sold at public auction to clear the indebtedness. Under white justice Negro heirs often received no more than a few pennies or an old plow stock as their portion of a parent's estate. The disposition of the Samuel Burt farm followed this relatively common pattern.

Like Joshuway Wilson, Samuel Burt predeceased his wife; and neither Burt nor his widow, Mary, who died in 1911, left a will. Unlike Delphia Wilson, Mary Burt was in debt at the time of her death to W. E. Henderson, a white neighbor in Verdery who held a lien on the family farm. Following established legal procedure, when Henderson pressed his claim against the Burt estate, the family farm was sold at public auction through the county probate court. Mary Burt's personal property and farm equipment were also sold at the same auction. Henderson purchased the farm for fifty-eight dollars, the amount of the lien. The personal property brought a total of $28.12, a sum divided between twelve heirs.[17] Disposition of the Burt farm was not yet complete, however, for Henderson was a merchant, not a farmer. He had little direct use for the small farm and subsequently sold it to North Carter for six hundred and ten dollars. Henderson's fifty-eight dollar investment was profitable; and Carter acquired an intact farm of his own, adding this property to his already prosperous store at the crossroads. The Burt family dispersed; dispossessed of their land, they disappeared from the affairs of the community.

Calvin Moragne, like the Wilsons and the Burts, also died intestate around the turn of the century; and, although the initial circumstances surrounding the settlement of his estate were similar to those of Mary Burt, the final disposition of his property, real and personal, proved atypical. He, too, was in debt at the time of his death, for he had recently purchased a new wagon on credit from Greenwood merchant F. M. Allen, and the debt was not cleared. Allen held a mortgage of eighty-five dollars on the fifty-five–acre Moragne farm as security for the wagon. When this claim was pressed, the probate court offered the farm at public auction; and the Moragne family mobilized their resources to salvage much of the estate.

Calvin's oldest son, W. L. Moragne, bought his father's carpenter tools and also cleared the debt with Allen. Moragne's widow Amelia purchased the bulk of the household items—the cooking range, sewing machine, furniture, dishes, clock, and family Bible. She obviously intended to continue her own independent household even though her children were all grown and gone. William (Bill) Moragne bought his brother's farm machinery and tools. Will, Calvin's son, purchased the family farm, although he was a schoolteacher, not a farmer, and had no intention of working the land himself. He held the title to the land, and his mother continued to live there in the family homestead.[18] The total amount of money realized from the estate sale was $65.10; and that sum, added to the purchase price of the farm, was divided between eleven heirs—Calvin's widow, the surviving children, and several grandchildren. Most used their inheritance to migrate from Promised Land.

Not all landowners died intestate, and the wills they left demonstrated a thoughtful concern for both their land and their heirs. The documents, written in their own hand and witnessed by their brothers and the preacher, reflected the extent to which domestic situations and circumstances guided landowners in the distribution of their holding. Elias Harris, a widower, faced old age while there were still dependent children in his household. He dealt quite rationally with the problems which would confront his children after his death. They would be orphans, without other relatives nearby to watch over the younger ones and raise them. Harris stipulated in his will that "my land shall be kept together until my youngest child becomes of age, when my real estate shall be equally divided among them."[19]

The Harris document was the only instance of an equal division of property among all heirs through a will, but his was an unusual situation. Lacking relatives nearby and wanting to assure a home for his younger children until they established economic and social self-sufficiency, the solution Harris devised was probably the only strategy available to him. His two oldest children, a son and a daughter, were in their early twenties at the time of his death; and with the proviso of his will they were able to forestall partition of the farm and maintain an intact household. The success of this strategy for meeting parental responsibilities was evident in the final disposition of the Harris farm. It was not until much later in the twentieth century, when all the children were grown and established in independent households, that the family land was finally subdivided among them.

Aside from the Harris case, wills were commonly employed to denote special conditions and to distribute an estate unequally. Beverly White transmitted his property, both personal and real, to his wife Anne, to be retained intact during her lifetime. Following her death, White directed that all property was to be transmitted to "two of my children, viz. William White and Nimrod White, who shall have and must have an equal share . . . but the remaining children must have one dollar each . . . before such subdivisions can be made."[20] A third son, Samuel, who had purchased a nine-acre plot from his father some years earlier, sold his land to Nimrod and left Promised Land shortly before his father's death. White's youngest son, Paris, also migrated from Promised Land prior to his father's death; and White's distribution of his property was clearly designed to provide land for the two sons remaining in the community. The others had no need for farms, and perhaps White's disapproval of their departure resulted in the single dollar he allocated from his estate as their portion of the inheritance.

Like Beverly White, Wells Gray distributed his land unequally among his heirs, although neither man waited until his death to establish adult children in secure land tenure arrangements. Inheritance further solidified ties to land and the community already established by their children. Neither White nor Gray showed a preference for elder children, and neither demonstrated a desire to provide equally for all children. The trend they established continued throughout the first quarter of the century. Landowners often chose to transmit their farms to a single heir, providing nominal sums of money to other children. Perrin Morton inherited his father's farm intact under conditions similar to those set forth by Beverly White, for he did not "come into possession of this land until after the death of Marshall Morton and Fannie Morton, the father and the mother." The six other Morton children received "one dollar each as their share of my entire estate."[21] Clearly, not all children could expect to inherit the family farm; less apparent were the reasons for the pattern of preference landowners expressed in their wills.

As was the case in the pre-twentieth-century period, some owners divested themselves of their lands before their deaths. Wilson Nash conveyed his farm to his wife Moriah in 1896. She, in turn, distributed the land to their children before her own death. The advantages Moriah Nash obtained by this arrangement were twofold. First, in retaining control of the family lands she kept an element of economic independence into her own old age and was not forced to rely upon the benevolence of her children. Second, she was able to distribute the land to her children at her own prerogative. Her economic independence was coupled with a degree of power and control which probably added stability to the total family unit, for her three youngest children established homes at Promised Land on farms provided to them by their mother.

A daughter, also named Moriah, and sons John Quincey and Gipson each received forty-acre farms between 1900 and 1905. These three youngest children from a family of ten were the only ones still living in the community in 1900. They, like Beverly White's children, had the most immediate need for farms of their own; and their mother arbitrarily provided the land to them rather than the children already grown and gone. John Quincey, the youngest of the children, sold his land to his sister after two years of independent farming and moved away. Daughter Moriah sold both her own and her brother's portion within a year, and she too emigrated. Only Gipson remained on the family lands, making a permanent home at Promised Land. It was his presence that maintained the continuity of the Nash family lineage on the land Wilson Nash first bought in the 1880's. After the other children were gone, Moriah moved into Gipson's home; and there she remained until her death, the aging mother of a dispersed family.[22]

The mechanics of intergenerational land transmission were governed as much by individual circumstances as they were by any prevailing norms of inheritance. William Moragne was in his sixties at the turn of the century. Over the previous thirty years he accumulated more than one hundred acres of farmland around Promised Land, buying a tract here or there as it became available. As he approached old age, direct management of these lands became increasingly difficult; and he began to lease them to young men in the community, following the patterns established by the men who had been his elders twenty years before. Edd Chappell, Joshuway Wilson's son-in-law, lived on the small four-acre plot his wife Amy inherited from the Wilson estate and rented a farmable tract from Moragne. Young Mose Moragne also rented some farmland from his Uncle Bill. Ultimately, even these renting arrangements proved troublesome for William Moragne. He was an old man and probably weary of the burden and responsibility of farming. In his seventies he divested himself of his land. His situation was complicated by the fact that he and his wife had no children. He turned to his nieces and nephews as the logical recipients of the land, and from them he selected the most likely farmers of the next generation. Joseph Moragne purchased fifty-four acres from Uncle Bill, and Luther Pinckney ninety-eight. William Moragne sold his remaining property in tracts of less than ten acres to other nieces and nephews, among them Gipson Nash, William Letman, A. A. Pinckney, and Rachel Turner.[23]

Although old William Moragne followed a pattern already well established by earlier landowners such as Wells Gray when he divided his land, he diverged from these earlier strategies in one important detail. While men of the first generation provided land to both their children and nonkin, Moragne sold similar tracts only to his younger relatives. Despite the fact that both men, Gray and Moragne, intentionally subdivided their lands and that they sold to men and women who would have otherwise been landless, differing choices of buyers were typical of two separate eras in the community. When Gray sold his lots to the newcomers, land was not so scarce. By the time William Moragne reached old age, circumstances were quite different; and it was unlikely that any of his younger relatives could have established permanent homes or secure land tenure without the assistance he provided. It was a demonstration of family solidarity that his nieces and nephews received this preferential treatment.

The older generation was generally thoughtful and prudent in the disposition of their lands, whether through sales of entire farms to a single child, subdivision of their land prior to death, or the unequal divisions usually afforded by wills. The younger generation, at the same time, was not entirely passive in this intergenerational exchange; and some showed a strong entrepreneurial spirit as they acquired farmland of their own. One Moragne nephew, W. A. Turner, began acquisitions when he purchased ninety acres of farmland from his uncles, Eli and Wade Moragne, between 1905 and 1910.[24] His land was scattered through Moragne Town; and Turner, like many other men in his family, combined preaching, teaching, and farming. By middle age his landholdings and professions placed him among the more prestigious members of the community, the result of a gradual but steady implementation of the lessons of his childhood—thrift, self-discipline, industry, and hard work. Even W. A. Turner, from this advantageous position, would not withstand the crises of the 1920's.

Picking Cotton to Beat the Band

Within Promised Land prosperity was measured by the older generation against their experiences during slavery times. Control of their
farms was relinquished only when the infirmities of old age drove
them from their fields. Even then, as epitomized by William
Moragne's actions, the land was divided first through leases before
control was completely surrendered through sale. Even sale, however, lacked finality for some. Wilson Nash, Beverly White, Marshall
Morton, and James Fields retained a sense of control even as they
contemplated their own deaths. In their cases the land was kept
intact by transmitting it to wives, who were expected to outlive the
old men.[25] Sale or final division of property was postponed as long as
possible. This land-use strategy directly affected economic conditions
within the community. Older children matured and moved off their
fathers' farms. Younger children remained and replaced their siblings as farm laborers for their parents. It was a pattern already well
established by the final quarter of the nineteenth century, one aris-
ing from the poverty and labor intensive farming styles which that
poverty demanded. The consequence for community farms was a
stable agricultural labor force uninterrupted by the emigration. The
productivity of the land increased, and for many families this in-

Table 6.
Internal Economic Conditions at Promised Land, 1897–1942*

Year	Annual Per Capita Church Contributions†	Taxable Property Landed	Nonlanded	Mule Ownership % Landed	% Nonlanded
1897	$0.12	$72.50	$39.50	37	33
1909	2.66	166.66	61.29	23	20
1915	1.36	99.00	57.50	26	32
1922	2.83	100.76	65.45	19	25
1932	(0.57)‡	63.00	31.50	21	29
1942	(0.17)‡	43.46	46.81	14	33

*Taxable property and mule ownership rates were derived from county tax
records, 1897 to 1942. Tax Auditor's Duplicate Books, Smithville and White Hall
Townships, Greenwood County, S.C.

†As abstracted from Mt. Zion Records, I–IV.

‡These two years are based on regressions, using taxable property among landowners as the criterion variable (r = +.70).

crease was accompanied by a decrease in total family size. There were fewer people to support; and, although the population diminished, the output increased. It was this combination of circumstances which explained the huge increase in per capita church contributions between 1897 and 1909 as well as the increase in taxable property among landowners and the nonlanded alike.

The people at Promised Land prospered despite land scarcity, poor soil, crop problems, and the chronic fear of violence. By 1909 the majority of the local residents owned some amount of land, although many of the individual holdings were quite small. Even those who remained landless increased the worth of their personal property over earlier hard times. North Carter's store stood at the crossroads; and, although Carter did not stock clothing, seed, or fertilizer, he sold flour, meal, kerosene, and sodas to his neighbors. John Turner did the same, and the local children went by the stores as often as they gathered a penny or two from selling blackberries during the summer. Their parents paid Carter and Turner cash when they had it and bought on credit when they did not. Both men trusted their neighbors, knowing they would "pay when they could."[26] Besides, if an account grew too large or if payment was slow, the men simply cut off credit. It was an effective method of financial management.

This general sense of well being and economic growth in the community continued only until 1911. That year the price of cotton, never particularly stable, fell to eight cents a pound; and the Negro yeomen at Promised Land, like other Cotton Belt farmers, felt the first effects of governmental controls on agriculture. The Cotton Reduction Act was passed and implemented in an effort to control the supply of the staple and thereby stabilize cotton prices.[27] The legislation limited the amount of cotton planted by any farmer to one-third of the total tilled acreage on each farm. This in effect reduced community cotton acreage by one-sixth. Combined with the decreased price, the reduction in acreage severely reduced cash flow in Promised Land. Church contributions declined, and there was a general decrease in the value of personal property among the residents of Promised Land.

After the Cotton Reduction Act was implemented, the price of the crop rose for three succeeding years. Then in 1914 the war in Europe and the naval blockade of Great Britain set off a chain of economic crises that reached into the core of Promised Land. The naval blockade effectively closed the sea trade lanes even to neutral shipping. This, in turn, halted foreign cotton sales. Domestic production far exceeded domestic industrial use of cotton; and, with an inadequate market for its staple crop and an economy based on seasonal advances of credit, the South in 1914 faced a nonreconcilable debt in excess of $500,000,000.[28] From the largest planter to the smallest farmer, a critical depression ensued; and the effects of this depression left its mark on the community. There was little new credit forthcoming for the Negro farmers; and lien men dealt decisively with delinquent Negro debtors, because they too were financially pressed. The effect of this new rigidity was felt in personal ways by some of the local farmers, who "never will forget that time. My Uncle Slappy had a real fine milk cow, and old Ramsey Blake from Greenwood come out there and took Uncle Slappy's milk cow 'cause he couldn't pay his lien."[29] Although entire farms were rarely repossessed because Negro farmers seldom mortgaged their land except to finance major purchases, the loss of a milk cow was critical to a family—it meant the partial loss of their food supply.

The economic crisis was not the only event which affected Promised Land in 1914. Race relations grew increasingly violent, aggravated by the severe and widespread economic hardships. Lynching, which increased during the 1890's, declined during the early years of the twentieth century until the tensions of the First World War reversed the trend once again. These tensions actually began during the Cotton Crisis of 1914, and Negro farmer Anthony Crawford of Abbeville County was doubly a victim of this economic and social unrest. Crawford was lynched by an enraged mob of white men in Abbeville that fall when he went to town to sell his cotton seed. He and the white merchant haggled over the price, significantly lower than Crawford had expected. In the collapsed cotton market his seeds were practically worthless. As the two argued some of the white men hanging around the store took offense at Crawford's impudence. "They took a stick and hit Mr. Crawford, bloodied him all up." A crowd gathered, and Anthony Crawford was beaten senseless. "Then they hitched him to a team and drug him through the heart of Abbeville."[30]

The violence proved quite an attraction among the white population, and as it continued "they shut down the cotton mill for all the whites to go up there and see them drag that nigger through the town." There was no help for Anthony Crawford. Like other Negroes he was the victim of mob violence, a form of terrorism discreetly ignored by law enforcement officers. "Before the sheriff could get to them, they done killed Mr. Crawford. That was 1914, before the Number One War started. Then the colored people started going North."[31] In Abbeville County, and in the memories of the men and women at Promised Land, violence was "a significant factor in the economics of survival" that eventually drove many local Negroes from the county.

Anthony Crawford's murder was a kind of violence that was neither new nor unexpected among local Negroes, even though it was relatively infrequent. No one from Promised Land had ever been lynched, and Crawford was only the second lynch victim in the county since 1883.[32] The possibility of violence had been a part of life for Promised Land residents from the beginnings of their community, and its impact now was not long-standing. By 1917 wartime demands for textiles once again stimulated the cotton industry. Prices for the staple recovered from the prewar depression and soared above the 1870 high of 22 cents a pound, reaching 31 cents in 1917 and peaking at 32.9 cents the following year.[33] Crawford's murder diminished in importance as the price of cotton increased.

The results of this new prosperity were as apparent in Promised Land as elsewhere among Negro farmers. Church contributions and the value of taxable property rose with the cotton prices. Old debts were settled; and the families at Promised Land probably reacted much like other Negro farmers, using their newfound capital for "rational expenditures, for better food, cookstoves, household implements, comfortable beds," and—one of the marvels of modernization—automobiles.[34] Fewer young men and women left their homes and community, and the population began to increase as they matured and established their own homes. Once again economic stability seemed within reach.

The cotton cycle still dictated life at Promised Land, as it had for forty years. Now the high prices, resulting from wartime demand, stimulated intensive planting and cultivation. Field work took on a new vigor, although the routines were unchanged. The year began in March—"then we plowed, next planted the cotton." Within the month, after the cotton was planted, the local farmers turned to their subsistence fields, sowing the corn, wheat, and cane which provided food year around for both people and animals. By May warm weather and spring rains sent the young cotton plants into a growth spurt, and with them the weeds and grass. "Then we chop cotton, thin the cotton out, and get the grass out. We use hoes, and everybody work then." This was an important time in the cycle, for the cotton plants needed room to grow. By June, with the hot weather and diminished rain, growth slowed. Then it was time to "bunch that old cotton." The plants were fertilized, and the ground between the cotton rows replowed. In July the crop was "laid by—that means we wrap it up and plow it no more"—as one final turning of the soil between the rows threw freshly fertilized soil up around the maturing plants. August was a time of rest, waiting for the cotton bolls to ripen. In September the final phase of the cotton cycle began. As during May, every available hand went to the fields. This time they moved up and down the rows, "picking cotton to beat the band," in a process which continued until Christmas.[35]

Even after the fields were picked clean and the crop ginned and baled, there was still field work, for during the fall months women and children picked cracked cotton, the leavings of the crop. "It was so cold then we sit by the fire at night and clean the cotton," which provided extra income to the poorest families. In the tradition of peasant gleaning, all fields were available to those who picked cracked cotton; and families frequently combined this crop, "sos her mother and mine together made a bale of cracked cotton." Although the first pickings were ginned, baled, and sold by the end of October, the cracked cotton was often stored for part of the winter. "Our house had one whole room full" of the cleaned second crop, which women sold in town to finance a new dress or a special suit of clothes for the children. Only at the end of this final picking did the community rest. The children went back to school; and the adults prepared for March, because "that be the time to get your lien."[36]

The War, the Boll Weevil, and Going North

While the children were preoccupied with school and the teenagers with each other, the older folks at Promised Land seized on new opportunities. The "Number One War" was upon the country, and it touched Promised Land directly. For those who stayed in the community, their cotton fields were a source of new prosperity. The farmers at Promised Land, tenants as well as owners, were among the Cotton Belt farmers to benefit from "the most valuable [cotton] crop ever produced." The treasuries of the churches, the burial aid society, and the Masonic lodge received their due along with the families.[37]

The Army was less important than the price of cotton. "Lots of boys went off to the Army then," but few adults at Promised Land made a clear distinction between going off to the Army and going north. "We didn't think nothing about it." Both involved moves away from home. The only difference between the Army and going north was that "they was called to the Army and they didn't have no choice." The boys from Promised Land joined other Negro draftees from the Carolinas, Georgia, Alabama, and Florida and constituted the 371st Infantry Regiment. The men were inducted after the 1917 cotton crop was harvested and received only an abbreviated basic training at Camp Jackson, South Carolina. The poorly trained and poorly equipped troops shipped out for France in February 1918 and were integrated into the French fighting forces. Unlike other Negro soldiers in World War I, the men from Promised Land probably spent their war years on the front rather than in labor brigades.[38]

There were others at Promised Land for whom war-related work was closer at hand. Nathan Redd, one of several carpenters in the community, "was the man what built the soldier camps in Columbia." Redd had maintained a small construction crew for a number of years, comprised of his friends Fred Moragne and Dolphus Frazier and his younger brothers Dave and Charlie. The five men moved temporarily to Columbia around 1917 and worked on the government construction there where they "made money on top of money" and established their reputations as "first class carpenters." For Redd and his crew the government work was followed by jobs that brought them back to Promised Land. Living at home once again, they built train depots here and there across the Piedmont and, on occasion, "even built white folks' houses."[39]

Redd was not the only local carpenter whose trade afforded opportunities to work outside the local cotton fields. John Turner, W. A. Turner's brother, "was the only colored on the carpenter crew that built the highest building in Greenwood." Luther Moragne, now an old man, also maintained a construction crew. Too old for war work, Moragne built homes, "not little two room homes for poor folks, but fine big homes." Carpentry was a skilled profession and served the men at Promised Land well. At first used primarily for local purposes—coffins, church pews, and school benches—the trade afforded an economically viable option to cotton farming; and, during the early years of the twentieth century, Promised Land men exploited this opportunity to an obvious advantage.[40]

Local men found other kinds of work opportunities that drew them from the cotton fields. Joe Brown was among those who laid track for the railroad. Jim White secured a job as a porter at the newly opened Oregon Hotel in Greenwood, as did Jim Turner. The pulpwood industry hired the community's farmers in August after their crops were laid by and again during the winter months after the cotton was picked. Many of their jobs took the men away from Promised Land temporarily, but their wives and children rarely followed them. Families stayed at home, and mothers and sisters waited together for the postman who brought money as well as letters from absent fathers and husbands. When the men came back, they had "a little money in their pocket; and they bought up a little land."[41] It was a recurrent pattern. Among those who stayed in Promised Land, money was always invested in land if possible. And for each man with some cash to spend, there was another eager to move on and willing to sell a small inheritance. Land redistribution in one form or another was an ongoing fact of community life.

By 1919 the Promised Land population once again began to increase. After the war many of the local men returned to the community and established the homes they had postponed. The emigration of youth slowed for a time, and outsiders once again were drawn into the community because "there wasn't no white problem here in Promised Land then." Many, like the Norman family from Lincolnton, Georgia, came seeking new opportunities and security, the same motives which attracted nonlanded Negroes to Promised Land a generation earlier. "Things was rough over there" in Georgia, where whites molested the isolated, backcountry Negroes with even greater frequency than they did in Abbeville County. The Normans came because Joe Norman married a girl from Abbeville County, and she knew that Promised Land was safer for her family. At her instigation the family's worldly possessions were piled high into an old one-horse wagon. The tiniest Norman baby perched on a pillow to soften the ride, and the family jolted its way across the rough country roads. Like other families who moved in, the Normans found a place to sharecrop; and, when the opportunity came, Joe Norman bought one of the small farms on the northeastern edge of the community. There the family established a permanent home.[42]

Economic disaster struck Promised Land in 1919 when "the boll weevil come across from Georgia" and invaded the local cotton fields. Daubing each cotton boll with a noxious mixture of sulphur and molasses had little effect on the worms. The crops were ruined, not for one season but for many. "It was so bad we didn't have no food or nothing then." The crops were completely destroyed. "The only crop we made that year was some peas. We ate pea bread, pea soup, peas boiled up. Farming was dead then" in the eyes of many community residents.[43] The poverty and ruin wrought by the boll weevil assumed an additional dimension of disaster and disappointment when measured against the hopeful prosperity of the previous years.

The community population dropped dramatically, from two hundred and ten households in 1922 to one hundred and forty-five in 1932, a 30 percent loss for the decade. The economic forces of this emigration from Promised Land were even more clearly visible than they had been during the Great Migration. "I went to Philadelphia 'cause there wasn't nothing to do here." Farming was at a standstill. Few had the energy or strength to struggle against the overwhelming odds which now confronted them. Youths raised to be farmers turned north at the worst possible time. The nation was immobilized by the Great Depression, and these southern immigrants found few choices and opportunities in the cities. Instead, they confronted a new form of destitution. Nevertheless, this emigration was more massive and inclusive than either the one at the turn of the century or the one during the pre-World War I period. During those migrations the men and women who left were the young, those without secure land tenure, heirs of partitioned and relatively useless farm lands. Now men and women of all ages and every status left Promised Land.[44]

Young men had grown to adulthood watching their mothers and fathers labor year after year over crops that were difficult and unpredictable. They spent their own childhoods in backbreaking field work. Now they abandoned the land because "it was awful hard there." Despite the problems they faced when they went north, most of these emigrants believed that "it was better when you left." Some, like Jim White, worked their way north as waterboys for the railroad, leaving home before they were old enough to shave. They had no destination, and their travels were guided only by the availability of work. They survived through a network of friends and family scattered from Atlanta to Chicago.[45]

For others, departures from Promised Land were systematically planned. Most young men knew that "you could ride to Philadelphia for ten dollars," and somehow found work for cash wages "at one little job or another. I saved up my ten dollars, and then I left." Even though the primary motive for their departure was economic, destinations were selected, not because of work opportunities, but because a grandmother, an aunt, a cousin, or a brother was already established. "When I got to Philadelphia, I stayed with my grandmomma; then I went out and found some work." The specific jobs they found were less important than a successful escape from the poverty of the rural South. "First I polished tomatoes early in the morning. Then every day I go to the docks and work unloading iron. After I learned to drive, I got a job delivering coal."[46]

Although most of the people who left Promised Land for the North established permanent homes there and returned to the community only for visits, a few found city life far less attractive than they had originally imagined. Women were particularly prone to dissatisfaction. Many had never worked beyond the cotton fields and the family garden, and even those who were employed as domestic servants in the South found equivalent work in the cities more demanding and much less personal. Cora Hall was one of these. She and her husband went to Philadelphia with many other Promised Landers when farming collapsed, and like the other Negro women she worked as a domestic. A month or two "down on my knees, scrubbing up other peoples' dirt with them womens telling me 'Do this. Do that'" altered her perspective on city life. "I got an old red milk cow and some acres of land down South, and I'm going home" she told her husband one day. "You can come back with me or not, but I'm going down there where I'm rich." The Halls went home.[47]

If they did not follow the men north, women, young and old, married and single, left their children with "old grannie women" and found domestic work in Greenwood. Lorenzo Station assumed a vital role in life for it was a point of departure for short trips as well as long ones.

> *I watched my momma flag that train to come to work. My momma come from church on Sundays—peoples work on Sundays in them days—and get her on a bike and come straight down the path to Lorenzo. Me and my grandmomma and the big dog would come with her. And you could hear that train coming. And when she hear that train she step out and flag it. Conductor stop it and step out, and she get on the train and ride to town. This was before cars come in circulation. She ride in to town on Sundays and stay with white folks, come back on Fridays to Promised Land.*[48]

While their mothers were in town "staying with white folks" and their fathers gone north to find work, children became a community responsibility. They moved in with friends and relatives, not as a result of nuclear family breakdown, but because the practical definitions of family and household expanded in response to economic conditions. "I stayed with my grandmomma while my momma was gone. Sometimes she left me with Sarah Devlin, sometimes with Miss Anne Wilson," other old women who lived alone. More personal factors also governed the arrangements parents made for the care of their children. "I started staying with [a neighbor] when I was ten, and I stayed with her until I was sixteen. Her husband died and she wanted somebody to stay there at night. There was a lot of us [children at home], and my mother and them didn't miss me." Whatever the arrangements, parents could be certain that their children would be well tended, for "back then everybody was a parent" and adult authority was always above question. "One time Sarah Devlin whopped me. I cried about it, and my grandmomma told me to hush. If I didn't need it Sarah wouldn't have whopped me. I never did like Sarah no more."[49]

SIX

It was Good to Live at Promised Land

I thought it was good to live at Promiseland. They raised every-thing they wanted, had plenty to eat. They had cows and raised their meat, made their bread. They were neighborly too. Gave us milk and butter and all. They were just friendly. Love what made them that way. Love your neighbor like yourself. They were good Christians then. They went to church. Folks raised their children right.
Azzalie Moragne Jones
Atlanta, Georgia

There was a noticeable change in the structure of the Promised Land community during the final years of the nineteenth century. The collection of independent subsistence farmers gradually became an interdependent network of small landowners, a process shaped by the prevailing patterns of land-use established during the first generation. Many who acquired land after 1885 by either outright purchase or inheritance achieved a dream embraced by many Negroes in the rural South. They owned land, but the size of their holdings was often so small that the significance of their new status diminished in all but its symbolic importance.

The economic utility of these tiny parcels of land was negligible, and new landowners realistically acquired little more than a secure location for permanent homes. In increasing numbers community residents who farmed cultivated at least a part of their crop on rented fields. The prestige of ownership was countered by the chronic insecurities of tenancy. Still, within that milieu 80 percent of the community residents were actively engaged in farming at the turn of the century; and even those few professionals—primarily teachers and preachers—local businessmen, craftsmen, day workers, and railroad laborers who formed the remaining 20 percent of the adult population did not escape the influence of agricultural economics, which pervaded community life.

The level of agricultural technology and the farming styles that prevailed in the community were remarkably unchanged from those used twenty years before. Farming for most was still an activity which involved the entire household, and domestic groups remained the basic unit of agricultural production as well as consumption. The labor patterns which characterized farming at Promised Land in 1880 were still in force at the turn of the century. Children entered the labor force at an early age and by thirteen most took their places in the cotton fields alongside the other adults. In an unchanging routine, the elderly men and women as well as the youth were described in the census as farmers and farm laborers with dulling regularity. Community residents forged a social environment balanced precariously on three factors: cotton prices; the obligations of family and kinship; and the twin values of self-reliance and community responsibility.

Household and Economy

Although farming was still the primary occupation for the majority of the Promised Land residents in 1900, as it had been in 1880, the household structures in the community changed rather dramatically during those twenty years.[1] In 1880 household structures had been clearly differentiated by land tenure (see Table 1). That was no longer the case at the turn of the century. As the economic circumstances of an expanded body of landowners changed, both family and kinship were redefined in the material ways that people lived. Economic imperatives imposed new restraints and introduced new demands on community families. Fully evident in 1900, were the two resulting changes: the household structures of the landowners and the landless became increasingly similar; and there was a newly emergent and identifiable group of female-headed households.

Household structures in 1880 reflected for all community residents the various strategies they employed in their ongoing struggles for economic survival. They were shaped by the different types of resources available to landowners, tenants, and sharecroppers, as well as by the economic options posed by the circumstances of their different tenancies. The majority of the 1880 households were composed of nuclear families, and the members of these families worked together in an agricultural system based on labor-intensive farming. Technology was limited, and the production capacity of each household was dependent upon its ability to mobilize a labor force which counterbalanced the rate of domestic consumption. Types of farm production were shaped by tenancy, and this in turn influenced household structure in a cycle of economic exigencies and human needs. By 1900 four specific alterations in household structure signaled a change in the economic patterns that subtly affected the most intimate aspects of life at Promised Land.

Table 7.
*Comparison of Household Structure, 1880 and 1900**

Household Structure	% Landowners 1880	1900	% Nonowners 1880	1900
Married	86	75†	77	70†
Multigeneration and Nonkin	10	33‡	21	26
Nuclear Family	90	63†	79	65†
Living Alone	0	4	0	9

*U.S. Bureau of Census, 1900 Household MSS, Smithville and White Hall Enumeration Districts, Abbeville County, S.C. 1800 household MSS; Greenwood and Abbeville Counties.
†Statistically smaller, binomial z > 1.96, p <.05.
‡Statistically greater, binomial z > 1.96, p <.05.

The first and most evident of these changes was the proportion of married persons in the community population. In 1880, 86 percent of the community landowners were married, as were 77 percent of the landless adults. The proportion declined among both landowners and the landless during the final years of the nineteenth century, and by 1900 only 75 percent of the landowners and 70 percent of the non-landed adults were married. The rate of decrease was statistically significant among both groups; and, further, although there had been a significantly greater proportion of landowners who were married in 1880, this was not the case in 1900. The economic factors that earlier had induced a greater frequency of marriage among landowners than among the landless now affected the two groups in a similar manner. It was the first indication of the extent to which all community residents experienced very similar economic pressures.

A second change in household composition that affected only the landowning families was the proportion of households that incorporated additional relatives and nonkin. In 1880 extended and multigeneration households were more characteristic of tenants and sharecroppers than landowners. By the turn of the century they were increasingly evident among landowners as well, rising from 10 percent in 1880 to 33 percent in 1900. The slight, statistically insignificant increase in the proportion of multigeneration and extended family households among the landless during the last two decades of the nineteenth century served only to further emphasize the extent of increasing similarity between landed and landless residents.

Among both owners and nonowners there was a significant decline in the proportion of two-generation, nuclear family households, families composed solely of two parents and their children. This third change was in part a function of the increase in extended and nonkin households, but it was also the result of an increase in the proportion of persons who lived alone. Like both marital status and the occurrence of extended and multigeneration families, the number of one-person households also failed to distinguish landowners from their nonlanded neighbors in 1900.

Increased similarity in landowning and nonlanded households resulted from the growing similarity of economic mandates that affected both groups. Central among these was the fact that both groups farmed on rented lands, using the same cultivation patterns employed by the previous generation of community farmers. Their status as tenants and sharecroppers dictated a concentration on cotton which in turn required a relatively mature labor force. Farmers with young children were not economically viable tenants, for they lacked sufficient labor to meet the requirements that white landlords held for tenants. Elderly couples whose children were already established in independent households faced a similar disadvantage. Because of this demand for household labor, both the young and the old often lived in multigeneration and extended households or households which incorporated nonkin. All three techniques expanded the labor potential of a domestic unit which would have been otherwise economically impotent under the prevailing conditions of tenancy.[2]

Within this broad framework of change a new household form emerged which further illustrated the extent to which economic pressures influenced domestic life. This was the female-headed household. In 1880 there were no single, never-married bachelors or spinsters among the community adults. With few exceptions unmarried persons were either widowed or separated from their spouses. The small number of never married heads of household were all landless young men engaged in cooperative farming. None of these men were over thirty; and their bachelor state was a temporary one, probably similar in both form and motive to the cooperative male farming prevalent at Promised Land since the 1880's. It was a pattern dictated by a combination of economic realities and personal desire for self-sufficiency.[3]

By 1900 there was an identifiable group of never married women within the community population, all heads of households and most between twenty-five and forty. In addition to these never-married women, there was a second group of widowed, divorced, and separated women in the same age group who were also heads of independent households. Together these two groups constituted 17 percent of all heads of household in Promised Land in 1900. There was not an equivalent group of single men. The economics of the land shaped this aspect of household structure through the same processes that minimized earlier domestic distinctions between landowners and the landless.[4]

The presence of the single female heads of household was an index of the extent to which emigration from Promised Land was already in progress, an emigration which preceded the Great Migration of Negroes from the rural South by at least a decade. As prospects for secure tenancy failed to meet expectations held since childhood, young men assessed their possibilities and realized the economic futility of an adulthood without land. Many left the community for the simple reason that they could not survive economically if they stayed. This pragmatic motive for emigration was compounded for children of landowners, themselves landless, by a threatened loss of status. The typical life crises of adolescence and the availability of convenient and relatively inexpensive transportation—the railroad—were both factors which stimulated early twentieth-century emigration from Promised Land. The departure of young men in their late teens and early twenties created an imbalance in the community sex ratio. Young women, with fewer options and greater cultural restrictions, stayed behind. The women bore family names familiar in Promised Land for a generation; and all of them, whether wives, mothers, or sisters of absented men, were integrated into established kinship systems.

Older men, faced with similar disillusionment and dissatisfaction, followed the same pattern as the young single men. They too emigrated from Promised Land, leaving their families behind in the safety and security they knew to be there until they were established in the cities. "The mens left first and the womens followed them," for

Table 8.
Household Composition, 1900

Household Composition	% Landowners	% Nonlanded
Husband/Wife Headed		
Nuclear	52	53
Extended and Nonkin	23	17
Female Heads		
Dependent Children	11	8
Extended and Nonkin	10	4
Living Alone	0	1.5
Male Heads		
Dependent Children	0	4
Extended and Nonkin	0	5
Living Alone	4	7.5

wives encouraged their husbands to seek work which paid "cash wages" and were willing to endure a period of separation from their husbands in order to accommodate that search for work. It was an emigration pattern predicated on a division of responsiblity as well as labor within family units, and one which afforded internal stability to families otherwise dislocated by radical change. The family relationships and strategies were firmly grounded in prevailing economic conditions.[5]

The details of male migration emerged from a larger model of domestic relations that defined men's and women's roles within the family as complements. Men were expected to support their families. Women were expected to support opportunities devised by the men. Through this division of labor, women in the agrarian setting functioned as partners in an economic team. They shared the responsibilities for field work with their husbands during the early years of family life, but these responsibilities were more flexible for women than men. As soon as their children matured and replaced them in the fields, women turned their energies toward household management and community affairs. Although this cultural pattern did not preclude female assumption of agricultural leadership, neither did it encourage a radical shift in sex roles. Women without husbands were rarely independent farmers in 1900.

As a portion of the marriageable young men emigrated from Promised Land, there was a corresponding body of young women unable to

secure husbands. Despite the unavailability of potential mates within the community, these women faced a cultural expectation of economic self-sufficiency that became more pronounced as they matured. With few exceptions they turned from farming to "day work" to
fulfill the dictates of culture. They were joined in their search for
work by women whose husbands were away from Promised Land,
whether temporarily as the men preceded the women north in the
pattern of chain migration, or permanently because of a breakdown
in the marriage. Often the two were indistinguishable because "in
the Promiseland the idea of marriage was very, very sacred. They
didn't have divorces." When relations between a husband and wife
deteriorated "the man just left and went north." There were powerful
forces operating in the community, "a peculiar ethic dominated by
church teaching," which defined marriage as permanent and indis-
soluble. "If there was a mistake, they tried to make it not be a
mistake"; and those efforts were facilitated by long-term separations
rather than formal termination of marriage by divorce.[6]

Whatever the causes in individual cases, by 1900 more than half
the female heads of household in the community labored as maids,
cooks, and laundresses for nearby white families. Julia Richie was
typical of these women. She rented a house in Promised Land and
supported her two grandchildren, a boy of ten and a girl of eleven, by
doing "day work." Her granddaughter Janice was also employed by
the family she worked for, and her grandson attended the Promised
Land School. Both the household arrangements and work patterns
were repeated in other female-headed households. Celeda Daniel and
her adult daughter Nancy shared a rented house in Promised Land
and worked as domestics for two separate white families. At the age
of seventy, Lucy Buckhanan, like Julia Richie, headed a household
composed of herself and her two grandchildren; and her granddaughter, too, worked for the same family where Buckhanan labored as a
maid.[7]

All of these arrangements, designed to counteract economic pressures emanating from the peculiar situations of female-headed
households, were forged on the basis of intergenerational kinship
bonds. The women were typical of the new domestic form. All of the
elder women would have lived with their adult children twenty years
before, easily incorporated into the household farm economies. Now
each of them supported the offspring of their adult children, who
themselves probably had emigrated from Promised Land and the
rural South in search of the economic opportunities they hoped would
replace the older patterns of subsistence farming.

The domestic service patterns derived by the grandmothers, who assumed new roles as economic and titular heads of household, were perpetuated into the next generation of Negro women when they trained their granddaughters, as young as ten, into the tradition. Despite the altered circumstances—the demise of farming as a viable strategy for economic survival, and the restructuring of households as a result of emigration—expectations that children contribute to the domestic economy were unchanged. Only the method of their contribution was redefined.

Day work was not a labor choice limited to women; and, although only half as many men as women were engaged in domestic service in the 1900 community population, those men who were employed in some type of domestic service were similar in both age and marital status to their female counterparts. Generally the men worked as gardeners and butlers and did "heavy" types of housework, such as window washing and outside maintenance; and they probably chose this type of work freely rather than under the economic coercion which directed women into domestic service. The work was cleaner and less physically demanding than railroad labor, a type of work chosen in equal proportion by nonfarming men. It was, as well, work well suited to an adult of either sex who also cared for dependent children. Male as well as female "day workers" tended to be unmarried or if married heading households in which their spouse was absent. Significantly, all adult "day workers" at Promised Land faced this double role with its demanding combination of unshared economic and parental responsibilities.

Of the four young men who worked in domestic service, three lived in families headed by single women who were also domestics. In these cases, mothers and grandmothers apparently secured domestic work for the young men in lieu of farming opportunities. The expectation that children contribute to the household economy had no sex distinctions. Millie Moragne provided such arrangements for her son John as did Anne Walton for her son Allen. Situations such as that of Whit Hutchison, Jr. were rare. At the age of twenty-five young Hutchison was unmarried and still lived in his parents' home. Because his father rented out the family land there was probably no farm work for him. Day work was a temporary expedience, intended in Whit Jr.'s case to provide only the price of his train fare for the trip away from Promised Land, for young Hutchison emigrated from the community around 1910.

One type of household structure remained unchanged despite the economic forces which affected many community families. Some

Table 9.
Age of Day Workers by Sex and Household Status, 1900

| | Female | | Male | |
	Heads	Dependents	Heads	Dependents
N	13	10	6	4
X̄ Age	43.9	17.0	43.0	19.5
S	17.1	6.7	23.7	3.7

young single men without dependent children headed their own households and farmed, following the pattern established twenty years earlier. Dave Chiles was typical of this group. He headed a household composed of himself and two other men, one forty and the other twenty-five. Chiles rented a farm, and the other two worked as his laborers. The three were more likely equal partners in their enterprise, with Chiles assuming only the titular head of household role. It was unlikely that an impoverished tenant or sharecropper could afford to provide room and board to his laborers. Similarly, Tolbert Harris headed a household composed only of himself and Henry Wideman. The two were both in their late twenties and farmed together on rented land. Jasper Cromer and Sam Matthews had a similar relationship, the only distinction from the other two cases being that Cromer owned his land. In all three households, the men apparently chose to live together and farm cooperatively as young men had during the previous generation. It was a pattern of domestic arrangements uniquely suited to the limitations of Negro farmers, a household strategy still shaped by economic exegencies and perpetuated by its success, for it established young, unmarried men in self-sufficient and independent situations.

Adaption and Self-Reliance

The economic conditions which distinguished landowning from non-landed households in 1880 were largely irrelevant by 1900. Among all farmers at Promised Land, whether owners, tenants, or sharecroppers, the household was still the unit of economic production. Over the twenty-year period, however, household composition shifted, and the changes were adaptions to altered economic realities. Increased structural similarity between the landowning and nonlanded farmers was evident in four different aspects of domestic life: the proportion of persons who married; the increased presence of extended families; greater numbers of households composed of people otherwise not related to each other; and an increase in the numbers of persons who lived alone. The similarity between owners' and non-owners' households reflected an increasing uniformity of economic conditions. The general increase in tenancy, even among farmers who owned a small plot of land, intensified the elastic quality of all community households.

The emergence of a sizable group of female-headed households, rather than a symptom of domestic disorganization and family break-down, was instead an example of the plasticity of the rural Negro kinship system. This, too, was the result of changed land arrangements and the migration from Promised Land of men unable to make a living farming. Women faced with greater responsibility for their families' economic well-being turned by necessity to domestic service. Farming was a cooperative enterprise, one difficult to conduct successfully without an adult partner.

Twenty years before, old women would have moved into the homes of their adult children. Now grandmothers maintained independent households where they supported, nurtured, and trained the offspring of their absent adult children. Younger women, deprived of the opportunity to marry by an economic system which evicted land-less young men, established homes and secured gainful, respectable work, thereby supporting themselves as well as the children they bore as a result of relationships motivated by a need for "affection wherever they could find it."[8] Young men, if they were able to establish tenancy, still formed agricultural partnerships, living and working together as they had twenty years before. Each of these domestic adjustments entailed a reconciliation between the realities of economic life and community expectations for individual self-reliance and self-sufficiency.

Learning: The Promised Land School

Promiseland is the only place I went to school. One time my momma stayed in town, and she wanted me to go to town school. She thought I might learn more because it was a longer term. Well, I really didn't like it, and after that she decided to build this house in Promiseland. I went back to school here. But I didn't go

> *go no further than the eighth grade, and then I married when I*
> *was seventeen. Annie E. Chiles taught me my ABC's and how to*
> *count and everything I know.*
> Cleora Wilson Turner
> Greenwood, South Carolina

Two events crystallized formal education for the Promised Land children. The first was political, the second fortuitous, and together they enhanced a climate already ripe for the educational system which resulted. The creation of Greenwood County, a fundamentally political act, partitioned Promised Land, transferring two-thirds of the community acreage from Abbeville to the new county. This clear case of gerrymandering was quite common during the late nineteenth century as southern Redeemer Democrats reclaimed political power from the Republicans and the Negroes. Promised Land's reputation as a Republican stronghold was probably a critical factor in drawing the county line through the center of the community. With the force of their votes divided between the two counties, any remnants of political potency were effectively neutralized.[9]

The leadership in newly created Greenwood County was drawn from the white mercantile class rather than the descendents of the antebellum aristocracy, as was the case in Abbeville County. The approach these men took to local government was somewhat more rational and afforded regular, though minimal, economic support to the county's public schools. Like most public schools in the South, the one at Promised Land was "miserably supported . . . and wholly inadequate" under the budgetary whimsy of the Abbeville aristocrats.[10] Although financial support was not greatly increased when the responsibility shifted to Greenwood County, fiscal reliability introduced a new possibility into community life. The school was able to support a well-trained classroom teacher. Through a series of coincidences that teacher became Anna Elizabeth "Lizzie" Chiles.

Lizzie Chiles taught most of the children at Promised Land everything they knew for half a century, and she was a "number one good teacher." Born in Charleston around 1880 and educated there at Avery Institute, Anne E. Robinson came to Promised Land under stressful circumstances in 1898. While still in Charleston she married a young man whose parents lived in the community. When the marriage collapsed she faced the difficult task of supporting two young sons alone. The decisions she made were directed by this basic problem. She accepted a teaching position at White Hall School for

Colored and traveled the distance from Charleston to Promised Land
by train and wagon. When she arrived "she give them boys to their
granddaddy," and Anna E. Robinson boarded with another family in
the community. One of the Morton boys drove her daily to and from
the White Hall School, a distance of only a few miles. Survival by
adaptive flexibility was a lesson Anna Robinson learned and exercised in her own life, and it was a strategy she taught her students.[11]

Anna Robinson joined Mt. Zion Church when she moved to Promised Land. There she met Mr. Jefferson D. Chiles, a widower and
"very attractive colored man" much older than she. Chiles had been
married before and was the father of grown children. The couple
courted and were soon married. It was a family of professionals. "One
of his girls was a teacher"; and Chiles was a house servant for a local
white family, a comfortable, clean and moderately well-paid position.
As a wedding present Chiles' employer presented the couple with a
small parcel of land at the edge of Promised Land, and they joined the
landowner class in the community. Thus Lizzie Chiles, through her
teaching profession, participation in the ongoing affairs of Mr. Zion,
and her marriage to J. D. Chiles, was established as a permanent and
influential member of the community. When the teaching position at
Promised Land School opened in 1907, she was offered and readily
accepted the post.[12]

Lizzie Chiles was assisted in her teaching tasks by Amanda Pressley Henderson, Oscar Pressley's daughter. The two women inherited
the twenty-year-old, one-room schoolhouse built next to Crossroads
Baptist Church, originally Crossroads School for Colored. Although
administrative responsibility for the school was transferred from the
Baptist church to Greenwood County in 1897, little else changed
when the school passed from church to public control. It contained
only the wood stove in the center f the room, the rough benches
"down this side and that" for the children, and a small table in the
corner "where the teacher sat when she heard your recitation." The
county made no physical improvements in the community's educational facilities.[13]

Both women taught in a traditional instructional style, demanding
of their students rote memorization and maintaining discipline in the
overcrowded schoolhouse with a switch and a sprinkling of love.
"Miss Amanda was a wonderful teacher, and she was real nice looking too"; but she had no toleration for lazy scholars. "If you come to
school, you had to learn." The penalty for those who did not learn was
clear, precise, and administered uniformly. "Miss Amanda didn't
pass you." Permanent failure, however, was rare; for in Amanda

Henderson's classes "you stayed in the second grade or the third grade until you learned it"; and then, when even the slowest scholar finally achieved the goal, "she passed you on."[14]

Both teachers "believed in that hickory," or at least their scholars were convinced of this. Generally the switch, always ready in the corner by the teacher's table, was reserved for the most recalcitrant of the children and the most extreme discipline problems. Both teachers and students were fully aware that a child who was "switched at school" would be "switched twice as bad when he get home." This knowledge served as a control over the temptation to misbehave, because the psychic disgrace of a public switching at school was equaled by the physical discomfort which followed at home. Neither Amanda Henderson nor Lizzie Chiles used the hickory switch capriciously. More than once the two teachers "just looked the other way, like they didn't see," preserving the potency of the switch and their authority for the more critical infractions.[15]

Discipline was the least of the problems at the Promised Land school. The one hundred and eighty scholars enrolled there, 47 percent of the 1900 school age (6 to 12) population in Promised Land, were all packed into a tiny schoolhouse, measuring no more than four hundred square feet.[16] Overcrowded and underequipped conditions limited the effectiveness of their work, which was further reduced by the labor demands imposed on the young scholars. School began late each fall for the Promised Land children, as it did for other Negro children in the Cotton Belt. They were needed in the fields to pick cotton until the end of October. Their months in the classroom were further reduced in the spring, for school ended when the time came to knock down the previous year's cotton and corn stalks in the annual preparation for spring plowing. The same conditions which had limited their parents' schooling persisted well into the twentieth century for these children.

The scholars were not the only ones subjected to inequities, for the teachers experienced the subtle but persistent abuse of financial arrangements controlled by whites. Their salary of twenty-five dollars per month for the four-month school term was half that of their white counterparts, doubly reduced by an abbreviated school term. White teachers were paid fifty dollars a month for a seven-month term. There were never public funds allocated for repair of the building, for school supplies such as books and maps, or for fuel for cold damp winter days.[17] All of these conditions together restricted the education of Negro children. Still, the schoolhouse opened in October. The children kept each other warm as they packed onto the benches;

and Lizzie Chiles and Amanda Pressley taught their scholars to read and write and count in spite of the crude circumstances. School for most of the children was a welcome relief, for "it meant we didn't have to go to the fields."[18] The most subtle of their lessons, and one which they learned in many different ways, was the value of self-reliance, independence, pride, and cooperation.

The physical facilities at Promised Land forced Lizzie Chiles and Amanda Henderson to approach their task with a creative spirit. There were times when the number of scholars who attended the school surpassed the capacity of the small schoolhouse. At one time "they put a partition in the school and made two rooms," dividing the children into primary and secondary groups. At another time Amanda Henderson used the split-day-system to accommodate her scholars. "When I was in the sixth grade, there was forty-six or forty-seven children in my class. Miss Amanda couldn't give but two lessons a day." Some children came in the mornings and others in the afternoons for their lessons. Miss Amanda rotated arithmetic, history, reading, and geography; and she expected the children to be prepared for all their lessons whether or not they were taught that day. Her expectations were generally met, for "you didn't know what she was going to have on that day. You had to learn it all." The technique was effective. Scholars dared not come unprepared. "She made you study all them lessons," and the hickory switch in the corner was a constant reminder to come prepared for a recitation.[19]

School was a form of freedom for the older children, for it was the only place aside from church where young boys and girls escaped for a brief interlude the watchful eyes of their parents. Walking to and from school, during recess, boys and girls "talked sweet" to each other. If the moment presented itself, they might hold hands or even make arrangements to meet at a coming church event. Mrs. Henderson and Mrs. Chiles did not intervene in these preliminaries to courtship. They were always available for advice and consultation but seldom imposed themselves on matters they judged to be private affairs of their students. The respect and dignity they accorded these youthful liaisons further instilled the sense of pride and self-sufficiency they taught indirectly in the schoolhouse.[20]

Learning: The Community

Neither Amanda Henderson nor Lizzie Chiles limited their teaching to the Promised Land schoolhouse. In public, at church, or just walking down the road, both women felt free to "grab you up if you were doing something wrong and tell you the right way to do it." Teaching for them was full-time and all-encompassing. "It didn't matter where you was. Lizzie Chiles was *always* your teacher."[21] Her assumption of this special status was verified and reinforced in a multitude of small ways, in the extra switching a child received at home following a switching at school, by community acceptance of reprimands teachers meted out after church, and by the general aura of recognition and respect accorded the teacher by the community.

The authority and prestige of the schoolhouse were also superimposed on community routines in more formal ways, such as public recitals by teachers and scholars. These extensions of schoolhouse procedures were popular and well-attended social events, for they afforded not only an opportunity for the scholars to exercise and publicly display their knowledge but also an occasion for local entertainment. "Not every Friday, but maybe every other Friday," in old Mt. Zion Amanda Henderson sponsored "concerts, dialogues, and recitations." The children were commanded to attended these events, and the parents came to watch their own and their neighbors' youngsters perform. Miss Amanda, completely in charge of the evening, arranged the program in such a way that "all the childrens say a little something." Her scholars were forewarned. During the week preceding the Friday gathering, "she would more likely tell you to prepare for a speech." From Miss Amanda this was not a request; it was a demand; and the children knew the consequences of failure to comply. Those who failed to prepare or who "tried to be stubborn" when their name was called on Friday night faced Miss Amanda's switch, moved from the schoolhouse to the church for the evening.[22]

Public speaking was for some a terrifying prospect, and Amanda Henderson tempered her expectations with a realization of her scholars' fear. "If you failed after you tried to speak, she would give you another chance." Whether driven by fear or by a desire for Miss Amanda's approval and public recognition, most scholars attended the Friday evenings ready to perform. They memorized arithmetic problems, lessons from their histories, poems, and Bible verses. Anything was acceptable, and "some would say the same thing over and over." Scholars who had difficulty preparing their recitations were often coached "out in the woods after school" by their older classmates.[23] A spirit of cooperation prevailed among the children, fostered in part by Amanda Henderson's patience and tolerance, in part by their own collective sense of pride.

The end of the school year was marked by a very special event. Then Miss Amanda gave a public concert at Mt. Zion, where "she would play the old pump organ and sing just like a bird." It was at this concert that the children learned who had passed that term and who had failed. The decisions were public knowledge. If the Friday evening dialogues and recitations were approached with anxiety, the end-of-school program elicited outright terror among the children. Failure in school was not accepted lightly by Promised Land parents, and any child not "passed on to the next grade" was assured of a trip "out back for a switching."[24] The months in the classroom were limited, and Promised Land parents expected their children to apply themselves while the opportunity was before them. The older generation in the community intended that the tradition of literacy be continued.

Learning: Community Alternatives

School ended for most children at Promised Land between the sixth and eighth grades, "for that was all the education the state allowed to colored children." For some even this brief time in school was cut short by family obligations. "I didn't go to school but four years. After that I had to come out and work on the farm." Despite an abstract belief in the value of education, parents often interrupted their children's schooling, either temporarily or permanently. When there was a conflict between school and work, the farm usually came first. Children cut briars, gathered kindling, and tended babies. In good weather they worked outside; and "on rainy days we had to sit in the barn, shuck corn and shell peas." Work began at an early age; and chores generally fell most heavily on older children, particularly when the others were still too young to help out. School was of secondary importance when measured against the very practical matter of family well-being. In times of family crisis responsibilities at home took absolute precedence over school. "I quit school when my mother was sick. I was the oldest child at home then. I have to stay home and help out there."[25] Lizzie Chiles and Amanda Henderson labored under a dual disadvantage in their attempts to educate the children of Promised Land. The public education system offered only the most marginal support for Negro education, and Promised Land parents felt quite free to interrupt the school routine. The result for the children was a limited education which helped to fix their adult status in permanent peonage.

Some children accepted the premature conclusion of their education with little question. They moved easily from the rough benches in the Promised Land School to their place behind the plow and by the age of fifteen were established as economically viable workers in their family labor forces. Other children made the transition less easily, and some defied custom entirely. But for even the motivated child, it was practically impossible to obtain more than a marginal education. "I went back one day after I quit, but the teacher told me she couldn't teach me no more, that I'd have to go someplace else." There was no other place to go for most of the children. The magic the women brought to the small schoolhouse was circumscribed by their own limitations as well as those imposed by the educational system and the domestic economy. "In those days the teacher didn't know much more than the children, and she said she had taught me all she knew already." For most scholars there was no place to go but the cotton fields.[26]

Too many children were sent from the schoolhouse to the fields before they were ready, and in 1921 Lizzie Chiles began to teach those who wanted to learn more in the Mason Hall. Promised Land established a private high school, supported entirely by resources within the community. Although the school was independent of county support, it was from the outset opposed by local educational authorities. The white supervisor for the county's Negro schools regularly arrived at Promised Land to inspect the school over which he had no jurisdiciton. More than once he harassed Lizzie Chiles in front of her students, telling her, "Anna, you can't teach children this way." Employed by the county to teach in the public school and by the community to teach in the high school, Lizzie Chiles was in a precarious position. She balanced her two employers and the obligations of her two jobs. The supervisor brought pressure to bear against the high school and Mrs. Chiles. When she responded in tears, but with a firm commitment to her young scholars, to one public humiliation, telling the white supervisor that "I must educate the children to the things I know are right," the county withheld her pay. Community response to the punishment was practical. Their problem was to maintain an educational system for the children. The Masons held "chicken suppers and bar-b-que dinners" to raise the money for her salary. Until the county recanted, the Promised Land community gave Lizzie Chiles and both of her schools their wholehearted support. This collective action challenged the local white opinions about Negroes and Negro education.[27]

Promised Land High School closed its doors for the last time in 1930 after only nine years of operation. In this period of economic hardship, the community was no longer able to support an enterprise, which "was too sophisticated for the times," without some outside assistance. That aid was not available in a period when advanced education for Negro children was only a dream for all but the most fortunate. Still, some parents sent their children outside Promised Land to continue their education. The Baptist-sponsored Little River Institute and Brewer Normal School, both in Greenwood, were available to those able to pay the tuition and arrange transportation into town. The problems of transportation were solved in the same way that other difficulties were solved, by determination, initiative, and cooperation. If children "didn't have no place to live in town" during the school week, they "rode a bicycle back and forth every day" between Promised Land and Greenwood. Those with friends or relatives in town boarded during the week, coming home every weekend. They walked to town together on Sunday evening, carrying enough food for the week, some clothes, and their school books. In bad weather the parents coordinated their efforts, and the children "rode into town together in a wagon" driven by one of the fathers. For many children this was their first step toward leaving Promised Land.[28]

There were no sewing classes and no vocational training classes at Promised Land. Despite the longstanding success of vocational education in the Sea Islands and the popularity of Booker T. Washington's educational philosophy in the state, the mastery of vocational skills at Promised Land was a parental responsibility, and one accomplished through an apprenticeship at home.[29] The children of Promised Land learned to read and write and figure their own accounts in school. Although most of them "didn't know about presidents and such things" until they were grown, their education taught them the skills they needed to comprehend the transactions inherent to their own sphere. They were cheated less often by the "lien man" because they could read and comprehend the contracts and mortgages they signed.

Lizzie Chiles had a favorite mind-bending arithmetic problem that she posed to her young scholars. It exemplified her approach to education, for it required that the students combine skills and knowledge from the classroom to resolve the practical problems they would soon face as adults:

If a man was going to plant an acre of land in corn, and he could plow twenty-five rows to the acre, and have fifty mounds in each row, with three kernels of corn in each mound, how many kernels of corn did he need to plant an acre of land in corn?[30]

Mrs. Chiles prepared her young scholars for their adult roles by skillfully manipulating a traditional curriculum to her own ends. The children's studies were enriched with history and geography. Their leadership skills were shaped through the demands Mrs. Chiles made for public performance and her implicit expectation that they would help each other prepare for these events. Cooperation was central to survival, at school and in adulthood. The practical applications of these values were as important as the knowledge the children carried with them when they left the schoolhouse.

Lizzie Chiles and Amanda Henderson taught hundreds of children during their careers at Promised Land. The adult destinies of their scholars were varied. Some remained at Promised Land and worked as farmers, sharecropping and renting land; others became day laborers and railroad hands. There were a few who took the state's teacher examination at the Greenwood Courthouse and spread across the region to shape the next generation of Negro scholars, who still walked miles across the country farm fields to schoolhouses built during Reconstruction. Future railroad porters, carpenters, bricklayers, and iron workers sat side by side on the schoolhouse benches and shared books with friends and cousins who left Promised Land for Morehouse and Wilberforce. It was not possible to tailor educational programs for each of their futures. The women reduced their educational equation to a single common denominator: "Mrs. Chiles was the best teachers I ever had. When she tell you something it was right."[31]

God and Power

The churches at Promised Land were the hub of community social life, maintaining their centrality through a pattern of rituals which remained basically unchanged from the 1880's. The routines of worship—a mid-week prayer service and weekly Sunday School and preaching—provided both physical relief and spiritual release to community residents on a regular basis. Children's Day, Founder's Day, and other special occasions continued, as they had during the nineteenth century, to blend the overtly spiritual with the more secular elements of community life. Although "I never did hear of no *party* in the church," there were few church gatherings which lacked an element of the social. Families dressed in their best clothes to go to church. The women wore the white dresses which signified membership in the Ladies' Aid Society, and the men wore their suits. Even the most impoverished sharecropping family had a special set of "Sunday clothes," which were kept clean and mended. Children who went barefoot all week bathed "in the big pot by the fireplace in the winter and out back in the summer" on Saturday night and "carried our shoes in our hands so they won't get dusty when we walked down the dirt road" on Sunday morning. Just in sight of the church, the children stopped, wiped the dust from their feet, and pushed them into the shoes which rarely fit. "You want to look your best when you go to church."[32]

The "turn-outs" and other church events were less formal than Sunday School and preaching. The picnics and barbecues and "fellowships" sponsored by the Mt. Zion Board of Stewards and the Ladies' Aid Society, designed as money-raising affairs, provided an ideal setting for visiting and gossiping because they were always open to anyone who wanted to attend. "In them days the Baptists and the Methodists didn't have nothing at the same time," and the visiting back and forth between the two congregations further solidified the already extensive social bonds at Promised Land. The members of the two churches regularly attended each others' special church services, revivals, and turn-outs. A similar pattern of visitation and exchange linked both Mt. Zion and Crossroads to other Negro churches in the vicinity and extended the community's sphere of influence as well as the scope of social life. In those days "people couldn't afford to do nothing else"; and, even for those who might have had the money other avenues were closed. Church activities were the major outlet for social activities.

The population growth at Promised Land during the early 1920's was accompanied by the establishment of a second Baptist church, Jacob's Chapel. Although not located within the community, Jacob's Chapel had unusually close ties with Promised Land. The source of those ties, like so many other aspects of life at Promised Land, was inextricably bound to the agricultural economics of the region. The Great Migration drew away many sharecroppers and tenants from the community population. As they left new families took their places on the farms in and around Promised Land, either renting or buying the vacated lands. For these families, as well as those who emigrated, moving was a step up in their lives.

Many of these families, drawn from the same southern corner of Greenwood County, had been members of Mt. Moriah Baptist Church before they moved to the Promised Land area. Now distance separated them from their church. Transportation for more than a mile or two was difficult for rural Negroes during the 1920's "because people had to walk back then." Still, their religious needs were strong and their collective identity as an independent religious group sufficiently well established that they did not want to merge with Crossroads.

The small group of families, drawn together out of a need to worship, a desire to maintain their own collective spirit, and geographical isolation from their old church home, formed Jacob's Chapel. The families went to Promised Land regularly, sometimes to visit, other times to share in the fellowship of the churches; and "many of us married girls from Promised Land."[33] In an already familiar pattern, church, family, and economics combined to shape the nature of social organization.

Together the churches provided the foundation and the hub of community leadership. The most stable and enduring of the local voluntary organizations, they provided the framework through which power and prestige found concrete expression. Like the land, the leadership positions within the churches were carefully controlled and informally transmitted from one generation to the next within the same kinship groups. These processes were clearly evident at Mt. Zion, where church leadership was stratified by both age and sex. Men and women uniformly began their participation in the church power structure as class leaders, Sunday School teachers. Men obtained their positions at a much younger age than women and tended to remain active in the governing bodies three times longer. Seventy-five percent of the men appointed to the Board of Stewards or to the position of church trustee served first as class leaders and were also kinsmen of previous church leaders. Women who advanced beyond class leaders to other official positions were also tied by kinship to a larger system of power and influence. Forty percent of the women appointed to the Stewardess' Board were married to men serving concurrently on either the Sunday School Board or the Board of Trustees. Eighty-nine percent of the men and women who moved from positions of class leader to other church leadership roles were members of families, by either birth or marriage, active at Mt. Zion since the 1870's. All but a few were landowners. For both men and women there was uniformly little opportunity to advance beyond the position of class leader without well defined family connections.[34]

Table 10.
*Male-Female Differences in Mt. Zion Leadership**

Leadership Differences		Male		Female
1. Age at entry into leadership positions				
	N	24		27
	X̄	39.8		50.7
	s	18.1		16.9
	t		2.22†	
2. Age at exit from leadership positions				
	N	24		26
	X̄	56.4		56.4
	s	13.8		17.3
	t		0.01	
3. Length of Service	N	24		27
	X̄	16.6		5.5
	s	13.2		3.5
	t		4.22†	

*Leaders were identified through the Mt. Zion Records, II–V, and their ages were computed from U.S. Bureau of Census, 1900 Household MSS, Smithville and White Hall Enumeration Districts, Greenwood County, S.C.
†$p < .01$.

Leadership positions at Mt. Zion were held equally by men (50.5 percent) and women (49.5 percent). However, the more powerful elective offices on the Sunday School Board, the Board of Stewards, and the Board of Trustees were more often held by men than women. Within the circle of leadership men were elected by their peers, male and female, to the positions of greatest power and prestige. Sunday School superintendent, secretary, and treasurer were positions always held by men; and the Boards of Stewards and Trustees were limited to men.

Men entered the Mt. Zion leadership structure as class leaders. Those with family connections and those who demonstrated an appropriate degree of religiosity were appointed to the Sunday School Board. Service on the board acted as a filtering device, and those who successfully met the expectations of their pastor and their peers were elected to board offices. After a period of service in this capacity the successful and well connected joined the Board of Stewards or the Board of Trustees by pastoral appointment. Service within the church in these sequential capacities extended over an average of sixteen years, and retirement from active leadership generally occurred for men between the ages of fifty-five and sixty.

Female passage through the church leadership structure followed a more circuitous route. There were among the class leaders many women under thirty, often women not yet married. Most served as class leaders for two or three years and then disappeared from the circle of leadership. For those who remained, the next phase of female leadership was the Stewardess' Board. Membership was obtained through the informal approval of other women active on the board, and among those who became stewardesses more than half were also involved in other aspects of church leadership. The most common of the positions held by these women was that of "club captain." Clubs, loosely connected with lineage, were money-raising vehicles; and club captains were highly competitive among themselves. The women prided themselves in their money-raising skills. Because the clubs were artifacts of lineage, club captains were women with long-standing family connections. They were viewed as representatives of the several dominant lineages and were probably selected for the positions they held because of their matronly respectability as much as their ability to raise money.

In addition to the club captains, 16 percent of the stewardesses also served on the Sunday School Board; and 11 percent of these women were members of the *ad hoc* Executive Committee. Election to these two posts represented the pinnacle of female power within the church. The Sunday School Board controlled the majority of the church funds, the appointment of class leaders, and major church policy. The Executive Committee was probably the most influential component of Mt. Zion's leadership pyramid; it monitored all aspects of church activities and the private affairs of the congregation. The trustees, in contrast, attended to the doctrinal aspects of church business. Thus membership on the Sunday School Board or the Executive Committee brought some women in the community to a position of relatively direct power.

Women, like men, retired from their active involvement in church affairs in their mid-fifties. For both men and women this withdrawal from public life marked the onset of old age, the time for disengagement from the labor force as well as active involvement in church leadership. It was a time when many men turned the management of their land to sons and sons-in-law and when women withdrew from field work. Old age held the opportunity for leisure, a luxury unknown among the younger community residents. Old men offered informal advice on matters of church policy, farming, and dealing successfully with white folks. Old women tended to babies, monitored the grandchildren, and oversaw pregnancies among the younger women.

Leadership at both Mt. Zion and Crossroads influenced a variety of secular affairs within the community. In some cases the strategies for exerting this influence involved the direct use of church power, but in other instances church leaders defined their roles in more subtle ways. Both churches served as delivery mechanisms for the community's social services. At Mt. Zion the "resolution on Behalf of the Poor and Needy" took concrete form. Funds were collected and disbursed to the sick and the elderly. The Executive Committee of the Sunday School Board was responsible for determining who among the congregation's old folks had the most pressing needs, and the Committee allocated church monies to families as well as individuals whose needs surpassed their own resources. The use of power in this case was direct, and there was little question as to the source of that power. The landowners and their descendents controlled the definition of need at Promised Land and determined who would be the recipients of community charity.

The Mt. Zion Resolution was an expression of benevolence and philanthropy framed within the context of religious and social responsibility. It was formalized in such a way that church sponsorship was beyond question. Church control of community affairs, however, extended well beyond such official policy statements; and church leaders held positions of such honor that they were able to exert influence on a variety of nonreligious community activities. The Board of Deacons at Crossroads, for example, "always passed on the school teachers" before they were hired for teaching posts in the county school. The church maintained an unusual degree of control over public monies through a web of interconnected influence systems. They determined who would teach the Promised Land children and what would be taught, not necessarily in terms of curriculum content, but in terms of values and standards of morality. Both Lizzie Chiles and Amanda Henderson were Methodists, but they held their teaching positions at the pleasure of the Baptist deacons.

The same men who were leaders at Mt. Zion were also the most active among the community's Masons. Although "the Baptists didn't believe in no secret organizations," it was through the efforts of the Baptist leaders that the Promised Land Union Burrial Aid Society was established. All of the founders of the society were either deacons or deacons' wives at Crossroads. These two groups supplemented the efforts of the churches, providing social services such as unemployment, sick pay, and death insurance to their members and augmenting the social activities of the churches through their own turn-outs and community barbecue dinners. Members of the society and the Masons enjoyed a position of elevated prestige within Promised Land, and the attraction they lent to church membership further enhanced the informal influence of the religious bodies over community life.[35]

The Little River Association: An Extension of Power

Both Mt. Zion and Crossroads were deeply involved in all aspects of life at Promised Land. The two churches also extended the scope of their involvement, and thus their influence, well beyond the community boundaries, most often using alliances with other Negro churches throughout the region as the mechanism of this extension. One such alliance, the Little River Association, was a convention of Baptist churches that met together quarterly for singing conventions.[36]

The meeting site for these widely attended events rotated between the member churches, and no single church hosted the Singing Convention more often than once a year. Crossroads was a member of the Little River Association throughout the first quarter of the twentieth century and duly took its turn hosting the singing convention. Although the Promised Land church was neither a special nor a dominant member of the association, Crossroads' participation and involvement in the Little River Association was an important aspect of community life. That involvement illustrated the diversity of vehicles by which Negro social and religious life intertwined and extended beyond the Promised Land boundaries.

As was the case within the community, leadership in the association was expressed and exercised in overtly religious terms. Through this framework Promised Land residents dominated the Little River Association throughout the first two decades of the twentieth century. Deacon J. F. Chiles of Crossroads was the association president from 1900 to 1921. John L. Turner, the carpenter and another prominent member of Crossroads, a descendent of the founding Moragne family, and a respected schoolmaster, served as the secretary of the

Little River Association during the same period. Both positions were elective, and the length of Chiles's and Turner's tenures in office clearly attested to the prestige and respect both commanded not only at Promised Land but in the region encompassed by the Little River Association.

Singing Conventions were gala events that began on Saturday afternoons with a social hour and dinner and extended through a Sunday worship service. The Saturday evening session was always opened with a ritualized roll call of church representatives, attending choirs, and an introduction of visiting churches. During the roll call there was a collection of contributions from various representatives and choirs, each recorded carefully in the association's minutes:

> *Crossroads Sunday School choir, B. W. Turner, send 80 cts. Damascus—60 cts., Mt. Calvary, Mrs. Anna B. Aikins, Miss Addie Burton, 40 cts., Mt. Tabor, Mrs. Mattie Pressley, Choir, Mrs. Lela Oliphant, Sunday School, 40 cts.*

Each contribution of each attending church was publicly presented to the entire assemblage. This roll call was generally quite long and was followed by a dinner break. The body gathered again, and the heart of the Singing Convention began. "The President lined a hymn" to mark the onset of a Saturday night filled with spirituals and friendly competition. "The Music Ramble was on." Choir after choir sang, and the night ended on an educational note. The music conductor gave a general talk on "the theory of music" or the nature of "voice culture."

Sunday morning all the participants gathered for preaching in the host church at a worship service that inevitably included special "talks" by members of visiting choirs. On one occasion "Mrs. Lonnie Glover read a good paper on charity," and at another time there was a "special duet by the Henderson sisters." A business meeting followed preaching, and it was during this part of the weekend that special problems were considered and personal dissatisfactions aired. Lela Moragne, Calvin Moragne's daughter-in-law and a school teacher in Honea Path, served as the official organist for the convention. One Sunday she rose and "made a touching appeal to the members of Damascus Church and chided them for not discharging their duty in meeting the organist at the station per promise." Hers was a paid position, and part of her pay was a ride from the flag stop to the church.

Sunday morning also provided an opportunity to disseminate information of interest to the region's Negro population, otherwise isolated throughout the county. At the conclusion of one business meeting "Prof. Hilliard was presented and spoke in the interest of the colored hospital in Greenwood." His appeal for financial support for the hospital was met that Sunday by the Singing Convention, for they immediately gathered a small collection which they donated to the colored hospital.[37]

The Little River Association brought the men and women of the Promised Land community into a broader network of relationships and was one of the ways in which members of the community maintained contact with other Negroes throughout the region. The association involved thirteen different churches scattered across three counties—Greenwood, Abbeville, and Laurens. Four times a year, on fifth Sundays, members of Crossroads and residents of Promised Land traveled together by train and wagon to join old friends for the two day meeting. They sang and prayed and visited with people distant from their own day-to-day lives. The bonds of caste and religion brought them together in a pattern of recurring and reciprocal interchange, an important part of Negro social life otherwise restricted by poverty and Jim Crow.

Leadership at Promised Land was vested within the kinship systems of the original landowners in the community. The same families who were actively involved in radical Republican politics during Reconstruction established the churches during the 1880's and supported the early efforts to establish community schools. Now they turned their energies toward community concerns. They fostered and promoted the ideal of mutual aid through the Mt. Zion Resolution, the Promised Land Union Burrial Aid Society, and the Masonic lodge. Together these three served the sick and the elderly, those most vulnerable to indigence in an already poor community. The burial services provided by the society and the Masons added dignity to death for those families unable to meet the undertaker's fee. Without them most of the old folks at Promised Land would have been "buried just like a dog." The men and women who shaped these organizations were not self-serving leaders, for they received little direct benefit from their efforts. Power and influence at Promised Land were used to promote community well-being, to encourage self-reliance, and to establish a framework of reciprocity.

SEVEN

Turn Outs and Granny Women

When my brother Mac was born, my mother sent me and my other brother up to Amanda Wright, said she was to come down now 'cause my mother was sick. Old granny woman made me and my brother go to bed, keep us from know what's going on. There was a key crack in the door. We stay up, run, and peep through the door to see what's going on. After a while I hear a baby cry. I peep through the door, see a baby lying on a quilt on the floor. The next morning my mother say old granny woman found the baby in a tree stump. The next day or two after that my brother and me, like little fools, run around looking in old stumps, trying to find a baby.

Cora Frazier Hall
Promised Land, South Carolina

Childhood was brief at Promised Land. In most families babies arrived in rapid succession, "one right after the other"; and, before the age of two, small children were replaced at their mothers' breasts by the newest infant in the family. Few of the impoverished families in the community were able to support and nurture any but the most robust of their children. Medical care was minimal; and infants died regularly of diarrhea, pneumonia, and a host of other undefined illnesses. Healthy babies survived to adulthood, and the sick ones were "buried over in a little corner" of the cemetery in graves marked only by a few small stones.[1] Although infant mortality rates decreased during the second generation and were generally much lower at Promised Land than elsewhere in the Cotton Belt, few families in the community saw all their children grow to maturity. Still, death was familiar at Promised Land, and the uncertainty of life extended from birth to old age. A boy who survived to adulthood might be abducted by the Klan or killed by a passing train as unexpectedly as babies died of the fever. Those babies who survived their infancy and early childhood were at work in the cotton fields or the houses of white folks before their adolescence was passed. By the time they attained maturity, most settled easily into the routines of adulthood.

Birth and Infancy

Babies were born either at home or, equally as often, "at my daddy's house," for young women frequently went home to their parents for childbirth, even if "home" was no more than half a mile across a cotton field.[2] Women were rarely attended by a doctor, although there were physicians in both Verdery and Greenwood. Dr. Devlin and Dr. Henderson came to Promised Land to set bones and attend critically ill adults; but Sarah Burt, "a midwife for both white and colored," and Amanda Wright, who lived "over by Mt. Zion behind the cemetery," delivered the babies. "Them old granny womens" came to each house when they were summoned, carrying little more than a bottle of homemade corn whiskey to attend each birth.

Childbirth was rarely discussed openly, even among the women themselves; nor was it viewed as a particularly special event. It was merely one of many accepted life routines. By mutual agreement between husbands and wives, "the mens didn't have nothing to do with it. They went for the midwife, and that was about all." Children were sent away or "put to bed sos we wouldn't know what was happening," and even female relatives were largely excluded from the actual birth. It was an event accomplished with only the midwife present. Women gave birth "down on your knees" in a squat position, and whether labor was brief or protracted there was little more than "a sup of whiskey" to dull labor pains.

Infants arrived in a casual manner, "when it was that time," and were readily incorporated into the family and kin systems at Promised Land. They were viewed as gifts to be loved and cared for; and, if they died, they were soon replaced by new babies in the prolific families. One of the first and most symbolic acts following the birth of a baby was naming, which might occur immediately after birth or be delayed for as long as a year. While family names established lineage in a general sense, a given name was also a vital component of a child's identity. Because babies were often named for relatives and parents, given names were part of a family tradition and linked the newborn with a specific elder member of the family. In the same way that family names located a child within one of several community kin groups, given names further focused a child's identity within that kinship system.

Selection of a newborn's name was not automatically made by the baby's parents, although they controlled who would select the name. In most cases, "my mother give me this name when I was born"; but, with some frequency, "my aunt, my mother's brother's wife," or a relative "here visiting from Atlanta when I was born name me for herself." On rare occasions older cousins were allowed to select the newborn's name, a special honor bestowed on a favorite niece or nephew by the baby's parents.

Boys were named for fathers, but also for grandfathers, uncles, and other male relatives. Girls were likewise given the names of favorite relatives and of people respected by their family and the community. Allen and Mary Richie named their first son Joshuway for his maternal grandfather, Joshuway Wilson. Gibson Nash named one son after his father Wilson; Lymus Pinckney named a middle son for his brother-in-law Moses Moragne. Generally eldest sons were not given their fathers' names but that of another relative, usually a grandfather. Younger sons were commonly named for their fathers. Such was the case for John Gilmore, Jefferson Chiles, and Thomas Williams. In some instances names were altered to suit the gender of a newborn. Allen and Mary Richie named one of their daughters Allie, a feminized diminuitive of Allen. Probably they expected a son and intended his name to be Allen. The adjustment was a simple one and an index of the extent to which parents planned and anticipated the birth of each new baby, even in already crowded households.

Naming patterns reflected the strength of affective bonds among subgroups of kinsmen and between the generations. It was common that several cousins be named for the same elder relative or that a given name be transmitted for three generations or more within a kinship system. This naming pattern established and maintained ties between the generations in a social environment otherwise marked by great social distance between age groups. It served, as well, as a form of symbolic inheritance for men and women who had little else to transmit to their children and grandchildren.

Childhood and Adolescence

The world of childhood was an androgynous one, for adults made little distinction between boys and girls.[3] Those children who survived infancy were regarded by their parents as a source of labor for the small unending tasks of farm life, and their training to this end began at a very early age. Before they were old enough to attend school, scores of small children were sent out to gather kindling; and, as soon as they could lift the bucket, they carried water to the fields for their parents and older siblings. By school age most children were already accustomed to a number of household responsibilities. Many "had to sit there and tend to my sisters and brothers" while their mothers labored in the fields. Young children, by the age of eight or nine, were charged with midday meals, told by their mothers only to "put the beans on, or the peas, and let it boil 'til you see the water turn white." Young boys cooked as proficiently as girls " 'cause the parents learned them." In a cultural setting in which the survival of all was dependent on the cooperative labor of individuals, childhood was characterized by uniform responsibilities and an absence of sex role distinctions.

Young children were left unattended for long periods of time because in this farming community every able bodied person worked. As a result, children at Promised Land ranged freely about the farms. They roamed the woods and fields with their cousins and friends. They hunted with their grandfathers' dogs, and they also found ways to get into trouble. Childhood impulses and pranks were as much a part of life as carrying water to the fields and "cooking dinner on the fireplace." Cane patches were especially vulnerable to assault by boys and girls drawn to the crop by a chronic sweet tooth. It was tempting to rip down a stalk or two, "break it up, and chew it to get the juice," even though the indulgence was forbidden by most parents.

One or two stalks of cane from an entire field were never missed, and few children grew up without "sitting down in a ditch" chewing on cane stalks appropriated from their fathers' or a neighbor's fields. On occasion a group of children roaming through the fields would "just wreck that whole cane patch." One small mob descended on a cane patch en masse and destroyed the entire field before they were stopped. The crime was a serious one. Sugar cane was central to the local subsistence economy, and in their vandalism the children demolished future molasses and feed for the mules. The punishment matched the gravity of their crime. All were thoroughly beaten.

The Carter and Turner stores, too, were a source of temptation for children with little money to spend but normal desires "to have a little something special." Children sent to the store for a bag of meal eyed the sodas and the candy longingly, but most families could rarely afford such luxuries in a world where even small children were essential contributors to domestic survival. Still, on at least one occasion desire outweighed resistance, and somebody "took a handful of peanuts from Mr. John Turner's store." This theft, like the destruction of the sugar cane patch, was a serious crime. Stealing was intolerable in a community where everyone, even the storekeeper, lived under the most marginal economic circumstances. From the youngest to the oldest, all the children present at the scene of the crime got a switching "when the old man told our daddy about it." All were held responsible for the misbehavior of one, and few ever stole a second time.

One of the most distinguishing aspects of childhood was the extent to which smaller children were isolated from the adult world. They were separated from their parents throughout the workday for economic reasons, and they were separated at other times for social reasons. Adult social events, when a grandmother or the preacher came to dinner, were intentionally structured to exclude children. Meals for company were particularly special occasions and remembered by small children because "my mother used to always fix big dinners then. She'd always have something extra—vegetables and chicken and pie and things like that, coffee too." The best of the meal was saved for the company; mothers "put the biscuits back in the oven" if the preacher was coming to dinner; "and we couldn't have none. They was for the grownups." Even if the children were served the same food, it was not in adult company. The smaller children "couldn't go in the dining room" but were fed in the kitchen while Grandmother or the preacher "always get the best." Despite a festive atmosphere among the adults, children were not permitted to fully participate; and, in this restriction, they were reminded of their subordinate and isolated position in the household.

While relationships between parents and children were structured and formal, the ties between grandparents and their grandchildren were marked by reciprocally affective bonds. Old Fannie Moragne, the mother of all fourteen Moragnes who first settled Promised Land, claimed more than one hundred grandchildren among the second generation Promised Land youth. In her old age Fannie lived with her son Eli, and there in the tiny house she had "a secret place right under her bed" that all the grandchildren knew well. That was where she kept surprises and presents, boxes "with different things," for the constant stream of small visitors who came to call. No matter which one came over to see Grandma Fannie, "she always have an apple or something, even if it wasn't nothing but a biscuit. It would be in that box under the bed waiting 'til you come." The gift itself was not important, for whether the children wanted it or not, "we'd take it and thank her for it." The most important aspect of Grandma Fannie's boxes under her bed was that each child who came for a visit felt special; all knew that "she'd always have you a little something."

Children seldom left Promised Land apart from adults. They were allowed to roam freely within the community; but, whether they went to town for the day or to the Little River Association Singing Convention for the weekend, small children were never permitted far from home alone, and never without a specific purpose. Folks went to Greenwood for Saturday shopping and occasional entertainment, and almost every child in Promised Land looked forward to the circus which came annually in the fall. "Our parents took us to town then," piled in the back of the family buggy. Singing Conventions and visits with relatives in Bordeaux or Ninety-Six were other reasons for family outings, always in buggies "with the little old slow mule." The train was far too expensive for entire families.

Throughout the first twelve years of their lives, most children at Promised Land were relatively sheltered. They worked and went to school during the week, bathed "in a big tub by the fireplace on Saturday night," and went to church on Sunday. Few were ever "exposed to discrimination out there" because their contacts with whites were controlled and protected by their parents. Children rarely encountered whites in situations other than those structured by formal employer-employee rules, and they had little opportunity to observe and learn the interaction rituals between Negroes and whites dictated by southern racism. On the rare occasion when a traveling salesman "called my mother 'auntie,'" children witnessed a less than stereotypical response. "She told him she didn't know that she had any white nieces or nephews." On the whole, most children "never did venture out much," and in their isolation they were also innocent. Few were aware of the complexities of local race relations or their own objective position in the southern caste system.

Children lived in a world away from whites and also in a world largely separate from their elders. Their infancy was marked by an intimacy and dependence, not on mothers and fathers, but on slightly older brothers and sisters to whom they were entrusted while their parents worked. They learned quickly not to ask impertinent questions of adults, for "in them days the parents would beat you" with little provocation or warning. Knowledge and information were the prerogative of the adult world and were not shared with small children. They learned what they knew from their teachers, the other children, their own experiences, and "sneaking around the corner of the chimney" to eavesdrop on adult conversations. Protected from racism, isolated from most adults, and threatened with severe and instant punishment for even small infractions, children learned at a young age to depend on and trust their peers. They shared textbooks with cousins, shoes and punishment with their brothers and sisters. In a largely child's world they explored the woods around Promised Land and found "a special little tree, a pine tree," they could talk with and share their most private young dreams. They slept together in houses "with low roofs" where they could "see through to the stars at night." Their responsibilities within their homes and to each other were clearly defined. They were expected to do their chores, look after the other children in the family, learn their lessons in school, and sit quietly in church. They were trained to be obedient, self-reliant, dependable, and proud.

As the children grew their responsibilities increased proportionately. They were told only "to put the greens on" or to "cook a chicken for dinner and put with it what you like" as their cooking skills increased. Boys and girls alike learned the rudiments of field work, how to harness a mule and distinguish between a weed and a vegetable in the family garden. Most skills were learned by example because as they grew the children spent more time in the company of adults. "Both boys and girls go out in the woods and help our daddies split cordwood." Before they were teenagers children learned to "set out grass and hoe cotton" and entertained themselves during the long hours they spent in the cotton fields "talking about courting. By then some of us had started."

Late childhood was a time of apprenticeship, in their own parents' kitchens and cotton fields first and then in the fields and kitchens of whites. Young girls were trained for domestic service, sent first by their mothers to live with old Negro women, where they cooked and cleaned to earn room and board. After they mastered these domestic skills—cooking, laundry, cleaning, child care—they "went to work for white folks." By twelve or thirteen some of the girls were fully employed, living in the homes of local whites and coming for the first time to know the intimate details of white family life. They were shocked and disapproving of what they observed. In contrast to their own domestic arrangements, they saw husbands in white families maintaining rigid economic control over their wives. Despite the fact that the women worked too, whether for wages in the textile mills or without pay at home, it was not unusual that a white husband "didn't never give [his wife] no money; and that wasn't right." The economic and social equality the girls observed between their own parents was the yardstick they used for the judgements they leveled on their white employers. Similar standards were used to evaluate other aspects of white culture. Families with poorly behaved children and dirty habits were scorned as employers even if "they paid good wages."

Once the fundamentals of field work were mastered, "then the white man 'low you to work in his fields." This was an essential step in the children's maturation, for such work enabled even youngsters to make a substantive contribution to their families' cash resources. The work began as soon as possible. Although young children who worked as field hands for local white farmers "didn't even make a dollar a day" chopping and hoeing cotton, "Ma always send me and my brothers to work for the white man. They pay you more than the poor colored" farmers. The arrangement was a beneficial one for white farmers, too. The Promised Land children provided a well-trained, obedient, and inexpensive labor force, easily employed on a part-time and emergency basis. "White man come in here with a two horse wagon" and filled it with fourteen or fifteen children. "Our mother made us work for them" because all of the families at Promised Land needed extra cash if they could get it.

Although child labor was common and promoted as much by the Promised Land parents as by the white planters, the children were not always wholly enthusiastic about the work and occasionally found ways to circumvent the boredom of field work or to avoid it altogether. Talking about courting was a favorite way not to think about the hot sun and backbreaking labor. "One time I got to talking about that so hard I chopped down a whole row of cotton plants. They wouldn't let me go to the fields no more after that." At other times, left unattended, children who heard their friends "playing ball and having bicycle races" found the work intolerable. "We made up some kind of little tale" and skipped away from the cotton fields to more exciting things.

The subterfuge and minor rebellions mounted by the children were relatively infrequent. They were uniformly afraid of their parents and rarely defied them. Parental authority, in this case, served a vital end. The children were an important source of extra labor at two times during the farm season: in the spring, when the fields were prepared for plowing; and in the fall, when the cotton was ripe. The little cash the children earned working for white farmers or the help

they provided in their family's fields were both important contributions in the precariously balanced economy of Promised Land.

Childhood ended with the sixth grade, and a series of interconnected events signaled the onset of adolescence. As their places on the
schoolhouse benches were usurped by younger children, teenagers
took their place behind a plow, at the end of a hoe, or in a white
family's kitchen. The beginning of adult economic responsibilities
coincided with spiritual maturation. Many youth "found God" and
were "baptized in the church yard" in their early teens. Economic and
religious maturity were complements. The first was a statement of
material obligations, the second an acceptance of spiritual responsibilities. They were incurred simultaneously.

During these early teenage years, usually by the age of twelve or
thirteen, boys and girls "was kind of on their own" in other aspects of
their lives. A part of the independence was permission to ride the
train into town with their friends rather than going in the back of the
family buggy. For most teenagers going to town was a regular Saturday activity, and "everybody who had thirteen cents *rode* to town. If
you didn't have the money, you walked. Took approximately one
hour." Most found the money somehow and "walked across the fields
to Lorenzo" where they caught the ten o'clock train into Greenwood.
They spent the day strolling up and down South Main Street and
Maxwell Avenue, meeting friends and cousins who had moved into
town, and looking in the shop windows. At the end of the day they met
at the train station and caught the westbound Seaboard back to
Promised Land.

Economic responsibilities, religious maturity, and a new degree of
freedom and personal mobility all coincided with the onset of puber-
ty; and then the separate worlds of men and women assumed clear
demarcations. Girls became women almost overnight, with the beginning of their menstrual cycle. They were rarely forewarned, for
mothers simply did not discuss such matters with their daughters.
Some girls were completely perplexed by the event and depended
upon kind older woman to "pin my dress over so the spot wouldn't
show." Others had a vague sense of the situation only because "that
girl at school told me how it would be." None of the girls were
prepared to manage the mechanics of menstruation. Each coped with
the situation in isolation for the first month or two, and each eventually devised some more or less adequate way to "protect" herself. It
was for many a lonely and shameful time, filled with confusion and
embarrassment. "I wash out my panties and hang them out. Put

them on, they get all messed up, and I wash them again." Gradually shame gave way to practicality, and the girls pooled their knowledge to solve the common problem they faced each month. In the pre-Kotex era they, like women of all ages and colors, depended upon rags, washed out nightly and used over and over.

Courtship and Marriage

The ritual of courtship began quite naturally at Promised Land, when the boys and girls were ready.[4] It occurred in spite of the parental barriers erected to inhibit it. The general community emphasis on group activities and family insistence on relationships of reciprocity and mutual responsibility between brothers and sisters delayed the development of romance for a time, and there were relatively few social pressures exerted on young teenagers to establish permanent romantic relationships. Families needed their labor, and "starting out married life" was difficult even at twenty-five. Still, romance was a part of adolescence, usually begun during the last years of school and continued at church activities. They provided convenient settings for social life among teenagers otherwise preoccupied with economic responsibilities and controlled by a community in which "everybody was a parent." Most of the children had grown up together and knew each other well. The same activities that had been part of the routines of their lives since infancy took on new meanings.

Church memberships at Promised Land often crossed family ties; and, in order to maintain a general domestic harmony as well as obtain as much support as possible for church activities, the congregations regularly attended each other's church services, revivals, and social affairs. These events provided the first opportunity for romances away from the schoolyard. Girls and boys would "go over to the Methodist church, go down in the trees, and talk to each other, then go over to the Baptist church next week, do the same thing."

By twelve or thirteen some types of parental control were loosened, and the older generation "allowed the children to sit apart from them" during Sunday school and preaching. Boys and girls alike sat at first with their friends in same-sex groups; and then, as the secret meetings down in the trees gave rise to romances, the teenagers sat together in church as couples. This event served as a public announcement that a boy and girl were "going together." If the parents approved of the relationship, they gradually allowed the pair greater freedom and intimacy for their romance.

The first step in this new phase of courtship came when boys walked girls home from church, always with the approval of both sets of parents. Still the two were not allowed more than minimal privacy, for the girl's parents either followed at a discreet distance or expected the couple to walk with a group of younger brothers and sisters. Sibling chaperons were not always as effective as the parents hoped, and teenage couples occasionally dawdled behind the younger children. Taught from early childhood that all would be punished for the misdeeds of one, the children themselves took control of the situation. If they were unable to coerce the older ones in to staying with them as they were supposed to, "my little sister told my mother when we walked too far behind."

During this age of exploration and awakening, few youth were provided any guidance by their parents in the management of their new sexual potential. Sex was not a topic discussed between parents and children except in the most ambiguous way. Fathers told their daughters little more than "I don't ever want to hear about no boys fighting over you," and mothers advised the girls not to "fool with those boys because the next thing will be a baby." The advice and admonitions were probably confusing at first. Despite the biological realities of farm life, of animals breeding and birthing in every family's fields, most youth adhered to the myths of their childhood until their own bodies provided a contradiction. Babies were brought by the midwife who in turn "got them out of old tree stumps." Even after they realized that the tree stump theory of human reproduction was false, however, few had an adequate explanation of pregnancy. Babies, their origins, and the connection between sexual intimacy and pregnancy were mysteries that persisted for many adolescents "until I got married. That's when I learned where babies come from." One popular intermediate theory was that "you could get a baby by kissing." The belief limited and inhibited sexual intimacy among adolescents for a time; but eventually some young lovers overcame prevailing fears and inhibitions, pushed forward by the forces of nature.

Teenage social life revolved around courtship, which quickly expanded beyond the boundaries of church activities to include popular Saturday night parties in addition to "picnics and ball games out in the church yard." Friends gathered in each others' homes, and there "always be someone there to play the piano." Even though parents allowed the youth some degree of privacy, everybody in the house knew that "my mother was always right there in the next room." The singing and occasional dancing provided some relief from parental control; but, in the small houses where a single room often served several purposes, there were still rules to follow which maintained a degree of propriety. The teenagers were all expected to sit in their own separate chairs. "No beds, no laps" was a common parental dictate, and father found reasons to pass through the parties occasionally just to make certain that the rule was followed.

In families with many children, usually spaced only a year or two apart, brothers and sisters were often members of the same peer group. They attended school together, were in the same Sunday School class, had the same friends, and courted together. Parents exploited the long-standing expectation that their children look out for each other and be responsible for each others' behavior. Fathers insisted that "if you go out together you come back together," for mutual responsibility and reciprocal protection were values inherent to the family as well as the community. Like other rules, this one occasionally disintegrated in the face of other parental demands. On one evening, when a young girl "drank too much wine and fell asleep," her older sisters left her and went on home "because we had to be back at twelve o'clock. My mother propped the door with a chair, and that wake her up when we come in. That's how she check up on us." The girls were home by midnight but they broke one rule to adhere to another. When their father discovered the missing daughter, he dressed and "went after her." All the girls were switched that night, "and the oldest was twenty-six." There was neither independence nor autonomy so long as an unmarried child lived at home.

Despite the barriers which parents erected through rules and fear, the teenagers found ways to conduct their affairs; and there were pregnancies among them. As they grew older some of the girls went to Amanda Wright for information. She advised them "to wash with alum water" to avoid pregnancy. "It drawed the sunflower up," although the practice also had undesirable side effects. "Some girls what wash with alum water can't have no babies after they get married." Despite the fears and misinformation among the teenagers, the imminent public disgrace, or the threat that a girl "might not get a husband, not nothing but an old widow" if she became pregnant, babies were born to unmarried girls.

Young couples were trapped in a web of ignorance and innocence. "We didn't know no better than what we were doing when we did it."

Although Amanda Wright provided "a crude type of abortion" to the girls who sought her out, "the parents won't tell us nothing"; and many girls were not aware of their pregnancy until they were well into term. The pregnancies were a source of shame and fear to both the young couple and to their parents. Boys, with few material resources or the emotional maturity to meet unwanted and premature paternity, often solved their dilemma by flight. They "just runned off to Atlanta or somewhere and stayed gone 'til it was over." If they were aware of the problem and "didn't kill the boy first," a girl's parents "might make that boy marry you." Both sets of parents, however, were often ignorant of the situation until the boy was gone and the impending birth public knowledge.

If she was not "sent down to an aunt in Augusta," a young girl who "got with a baby was an old women then" and was shunned both publicly and privately. "Had to mix with the old women. And your mother would tear you up if you was caught with that girl." When her condition became obvious, "they turned her out of church" until the baby was born. As a result, most "just stayed in the house and won't see nobody, except maybe a few people" who were able to overlook the nature of the sin. Public embarrassment was compounded by private humiliation. Even within their own families "some would be mean if everybody else left." There was little to do but endure the pregnancy and wait for the baby to arrive, because the birth ended a girl's period of imposed isolation. Her return to respectability began where her public shunning had first occurred, at church. "When she come to church she had to get up and confess, and she sang this song—'I Believe I'll Come Back Home. I Know I Done Wrong.' " After that the girl, although tainted, was drawn back into church and family; and the community moved forward once again with the problems of survival. To bear a child outside marriage was shameful and sinful, but the stigma of the mother was not transferred to the child. "Don't nobody want to punish an innocent little baby."

Negro women faced two kinds of sexual vulnerability. The first was that experienced by girls who became pregnant through the innocence and ignorance that guided their love affairs with Negro men. They were affairs constrained by protective parents and "fellows afraid to risk it," by the threat of community disapproval and "a strong teaching about not having children out of wedlock." The collective norm, however, reflected the perennial double standard of male and female sexual behavior, which fostered sexual exploitation of women in the community. "There's no unwritten responsibility on the part of the man" in affairs that resulted in the birth of a child. At Promised Land "the men had dominance over the women" and were known to "sometimes brag about it" to their friends. Still, the standard existed; and "most of the people would live by the rules" designed to maintain the integrity of family life and limit sexual encounters to marriage.

A second kind of vulnerability unique to Negro women was that which they faced in sexually charged encounters with white men. This was a problem beyond the controls of the community, and one rarely acknowledged in a public way. It began as soon as young girls ventured away from Promised Land unaccompanied. One of the earliest opportunities for confrontation came when daughters were sent to Verdery or Greenwood to bring the laundry back for their mothers. Walking down the highway alone, more than one teenage girl saw a white man "drive past me, then set his mirror so he could look good at me." There was little protection for the girls on the isolated road, and they watched helplessly as the car turned and came back. "I have ran so hard that I be out of breath, and my heart would beat so bad. And here they come back down the road, just barely roll along, looking for you. Many times I have ran through the woods" to get away from them.

Like menstruation and pregnancy, the girls were never given explicit information about the sexual aspect of a Negro woman's encounters with white men. "When you grow older you just figure it out." This aspect of womanhood was not always a slow awakening, but one thrust upon a girl in a moment of isolation and vulnerability. "And then you realize right then and there, you got to be careful for the rest of your life."

Male attitudes toward sexuality and sexual intimacy mirrored a larger culture. In the isolated hills of the South Carolina Piedmont the double standard shaped and guided male behavior even among the teenagers. Talking among themselves, the boys "thought it was nice to go with some girls, but we all said we wanted to have our *own* families when we got married. We didn't want no other fellow's babies." The reality was different from the ideal, however; for many young men married women who already had "another fellow's baby"; and they raised that child as their own. Most Negro men did not even permit themselves to consider the violations of Negro women by white men, for they were powerless to solve the problem of interracial sexual exploitation. On the occasions when a Negro woman willingly took a white lover, most men assumed an attitude of scorn. "Those womens was kind of isolated. In our community we didn't have too much to do with womens who went with white men."

Courtships developed between youths who had known each other all their lives. The parents were friends and neighbors, and at Promised Land most of the parents knew each other well. All were cautious during their children's courtships and romances. Prospective wives and husbands were judged as much by their families as they were by their own qualities; parental objections to a daughter's suitor were based as much on the quality and reputation of the boy's father as the young man's individual worth. "If a boy's father don't do right with his family or drinks too much, the parents was afraid the boy might be like that too" and would attempt to block a courtship with even greater restraints than usual. "They never would let me go with this one boy at all" because of his father's poor reputation in the community.

As in their other efforts to control their children, parents were not always successful in their attempts to cool the passions of disapproved love affairs. Youths eloped when love overpowered respect for parental authority. Schemes for successful escape were devised with the help and cooperation of brothers and sisters, and church events commonly provided an opportunity for the couple to avoid detection. "There was a convention down at White Hall" which was expected to last late into the night, and Azzalie Moragne and Joseph Morton saw it as a prime opportunity to "run off and get married." Plans were carefully laid. Azzalie packed her clothes and hid them "up under the house" where they could be easily retrieved after everybody was at church. "My sister's husband had a car" and agreed to spirit the couple away, "to carry us down to Bradley. There was a preacher down there" willing to perform the ceremony despite parental objections. The plan was discovered; and her uncle, acting for her father, made a final attempt to bring the situation under control by "sitting down at the house on the porch waiting for us to come back for my clothes." The clothes were abandoned, and the couple "went ahead and got married, and I wore that same dress for a week."

Even in the face of extreme initial objections, such elopements were ultimately accepted by the families; and the errant couple were drawn back into the kinship system. "My uncle come to town (Greenwood) and sent for me to come get my clothes." Father's brother served as the liaison between family and individual; he met his niece at the cafe where he "bought me my dinner and told me to eat it." As they talked the doors closed by defiant actions were reopened. "He give me some money and told me we could come back now if we wanted to."

Most marriages were less dramatic than the elopements. Few young couples could afford a church wedding, for "it took money to get married at the church," new clothes, and the ability to provide a meal for friends and family. Parents could not provide such luxuries for their children, even if they approved of the match. There were too many children in the family and too few resources. As a consequence couples were often forced to pool the little money they had to pay the two dollar license fee and were married on the courthouse steps by the clerk of courts. Only a few young men were so fortunate as to have saved back "enough money to pay for the license and even buy my wife a dress." For the majority marriage, like other life events, was a ritual completed as quickly and economically as possible; "and that was that. We was married."

Adulthood

Passage into adulthood was marked by several life changes.[5] "You was growed up" when economic self-sufficiency, separate residence, or marriage occurred. Most commonly the three events converged sometime during their early twenties for both men and women. Adulthood brought even greater independence from parental authority, although even then it was not necessarily absolute; but adulthood held, as well, a new problem, economic survival. The first years of adulthood and marriage were always difficult ones. "We didn't have nothing when we got married"; and, for even the most affluent among the community youth, the essentials of self-sufficiency—plows, guano distributors, cultivators, and planters—were acquired slowly, one each year when the cotton was sold. Newlyweds seldom "took to farming right away" because even sharecropping or renting, if it was to be a profitable enterprise, required a few tools. Those were the only edges a Negro farmer had against the lien man. As a result many young couples "did day work and had a cotton patch—about two acres." The wages from the day work, although small, provided for routine subsistence; and the small cotton patch was for the future.

Husbands and wives worked the land together from the beginning of their marriage, an alliance which was more economic than romantic. The division of their labors reflected adult sex roles. "My husband plowed it. I hoed it and picked the cotton and got half the money." Men used their half to buy a plow, a mule harness, or some other piece of equipment for the farm they hoped to have someday. The women "bought a stove and some little things for the house." The separate areas of male and female responsibility and concern established in their separate field labors extended to differentiated responsibilities in other aspects of their marriage. The division was, however, complementary.

Couples settled quickly into the routines of married life. Young husbands worried about crops and rains and "making enough to break even." In a good year a man might be able to pay off his lien and have enough money left for a one-horse plow or a middle buster. If not, there was always the lien man; and young men turned frequently to such white men as Will Henderson and Walter Devlin for financial assistance to buy farm equipment—"a man can't farm without those tools." As a couple accumulated the tools, they looked for more land to rent in an ongoing cycle of small cash profits and expanding resources. Together "me and her could farm fifteen acres alone," and a few more acres if they had a mule.

The men at Promised Land bought their mules in Abbeville from a merchant who "brought them down from Tennessee." The expensive and contrary creatures, which cost fifty to seventy-five dollars, were often so poor that "they didn't live but one year," not long enough to pay off the lien and benefit from their added production power. Mules were always a risk, but a necessary one for a couple who aspired to more than a marginal existence, for they enlarged the amount of land a married couple could farm alone "without no other hands." Young couples had the most acute need for draft animals, because they farmed with the disadvantage of limited household labor. They also had the most limited resources in the community and were often forced to take a younger brother or sister into their household to help out in the fields or to care for the babies.

Wives faced the problems of crops and rains and worried with their husbands about debts and the lien man because "in them days the womens worked as hard as the mens in the fields." They also worried about the babies which started arriving for most within a year after their marriage. They talked softly to each other about their pregnancies, confiding to their friends that "I'm looking to have my baby soon now," but were never really certain about the details or mechanics of birth. That problem they entrusted to "them old granny womens," Sarah Burt and Amanda Wright. While they waited and worried, they patched quilts with each other and tended their gardens in solitude; and the few who found the time grew some flowers out at the side of the house.

As the babies were born, young women struggled to balance the demands of new infants against their responsibilities in the fields. Those without the two dollars the midwives charged for their services faced the added burden of paying the old women. Some "picked salad in Mandy Wright's garden for her to pay for the baby," and others saved the money a few pennies at a time by selling eggs or some of their household produce. As soon as they were able, new mothers left their babies with aunts or grandmothers while they worked. Few of the young women wanted to "carry the baby to the fields"; despite the meager human and material resources at Promised Land, families united and found whatever was necessary to help newly married couples survive those early years.

Eventually the initial poverty subsided, "everybody took a lien to get a milk cow," and most who were determined managed to find a farm to rent nearby. Folks got together on Sundays at church and visited back and forth across the farms occasionally in the evenings when the work was done. Both husbands and wives enjoyed the "turn-outs" sponsored by the Masons and the Promise Land Union Burrial Aid Society, and they quietly considered the advantages of joining the society as part of their new adult status. The dues of ten cents per week were prohibitive during the first years of marriage; but, as family financial affairs stabilized, many couples found the money necessary for membership in the society.

The advantages of membership in the Promise Land Union Burrial Aid Society were many. It was an organization which paid both death and sick benefits to its members. Under some circumstances of extreme hardship the society also made small loans, an added benefit for people with few other resources. The society attracted both long-time community residents and newcomers to Promised Land and had the potential for an unusual amount of power and influence within the community. It was an insurance company; but it was also an adjunct to family and kinship systems, particularly during times of crisis. The society arranged for the funerals of its members, relieving the family of the details of death such as having the grave dug. A special committee monitored the health and welfare of all members, with a particular concern for the elderly. Both men and women, in couples and singly, joined this philanthropic, self-help organization.

Social Life

The economics of adulthood centered around the growing season and were focused on the cotton crop. Membership in the Burrial Aid

Society was one device which countered the uncertainties of those economics. It was a pragmatic technique designed and executed within the context of community life. Other organizations and activities at Promised Land further enhanced the sense of predictability and routine that was lacking in the financial affairs of most community residents.

The Promise Land Union Burrial Aid Society, the Masonic Lodge, and the Mt. Zion Ladies' Aid Society and Board of Stewards all held summer turn-outs, popular and well-attended social affairs pragmatically designed as money raising activities by the organizations.[6] With relative frequency, "during good weather, maybe every other week," the men and women of Mt. Zion sold chicken dinners "down in the church yard." The Masons barbecued a pig for their major turn-out of the summer, but the most spectacular of the events was the Fourth of July Picnic.

"Folks come from all over, not just Promised Land," to eat hash and hot dogs and watch the baseball game. The highlight of the day was the homemade ice cream, turned in churns by the men and boys, with fresh peaches in it picked from the Promised Land orchards. The food and company were important aspects of the picnic, which coincided with the time when the cotton crop was laid by. The farmers looked forward to a six-week rest before picking time. In itself, this fact of the agricultural cycle was just cause for celebration and, doubtless, heightened the pleasure and festivities of the Fourth of July Picnic.

The baseball games that were always a part of the turn-outs were generally spontaneous. Everyone with a secret desire to be Josh Gipson or play for the (Negro) Atlanta Crackers took a turn at the plate. Baseball also was a part of the community's structured social life and not just an impromptu diversion of the turn-outs. Promised Land had its own baseball team, and the men who played on it "was so good they could have beat the New York Yankees, if they'd ever played them." The ball field was "down behind Mt. Zion"; and the team played regularly against "other colored teams from all over, from Troy, and Bradley, and even Ninety-Six." When the games were held at Promised Land, most of the community walked over to the ball field to watch and cheer; and when the team played in other Negro communities, the "few cars and trucks we had out there" were filled to capacity with baseball fans following their team.

Summer gatherings drew to a close with the August revivals and weeks of "Homecoming." The churches scheduled their revivals sequentially, and "the Baptists went over to the Methodists, then the Methodists went over to the Baptists." Life came to a pause during this season of spiritual rejuvenation, and all of the energy in the community focused on the individual's relationship with God. For some this brought a joyful and ecstatic encounter with a personal Savior, for others recommitment to long-believed precepts. The revivals, and the sense of community which they fostered, were enhanced by the return of those who had moved away. Families looked forward to the renewal of old relationships, to long, leisurely visits with absent sisters and brothers, and to news from the North. "Some came home so regular there wasn't any need to write." Others came less often, but all were equally welcomed home.

Summer social life was active and vibrant. During the winter months, when cold weather kept folks inside and the turn-outs were discontinued, other activities replaced the summer diversions from exhausting work and economic uncertainty. Families visited back and forth between houses. Church remained a regular part of most life routines, and the extensions of church—Singing Conventions and similar get-togethers—maintained ties across communities. As children entered school, entire families attended Amanda Henderson's Friday night performances; and, in the evenings when it was too cold for anything else, families listened while one person read aloud the *Christian Recorder.*

Throughout the spectrum of social activities, whether they involved community-wide participation in a local turn-out or a family dinner after preaching on Sunday, the lives of men and women blended in complement. Husbands and wives struggled together to pay their individual dues to the Burrial Aid Society. They watched their children grow and gain in self-confidence and ability at each year's school recitations and orations. They shared a social life in much the same way that they shared an economic destiny. Only through membership in the Masonic Lodge and the Mt. Zion Ladies' Aid Society were men and women separated completely; and for all practical purposes those two organizations were also complements because husbands joined the Masons and their wives joined the Ladies' Aid.

Mid-Life and Community Affairs

Passage from young adulthood to mid-life was less abrupt than the change from childhood to adolescence or from adolescence to adulthood.[7] There were fewer visible rites of passage, for little in the routines of life changed for most Promised Land residents between young adulthood and the onset of old age. The principal difference between young men and women and those in mid-life, aside from the number and ages of their children, was their status in the community. Age brought with it the possibility for leadership and participation in activities not available to the young. In mid-life the men and women at Promised Land at last found the leisure to devote some of their energy to community affairs and concerns.

Leaders were most visible in the voluntary organizations, the churches, the Burial Aid Society, and the Masonic Lodge. Within each organization there was a recurring pattern of leadership. Men and women alike were middle-aged, long-time landowning residents of the community. Most of their parents or in-laws were among the original settlers. Within the Burial Aid Society the five major offices were held by prominent men at Promised Land. Although women were also members of the society and recipients of its benefits, they were not among the office holders. Of the men—B. W. Turner, Moses Burt, B. J. Morton, A. L. Letman, and William Smith—all were landowners, two were descendents of the Moragne family, and the other three were sons of other landowning settlers. All were Baptists; and together they controlled in excess of two hundred and fifty dollars per year in cash funds, more money than was collected by either of the community churches. These five men, guided by the values of their parents, served as an informal board of directors for the most potentially influential voluntary organization at Promised Land, an insurance company. The sole purpose of the organization was philanthropic, the redistribution of capital.

Philanthropy was also the guiding force of the local Masonic Lodge. Among its leaders, like those of the Burial Aid Society, were descendents of original settlers, and landowners; and, in contrast to the leaders of the society, all were Methodists—Nathan Redd, David Redd, North Carter, Allen Richie, Edd Chappel, and Bud Reynolds. The Mason Hall served as community center for most local events, was used at various times as a school, and functioned when necessary as a funeral parlor. The local Masonic Lodge sponsored and supported the Promised Land High School from 1921 to 1930, an extraordinary act of community pride given the meager resources among local residents.

Both the society and the Masons floundered toward the end of the second generation. In a moment of bulging membership the society "bought up some land over by Bradley." Possibly this act, although indicative of the society's prosperity, also proved its downfall because "after that folks stopped paying." The society lost credibility, and the land was sold to "a fellow back from the Army. He bought it out. Coolidge was president then." At about this same time the Masons disbanded. "The old heads died out, and the new heads was too dumb to keep it going." Mrs. Hargraves, the representative for North Carolina Mutual Insurance of Durham, began selling folks at Promised Land their insurance after that; and occasionally Mr. Robinson, "the colored mortician" in Greenwood, accepted an acre or two of land in payment for a funeral from families unable to afford North Carolina Mutual's insurance premiums.

During the decline in membership, power, and community support of the society and the Masons, a number of the men began to gather informally at W. A. Turner's or Moses Burton's "when they had problems around Promised Land or differences with some of the whites, or anything that they thought was wrong." The men, all former leaders in the society or the Masons, all contemporary church leaders, deliberated together on community problems. They consulted their Bibles for advice and insight, and "they had some white people they would go to and discuss these problems with."

The problems the small group confronted generally involved whites, their relationships with Promised Land, and the threats to community and family security posed by the always marginal nature of interracial encounters. Typical of these problems was an incident involving a white highway crew working near Promised Land on a state road. The crew was composed primarily of white North Carolinian laborers working under the supervision of a local white contractor. They hired "some colored women from Promised Land to cook for them." Nathan Redd made a practice of dropping in on the women from time to time, probably to make certain that they were being well treated. He was told "to quit coming around"; and, when Redd ignored the order, the crew "took him up the road and beat him up." Redd was a respected member of the Promised Land community, a landowner and a member of Mt. Zion's Board of Stewards. The beating was unnecessary and senseless, harkening back to the violence of the 1870's. The community was outraged but realized the danger of direct action. The men got together to talk it over; and eventually "they got the word to Mr. Will Henderson," one of their more trusted and sympathetic white neighbors. Henderson agreed that "something's got to be done" and saw to the matter. "They locked up them hoodlums to pay for beating up Nathan Redd," although the Klansmen went, as always, undetected and unpunished.

Three quarters of a century after their parents and grandparents were emancipated from slavery the men at Promised Land turned to the descendents of their former masters. J. V. Anderson, John Darraugh, Will Henderson, and Walter Devlin, the men who gave them liens and rented them land, were sought out for advice, assistance, and intercession when they had problems "with the men they was working for" or the hostile world in which they lived.

Death

Death was as natural a part of life as birth at Promised Land and created little stir in a community preoccupied with survival. Death was a simple matter which required an expression of grief, a funeral, and a time for mourning.[8] The women wore "widow's weeds" when their husbands passed away, and the men wept openly and without shame at the death of their wives. In death a man or woman lost a life partner, and the pain of that loss was expressed openly and freely.

Death was marked by the tolling of the Mt. Zion bell. Whether the funeral was arranged by the Burrial Aid Society, the Masons, the family, or the church, the routine of burial was the same. The family gathered together in a public statement of grief. Friends, neighbors, church members all came to call, to sit quietly or to listen while a widow or a son talked and wept. There was a great compassion between friends and the relatives of one who had died, and it was a compassion which lacked embarrassment. Tears were accepted as a part of the process of living on, as was the laughter which came from reminiscence. The wake of the Irish was transformed into the "sitting-up" of the rural South. The entire community waited together for the funeral.

The time which elapsed between death and burial varied because of different family circumstance. Children or brothers and sisters might have to be summoned from up north, and time allowed for them to arrive and participate in the "sitting-up." Families without insurance had to generate the cash to pay for the funeral expenses, for death was never financed on credit. There was no standard, but most funerals could not be organized in less than a week. Death did not always occur in Promised Land. People died "over somewhere in Georgia" or up in Chicago, and the bodies came "home on the train." Then one of the men from Promised Land drove into town with a wagon "to meet the corpse," in the same way that folks went to the depot in Greenwood or Abbeville to meet family members arriving for the annual Homecoming.

Funerals drew entire kin groups together. The family followed the casket into the church in a massive procession. Survivors were grouped by generations, as they had been raised. Directly behind the casket were the parents and surviving spouse, united in their grief with the deceased person's brothers and sisters. The sorrow of loss was no greater for a widow than a sister. Behind this group of family elders, children, nieces, and nephews followed together; and, behind them, grandchildren and the more distant relatives. Each generation consoled its own. The most prominent landowner and the most impoverished old woman were mourned equally. In death, life was eulogized by friends and relatives, who spoke of their departed friend with fondness, recalling a lifetime of accomplishments, spirituality, and endurance.

There were no additional words of comfort at the grave, for those had been said in the church. The casket was lowered into the ground; and the earth piled on top of it by the men in the family, who shoveled together to complete the task.

The impact of death did not conclude with the burial. Particularly among landowners and those with an estate of any size, the family then faced the complexities of the county probate court. Appraisers and executors were necessary, and they were drawn from within the community. Brothers and brothers-in-law most commonly assumed the responsibilities of appraisal. Spouses served as executors. Households were inventoried, and the work of a lifetime was measured by common material dollars and cents. A buggy worth ten dollars, six chairs valued at three dollars each, a table, a stove, and a sewing machine were all included in the estate. The accumulations of a lifetime were totaled and given a value which in no way reflected their intrinsic worth. The liquid assets of most elderly landowners included both cash on hand and notes they held against other community residents. The white lien men were only one source of credit;

Table 11.
Distribution of Personal Property Holdings,
Probate Files of Deceased Landowners, 1900–1930

Personal Property	$\overline{X}$ Dollar Value	Percent of Total
Household Goods	$ 83.31	30
Tools and Farm Machinery	54.21	20
Domestic Animals	35.23	13
Liquid Assets	100.31	37

neighbors, uncles, and old family friends were also available for help, always given willingly but within the context of formal, businesslike exchanges.

The brutality of life extended for some to the cruelty of death. From its beginnings Promised Land had a fringe population, homeless Negroes whose existence was even more precarious than most. Hulda Green was one such person. Known to the folk in the community as "Aunt Huldy," the old woman just arrived at Promised Land one day. No one ever knew where she came from, or how she found the place. Aunt Huldy had no home of her own. She was too poor and "lived from house to house among the negroes of the locality," although her most frequent sleeping place was Nathan Redd's. She arrived at the Redd house one February night in 1923, late at night in the middle of a snowstorm. The Redds were already in bed, trying themselves to keep warm. Aunt Huldy called out that she would go over to the Wideman place.[9]

In the swirling snow the old woman turned in the wrong direction that night; and, instead of going down the road to the Widemans, she became hopelessly lost in the Redd's cotton field. Her tracks were still evident in the snow the next morning, "miring across a field for a distance" until she fell, weakened from cold and exposure. "The old woman fell, and prints of her knees and hands could be traced where she had crawled in the dark" through the rows of dead cotton stalks, still struggling against her inevitable death. For nearly a quarter of a mile she pushed on through the cotton rows, convinced that she was headed in the right direction. "She would walk upright for a short distance and then crawl again" until she finally collapsed and laid down to die. When her body was discovered the next day, she wore only one shoe, a man's shoe, and her other foot was bare. "With a bit of old sweater tucked under her head and another rag of the sweater thrown over her face, she froze."

Aunt Huldy Green was buried at Promised Land. Miss Anne Wilson knew that the old woman had a daughter in Atlanta and, using the Promised Land network which crisscrossed the southeast, found the woman and notified her of Hulda Green's death. She came from Atlanta for the funeral and stayed with the Redd family. No one at Promised Land talked much about Hulda Green after that. Everyone knew that the resources which made life at Promised Land better than it was elsewhere in the rural South were limited; and it was because of their finite nature that Hulda Green froze to death, alone and anonymous, in a South Carolina Piedmont cotton field.

Community

From birth to death there was a basic scheme of rationality about life in Promised Land. The values of childhood—obedience, the acceptance of absolute authority, diligence—were translated during adolescence into new realms. Children were obedient to their parents, their teachers, and to the lessons of their Sunday School teachers. There was no room for questioning, and the values they were taught were absolute and immutable. There was honor and respectability to be attained through honesty, frugality, thrift, and hard work. Loyalty to brothers and sisters translated in adulthood into loyalty to community. Responsibility during childhood found expression in self-help and philanthropy in the adult world.

The lessons of family, school, and church provided a means to endure the lessons of economic trial and hardship. Life was defined as temporary, and death as a progression. Adherence to the values which were taught was the only possible route to spiritual progress. "You cannot be admitted to the kingdom if you feel hatred," and so hatred and anger and resentment were repressed, and in their place love and compassion were substituted. Still, the folks at Promised Land retained a sense of self-preservation and an awareness of the conditions and circumstances which controlled their lives; and this awareness was bluntly stated when most agreed that "it was good to live at Promised Land because there won't no whites out here."

EIGHT

Going North

*When I left home I had a ten dollar bill and some change. I put the
ten dollar bill in my shoe, so when I got to Philadelphia I didn't
have it no more. I plumb wore it out. So I just had some little
change left. Then I got some kind of job, but I didn't stay with any
of my people.*

James Evert Turner
Chicago, Illinois

Negro emigration from the rural South began almost immediately
after emancipation, as Negroes began to drift away from the farms
and cotton fields which had symbolized their bondage. A few went
North, but more turned westward during the 1870's and early 1880's.
Then, in the 1890's many journeyed to the cities of the South.[1] During
the first two decades of the twentieth century, the trickle of emigration grew into an exodus of unprecedented proportions as hundred of
thousands of sharecroppers and tenant farmers boarded trains for the
urban centers of the North. This period of mass migration affected
the Promised Land population in much the same way as it did other
Negro communities across the Cotton Belt. Between 1897 and 1915,
43 percent of the community families were among the three hundred
thousand South Carolina Negroes who went to the North, armed with
little more than the hope that they could, as they said, "better our
condition."[2]

The principle factor which stimulated this emigration was economic. Negro farmers throughout the Cotton Belt were affected by
the erratic cotton market, credit arrangements which fostered chronic indebtedness to white creditors, and depleted soil. It was practically impossible for the small-scale Negro farmers in the Cotton Belt,
particularly tenants and sharecroppers, to make a crop under the
capitalist system of southern agriculture where "an elite group of
white planters, bankers, investors, and merchants held a tight

monopoly over . . . the entire agricultural production of the region."[3] The landowning subsistence farmers at Promised Land, who had avoided the economic dependency which engulfed their landless neighbors, were more economically secure. Relatively immune from the monopolistic conditions that dominated agriculture, many were reluctant to abandon their farms. The circulation of land which a generation earlier had supported community population growth halted, and local youth who matured during the first fifteen years of the twentieth century were pushed from their homes by a new kind of land scarcity.

There was as yet no clearly defined pull from the great urban and industrial centers of the North, and many youths left Promised Land prior to World War I with only vaguely defined goals and fanciful notions of the opportunities for work which they might find in the North. Few of these maturing youths had more than a casual acquaintance with life beyond Promised Land, and for that reason their emigration was commonly characterized by a two-step or even multi-step series of moves. In their search for work and economic stability, they explored first one possibility and then another, moving from place to place in much the same way as sharecroppers moved from farm to farm, always seeking a job with slightly higher wages or greater security for the future.

Table 12.
Average Annual Promised Land Rates of
Population Change per 100 Households, 1897–1942

| Years | Total Households | Average Annual Gain/Loss | |
		Landowners	Nonowners
1897–1909	− 2.4	− 0.03	− 4.0
1909–1915	− 2.2	0	− 5.3
1915–1922	+ 2.5	+ 3.6	+ 0.5
1922–1932	− 4.6	− 3.4	− 2.7
1932–1942	+ 1.8	+ 3.5	− 0.02

Few of those who left Promised Land prior to 1915 went directly to the urban North. There were no networks of friends and kinsmen scattered across the cities who could "write to different ones back home about jobs and things like that" or provide assistance to new urban immigrants with work and housing when they arrived at their destinations.[4] These vital extensions of community life emerged somewhat later during the migration process; but, for the earliest to leave Promised Land, there were few forms of assistance or support as they worked their way north and adapted to a new environment and set of living conditions.

Atlanta was the closest large city to Promised Land, and the two were connected by a direct railroad line after 1890. As a result many of the earliest emigrants chose this as their first destination. The jobs they found there were primarily unskilled labor and service work. Women had little difficulty finding jobs. They had cooked and tended their younger brothers and sisters from an early age, and the skills they learned were easily transferred to an urban setting. The men worked as laborers in the lumber yards and warehouses, as hands at the railroads, as cooks and coal deliverers. Few left home with more than "a ten dollar bill and some change"; but that was always enough for train fare, a room for a few days, and enough food to ward off hunger for a time. When their money was exhausted, their only resources were the skills they learned as children and the belief that they could and should work. Few went hungry or were unemployed.

Among those first youth to emigrate were Joshuway Richie and Martha and Charlie Reynolds. All three were born during the early settlement years at Promised Land, Richie in 1881 and the Reynoldses only a few years later. All three were tied through kinship to the original landowners in the community and as a result were raised in relatively privileged, high status conditions. Josh Richie was Allen Richie and Mary Wilson Richie's oldest child. His mother owned four and one-half acres of land she inherited from her father, Joshuway Wilson; and it was on this tract of land that the family built their home. Martha was Primus and Francis Letman's oldest daughter, and Charlie was among the oldest of the Reynolds boys. As elder children all three faced similar problems as they approached adulthood, and they derived common solutions to these problems. They were typical of many community youth in both their plight and in the solutions they devised. They emigrated.

Growing Up and Leaving

Josh Richie

Allen Richie "was a half white man," and from him Josh inherited the angular facial features and copper colored skin which made him "more or less out of the caste." His mother's family, the Wilsons, were all very dark skinned; and from them Josh inherited features which firmly identified him as Negro. Although Allen Richie "could cross color lines," his son could not. Young Josh was "well built, not tall for a man, but a handsome devil" who even as a child liked to brag and joke. He learned his letters and his numbers from his neighbor Sarah Wideman in the local public school; and he was one of many children at Promised Land who were scrubbed clean every Saturday night and marched into the old Mt. Zion church every Sunday morning for Sunday School and preaching. He learned his Bible verses and listened along with the others to the talks, speeches, and orations which emphasized hard work, education, and worldly success. In fact, probably all that young Josh learned from his parents, his teachers, and his Sunday School had a common theme. He must love and fear God, live honestly, and always strive to better himself through diligent hard work.[5]

Another aspect of his early childhood which probably had a powerful impact on Josh was the railroad. When he was about eight, in 1889, the SC&N Railroad purchased rights-of-way through Promised Land; and as a young boy Josh watched the first tracks laid across the community farms.[6] He probably heard his father and mother talk about the cash wages the railroad hands earned. He saw for himself the material results of those wages. Some families bought more new clothes; some children actually had a store-bought toy; some men went to town more frequently now; and certainly those same men, the railroad hands, had money in their pockets that the cotton farmers like his father lacked. Allen Richie rented his farmland and struggled year after year with cotton and corn and cane crops, and with lien men. The railroad hands, with their cash wages and steady jobs, were free of those chronic problems.

Like the other children at Promised Land, Josh Richie first experienced the stark realities of the community maxim for hard work when he went from the schoolhouse to his father's cotton fields; and by fifteen he could do a man's job with the plow, the mules, and the hoe. Together with the help of his sisters Mattie and Allie and his brother Joseph, Allen Richie and his oldest son cultivated about thirty acres of land, barely enough to make a small cotton crop and keep the nine children from going hungry. The Richie family's difficult life, characterized by chronic poverty, was mitigated only by the equally marginal circumstances of their neighbors. None lived far above the subsistence level.[7]

All of life was not the drudgery of field work however. The routines of the community were punctuated by occasional excitement and sometimes danger. During his teenage years Josh may have watched his grandfather Joshuway Wilson mobilize the men of Promised Land when they defended their community against the "Phoenix rats" dressed in red shirts. If he did not observe the incident, he certainly "slipped around the chimney corner" and listened to his father and uncles talk about it. They were some of the "boys with shotguns and Winchesters" that Josh Wilson and Colbert Jordan led in the community defense, and they were local heroes. Young Josh interpreted this event through an adolescent filter. The fundamentally racial issues underlying the Red Shirts' organization were probably secondary to the general excitement and bravado of the adult men for him. Pride, not fear, was the emotion most likely evoked in the teenage boy.

Josh Richie's most immediate example of life was his own home environment. His father provided for the family by scratching out a cotton crop. Still, his own notion of work was shaped by other examples within the community. Among the Richie family's closest circle of friends and family, Josh and the other children knew men who were not farmers, who did other kinds of work. They, too, provided examples of adult life that were respectable and productive. Fortune Wilson was Josh's uncle and also the family's closest neighbor. He was a successful businessman, and his molasses mill was concrete evidence to Josh of an alternative to farming. Uncle Fortune's yard was filled with lively activities, with the mules going round and round in their work and the stacks of sugar cane slowly being converted to jugs of molasses. Fortune's trips around the county to peddle his jugs showed Josh one occupational choice other than farming, which he watched daily.

Preaching and teaching, both respected professions in Promised Land as in other Negro communities, were also adult occupations which Josh Richie knew intimately as a young boy. His knowledge was acquired through family friendships between the Richies and Isaac Y. Moragne's family, whose farm adjoined the Richie lot. Both families were Methodists; both men were Masons and good friends. The children grew up together, walked to school and church together, and eventually Josh's younger sister Lettie married Isaac's son Fred. The ties between the Richies and the Moragnes were extensive, and the friendship longstanding. Josh probably admired Isaac Y. Moragne as much as his own father, and through Isaac he envisioned still another alternative to farming.

In 1900 Allen and Mary Richie's family included nine children. All lived at home. Three were over fifteen; and all but the youngest were able to read and write, testimony of the extent to which these parents valued and supported education for their children. The small house grew more crowded as the children matured, and by the time he was nineteen Josh felt the push of community custom. His younger brothers and sisters were old enough to take his place in the cotton fields. There was no possibility that he would inherit any land of his own. The only family property was the small home lot his mother had inherited from Joshuway Wilson. It was nearing time for him to move out of his parents' home.

Richie contemplated his adulthood under grim circumstances. The community was filled with families already established on most of the available farms. Because he was not married, sharecropping was not a serious option for him. Sharecropping required a partner, generally a wife, to share in the field work. Richie had no wife, and at nineteen was forced by circumstances to widen his vision of his own future. He had little realistic choice but to emigrate, and he boarded the train for Atlanta armed only with the conviction that life must hold some possibilities for him and he must seek out his own opportunities.

Martha Letman and Charlie Reynolds

Martha Letman and Charlie Reynolds[8] grew up just behind Josh Richie, and their childhood experiences paralleled his. While they matured Promised Land changed too, from a sparse farming settlement into a thriving village. They must have watched their fathers fell the pine trees for the first log churches, for both were children of church leaders. Martha's family were Baptists, and Charlie's Methodists. They also watched Luther Moragne build the four room houses he regularly constructed for the new families who settled in the community. Like Josh Richie, Charlie went to public school; and Martha, because she was a Baptist, was enrolled at Crossroads School for Colored. She learned to read and write first from Henry Latimer and then from her brother-in-law, B. W. Turner. As children of landowners and church leaders both Martha and Charlie, like Josh Richie, enjoyed a childhood position of relative privilege at Promised Land. As elder children they, too, had little probability of inheriting the land necessary to maintain that status.

Their courtship was conducted between church meetings and school, always under the watchful eyes of their parents. When they decided to marry, Primus Letman signaled his approval of his daughter's choice for a husband. He deeded two acres of his farm to Martha for her dowry. The gift was intended to tie the young couple to the community as well as provide a place for their home, but the land tenure arrangements for farming were left to Charlie and Martha. The Reynolds family had as many children as the Letmans, and Charlie received no assistance from his father. Without tools, animals, or cash resources, it was impossible to rent a farm; and Charlie and Martha began their married life as sharecroppers.

They may have accepted their reduction in status unwillingly but philosophically, for the situation was not unusual. Still, with no hope of inheriting sufficient land to become economically secure, and less hope of doing more than breaking even at the end of every season, the couple grew increasingly dissatisfied and discouraged with sharecropping and living at Promised Land. They faced a choice, which many youths in the community confronted. They could either stay, resigned to a diminished status and marginal existence but secure in community and family networks; or they could leave, venturing beyond Promised Land in the hope that they "could better their condition." They chose the latter alternative.

Following Josh Richie, they headed southwest on the train to Atlanta. They did not stop there, however, for, unlike Josh Richie, Charlie Reynolds "already had some people" in Mississippi.[9] With no more than a promise of assistance when they arrived, Martha and Charlie packed their few worldly goods and left Promised Land with their children in tow. They were in their mid-thirties when they moved to Mississippi.

First Stops, Long and Short

Josh Richie

When Josh Richie arrived in Atlanta, he rented a room in a boardinghouse which accepted single Negro men; and then he got a job with the railroad. Relatively well educated for his day, trained to be ambitious, the good natured young man "rode the train from here to there and there to here" as a Pullman porter. His travels were solitary ones, and Josh remained a bachelor during his Atlanta years. His younger brothers and sisters "loved to see him coming" back to Promised Land for visits. He always had pockets full of candies and cookies, treats they never saw between his trips home. For his mother he brought cream pitchers of pressed glass and other small trinkets of his travels. Each gift was saved and cherished.[10]

For a time Josh returned to Promised Land as often as possible, and eventually married a girl from home. "There was a baby coming," and the obligations of a man had to be met. The couple never lived together; and after his marriage Josh "went away for a long time," although his wife and child remained in Promised Land with her parents.[11]

Throughout this period of prolonged absence, Richie maintained a unique type of contact with the community. As a porter on the Seaboard Air Line, John Richie had access to the dining car food. During the miles before the train approached the Lorenzo flag stop, he would "pack the leftover food from the dining car into a pail." Then, several hundred yards before the train swept past Lorenzo, Josh Richie stepped out onto the platform of the train and began to swing the bucket of food, now tied to the end of a rope, to the rhythm of the moving train. With careful timing he was able to "just set that bucket down on the ground while the train was still moving." Everybody along the northern edge of the community "knew when he was coming," and there was inevitably somebody waiting at Lorenzo to carry the bucket of food home. "It was always for whoever was there at that time, for who needed it." Richie never forgot the poverty of his youth nor the people who lived in that poverty. His gifts and surprises always focused on the most basic human needs. "He used to brag" about his ability to set that bucket squarely on the ground while the train rolled along, and he laughed when the children rummaged his pockets for the sweets they knew were hidden there.[12]

Richie "had a wild life, running from place to place," during his years as a Pullman porter. In his job he met a variety of people; and one of them, a young German immigrant named Rose, made a lasting impression on him. Rose worked in the dining car for a time and may well have helped Richie pack his food pail for delivery at Promised Land. They probably indulged in a brief romance while they were co-workers, but eventually the affair ended, and Rose left her work on the train when she married. She disappeared for a time from Richie's life.[13]

During this same time, between 1915 and 1920, his wife and daughter moved north to Philadelphia where they were absorbed into his wife's kinship system. The marriage was dissolved by no more formal means than mutual consent, and the obstacles which once prevented his return to Promised Land were removed. Richie resumed his regular trips home. Between visits he sent boxes of candy and fruit, always his favorite gift, home to his sisters and their families. The gifts were remembered long after the food was gone for the exotic aromas they "sent through the whole house."[14]

Although Josh Richie had been away from Promised Land for twenty years, he still maintained ongoing contact with his family who remained in the community, reinforcing his ties with them through his visits and gifts. His affection for them was apparent; but equally obvious was the extent to which his absence forced him to devise new ways to fulfill family obligations. For twenty years he maintained a vital role in the Richie family's well-being, supplementing their farm diet from time to time through his own resources. He was typical of later emigrants who "helped out when they could." Few forgot the families they left at Promised Land or the conditions under which they lived.

Josh Richie quit the railroad in the 1920's and moved from Atlanta to New York. Perhaps he tired of the traveling life of a Pullman porter. Perhaps he looked to new horizons. New York was a place of opportunity then, a place he knew directly through his own travels and indirectly through the wanderings of others. Whatever the specific reasons which guided Josh Richie, he joined, once again, the flow of Negro migrants going north. In his forties Richie settled permanently in New York, where he found work as a skilled laborer in the garment industry.[15]

Martha and Charlie Reynolds

Whatever promises Charlie Reynolds' kinsmen in Mississippi held out to him when he moved his family away from Promised Land, they were not kept when he reached Mississippi. Farming opportunities there were no more favorable than in South Carolina for Negro sharecroppers, and life continued to be an economic struggle. As the children matured, they pressed Martha and Charlie for another move. When the labor recruiters passed through the state with promises of wealth and prosperity in Chicago, the family joined the flood of Negroes who boarded trains for the long ride north. By 1910 they were established in Chicago. Charlie and the older boys "did all kinds of work like mens do" in the new urban environment. With so many members of the family working and bringing home cash wages, there was soon money enough to "buy some property out in Maywood."[16]

Josh Richie and the Reynolds family both took a circuituous route north. Neither had friends or family there, able to provide the material and moral assistance so essential to a successful transition from country to city. Chicago and New York afforded rural southern immigrants like Richie and the Reynoldses expanded work opportunities. While Negro poverty was a chronic aspect of city life, the opportunities to transcend that poverty were more readily present than they had been in the rural South. These three early migrants were typical of those who seized available opportunities and early established working-class lives. Their steady employment and stable family units were their primary protection in the city against descent to the existence of urban slum dwellers.

Josh Richie's ability to secure skilled work was unusual for a migrant from the rural South. Such men and women usually left their homes ill-prepared for city life. They had few skills and lacked the ability to adapt to the requirements and demands of the city. Josh Richie was no better nor worse prepared than most other Negro youths who emigrated from the South when he did. The advantages he enjoyed were subtle ones. When he left Promised Land he took with him a sense of pride and community and a belief in his own abilities. He embraced the work ethic and set about realizing his private dreams. His job as a Pullman porter bolstered his confidence and self-image. Well paid, protected to some extent by union affiliation, Richie's work placed him solidly in the Negro middle class. In this sense his transition from Promised Land to Atlanta was successful, for only through emigration had there been any possibility that he could avoid downward mobility.

Martha and Charlie Reynolds and their family were more typical of the majority of early twentieth-century Negro emigrants in an occupational sense. They left Promised Land as the lowest among the occupational groupings; and, as unskilled laborers in Chicago, they remained at that marginal level. Given this limitation, that they acquired property quickly and moved to a more suburban Negro middle-class residential area was somewhat unusual. The values that they retained from Promised Land and adapted to urban life were the principle factor in their success. The family and household unit had long functioned within an encompassing economic and social framework at Promised Land. The Reynoldses exploited this technique of domestic economics in the city. All able members of the family held jobs. They lived together and pooled their resources, even though "some of them boys was real big when they come to Chicago." Independence and self-sufficiency were defined first in terms of the total household, and only after the larger unit was securely established was the definition applied to individuals.

These two cases of successful transitions to city life were repeated elsewhere—in Philadelphia, in Washington, and in Baltimore—as other emigrants from Promised Land moved away, found jobs, and established new homes. By the onset of World War I there was a complex network of brothers and sisters, friends, first and second cousins, and in-laws scattered throughout the urban North. This web of initial urban settlers welcomed the next wave of migrants from the South in the same way that the original Promised Land settlers shared their resources with community immigrants between 1875 and 1890. They fed and housed them and helped them find work.

Leaving Again

The stream of emigration increased steadily as family after family moved away from Promised Land between 1900 and 1916. Many who left were branches of long-established community family groups. In addition to Martha and Charlie Reynolds and Josh Richie, "the Martins, a lot of the Moragnes—Pope and his sons they come up to Chicago about 1910—the Burts," and many others trekked north. The Promised Land population was further depleted when a number of young men were drafted into the Army. Their departure, coming when it did, caused little specific concern in the community. The residents there had watched emigration for fifteen years. Going to the Army seemed, to them, no different than going to the North. Promised Land was remote, and they "didn't know nothing about no war. No radio then," and only a few copies of the A.M.E. *Christian Recorder* from Philadelphia scattered around.[17]

With the onset of World War I the price of cotton soared, and with it the Promised Land community's economic well-being. Church contributions rose, as did the value of personal property among both landowners and nonowners alike. Opportunities to work for wages also increased, and many of the reasons for emigration subsided for a time. The local population increased by more than 20 percent. Most of the new residents were landowners, primarily maturing children who chose to establish permanent homes at Promised Land rather than emigrate and abandon their small tracts. The size of individual landholdings decreased, indicating that once again the farms were being subdivided. When the boll weevils invaded the local cotton fields, the brief period of growth and prosperity ended and emigration resumed. This exodus differed from that of the earlier period because it included landowners as well as the nonlanded.

There was a second aspect of this migration from Promised Land that also distinguished it from earlier periods. Now there were opportunities for work closer to home, and some of the departing youths took a much smaller first step toward separation from their community than the earlier emigrants. They often went to Greenwood rather than Atlanta. The small town was only fifteen miles away and was well-known to most community residents as a place where they visited and shopped every Saturday. As a consequence of their greater familiarity, many Promised Land residents were also aware of various opportunities to work there for cash wages. Everybody knew a merchant or two where they traded, and most who wanted to were soon integrated into the local labor force. They worked at menial jobs, saved up their ten dollars, and then set out for the North.

The conditions which stimulated this migration were complex. The boll weevil and land scarcity both depressed the agricultural industry, and it was practically impossible for small farmers such as those at Promised Land to make a crop. Some local farmers, like W. A. Turner, just gave up and stopped farming. Turner's son Ev was sixteen when he settled on that solution to economic ruin. In 1920 W. A. Turner was too old to start over again but not old enough to die yet. When he decided to stop farming, Ev had to be told. He was near adulthood, and without farm work there was nothing else for him to do at Promised Land.

One early spring day, when it was still too soon to plow, Ev was helping his mother with the churning. She came into the kitchen, took the churn, and told Ev: "Your father out there in the yard. He want to talk to you." Ev went on out and received the devastating news. W. A. Turner told his son that he intended to "farm no more" and that young Ev "could get a job in town now. So that was it. I walked to town every day, just to make seventy-five cents a day" working on the road crew which paved Maxwell Avenue. The contractor was a white man from Atlanta who maintained a largely Negro labor crew. More than one Promised Land boy worked for him in that year after the boll weevil.[18]

On the first payday, with more than one hundred local Negro men waiting to receive their first cash wages, "the old man come out" to talk to them. In Atlanta, he told them, men received wages of two dollars a day for this kind of work; and that was the rate he had intended they be paid. "But the men said—Jim Self was one of them—'You can't pay those darkies that much.'"Greenwood exercised its own form of covert labor control; and the local Negroes were admitted into the town's labor force only if they entered and remained at the lowest, most menial levels of work. The contractor from Atlanta balanced between two sides, providing small raises on a regular basis to placate his underpaid crew. "Finally he did get us up to $1.25 a day," but local wages never rose to Atlanta levels. The more ambitious youths from Promised Land seldom stayed long in Greenwood, for there was no way to improve; and self-improvement was the whole point of leaving home.[19]

From the road crew Ev Turner moved to a job at the new Oregon Hotel in Greenwood. He worked nights there, and walking the highway out to Promised Land at odd hours was not safe for a Negro. "There wasn't no way I could live out in the country then. That's when I moved to town." Others followed Turner into Greenwood, and the town gradually supplemented Atlanta as the first stop for some community emigrants.[20] Those who utilized Greenwood as their first stop were probably able to finalize their departure from Promised Land in a more leisurely fashion than those who moved further away in the first step. From Greenwood many were able to maintain a residence in Promised Land for a time, relying on secure interpersonal relationships while they made their first economic adjustment from farming to cash wages. Then, with economic matters under control, they moved into town. Despite the geographic convenience the Greenwood move offered, only the very young, who were still emotionally dependent on their parents at home, or those with insufficient resources to take them further chose this alternative.

Even among the youth not yet drawn or pushed away from Promised Land, attitudes about farming shifted visibly from the general endorsement such work received twenty years before. Few young people viewed the farm as a desirable place to live any more, and now young couples questioned their options from a new vantage. Older relatives had been drifting away for two decades; many of them retained contact with their former home. The Homecoming and annual August visits enhanced local knowledge of distant opportunities and solidified the bonds between the community and its urban outposts. Awakened to new possibilities for their own lives, more than one young wife minced no words with her new husband when she told him she "didn't want to work in no more cotton fields." Women encouraged the men to find work which paid cash wages, and for most that meant "moving to town" or "going north."[21]

Why folks left Promised Land and where they went when they did were two quite different matters. Destinations were selected on the basis of available networks of family and friends, not work opportunities. Even specific plans were often consciously defined by the migrants as temporary solutions to an immediate problem. The Rileys, who were "planning to leave Atlanta" when they arrived, were typical of this second group of emigrants. They worked for a time in Atlanta—"he worked in the warehouse, and I did day work"—while they considered their possibilities. They first thought "maybe we go up to Philadelphia" from Atlanta. "So many people from my home went up there" that they would not be alone. For most emigrants, the presence of family or friends was sufficient reason to make a second move; and they boarded the train for a new destination as quickly as they saved the fare. In the Rileys' case even more fundamental family issues intervened in their plans—demands from Promised Land. "My mother said, 'Go on up to Chicago where your sister Mattie at. She up there by herself.'" Mattie was alone in Chicago only in that she had no immediate kin there. Her husband, also from Promised Land, was surrounded by kinsmen; and there were a number of other Promised Land families also settled there. But the order was issued, and the Rileys "went on up to Chicago where Mattie at." The two sisters established yet another extended family unit from Promised Land.[22]

Like many new immigrants, the Rileys "stayed with Mattie when we got here." The in-laws shared a small apartment, and "a friend of his who lived here got my husband a job in a steel mill." It was 1924, and Negroes had more difficulty maintaining steady employment than they had during the war years. Riley was laid off with frightening regularity; and, although "my husband didn't want me to work, wanted me to stay home and take care of my daughter," Pearl Riley felt the pressures of hard times. Domestic work, "day work," provided the family's more reliable income; and during the layoffs Riley found odd jobs wherever he could, "washing windows where I worked, sometimes yard work, or cooking in a restaurant.[23]

Ev Turner fared slightly better than the Rileys as he headed North. A single man, without family responsibilities, he was able to change jobs and locations more freely than married men. He went from Greenwood to Philadelphia where a cousin helped him find work in a steel mill "chipping and smoothing iron." The work was hot, hard, and dangerous; and so he left the pay behind and worked a while in a shirt factory. After about a year of garment work, wanderlust took Turner westward. "In them days people going from this town to another," and Ev Turner joined them. He worked his way across the upper Midwest, stopping in Reading for a few months to work in the coal mines. Eventually he drifted on to Chicago. There he found quite a collection of cousins and old friends, and he settled into the small community of transplanted Promised Landers. Competition for jobs was intense; and for a time he, like John Riley, did odd jobs, some domestic work, and yard work. Eventually he found steady employment in clothing manufacturing as a skilled laborer, married a girl who was native to Chicago, and made Chicago his home.[24]

Networks

Martha and Charlie Reynolds in Chicago

There were those from Promised Land, like Ev Turner and the Rileys, who made their way north with little assistance from friends or relatives. The pattern of their emigration included at least one stop during the move and was characterized by a work pattern of odd jobs and make-shift arrangements. Other community residents relied on kinsmen or friends for both advice and assistance as they consciously formulated their emigration; their exit from Promised Land and entrance into the northern urban centers was more carefully planned and systematically carried out.[25] Often this second type of emigration encompassed an entire family and extended over several years, as first one and then another relative was moved from Promised Land to the city. The Letmans moved gradually in this way.

Once established in Chicago, Martha Letman Reynolds wrote home to her family of her own success and prosperity. The family she had left in Promised Land faced a series of disappointments that made Martha's life in Chicago all the more attractive to those still in the South. Her father, Primus Letman, died about 1909; and the family farm was sold at a tax auction. Martha's older brother William managed to purchase only a tiny two-acre tract of land from his cousin Will Moragne, and his own impoverished sharecropping status prevented him from intervening in the disposition of the farm. The other Letman sons, mature men in their thirties and forties, were no more economically able than William to assume the obligations for the land, for one by one, as they matured, Primus Letman had sent his sons out to sharecrop. None acquired sufficient resources to buy up the family farm that Letman had refused to relinquish during his lifetime. Like their brothers, the Letman daughers had no resources. They, too, were burdened with the obligations of young families and trapped in the marginal life of sharecropping.

The youngest of the girls, Ada, was married to Fortune Wilson's son George; and they alone were successful in acquiring land. In 1908, at the age of twenty-five, George and Ada Wilson purchased a fifty-acre farm from Harrison Cole. Fortune Wilson may have loaned them the money for the purchase or may have intervened with Cole in the financial arrangements. But they were the only couple from the Letman family established locally in a relatively secure economic situation. Probably in part because they already owned land, in part because they too had no money, the couple made no attempt to acquire Primus Letman's farm at the tax sale. The Letman land was gone, sold to Rev. C. G. Glover, a young African Methodist minister who had recently moved with his family into Promised Land.

It was within this climate of disappointment and failure that Martha and Charlie's letters from Chicago were received and read by her discouraged brothers. One of the brothers, Timothy, was blind; and his situation was even more critical than the others—without sight there was no chance for productive work in an agricultural community. At Promised Land he was a burden to an already over-burdened family. When news of the family misfortune reached Chicago, Martha and Charlie sent immediately for Tim. He rode the train first to Atlanta and then on to Chicago, where he joined his sister's household.

After Tim was settled Martha and Charlie sent for Allen, who wanted to go to "a place where he could make something." He too rode the train up, and when he arrived Charlie helped his brother-in-law find work in a foundry. Allen stayed with Martha and Charlie until he acquired enough resources to support himself. After he had worked several months and established self-sufficiency, Allen began visits back to Promised Land. He was a sharecropper before he went to Chicago, and the new opportunitites he discovered there were overwhelming to him. They filled his conversations when he returned home to visit with George and Ada Wilson, his sister and brother-in-law. The war years were good ones in the North. A labor shortage, caused when the flow of immigrants from Europe stopped, created a situation in which no man or woman who wanted to work remained unemployed for long. In Chicago skin color was a secondary concern to employers in 1917. Allen eagerly reported these opportunities as well as his own prosperity to his relatives in the South; and finally, in 1920, George and Ada Wilson "got tired of where we were." The bonds which once tied the couple to Promised Land were either dissolved or diminished. Ada's brothers and sisters were in Chicago, and her parents dead. The Wilson family, too, was scattered from Florida to Philadelphia. With "quite a few of my relatives gone" and their childhood friends moved north or "gone to the war," in 1920 George and Ada Wilson "just decided we would leave" and join the others in Chicago.

George went up first; and, staying with Martha and Charlie, he found work and lived frugally. The money he saved from his wages was "sent home for our fares"; and, as the time for his family's departure neared, he sent his children new shoes to travel in. Living in the South was very different from living in Chicago. Farm children in those impoverished families rarely got new shoes; but in the North in the icy, snow-filled winter months even the poorest children wore shoes adequate to protect their feet. George sent shoes from Chicago "because we didn't have any shoes fit to travel." Guessing at the sizes of his children's feet, five new pairs of traveling shoes were delivered by the postman to Promised Land. Some fit and some did not. The children wore them anyway.

Friends took Ada and the children to Greenwood where they boarded the Eastern Seaboard to Atlanta. There, in order to transfer to the Illinois Central, they "had to come 'cross town.' " The prospect was terrifying to Ada. She had never been beyond Greenwood County; but by 1920 the Promised Land network was extensive and arrangements were made for "a cousin, Mr. Turner, to meet us in Atlanta. He took us across town to get the train to come up North." Travel for Negroes was difficult. Jim Crow was a pervasive part of life, and "there were only two cars for the black people" rushing to escape the South. Those two Jim Crow cars were crowded for the long trip and lacked both toilet and eating facilities. Ada carried some food, and the children held their bladders until they reached Kentucky. There "Jim Crow ended. They put on two more cars and a dining car."

Ada dressed the children in their best clothes for the trip. Despite the conditions, which were both distasteful and uncomfortable, "we always dressed up when we traveled." It was also important to look nice when they arrived because the children knew that "our father would meet us when we go to Chicago." George was waiting for them when the train pulled into the station, and there on the train platform in that alien city the Wilson family was reunited. They went directly to the apartment George Wilson had rented and furnished. Now, with a decent job that paid regular cash wages, Wilson had hopes for a more prosperous future for them all.

Wilson had assumed sole responsibility for his family's travel arrangements and for their financial support. Now he attended to their future. The day after their arrival Wilson took his children to the public schools and enrolled them, his first act as a city father. School in Chicago did not end at the sixth grade for Negro children, and Wilson was eager to have his children urbanized as quickly as possible. His second fatherly action soon followed the first. Despite his efforts the children were marked as coming from the South. Ada had no idea how to dress her girls for the cold northern fall; and she sent them to school that first day clothed in layers, dresses on the outside and beneath the dresses a red flannel slip and then long underwear. Their country origins showed almost immediately. In gym class, when the other girls changed to their regulation black bloomers, seven year old Rosalie faced public disgrace. She had no bloomers. The teacher, who had seen more than one young girl from the South enter this new world in similar confusion, told her "to just wear [her] slip today." When Rosalie emerged from the dressing room for gym class, everybody laughed at her. George Wilson bought his daughter her black bloomers that evening when he got home from work.

Josh Richie

Josh Richie was a bachelor in his mid-forties when he moved to New York, and his life there was a world apart from those of his sisters and their families back in Promised Land.[26] His visits home were infrequent; and, during the time which had passed, Richie's sisters had married; and the babies had "come one right after another." In a short time Richie had accumulated a sizable collection of nieces and nephews. He lavished the gifts on them which he once sent to his own brothers and sisters and might now have provided to children of his own. Each Christmas "whole boxes of candy, boxes of dolls, boxes of toys" came from Uncle Josh. Remembering the deprivations of his own childhood, "he even sent fruit" and boxes of material scraps to his sisters with which they patched their quilts.

Richie's life in New York took a strange twist when one day he met Rose, his old friend from the railroad, on the street. Neither knew the other was living in New York. Widowed and living in precarious circumstances, she had left her apartment for only a few minutes "to buy something for the children." Their friendship and romance was immediately rekindled. Richie went home with her that day, and "they were never apart after that" except when he went down to Promised Land for a visit. His marriage to a white woman was neither accepted nor rejected by his relatives in the South. It was simply a fact of Richie's life in New York until he brought Rose home with him one summer without warning.

As always, Josh stayed with his sister Lettie and her husband Fred Moragne, Isaac's son, when he came for a visit. This time Fred "was hysterical. He almost died when Josh brought that white woman here." Although the family tried to hide her presence, "Richie couldn't move. Every time he went somewhere Aunt Rose went too," and their visit was punctuated by the constant fear that the white woman staying out at Promised Land would be discovered by the white townspeople.

Josh was a favorite among his sisters, and during his visits home he was often called upon to serve as family arbitrater. "When there was a little confusion or a little conflict, he could help" ease the tensions and return order to his sisters' households. When there was sorrow or anger, he was able "to give them a little comfort here and there"; and they trusted his judgment on many matters. He was in their eyes a traveled and successful man of the world.

On each trip home Josh took special pleasure in his nieces and nephews and always teased his sisters and their husbands, telling them, "I'm going to take all these kids back to New York." Since his marriage to Rose his life there had settled into an orderly routine for she brought to their marriage the strict rigidity of her own German upbringing and a powerful morality of fundamentalism. She was an evangelist, "a jack-leg preacher" in the eyes of her in-laws still living in the South. Josh began transporting his young nieces and nephews to New York during the 1930s'. The first to go back with him was Mattie Cooper, who traveled to the North with Uncle Josh to go to school. "He kept her up there about a year, and then it was time for her to come home," for there was a long line of youngsters in Promised Land waiting for their turn.

Richie's brothers-in-law were farmers; and their children were their laborers, just as Josh had been for his father forty years earlier. He understood that they were needed at home, but he also knew that the future for them there was limited. He probably listened patiently, perhaps with a degree of condescension, when his brothers-in-law "made all kinds of excuses" to keep the older ones at home another year or two. But year after year Uncle Josh came for his visit, and the children saw a difference between him and their parents. It was the same difference Josh Richie had noticed himself between his father and the railroad hands when he was a teenager. Uncle Josh, who lived in the North and worked for cash wages, "dressed better, looked better, and had more money." The facts, readily apparent during his summer visits, were reinforced by the presents which came at Christmas. The contrasts between Uncle Josh's world and life at Promised Land made his nieces and nephews "want to go up there and see" for themselves if life could really be that fine, even for a Negro. After Mattie came home there was room for another youngster, and Hazel Moragne "cried to go back with Uncle Josh." When Richie promised to send Hazel to school, her mother and father finally agreed to the trip. Uncle and niece boarded the train together for the trip north. For a young girl who "hadn't hardly been to Greenwood but three or four times," it was an exiciting adventure of grand proportions.

Josh Richie enrolled Hazel immediately in a vocational high school, just as George Wilson had rushed to place his daughters in Chicago's public schools. Hazel wanted to study the beautician courses; but "Aunt Rose wanted business," so Hazel enrolled in typing. Richie found her a part-time job, "four hours every day in the week and six hours on Saturday," sewing buttons on cards down in the garment district. She made twenty-five dollars a week at the button job, a small fortune in Hazel's estimation, and "out of that money got two dollars a week allowance." Aunt Rose kept the rest. "At Christmas time Aunt Rose spent every dime buying gifts for Momma and Daddy and everybody who had a baby." Hazel was unhappy with the arrangements. Her friends at work "used their money to buy socks and ride the subway and eat out." Her meager allowance constricted Hazel's social life. "That's the part I hated."

Living with Aunt Rose was not easy. Hazel "had to go out with her when she went preaching" and was also expected to babysit for Rose's grandchildren free of charge. One night the babysitting demands conflicted with Hazel's plans to attend the movies with her friends. "Aunt Rose said I had to keep the kids, that I couldn't go." The eighteen-year-old girl from Promised Land and the old German immigrant woman took their war to Josh, working the night shift in the garment district. They descended on him at the belt shop, each eager to tell her own side of the story and receive a favorable decision. "I was crying, and she was crying," as they blurted out the details of the disagreement. Richie listened to them only briefly, then "told us to go on home. He'd talk to us in the morning."

Problems persisted between the two women. Hazel, hungry for fried fish, bought her own fish one day and took it back to Richie's apartment. Rose, in control of the kitchen, "baked the fish with tomatoes and peppers." The concoction made Hazel "sick to look at it," and as a result Rose "ate the whole thing." Rose was a strict disciplinarian. Hazel came to New York ready to be an adult. Josh was unable to mediate problem after problem between the two, and Hazel finally went back to Promised Land. Her year in New York was not wasted though; she returned home with new skills and a broadened outlook. She turned away from the domestic work which usually absorbed the local female Negro labor force, and before long she married a young man from Greenwood and moved into town.

After Hazel left New York, no more nieces or nephews came to the North with Uncle Josh until the 1940's.

Ada and George Wilson, Visiting Down South

Networks between emigrants and their former neighbors, friends, and relatives who stayed behind were maintained through a variety of means. The most apparent was the system of aid urban dwellers provided as new members of the community came to the North. Housing, help finding jobs, even outright financial assistance were all part of the help which was given willingly during the emigration process. These important contributions by those already settled in urban areas to new immigrants facilitated their integration into the new environment. Equally vital to the continuing sense of community, which persisted over time and space, were visits home.[27] George and Ada Wilson, like others who moved north, settled quickly into the routines of city life. Yet they, like others, maintained ties with friends and relatives in the South. For the Wilsons these ties were particularly unusual, for so many of their kinsmen emigrated that with the death of Fortune Wilson their lineage bonds in Promised Land were almost completely severed. So long as Fortune Wilson lived, however, the Wilsons made an annual pilgrimage to the South, timed to coincide with the community's August revivals.

Revival time was a particularly important period at Promised Land, remembered by the emigrants for the intense spirituality which it generated. It had long symbolized a time for renewal and regeneration; now that was extended to represent reunion with family and community as well as with God. By the 1920's the return of emigrants to their homeland was an explicit aspect of the August revivals, and this return was afforded community-wide recognition by "Homecoming." That was the time that "folks come down from Chicago, from New York, from Philadelphia, from all over these different places" to rest, to visit, and to revitalize old childhood memories and bonds. Most stayed "for both revivals, two weeks," because friendships and family ties inevitably crossed the denominational line between the Baptists and the Methodists as they had for half a century. The train, ever central to community life, brought back the same families it had carried away. Promised Land was filled with reunions, large and small.

Children who came down from the North brought with them a new outlook on life, a new reality. They knew little of the routines of subordination expected by whites of southern Negroes. They were no longer trained by their parents in behaviors locally considered "good manners for the nigras." Part of coming home was a trip into Greenwood. That town, too, was an important part of childhood memories; and the children who once rode the train to town on Saturdays now took their own children to Greenwood, just for a visit or to look around. For these youngsters from the North, unaware of the special rules for Negroes in the South, trips to town occasionally proved dangerous. Once, during the 1920's, the Valentine girls were home from Chicago for a visit. "They dressed up nice in their best clothes" to go into town. When they encountered a group of white women on the sidewalk, the girls were expected to "jump out in the street and let them pass." But the Valentine girls, not yet teenagers, had no idea they were expected to give way "'cause they wont used to it in Chicago. They just walk along." The women were outraged and "knocked them girls about" for their impudence.

Another time two of the Wilson girls wandered off from their father while they were at the post office. They were thirsty, and the drinking fountain inside had cold water. Although it was clearly marked "Whites Only," they helped themselves to a drink. "We didn't know any better, but we were drinking out of the wrong fountain." Their mistake was quickly pointed out, and they were ordered "around back to get our water." Like the young Valentine girls, the two Wilson children were from Chicago. They stood still, not comprehending the gravity of the situation. Finally they were led around to the back of the building and the bucket of water kept there for thirsty Negroes. On that steamy August day "the water was so hot we couldn't drink it."

Children who grew to maturity in the North remembered very little of life in the South, but that which was fixed in their memories was vivid. They were told by their parents of the Ku Klux Klan; that "they get it in for somebody, they follow them all the way to their home or to church or to wherever they are. And then they would get them." They were told as well about the white men who would "take a woman out in the woods and rape her"; and about Negro men— fathers, brothers, and husbands—who were powerless in such assaults, who "couldn't fight back." In the minds of the first generation of urban children, southern whites were a force to be avoided and feared.

Childhood memories were not limited to the negative and fearful, for from their own experiences during their annual visits these same children remembered grandfathers like Fortune Wilson, who made his own sausage; he "cut the loin and put it in a meat grinder he turned by hand." They smelled the aromas from the smoke house and learned about head cheese. They picked blackberries; and, when they lay in bed at night, they "looked at the stars through the holes in the roof." Memories of dinners in the church yard and all the men working together to barbecue the pigs were also carried home with them; and, while few ever returned to Promised Land as permanent residents, most came back year after year, into their own adulthood.

The migration from Promised Land, begun as an economic push for displaced and landless youths during the early years of the twentieth century, was an unavoidable outgrowth of community dynamics, southern peonage agriculture, and the maturation of a generation of Negroes unaccustomed to bondage. Although Promised Land was dominated by landowners, those men and women were not generally disposed to relinquish control of their farms to maturing children until they themselves were too old to farm any longer. For this reason elder children faced a peculiar contradiction in their adult lives. Accustomed to a relatively privileged social position within Promised Land, few willingly accepted the permanent reduction in status which accompanied sharecropping. Although some, like Martha and Charlie Reynolds, did sharecrop for a time, most abandoned farming altogether and found other kinds of work. There was no local alternative to farming for Negro youth. The textile industry was the major industrial employer in the Piedmont, and Negroes were severely limited in that sort of factory work until much later in the century. For this reason many of the children of landowners emigrated from Promised Land. Children of tenants and sharecroppers, while not faced with the same status inconsistencies, confronted an equally difficult problem. Land was scarce, and it was difficult to make a living farming even if suitable tenancy could be arranged. They, too, were forced to leave.

Trained in a combination of self-confidence and a powerful work ethic, these early migrants from Promised Land found work alternatives which were as consistent as possible with their self-image as well as with their aspirations. Some, like Josh Richie, established themselves rather quickly in urban, working and middle-class situations. Others, like the Reynoldses, were less direct in achieving this goal. Few, however, were downwardly mobile in their transition from the rural South to the urban North. When the situation demanded it, emigrants worked as family units, pooling economic resources in order to maintain a stable social and economic status.

During the second decade of the century, Negro emigration from the South accelerated. At Promised Land as elsewhere in the South, this was accompanied by an increase in interracial violence. The lynching of Andy Crawford and the assault on Nathan Redd underscored the inherent danger of the life Negroes faced if they stayed in the South. At the same time labor demands in northern industrial areas increased, and migrants from Promised Land had little difficulty securing work and successfully adapting to urban settings. Some, like Martha and Charlie Reynolds, drifted west, then north. For others the move from Promised Land to the cities was direct and intentional. Regardless of the details of their migration patterns, those who arrived during this period of high labor demand successfully transplanted the joint family and community ethics of their childhood. Most improved their condition, as they had intended; some, like Dave Moragne, were so prosperous that they "bought homes up in Michigan" and lost touch with friends and relatives down south. Others, like Joe Lee Burt, who once taught piano lessons to the children of Promised Land, shaped their lives in more exotic environments. Burt went from Chicago to Harlem, following the drift of Negro musicians; and then, still a part of that movement, gravitated to Paris. "After that nobody ever heard from him."

The majority of the migrants, regardless of their destination, retained contact with those still at Promised Land; and, as prosperity in the community ebbed and crops were destroyed by the boll weevil, the bonds between city and country became a pipeline for travel in both directions. Folks from the North came home to visit, to rest, and to remember the special kind of peace they had known at Promised Land. Hardship, discouragement, and chronic poverty pushed new waves of migrants into the network in the North. Still, the pull from the cities was not one formulated solely on economic motives. It was, as well, a pull fostered by a web of social bonds and kinship ties. Through these personal and affective relationships new migrants forged their economic futures and created life alternatives.

PART III

THE THIRD GENERATION
1930–1960

NINE

They Done Killed B. J.!

*All the cream of swift intelligence, initiative, and courage has run
away or crawled away or lies murdered to fertilize southern soil.*
W. E. B. DuBois

The stock market crash of October 1929 and the economic crises that
swept the cities and towns of the nation in the following months made
barely a ripple in the already deteriorating fabric of life at Promised
Land. The cotton market collapsed with historic regularity in 1920,
and the boll weevil soon followed. An emigration stimulated by the
agricultural problems of the 1920's continued at a steady pace during
the early 1930's, siphoning away many of the young and the landless
and even a few of the established landowners in the community. Each
year six or seven more families sold their milk cow and packed their
few belongings into pasteboard grips to make the trip to the North.

By 1932 the Promised Land population dwindled to one hundred
and forty-four families, half the size of the bustling community of the
previous generation. Despite the greatly diminished population,
however, the traditions which had been an integral part of the community life for two generations survived. Although community resources were negligible, support for the school and the churches
continued at a greatly reduced level. Overall, the quality of life at
Promised Land was typical of the plight of southern Negroes during
the late 1920's and 1930's. It was marked by chronic poverty and a
spreading sense of disillusionment.

The general mood in Promised Land was representative of a discouragement which pervaded the rural southern Negro population.
Politics and economics intertwined, as they had in the late 1870's,
bringing severe hardships to Negro farmers. In the South farm
tenancies of all types approached 60 percent of all farmers, and the
majority of these tenants were Negroes. The Harding-Collidge
schemes for agricultural relief during the late 1920's made little

impact on this economic condition, and in the following years the boll weevil and droughts further aggravated the level of poverty among rural Negroes.[1]

The diminished population, economic problems, and the emigration and death of many of the dominant landowners foreclosed the possibility of farming at Promised Land. In contrast to the vitality of the farms during the first and second generations, there were few subdivisions of land during the 1930's. The death of a landowner, with or without a will, did not automatically result in partition of a family farm. Many residents and absent heirs found a way to avoid the expensive and complex legal routines of probate judges and inheritance laws. Circumvention was simple. One or more children, those best able to shoulder the financial burden, paid the taxes on the land each year when they came due. "Courthouse don't know who's dead," and so long as the taxes were paid families kept their idle land intact.[2]

The informal strategy was only in part successful, however, because the land no longer provided even a subsistence existence for most families. Two generations of partitioning had diminished the size of the farms to only about half that of the original tracts, about eighteen acres (see Table 5). Each household at Promised Land struggled against constantly oppressive economic conditions on land barely large enough to accommodate a family garden, pasturage for the milk cow, and a hog pen. New strategies for survival derived from a heritage that emphasized frugality and hard work and assumed ultimate triumph over worldly tribulation. These beliefs had served Promised Land residents since Reconstruction. Now they were tested to the limit. The families at Promised Land survived the conditions of the 1930's with an adaptive resourcefulness characteristic of the poor.

We Were So Poor We Didn't Know There Was a Depression

Negro farmers, still not recovered from the economic disasters of the 1920's, were ruined again by droughts and a flagging cotton market in the early 1930's. Poverty and hard times were everywhere, but they were particularly acute among Negroes. Twice as many black as white families were on relief rolls in the cities, and many Negro farmers simply abandoned their land in despair. Roosevelt gained the presidency in 1932 when he promised relief and recovery. The

Negroes in the cities heard his radio messages; but out in the country, at places like Promised Land, there was no electricity. The folks there depended on other sources for their political information. The local preacher, their relatives from the North, and perhaps a Negro weekly told them the same story. Roosevelt understood poor folks, and he intended to help.

The first of the New Deal programs, enacted in 1933, established minimum wage standards, eliminated child labor in industry (but not in agriculture), and regulated the work week (for all but farmers and domestic workers). They offered little economic relief to rural Negroes. The Agricultural Adjustment Act (AAA), which introduced crop reduction programs and parity payments, had a negative effect on tenants and sharecroppers. The crop reduction program resulted in a *de facto* eviction of thousands of Negro tenants and sharecroppers, no longer useful labor to their white landlords. Still, some of the landowning farmers at Promised Land realized benefits from the program. Their farms were small ones, and the amount of government money which found its way into the community was minute, but it was more than the farmers had before Roosevelt's New Deal. The president had delivered on his political promises in the estimation of folks at Promised Land.[3] The community's agricultural economy was further stimulated when money from the federal farm loan programs filtered down to Promised Land. The soil conservation program and parity payments and public and private lending agencies together "put a little nickle" into the pockets of men and women who until then "never even had a penny."[4] Only then did local farmers return to their fields, although most were still guided by a quiescent orientation to subsistence farming rather than the capital expansion that would have promoted rapid economic recovery within the community's economic structure.

Craftsmen—primarily carpenters and railroad hands—and preachers were less resigned to the impoverished situation than the farmers; and, although they were but a small fraction of the community population, their response to the prevailing hardships contrasted sharply with that of their farming neighbors. Preachers and craftsmen both enjoyed greater opportunities for geographic mobility than the farmers, who were tied to Promised Land and the poverty of the land through their ownership. Moving about in the routines of their work, preachers and carpenters took advantage of some of the possibilities of life beyond the parameters of the community; and they came to view their own existence in less provincial terms. Residents unable to escape the situation, or unwilling to emigrate from Promised Land permanently, transferred their aspirations to their children.

Local youths trained to an ethic of hard work and an expectation of a fair return for their labor, experienced a frustration that the older generation felt less acutely. Their parents were accustomed to a lifetime of "getting by"; the youths wanted to "get ahead." In their frustration some instigated efforts for social changes of a most fundamental nature. They pressed publicly for equality—social, political, and economic. Others, in a different response to the same conditions, sought relief through emigration; they abandoned their homes and community in a recurring effort to better their condition elsewhere. Still others stayed at Promised Land and, not able to realize their dreams for a better life, retreated into political, social, and economic isolation.

Hard Times Gettin' Better Now

Among all the residents of Promised Land poverty and indebtedness were chronic companions during the 1930's, as they had been for half a century. Some experienced increasing hardship as early as 1924. That year, for the first time since Reconstruction, twenty-three community residents were listed as tax delinquents by the sheriff's office. None was a landowner; and all emigrated from Promised Land within the next twelve months, well ahead of legal attempts to collect the back taxes. This pattern of flight continued through the 1920's, although emigration diminished in numbers as the decade progressed. By 1926 eight of the sixteen persons—half of those listed on the delinquent tax rolls—were subsequently noted as "gone" by the county tax collector. In 1928 only 12 percent of the tax delinquents migrated.[5] For those who stayed in the county, overdue taxes were often simply cancelled after a year or two. The pattern of indebtedness and tax delinquency followed by emigration probably slowed as the community realized that the money owed to the tax collector could not be collected easily, and the amounts were so small that legal action on the part of the county was not feasible.

As the community entered the 1930's, emigration subsided and then appeared to stop (see Table 12). Word came down from the North that life was equally difficult there. Those who remained at Promised Land now were gripped by an incredible poverty, a poverty readily apparent in the community tax structure (see Table 6). Tax delinquency assumed a new dimension. Prior to 1930 only the landless, most often the sharecroppers and wage laborers, were unable to pay their taxes. After the onset of the Depression and throughout the early 1930's, the prevailing economic problems spread. Landowners, too, fell behind in their tax obligations; and for many of these people the delinquency persisted year after year. The tax assessor carried all of the Promised Land tax delinquents on the county's book throughout the economic crisis, which extended in its most extreme form from 1930 to 1937.

The list of 1930's tax delinquents included members of the most respected and established families at Promised Land. They were descendents of the first generation settlers, church founders, and radical Republicans, families with long-standing roots in the community. Taxes on the Burt family farm were in arrears from 1931 through 1934. Oscar Pressley, W. A. Turner, the Clayborn Reynolds estate, and the Redd family were all behind in their taxes from 1930 through 1937. Although none owed more than a dollar or two to the county, the lands at issue averaged thirty-nine acres, twice the size of the overall average size of farm tracts at Promised Land. Large as well as small landowners were defenseless against broader economic conditions.

Within the community there were fundamental social and economic differences between families who owned land and those who did not. In comparison to the larger population of the region, however, the landed and nonlanded residents of Promised Land were far more alike than they were different. They, like other Black Belt Negroes, were the most impoverished group in the nation.[6] In only one aspect of their lives did community residents differ from the vast body of southern Negro yeomen—two-thirds of them owned tiny pieces of land on which they lived. Yet without a cash income, even in pitifully small amounts, they were no longer able to pay taxes. Landownership, a distinguishing feature of community life, stood in danger of collapse.

In addition to nearly losing their land, community residents were barely able to provide even minimal support to their churches. Cash contributions to both Mt. Zion and Crossroads dwindled away; and preachers counted their pay in chickens, peas, and biscuits (see Table 6). Only the patience of the county tax collector and the raw force of faith within the community saved the farms and the churches. The seven-year crisis resulted in only one major change in community life. In 1936, utterly unable to stretch their few resources any further to pay taxes, members of the Promised Land Masonic Lodge witnessed the sale at public auction of the one-acre tract which housed the Mason Hall. A witness remembered that the hall's condition mitigated her regret: "The Hall was all broke down then. They didn't use it no more."[7] Although by 1937 all other tax obligations in Promised Land were current, the sale marked the end of a special era of community life, characterized by intense cooperation, community self-awareness, pride, and collective optimism.

Tax delinquency was only one index of the impact of the Depression at Promised Land. A second and related indicator of the extent to which prevailing economic conditions imposed additional hardships on the already impoverished Negro yeomen was the decline in the value of personal property. Both landowners and the nonlanded residents felt this effect of the 1930's. Throughout the Depression the total value of taxable property, real and personal, decreased dramatically for all who lived at Promised Land. The rate of decline was far greater among the landless (50 percent), although landowners, too, lived in reduced circumstances. The value of their property diminished by one-third. As a plow stock broke in the fields or an exhausted milk cow went dry, there was simply no way to replace it. "Things just went all to pot then."[8]

At Promised Land the extreme poverty of the Depression persisted well past the time of economic recovery for the rest of the nation. Restoration of the economic balance was retarded by two factors. First, most families had lived in marginal circumstances before the onset of the Depression. The boll weevil and an erratic agricultural market had already depleted whatever surplus resources were available among local farmers. The Depression did not cause their poverty but simply aggravated it. Second, many community residents were reluctant to take advantage of the various New Deal assistance programs. Some of the old men and women, badly advised by their children or neighbors that they must "sign over their land to get a check from the government," rejected the single source of aid available to them.[9] Through fear, misinformation, and ignorance they were pushed even further into the web of rural poverty. Only the younger and better informed took advantage of the new federal programs. For them the New Deal proffered hopes and opportunities for survival; and they borrowed federal money to start farming again or went willingly to the Civilian Conservation Corps camp in Augusta, some forty miles southeast of Promised Land.[10]

While the men were occupied with the Civilian Conservation Corps, their wives and girlfriends commuted between Promised Land and Augusta. They "got rides with the mailman" from Augusta to save the price of a bus ticket, trailing small children and a parcel or two; and, lacking permanent homes, they stayed with relatives in both places. When in Promised Land they "helped my sister with the wash, down by the spring," and stayed "at my Daddy's house" where childhood beds were still available, even to daughters grown and married. In Augusta the women shared experiences, talked of migration, and learned from each other that "there's women up in Baltimore that take your husband from you." They learned to travel; and, in even brief trips from Promised Land, they realized that life could mean more than "just getting by."[11]

Despite the extreme poverty and lack of cash or credit, some Promised Land farmers found ways to buy up the land that occasionally became available within the community boundaries. Although the land trade was minimal, some farms did change hands. One principle medium in these exchanges was Henry Robinson, the Negro undertaker in Greenwood. People died whether or not they could afford the price of a funeral in cash. During the 1930's Robinson buried many such impoverished landowners. When members of such families could not pay for his services, Robinson "finally got in possession" of a number of farm-sized tracts, deeded to him to pay the funeral expenses. He brokered the land to other Negroes, generally for about fifteen or twenty dollars an acre.[12] Rarely was the entire purchase price paid in a single lump sum, and Robinson served for a time as a *de facto* mortgagor for several new landowners in the community.

Robinson's role in the lives of the people at Promised Land extended well beyond the boundaries of economic exchange. He became personally involved with many community residents and was "sort of like a Godfather" during a time when churches and families neared collapse under economic strains. In addition to burying people and selling and financing land purchases, he also helped some community residents locate small tracts they could afford to buy. He visited Promised Land regularly and even provided taxi service to and from Greenwood for those too old or too sick to walk into town, and in times of extreme crisis Robinson loaned money to the men and women of Promised Land.[13] The undertaker became the banker, the land dealer, the social worker, and the general advisor to the community during a time when local leadership foundered.

Two other mechanisms for property transfer—inheritance and estate sales—supplemented Henry Robinson's role in the land exchanges. Inheritance was relatively unimportant during the 1930's; most landowning families delayed probate proceedings; and approximately 20 percent of the community property remained in unprobated estates.[14] Estate sales, although infrequent, provided one means to acquire sizable portions of property; and Rev. C. G. Glover purchased the old Letman farm in Promised Land this way. Glover, an African Methodist minister, moved to Promised Land around 1920; and, although he never pastored at Mt. Zion, he maintained a permanent residence in the community, traveling as much as thirty miles in his Model T Ford to preach in the small A.M.E. churches of the Piedmont.[15] He seized the rare opportunity to own land.

Every vacated tract found a willing and eager Negro like Glover, ready to assume the obligations, problems, and advantages of land-ownership. Land hunger was as great in 1930 as it had been half a century earlier in 1880; and men like Glover who grew to adulthood in the tradition of Negro yeomanry responded quickly to an opportunity for a "place of their own," regardless of the size of the tract or the condition of the soil.[16]

Glover, like Henry Robinson, provided a new source of leadership at Promised Land during a time when older sources failed. Glover was viewed by most community residents as "stern and serious, yet [he was] always available to anyone at Promised Land in need of advice and counsel." His reputation for fairness, kindness, and wisdom drew many to his home to discuss and debate various matters. Like Robinson, Glover enjoyed contacts with the white community and was able, thereby, to intervene in behalf of local Negroes. For both men such access enhanced the other qualities they brought to their positions of influence within the community.[17]

Farmers and Land

The first perceptible relief from economic hardship occurred in 1935.[18] That year eleven men borrowed money from one of two new sources of agricultural credit and began farming again. One man got a crop lien from the New Deal Farm Credit Association (FCA); and the others negotiated chattel mortgages and crop liens with a privately financed local agency, the Greenwood Production Credit Association (GPCA). These Negro farmers were no longer forced to rely on local white merchants or benevolently exploitative white planters to finance annual planting expenses. Those with land, an old plow, wagon, or a mule to pledge as collateral, could obtain money from institutional rather than private sources. The Greenwood Production Credit Association made loans primarily to those farmers willing and able to back up their loans with some form of capital. The agency also

Table 13.
Crop Lien and Chattel Mortgage Averages, 1935–1945*

| Year | Lending Agents | |
	FCA	GPCA
1935	$ 68.00	$127.00
1937	62.50	174.00
1939	69.00	226.00
1941	52.50	355.00
1943		397.00
1945	182.00	518.00

*Crop Liens and Chattel Mortgages, 1935–1945, Greenwood County, S.C. Greenwood County Courthouse, Promised Land residents only.

required that farmers plan and adhere to a realistic planting program as a condition for granting crop liens. The Farm Credit Association, with greater financial latitude and a political mandate to provide assistance to farmers, was less stringent in its demands on borrowers. It required neither collateral nor a planting program. The two agencies negotiated annual agricultural loans with both landowners and tenants.

The new credit system affected community agriculture in three distinct ways. Beginning in the mid-1930's, the community farmers who negotiated loans had money at the beginning of the planting season, with which they paid cash for seed and fertilizer and avoided the interest rates charged on credit purchases. The lending agencies displaced the lien man and fostered a renewed self-sufficiency and independence among Promised Land's farmers.

The GPCA enhanced this effect and encouraged some crop diversification in indirect ways. Borrowers contracted their loans on the basis of a predetermined set of crops. This required some evaluation of projected market potential, a task probably accomplished with the assistance of a county agricultural agent. Still, they were forced to draw on their own knowledge too as it derived from their years of farming and an understanding of their fields. Such personal factors were never a part of their negotiations with the lien man, who consistently demanded heavy concentrations of cotton. As a consequence, commercial farming as well as subsistence agriculture now reflected both the personal experiences and preferences of the men who tilled the fields.

Promised Land farmers were steeped in the tradition of cotton cultivation, and few actually reduced their cotton crops dramatically during the New Deal years. Community farming patterns changed in much more subtle ways. An occasional acre or two of barley appeared among the grains, diversifying the corn and wheat crops that were always a major part of local farm production. Three different types of pasturage—hay, vetch, and lespedza—replaced sugar cane, which disappeared entirely from the local crops.

Table 14.
Community Cultivation Patterns, 1935–1945*

Year	X̄ Tilled Acres	Cotton	Corn	Other Grains†	Legumes	Hay/ Vetch‡
				Percent of the Crop		
1935	35.65	30	30	22	10	0
1937–38	67.20	30	28	20	18	0
1939–40	73.20	30	25	17	16	5
1941–42	70.81	32	25	20	15	6
1943–44	66.65	33	24	21	6	9
1945	58.31	34	24	19	11	9

*Crop Liens and Chattel Mortgages, 1935–1945, Greenwood County, S.C., Greenwood County Courthouse.

†Included primarily wheat and oats, with about 5 percent of the crop planted in barley.

‡Farmers also planted cane, peanuts, and potatoes in small portions, which accounts for the difference between the percentages shown in total tilled acreage and the breakdowns as given.

In addition to the new autonomy that the increased cash flow encouraged and the trend toward some degree of crop diversification, the new financial arrangements had a third impact on local farming patterns. The new money stimulated a moderate degree of expansion among the farmers, as some men used the cash they obtained to rent additional farmland. This was particularly common among farmers who borrowed from the GPCA, whose average loans to Promised Land residents were two to three times greater than the sums they obtained from the Farm Credit Administration. Men who had abandoned their fields following the various agricultural disasters of the 1920's and early 1930's turned once again to their land with renewed expectations for economic survival.

W. A. Turner, who sent his son Ev into town to find a job in 1924 because he intended to quit farming, was typical of those whose lives were changed by the economic stimulation of the New Deal.[19] Turner negotiated a small crop lien for ninety-five dollars from the Farm Credit Association in 1935. After a decade of a retirement forced upon him by crop failures and other misfortunes, Turner took the money from the FCA and bought seed and fertilizer and set his plow to the field on his farm. That first year his crop was small and tentative, nine acres in cotton and ten in corn.

Turner made his 1935 crop and repaid the lien. Encouraged by his success, he turned to the greater resources of the Greenwood Production Credit Association. In 1936 he negotiated both a crop lien and a chattel mortgage with the private lending agency for three hundred dollars. In return for the money he pledged all of his farm equipment and livestock: a wagon, seven plow stocks, a guano distributor, a cotton seed planter, and a section harrow as well as two mules, a horse, cow, and hog. His crop lien was based on planned cultivation of thirty acres of cotton, twenty-five acres of corn, four acres of wheat, fourteen acres of oats. fifteen acres of peas, and two acres of cane. He farmed that year on his own one hundred and nine-acre farm and fifty additional acres leased from A. C. Hudgens, a neighboring white landowner; and he employed two young men from Promised Land as his field hands. Turner was back in the farming business.

Table 15.
W. A. Turner's Planting Patterns, 1937–1945

Year	Cotton	Corn	Other Grain	Legumes	Cane	Barley	Pasturage
1937	33	28	20	17	2	0	0
1938	27	26	21	22	3	1	0
1939	23	24	27	24	0	0	2
1940	28	22	24	16	0	0	10
1941	31	25	26	13	0	0	5
1942	24	15	31	30	0	0	0
1943	23	28	21	11	0	6	11
1944	22	20	30	7	0	5	16
1945	17	17	17	23	0	9	17

Nineteen thirty-seven was also a good year for Turner. He made his crop and cleared the notes with the GPCA. The following year, still cultivating both his own land and the leased fifty-acre tract, he negotiated a two-hundred-dollar crop lien and chattel mortgage. As collateral he again pledged his farm machinery and livestock, which remained unchanged, and added as new collateral two additional sources of New Deal money, an anticipated 1938 parity check for seventy-eight dollars and the income he expected from the federal soil conservation lease on part of his own land. W. A. Turner had learned to manipulate and exploit the New Deal to his own advantage.

Turner's 1938 crop changed slightly from the previous year. He cultivated eighteen acres of his land in cotton, slightly less than the previous season. His grain crop included corn, wheat, and oats; to that he added half an acre of barley, an innovative experiment in crop diversification. He increased his pea crop and maintained a two acre cane patch. Once again he had a successful year, and in 1939 negotiated another loan with the GPCA, this time in the amount of two hundred and twenty-five dollars. He pledged the same property as collateral, and his crop that year excluded the barley and cane but added two acres of vetch to the other crops. For the third year in a row he decreased the percentage of his fields planted in cotton and increased the proportion of his land in peas.

In 1940 Turner lost his lease on the fifty-acre Hudgens tract and cultivated only ninety acres on his own farm. Despite the reduction in tilled acres, he increased the amount of his crop lien and chattel mortgage from two hundred and twenty-five to three hundred and twenty-five dollars. His collateral remained unchanged; and his planned crop that year again included cotton, corn, wheat, oats, and peas. Rather than vetch he planted lespedza for his pasturage. The loss of the leased fields coincided with a renewed emphasis on cotton as his major cash crop as well as a reduction in his pea crop. In 1941 he again negotiated a three hundred and twenty-five dollar loan from the GPCA and expanded his tilled acres, renewing his lease on Hudgens' fifty acres. From 1941 to 1944 Turner borrowed four hundred dollars each spring, and each year he cultivated both his own land and the rented tract. The resumption of his lease coincided with a steady reduction in the size of his cotton crop. Ever-increasing proportions of the land were given over to grain crops. Although the livestock he pledged as collateral for his annual mortgage—a mule, cow, horse, and hog—were unchanged, the increase in pasturage, from 11 percent in 1943 to 17 percent in 1945, indicated a possible expansion of his livestock holdings.

In 1945 Turner's loan declined from four hundred to two hundred and fifty dollars. Still, his collateral was unchanged. He pledged the same wagon, seven plow stocks, guano distributor, cotton seed planter, and section harrow that he owned in 1937. In the decade from 1935 to 1945 Turner's farm machinery had not changed. He still pulled his plow with a mule and farmed primarily with the strength of his own labor. Although there were few changes in the equipment or resources at his command, Turner had altered his cultivation patterns drastically. His cotton crop was reduced by half, to only 17 percent of his total tilled acres. He had added a small but stable barley crop and instituted pasturage that was equal in size to his cotton fields. His largest crop was a ten-acre pea patch, important to his farming enterprise not only for its market value but also for its ability to restore nitrogen and other nutrients to soil thoroughly depleted by the cotton.

W. A. Turner was a bit more innovative than many of his farming neighbors at Promised Land. He did not hesitate to incur sizable indebtedness through his crop liens and chattel mortgages with the GPCA. Until 1945 his annual loans from the Association were consistently above community averages; similarly, the amount of land he cultivated was three times greater than the average. Turner's cultivation patterns, too, deviated from community norms. He reduced his cotton crop earlier and more extensively than most and increased his pea crop as well. He also devoted more of his energies to the development and maintenance of pasturage than many other local farmers. Turner had personal attributes that also set him apart from his neighbors. He was at one time a school teacher, a Baptist preacher, and until his death in the 1950's served as the church clerk at Crossroads. These positions attest to his level of literacy, which in turn suggests a direct knowledge of the opportunities provided by several New Deal programs.

Despite his advantage of literacy and his obvious ability to exploit the resources made available to him for his own benefit, Turner never expanded his operations beyond his own small farm and the one leased Hudgens tract. Perhaps he did not realize sufficient profit to increase either his farm equipment or his livestock. Or perhaps, as a Negro farmer he encountered the common problem of discrimination and was unable to lease any other land than that from Hudgens. More likely, he simply did not want to expand his farming; for, while

W. A. Turner was one of the more successful farmers in Promised Land during the 1930's and 1940's, he was and remained a subsistence farmer. In this respect he followed an agricultural pattern ingrained by half a century of tradition. The land was there for his survival. Contented with that, he probably never expected to show a profit from his labors.

Carpenters and Preachers

W. A. Turner's approach to the problems of the 1920's was to abandon farming, and his response to the renewed opportunities of the 1930's was to resume that same enterprise. Yet not all community residents were farmers. Throughout the first and second generations there were two small but constant bodies of nonfarmers among the residents, primarily preachers and carpenters. Although both groups generally engaged in part-time agriculture, they were not farmers. Both groups used Promised Land more as a home base than a permanent residence. Still, they felt at home in the community; and left their families there when they traveled. Preachers moved outside Promised Land on a regular and predictable route. Their social contacts and public consciousness were among the factors that prevented total isolation of other community residents during this time of extreme poverty. Men like C. G. Glover routinely reported and interpreted the news from outside to their friends and neighbors. Glover, along with Will Bradley, the Turners, and the Reynoldses served as informal "readers" for those who were less able. They received both the *Christian Recorder* and the Greenwood daily, the *Index-Journal*, and "kept up with outside events" that were routinely reported to the rest of the community during church services at Mt. Zion and Crossroads. Generally, these men merely summarized the week's news for the two congregations; but "when there was something which was quite important or significant, they read it word for word."[20]

The carpenters, less predictable in their work and travel, faced a dilemma during the 1930's. These craftsmen were accustomed to working away from home, but now there was no work. The Piedmont was economically immobilized by the Depression, and it was hard for a Negro in the South to get on a PWA project. Few of the craftsmen owned more than a small home lot or an acre or two in Promised Land; and they, therefore, simply did not have the option of weathering the Depression on their land as their farmer neighbors did. They were forced by circumstance to alter their type of work, and they devised solutions to their problems within a tradition of geographic mobility. Many went north temporarily where they were more likely to find employment, either on government projects or, if they were exceptionally fortunate, in private industry. Daymon Marshall's solutions to the situation were representative of the adaptive strategy devised by local craftsmen.

Marshall was the son of Easter Marshall, and a lifetime resident of Promised Land; but even as a boy he "didn't like the country"; and he resisted the social pressures which usually directed young men in the community into sharecropping. Instead, he went to work for Nathan Redd and from him learned carpentry. Daymon's marriage to Redd's niece Lilly Jane Martin probably solidified the bonds between the two men, and Daymon joined Nathan Redd's crew until the Depression cut short their trade.[21]

Daymon and Lilly Marshall bore and raised a large family at Promised Land, with Daymon supporting his wife and children through his carpentry work. The Marshalls were hit hard by the Depression. There was no work for independent Negro tradesmen. Marshall looked north, and in the late 1920's he and his oldest son Herman left Lilly Jane and the smaller children in Promised Land and "went off to Baltimore. They stayed with Daymon's cousin at first," who helped father and son find work as laborers in the city's copper works. Daymon sent money home to Lilly Jane regularly, and everybody in Promised Land knew when the money arrived from Baltimore. "We'd hear that old mailman coming down that road blowing that horn, and everybody'd know Daddy was sending money."

Lilly Jane and the children were accustomed to Daymon's absence, and their life at Promised Land probably changed little when he went north to work. Their routines were established and maintained independent of his presence in the household. Lilly kept a small vegetable garden, "just a little corn and tomatoes, nothing much"; and she also maintained an elaborate "flower pit, just like a long grave, only filled with all kinds of flowers." Lilly never made a trip into town without "getting herself some flowers." One of the primary responsibilities the children had around the house was to cover their mother's flower pit during rain or cold weather; and, when an early frost killed all the flowers one year because the children failed to cover them the evening before, "you could hear Momma yelling way down to the Foster place." Lilly Jane Martin was a stewardess at Mt. Zion, an attentive daughter to her aged parents, and a friend to practically everybody in the community. Her life was filled with the routines of Promised

Land—going to church, visiting, and gardening. Although she probably missed Daymon during his protracted absences, she was deeply rooted in Promised Land.

The Marshall children, too, were happy and busy during their father's absence. Daymon left the family's Model T at home when he went up north to work, and the car became a source of entertainment for all the smaller children. Lilly could not drive and had no desire to learn, but her oldest daughter Ethel drove the car every day. Each afternoon when school was over the younger children "used to beg Ethel to take us for a ride. She would drive into a ditch or run into a tree. And the next day we would beg her to take us for a ride again." The only other car at Promised was owned by Rev. Glover. He was a stern man and would never allow his automobile to be used frivolously. But Daymon Marshall's car careened through Promised Land many afternoons, filled with squealing children out on a lark.

From Baltimore Daymon sent blankets and clothes in great boxes for his family, and occasionally he included silk stockings for his older daughters. He missed his wife and children and was delighted when Lilly brought one or two of the children up for a brief visit. The children were as "excited about going to Baltimore" as they were about visiting their father. It was like going to a foreign country filled with exotic people and adventure. "Every little country girl would like to live in the city," and for them the next best thing was this visit. Daymon and Herman had an apartment "in a pretty nice neighborhood"; and Lilly readily assumed housekeeping responsibilities during her visits, cooking and cleaning and "sending the children to the store on the corner" in much the same fashion as she kept house at Promised Land. Still, Lilly's presence in Baltimore was never more than "just a visit. She wanted to stay close to her mother." So, for the time, Lilly stayed at Promised Land, Daymon in Baltimore.

Eventually Daymon quit his job and came back to Promised Land. Lilly was sick and he was needed at home. He was "a kind and gentle person, very proud, quiet, not like the other men." When he returned to the family's Promised Land household as a permanent resident, his children were teenagers, finished with school, and thinking about what it meant to be an adult. Daymon gave them a vision of a life away from the country, and the vehicle for this vision was education. Not long after his return to Promised he formulated and implemented a plan for his children that took them away from the community.

School was not greatly different for Daymon Marshall's children than it had been for him. Lizzie Chiles taught them their letters and numbers, along with all the other children in Promised Land. In mid-life Lizzie Chiles was more stern with her students, less willing to overlook their small misbehaviors than she had been when Daymon Marshall and Lilly Jane Martin sat in her schoolhouse. Perhaps thirty years of teaching, the failure of the Promised Land High School, and the limited futures her students faced made her even more aware of the importance of the brief five-month school term.

Lizzie Chiles still taught in the schoolhouse built by Crossroads during Reconstruction. Her students still learned hovering around a wood stove to keep warm, and the stove still burned the wood the children brought with them. There were no books, no blackboard, and no money for repairs. The men did what they could to keep the old building together, and Lizzie Chiles struggled along with her duties. She had always believed that school and education were the most expedient way for the children to "better their condition," and she devoted her life to teaching them. There was an unchanging quality about the Promised Land school, and despite her efforts Lizzie Chiles was not able to surpass the static nature of education in the community.[22]

Mrs. Chiles was not alone now in her awareness that the children needed more education than she could provide. Some of the parents, in contrast to those in earlier years, were also convinced that the road away from chronic poverty was a better schoolhouse. Some had seen the schools in the cities; and, although by comparison to schools for white children those, too, were woefully inadequate, they were still an improvement over the community's educational facilities. Daymon Marshall and Rev. C. G. Glover were both experienced with the world outside Promised Land, and both men sent some of their children away to the cities when they completed the eighth grade with Lizzie Chiles.

The Marshall girls were sent into Greenwood to attend Brewer Normal School, a close approximation of secondary education for Negro children. First Ethel went, and then her younger sister Mary followed. Daymon Marshall was pleased. His daughters did well and enjoyed Brewer. "He wanted us to go on" to school; and, after a year or two at Brewer, Marshall made arrangements with his wife's sister in Atlanta, Mary Wideman, for the girls to board with her and attend school there. Lilly Belle, the third daughter, followed the same pattern, going first to Brewer and then on to Atlanta when it was her turn.

Each of the girls returned to Promised Land for a time after she finished school, and once again Marshall helped them plan a future away from the community. He had seen another world; and, although

Promised Land was his home, he hoped it would not be theirs. He encouraged the girls to go on to Baltimore. Herman was still there, and so was another brother, Tim. Both were working, and they helped their sisters establish homes and find work when they arrived. Marshall was less adamant in shaping the adult lives of his sons. He encouraged them to move away from Promised Land but was less concerned with their education than he was with his daughters. Perhaps he believed that men were capable of obtaining honest work with regular pay regardless of their educational background but that women were confined to domestic service or in danger of becoming prostitutes without additional education. Education alone would assure them a living wage and a certain personal protection. Perhaps he hoped only that their time in Atlanta would wean his daughters from Promised Land and facilitate their move north. Whatever his motives, the girls moved north one by one; and Daymon was the last of the Marshalls to maintain a permanent home at Promised Land.

Daymon Marshall was not the only parent in Promised Land with ambitions for his children. Rev. C. G. Glover also sent his children away to complete their schooling. In 1932 B. J. boarded the train for Cincinnati, Ohio.[23] There B. J. lived with his father's sister and attended high school in preparation for his entrance to Wilberforce University. B. J. intended to be a minister like his father, and Wilberforce was an ideal choice for his training. Glover considered the needs of each of his children individually as he directed their education. His sons Charles and George and his daughter Gertrude went to Cleveland and lived with an uncle during their final school years. His daughter Esther stayed with relatives in Youngstown; and she, too, completed high school in the North. C. G. Glover, like Daymon Marshall, had seen a world broader than Promised Land; although the community was his home and his professional life was in the South, Glover envisioned a broader future for his children and sent each child to the North to school.

B. J. Glover trained in theology at Wilberforce; and, when he completed his studies, he returned to the South and accepted a pulpit in the A.M.E. church at Due West, South Carolina, a small village in Abbeville County about fifteen miles from Promised Land. B. J. Glover had left the South much like the other local youth, marginally educated and limited in experience. He returned an educated man, able to read standard English, Latin, and Greek, filled with the youthful idealism of the late 1930's. He went to work immediately, using his pulpit as a platform for social reform. He promoted a variety of causes never particularly popular among southern whites, including voter registration, educational equality, and the "advancement of southern Negroes" in general.[24]

His own years in the North demonstrated to B. J. Glover what education for Negroes could be, and those possibilities stood in stark contrast to the realities of the southern educational system. To counter the failures he viewed as inherent in the segregated schools of the South, Glover began a "no drop-out program" for the youth of his church, appealing to local Negro teachers to work with him in returning Negro youth from the fields to the classrooms.

The students were only one concern he addressed within the educational mechanics. He was aware that teachers like Lizzie Chiles, who dared challenge local authority, fell into disfavor with county superintendents and had difficulty collecting their pay claims. Glover devised a workable ruse to overcome the problem. He and a friend "who could pass for white" presented themselves to recalcitrant school superintendents "as federal agents." In this official capacity they demanded back salaries for certain Negro teachers. The sham was successful during a time when affiliation with the New Deal brought both respectability and a degree of authority. The teachers collected, and with each success word spread around the county that Rev. B. J. Glover could help.

B. J. Glover extended the scope of his social activism from impersonation to the direct challenge of racial discrimination in 1936 when he went to the Abbeville County Courthouse and attempted to register to vote. The clerk routinely administered the literacy test required by the 1895 state constitution; and Glover, literate in three languages, easily read and interpreted the passages from the constitution as they were presented to him. The clerk had no guidelines for such a situation and quickly conferred with other officials, leaving Glover on a bench in the courthouse corridor. The clerk returned and dismissed Glover with a simple and final decision: "I just can't register you." There was no additional explanation. Glover left the courthouse quietly but filled with deep emotion. The following Sunday he rose to his pulpit in Due West and "talked about black people registering to vote and the unfairness" of his experience in the Abbeville Courthouse.

Glover's courthouse confrontation and his involvement in the various social causes raised his visibility among a particular segment of the white community, the local Ku Klux Klan. "We all knew about the Klan," said Glover later; but a childhood in Promised Land made him less concerned with their presence than he might otherwise have

been. The organization was "simply not a fright. During the early
Reconstruction days the Ku Klux did quite a bit, but the Promiseland
was already settled, and nobody paid much attention to them then."
In more recent times, during B. J.'s boyhood, the folks at Promised
Land "knew about them because they come down the highway to
Verdery. Sometimes they had demonstrations, but it never bothered
things in *our* area. The Ku Klux started back when blacks began to
ask for places in the Army and places in school, and started asking for
the ballot to vote. That was when they really started."

Still, despite the Klan activity, living at Promised Land held a
degree of security. "There was no whites [living] in the area to see
what was going on" in the community, and this isolation brought an
element of privacy to the Negroes who lived in Promised Land.
Further, the entire community monitored the movement of any white
person passing through. "If a white person came through and wasn't
moving along, we could get them out." On rare occasions the Klan
rode into Promised Land "down by the Crossroads Church," which
was situated directly on the highway between Greenwood and
Verdery; but they never stayed and never did more than attempt to
frighten people by their presence. Accustomed to the security he
knew as a child, B. J. Glover was unprepared for the dangers he faced
now. He failed to realize the full potential of Klan rage.

The Attack

One afternoon in September 1939 B. J. Glover took the bus from Due
West to Greenwood. He went over to Greenwood to renew his driver's
license and then intended to go out to Promised Land for a visit with
his parents. The Klan "knew I was leaving Due West and was coming
to Greenwood. I had gotten off the bus and was walking down the
street. A group of white men stopped me at that time and asked me
my name. I told them, but I didn't say 'yes, sir' and 'no, sir.' It was five
to begin with." Glover's cool, dignified responses further enraged the
angry group of white men, for he failed to follow the proper southern
pattern of Negro deference. "They took me from there in a car,
blindfolded, out in the country." Away from town and isolated from
any help or possible rescue, Glover was a captive.

*They did every kind of thing you could imagine. I was stripped
completely. I wore nylon shorts, and I can still hear them talking
about my nylon shorts. They beat me and made me say "yes, sir"*

and made me do all kinds of personal things. They were sexually cruel, talking about my sex organs and things like that. They made me do things. They would do it and talk to me. "What you doing, nigger? Why don't you leave things like they are?" The KKK said they had to make an example of me. I was an uppity, smart nigger from the North. I had come back with northern ideas. They came up with the idea of beating me, and they did.

The Ku Klux had me for five or six hours. I fought until I couldn't fight any more. Then they left me for dead in the woods. I would have died if it hadn't been for a lady they would now call a prostitute. In those days my parents called her a no good woman. My people didn't care for her, and I never got close to her, knowing about venereal disease and all. My imagination was big, and I was scared of her. This lady was out in the woods—there was no motels or hotels or any type of love accomodations [for Negroes] in those days. She found me.

The woman recognized B. J. instantly, unconscious and bleeding. Horrified at his condition, she "ran three miles through the woods" to the elder Rev. Glover's home in Promised Land; and there she "fell on the steps and cried out: 'They killed B. J.! They killed B. J.!' " C. G. Glover and his sons who were still at home knew without further question who "they" were and what had happened. They packed into the family car and, with the woman to guide them, raced back through the woods to where B. J. lay unconscious.

His family took B. J. back to Promised Land and summoned Dr. Henderson, the Negro physician in Greenwood. "He came and stayed all night" until Glover regained consciousness and returned daily throughout B. J.'s recovery. While B. J. lay bedridden in his parents' home, Promised Land was a tension-filled community. No one knew if or when the Klan might return and make a second attempt on B. J.'s life. "People monitored my home for many days after the attack." The Hacketts, the Burts, the Carters, and the Williamses were all close friends and nearby neighbors. All the families had strong young men in the house, and together the boys rotated shifts around the Glover home day and night "until we were convinced that they didn't intend to bother me any more." The intentions of the guard were firm. "If [the Klan] had come back, there would have been a dead white person out there."

The assailants did not return; nor were they ever officially identified, although they were known to the men at Promised Land. B. J. and the others "had seen them before, in parades and on the streets.

We later learned that their attempt was to frighten any other [black] person from registering to vote. We learned that from white friends, from Dr. Long, a minister at the Presbyterian church in Greenwood. It came out that I had been discussed in the Klan meetings."

The War and Mr. Greek

*I was born down by Verdery, on the Hearst Place. We was married
down by White Hall. Then, after we was married we moved down
below Verdery, over in Abbeville County. And then in 1952 we
moved to Promiseland. The reason we moved to Promiseland was
we didn't have no other choice. We was wanting somewhere to live
and make our home, and so we just bought this little place. Wasn't
nowhere else we could buy a place.*
Augustus White, Sr. and Pearl Wideman White
Promised Land, South Carolina

B. J. Glover left the South when he recovered from the Klan attack
and did not return for many years. Floyd Reynolds, who shared a
school bench with B. J. when they were boys, left about the same
time. The two men had much in common. Both were young, and both
were ambitious reformers. Both tried to implement their ideas about
life within the context of a rural southern heritage and tradition, and
both failed in their attempts. In an earlier generation both men
would have probably sought other ways to carve out an existence at
Promised Land, within a limited framework of dignity and self-
respect; and both would have emerged as community leaders. Now
times were different. The barriers of southern racism were countered
by new alternatives; and Glover and Reynolds left Promised Land,
unwilling to sacrifice their manhood.

B. J. Glover, Floyd Reynolds, and the Marshall children, all left
home as young adults, before establishing independent households at
Promised Land, to begin their adulthood elsewhere. Their departure
was quite different from that of earlier migrants, Martha and Charlie
Reynolds, or George and Ada Wilson. They moved away to start new
lives only after they had attempted and failed to sustain viable
adulthoods in the rural South. The youths who left home in the early
1930's would have been the next generation's leaders, and in that

sense their departure from Promised Land was a loss to the entire community. As a result of their departure the internal leadership structure changed dramatically. For a time Henry Robinson and Rev. C. G. Glover emerged as local leaders. Neither man had longstanding roots at Promised Land. Although Glover owned land and lived there, Robinson lived in town and probably had little sense of the community's heritage. He had come to Greenwood County from Georgia; and his relationship with the folks at Promised Land was based, in the final analysis, on the practical concerns of a businessman. Through the Depression these two men maintained the political and economic contacts with local whites that for two generations had been controlled by a body of local farmers and church deacons, men with powerful vested interests in total community well-being.

The change in leadership was compounded by a change in the land base of the community. Unprobated estates and land bequeathed to daughters who stayed near their parents but were not inclined to farming contributed to a stagnating economy. The infusion of capital from the New Deal programs did not offset the effect of these idle lands. The Reynolds girls, who inherited Clayborn Reynolds' farm, moved away and neglected their inheritance, attending only to the tax obligations. In the past the farm might have been leased to another community resident. Now the fields grew up in weeds. Pearl Redd inherited the ninety-acre tract that was transmitted to her mother Hannah by James Fields, but she had no interest in farming either. Pearl's father, Nathan Redd, attended to the cultivation of that land during his lifetime; but Nathan Redd was gone now. By the mid-1930's the vision of a self-sufficient and independent yeomanry, nurtured through two generations of residency at Promised Land, seemed lost.

Madness and Success

When B. J. Glover left South Carolina for the second time, he returned to Ohio. Although his physical wounds healed, the Klan attack left far deeper and lasting effects than broken bones and bruises. Following the beating, Glover went through "a period of madness. It came up often. I didn't want to see anybody white. I had a severe psychosis about white people and had to work very hard and pray very hard to overcome it." Glover enrolled in Antioch College in Yellow Springs where "the student body was racially mixed." The setting was ideal for his psychological healing.

Antioch blended academics with social service. Both were familiar ground for Glover. More important, however, was the expectation that Negro and white students would cooperate with each other in the two realms. During the week they attended classes and studied together; and on weekends they "went off and repaired poor and disadvantaged people's homes" in another of the New Deal, federally funded programs. "The government bought the paint, and we did the work." In these racially mixed student groups, where Negroes and whites "worked, ate, and slept together," B. J. Glover, guided by a deep spirituality, was finally able to separate the Ku Klux Klan from a more generalized body of white people. "I knew I couldn't go on with that kind of feeling. You cannot be admitted to the kingdom if you feel hatred. I had to overcome my psychosis in order to be admitted." Eventually his "madness," the fear, anger, and hatred evoked by his beating, were dissipated; the terror, an indelible part of his memories, no longer obstructed his work. "I knew that our society could not live with the Ku Klux Klan beliefs." Only then was Glover able to return to the ministry.[1]

Floyd Reynolds was the grandson of community founder Clayborn Reynolds, who had bought a thirty-two–acre farm from the Land Commission in 1871. When Clayborn Reynolds died in 1915, he bequeathed his farm to two daughters, Martha and Anna.[2] Floyd's father, James Reynolds, and four other children received no portion of the estate. James Reynolds married Minnie Pinckney, the daughter of landowner Lymus Pinckney, and the couple began sharecropping. Floyd Reynolds' family was downwardly mobile. Both sets of grandparents were landowners, founders of the Baptist church, prominent and respected members of the community. Although James Reynolds and Minnie Pinckney received no land from either set of parents, they were trained in an ideology of community which tied them to Promised Land despite their landlessness. James Reynolds never acquired a place of his own. Floyd Reynolds grew to manhood within the context of these contradictions, convinced that with hard work and frugality he stood a chance of "getting ahead." When the opportunity arose, Floyd was ready to make that attempt within the framework of community life.

During the early 1930's both North Carter and John Turner closed their stores at the crossroads. Carter was an old man; and, in the face of even greater hardships than he had known during his youth, he closed his store and retired. Turner, a younger and more modern man, experienced a modest degree of financial success during his initial years as a local merchant. He "put his money in some bank," an unusual decision for a Negro. "When the banks failed, he lost all his money. After that he just quit."[3]

With both stores closed Floyd Reynolds, an ambitious young man of twenty, saw an opportunity "to go into business for myself." He went to Greenwood and "talked with different white men about wholesale and retail prices." When he understood "how it worked," he arranged credit with a white merchant and with a cash investment of fifty dollars opened a new store at the Promised Land crossroads. He stocked a few groceries, canned goods, and kerosene, but "didn't bother with fatback and things like that—most people raised their own hogs." The store was convenient. Folks who lived at Promised Land went into town for their major shopping only once a week, on Saturdays. Between trips they bought supplies from Floyd who, like the other storekeepers before him, granted credit to the families he trusted and never permitted an account to grow larger than he judged the family could afford. Even with a low margin of profit and careful management Reynolds "couldn't make ends meet." The Depression was against him. Neither long hours nor frugality helped achieve the success Reynolds sought, and he returned the balance of his inventory to the white merchant and closed the store. With less than his original fifty dollar investment back in his pocket Reynolds headed north, where he found the economic opportunities he had believed existed in South Carolina.[4]

When Floyd Reynolds left South Carolina, he went to Philadelphia where his older brother lived. There he found work as a dishwasher at Temple University, and for a year he worked in a hot kitchen during the day and slept on a cot in the corner of his brother's small apartment. The situation was not exactly what Reynolds had envisioned when he left the South to better his condition. His dissatisfaction mounted; and eventually Reynolds moved on, this time to another brother in Brooklyn. Work options in New York exceeded those in Philadelphia, and Reynolds obtained a steady job as an industrial materials grader. True to the principles of a Promised Land childhood, Reynolds lived frugally and put aside a little money each payday. He was determined to get ahead, not just to break even. When he accumulated another nest egg, this time not fifty but several hundred dollars, he bought a truck. Once again he saw "an opportunity to go into business." Reynolds opened a moving company in Brooklyn.[5]

Young men like B. J. Glover and Floyd Reynolds had found no opportunities to improve their lives at Promised Land. Unwilling to accept the circumscribed conditions of life in the rural South, they moved away. Their attitude toward the community was common among rural Negro youths between 1930 and 1945.[6] Most local teenagers agreed that "Promised Land was a great place to grow up." Days were spent visiting back and forth to each other's houses, "hunting and whatnot" with their grandfathers' dogs, and working at whatever jobs were available. Boys and girls alike still "helped with planting, waited around for harvest" in the endless cycle of farming. If their own parents had no fields, they helped the neighbors. Between farm jobs they learned other kinds of skills, taught by parents, relatives, or any other available adult. "In them days everybody was a parent"; and, although Lizzie Chiles had a monopoly on the schoolhouse and book learning, all the adults at Promised Land taught the local children survival skills from their special stores of individual talents.[7]

Work and play both took Promised Land youths beyond the community. Some found jobs in Greenwood, shining shoes at the barber shop and sweeping floors in the retail stores; others worked for Tom Darraugh, the white owner of the sawmill at the eastern edge of the community. (The Darraugh family had a long-standing relationship with the people who lived at Promised Land. There had always been Promised Land residents who sharecropped on the Darraugh lands, and the family was known to be aloof but fair in its dealings with the community. The Darraugh men were always available to intercede when someone in the community had problems with a white boss or felt they had been cheated by a merchant.) Everybody still went into Greenwood on Saturdays, catching the same train at the Lorenzo flag stop that their parents rode years before. Their most frequent expeditions outside Promised Land, however, brought them into intimate contact, not with the white world, but with the larger regional Negro culture. They regularly attended revivals and church conventions. Occasionally they borrowed Darraugh's truck and took "all the fellows to the ball games—to Greenwood, Waterloo, Ninety-Six, Bradley, and Troy. Our teams played their teams" in a continuing round of intercommunity rivalries that had linked the Negroes in the Greenwood-Abbeville area for thirty years.[8] Life had changed little out in the country.

Each of these experiences amplified and reinforced the beliefs and attitudes youths learned from childhood, and it was this set of values which shaped the lives of the third generation as surely as it directed and formed their parents and grandparents. Among the earliest observations children made of their own world were qualitative distinctions between landownership and landlessness. At a very young age most community children were aware that "a person who had to sharecrop *had* to live in a white man's house and work a white man's farm." The benefit of landownership was personal independence: "You have your *own* farm, your *own* kids, your *own* home." The fierce independence of the community, the freedom from white control, still derived from the fact of economic self-sufficiency. This, in turn, was most frequently established and maintained through landownership. The status held an intrinsic and enduring importance in community ideology, which all children learned and believed regardless of their parents' status. It was a value which shaped the future as emphatically as it explained the past because it instilled in this generation of community youths a dissatisfaction with life as they knew it.[9]

The diminished circumstances and economic difficulties of their parents did not dissuade the youths from adhering to a fundamental optimism about their own futures. They were taught that with hard work and faith in God life would improve. For most, as they "got older and started thinking in terms of adulthood," the discrepancy between reality and dreams became more apparent. As they approached adulthood many youths realized that they "didn't want to live in Promised Land. I had an urge to move on."[10] These were the conditions which prompted B. J. Glover and Floyd Reynolds to seek their fortunes elsewhere.

Fighting for Freedom

For many of the young men in late adolescence this "urge to move on" was translated into military service. Whether they enlisted or were drafted, the effects were the same. The military trained them and armed them in Negro units. Accustomed to and comfortable in a racially homogeneous setting, taught from childhood to exercise their leadership abilities within such settings, young men like Isaac Moragne, John Cole, and Robert Evans, Moragne's second cousin, all rose easily through noncommissioned ranks. Moragne was the grandson of Isaac Y. Moragne, one of the original settlers at Promised Land; and Evans was his great-grandson. Cole, from a different background, was the grandson of a sharecropper, the son of a carpenter. Cole and Moragne had been friends from childhood; and now both attained the Army rank of staff sergeant, "the best rank in the Army. It was in the middle." Evans, who enlisted in the Navy, became a seaman first class and saw duty throughout the Pacific war zone— Saipan, the Mariannas, Iwo Jima.[11]

All three men traveled extensively during their tours of duty. Cole and Moragne were both drafted, and after their basic training went in opposite directions. Cole shipped out from the West Coast. Traveling across the Pacific he saw Australia, New Zealand, India, and then the Middle East, serving as "a quartermaster in a diesel outfit." Typically, his unit followed the war route but saw no combat until "we caught up with the front just before the Bulge." In two brief years John Cole saw more of the Near and Far East than he had ever dreamed existed.[12]

Isaac Moragne's Army tour took him to Europe. After his basic training, he was sent to England and took the opportunity to travel through most of the British Isles while he waited for D-Day. Moragne crossed the Channel and slogged through France with the other Allied soldiers; and, when France was liberated, the two boyhood friends were there, separated by only a few miles of French countryside they later realized. They celebrated victory in the tradition of soldiers, "drinking and dancing with everybody. Nobody cared what color you were."[13] There was a spirit of equality in France which they enjoyed immensely.

After they were discharged the three men's lives took very different turns. John Cole never returned to Promised Land to live. He went directly to New York. His father, "one hell of a fine teacher" in Cole's estimation, had died during the war; and "several brothers in New York and a sister in Yonkers" asked him to join them in the North. "When I decided to go someplace this was the place to come."[14] Isaac Moragne and Robert Evans went home to Promised Land. Both had families there, parents, wives, brothers, and sisters. Both intended to make the community their permanent home.

Isaac Moragne's vision of life had changed during his Army hitch, and down in the country "it didn't seem like a free world any more." The Army provided him with a taste of freedom, and all Moragne wanted now "was to go back to France." He wanted to re-enlist. No one at Promised Land understood or was sympathetic to his frustrations and anguish. He tried to talk to his father, to explain what he had seen and felt. Fred Moragne was impatient with Isaac and perplexed by his dissatisfactions. He roared an angry response to Isaac's proposal of re-enlistment: "Boy, as hard as we worried about you all these years, and now you're a free man—out of the Army— and you say you'd just as soon go back?"[15]

For a time Isaac tried to readjust to the way of life at Promised Land. In those days "people had a lot of respect for their parents"; and, if a father expressed disapproval over something, even an adult son "would think about it six months before he brought it up again." So it was between Isaac and Fred Moragne. Isaac stayed put and talked no more about re-enlistment, "going round and round trying to figure out what to do." He did not want to farm and yet found no other work.

The Veteran's Administration "sent me a little card" which provided the first glimmer of hope for Moragne's future. The message printed on the reverse side—"Need help or assistance getting a job? See the government people."—sent his spirits soaring. He realized that "these were government people, not county people"; and he had an abiding faith that the "government people" would treat him with the dignity and respect he first experienced in France.

Moragne approached the Greenwood VA office with unjustified optimism. The two doors marked "white" and "colored," the "partition straight from the window to the back" of the room should have signaled to him that in matters of race "government" and "county" were irrelevant distinctions in South Carolina. Jim Crow still prevailed. Moragne stood on the "colored" side of the partition "for an hour, two, then three," waiting his turn to talk with the official behind the counter. "As long as I was there, everytime somebody [white] came in on the other side of the fence they would be waited on." When the room was finally empty "and they got nothing to do, then they helped me."

Moragne produced the postcard which brought him there. "Can you help me get a job?" The VA official pondered the man and the situation. There was no discussion of work experience, Army training, or job preferences. In South Carolina in 1946 work opportunities were dictated by race. Moragne was told to "go to the mill down in South Greenwood. They got a building they're building. You can push wheelbarrows and carry bricks. They're paying twenty-five cent an hour." This was not the sort of help Moragne expected. He determined, standing on the "colored" side of the room partition, that he would leave the South. "I would have gone to Egypt or anywhere right then." He recounted to himself his recent accomplishments. "I was a staff sergeant in the Army. I traveled all over England. I sat fourteen days in the English Channel. I liberated France. And I wasn't going to push a wheelbarrow."

Moragne walked back out to Promised Land prepared for another confrontation with his father. He was twenty-five years old and knew that he needed "to get back in the routine" of life, a steady job, his own home, and some dignity in his life. Isaac Moragne's problem was that, while the routine was the same, he was changed. Again he sat down with Fred Moragne and tried to explain the advantages of military service. The pay was good, and it was regular. The color of a man's skin was not so important as it seemed in the South. Black or white, Isaac explained, "if I was in Casablanca and you got sick, I could get an Air Force plane home." Fred Moragne listened this time, not to his son's words, but to the meaning of those words and resigned himself to the inevitable. Fred Moragne's brother-in-law, Josh Richie, was still in New York; and, although Richie was an old man, he was also young Isaac's uncle. Fred Moragne told his son to "go to Uncle Josh. At least you'll still be in the country."

Military service had a different impact on each of the young men from Promised Land who donned the Army uniform and shouldered a rifle. In John Cole's case the effect of his Army years was negligible. While he was overseas, Cole's father died; and "after that there just wasn't much reason to go back" to Promised Land. The Coles had no land to tie John to the South. His brothers and sisters were settled in New York; and he followed them there, adhering to the basic precepts of family bonds and obligations he had known since childhood.[16] His Army hitch was an interlude in his life, without long-range consequences. Cole would have left Promised Land with or without military experience.

In contrast to John Cole, military service had a dramatic effect on Isaac Moragne. It broadened his vision of the world and exposed him to a diversity of experiences. It made him hungry for something which seemed beyond reach when he returned to Promised Land— dignity, respect, and equality. These were values he had learned as a child, but they were redefined and cast into concrete terms in Europe. The world of Promised Land seemed tiny and narrow to Moragne when he came home. Although extensive family ties kept him in the community for a time, they failed to satisfy his other expectations. Despite his kinship bonds he ultimately left the community because Army life had opened the door to a kind of freedom beyond Moragne's grasp in the South.

Robert Evans' postwar destiny and his motives for pursuing that destiny contrasted with both Cole's and Moragne's. The oldest of eight children, Evans, like Floyd Reynolds, was from a downwardly mobile family. He was old Isaac Y. Moragne's great-grandson, but the Evans branch of the family had been landless since the turn of the century. Like most young men in the community, Robert Evans keenly felt his family obligations; and he also understood the importance of land. During his Navy hitch he sent "all the money he could" to his mother "to help out with things at home."[17] She bought land, not the food or clothes Evans probably intended, with his small contributions; and, when Evans was discharged, he found himself co-owner with her of a respectable accumulation of acreage; the land bound him to the community. At first he farmed; but he soon turned to other work as a skilled electrician, learned in the Navy. One step at a time, Robert Evans became an independent electrical contractor.

Evans' postwar destiny was as predictable as that of both John Cole and Isaac Moragne. All shaped their behavior on the basis of family ties and responsibilities. All were motivated by economic incentives, and all sought to achieve a balance between these two forces. Each pursued independence and self-sufficiency, designing futures for themselves on the basis of the resources at hand. Robert Evans stayed at Promised Land for the same reason that Isaac Moragne left.

Things Are Changing Out Here

In an initial burst of postwar prosperity the Reynoldses, the Wims, the Hacketts, and the Widemans all bought their first cars.[18] None of the cars was new; and none was worth more than forty dollars; but they were a definite improvement over the mule-drawn wagons, the only mode of private transportation most folks previously could

Table 16.
Population and Property Values, 1897–1950*

Year	Total Households	Landowners % of Total	Landowners Taxable Property	Landless % of Total	Landless Taxable Property
1897	283	42	$ 72.50	58	$39.50
1909	199	57	166.66	43	61.29
1915	172	66	99.00	34	57.50
1922	210	68	100.76	32	65.45
1932	144	66	63.00	34	31.50
1942	176	73	43.46	27	46.81
1950	193	68	36.50	32	48.88

*Based on a random sample of: Tax Auditor's Duplicate Books, Smithville and White Hall Townships, Greenwood County, S.C., 1897–1950. Greenwood County Courthouse.

afford. The trend continued, and by 1950, 25 percent of the families owned their own automobiles. Promised Land drove into the modern world. The wave of postwar emigration was reversed, and the population increased at a slow but steady pace even though postwar economic prosperity seemed limited to the landless. This group worked more often for cash wages now, rather than sharecropping as they had in earlier times. Most landowners continued their pattern of subsistence farming, which had its own unique set of advantages, not including the accumulation of taxable property. Still, most of the farm families thought themselves comfortable, if not prosperous. They measured the quality of life in terms of survival. "We ate well and had clothes." Added to the physical comforts was a type of psychological freedom, enjoyed most fully by those families who were economically independent of the white world. Only they "didn't have to worry about what's going on out there."[19]

Every family with a garden and a hog pen shared the bounty of the land with their relatives in the North, mailing "boxes of sweet potatoes, whole hams, and packages of red mud" from the Verdery post office. (The red clay soil was a popular substitute for chewing tobacco, and men and women alike frequently sucked on a small plug while they worked. The migrants missed the stuff and requested that it be sent along with the food.) Letters came and went through the post office too, as news traveled back and forth between Promised Land and Philadelphia, New York, Chicago, and Baltimore. White postmaster Joe Ligon was central in the communication system. He wrote many of the outgoing letters as they were dictated to him by men and women who had long since forgotten the few words they learned to read in school, and he read the incoming mail to those same people. "Little Joe" was well-known in Promised Land and generally liked by most of the people there, even though he occasionally "worried us all to death."[20]

There were other, nonmaterial changes also occurring at Promised Land during the late 1940's and early 1950's. The most important of these was the general tenor of relationships between community residents and local whites. Traditionally, superficially at least, guided by the reciprocal principles of paternalism and obsequiousness, these interracial interchanges now took on a new tension. Nowhere was this more apparent than in the attitudes of women who were domestic workers in white homes. Their daily work routine brought them into the most intimate contact with whites, and this intimacy increased their vulnerability to historically common white male sexual exploitation. White men still initiated and promoted sexual encounters with their Negro domestic workers, just as their grandfathers had with slave women.

The women, however, resisted these overtures when they could with a new understanding of the conditions which promoted them. Economic control was the factor which led to sexual exploitation of Negro women by white men in 1850 and in 1950. When an employer pressed the issue of sexual intimacy, the women knew that "you *had* to do it, no doubt about that." Nevertheless, the physical conquest was not accompanied by psychological domination. When a Negro woman was thus compromised, "this was not what the black person wanted to do. This was what she *had* to do." The traditional problem as yet had no solution, but the nature of the problem had definition. "You work for that white person, and he want you to go with him, you had to go with him" or quit the job.[21] The economic factors which established the foundation of sexual exploitation still perpetuated it.

Economic pressure was well understood by the men and women who lived at Promised Land. They had experienced it all their lives; and, although they were generally the victims, by the 1950's they were prepared to apply the principles to whites that had been used to direct and control their behavior for so long. After Floyd Reynolds went north, a white man from Georgia took over the store at the crossroads. Jess, nobody ever knew him by any other name, had very little affinity for any of the Promised Land residents; and relations between Jess and the community were based more on reciprocal economic need than any other motive.

In 1952 even this cool and distant tolerance between Jess and the Negroes came to an abrupt halt when he "shot one of the colored men who lived out here." The victim was Hut Warren, a long-time member of the community; and one of many who traded regularly at the store. Jess and Warren had an argument which the folks regarded as "little of nothing." Warren, like Anthony Crawford forty years earlier, temporarily suspended the protocols of race and gave the white man "a short answer." He paid for his impudence with his life. Jess shot him in the back as Warren was leaving the store and killed him instantly.[22]

A coroner's inquest was scheduled to investigate the incident; and a number of community residents walked into the Greenwood Courthouse, prepared to testify against Jess and convinced that he would be brought to justice. Jess ignored the hearing and stayed in his store that day, in overt defiance of the law. The justice system overlooked the crime; and, in a courtroom filled with Negroes from Promised Land, a white judge dismissed the charge of murder. Southern laws, written and enforced by whites, afforded no more protection to Negroes in 1952 than they had in 1870.

Promised Land turned inward and drew on its resources for the solution to the problem. The community realized that they were practically the only people who patronized the store; and they decided to deal with Jess in their own way, to "hurt him where it hurts the most—in his pocket." In a spontaneous mass action "we boycotted him and run him out of business." Mothers firmly told their children, accustomed to walking down to the store for a soda, that "we were not going to buy drinks there any more." Most of the adults joined in the boycott willingly, but a few still went to Jess because that was more convenient than going all the way into Greenwood. People watched, and the ones caught going into the store at the crossroads were quietly taken aside by community leaders and "told that it was in the best interests of the community not to buy there." The matter was never discussed in church, and there were no public meetings. It was a scheme designed and executed entirely through the use of social pressure. After a time "nobody stopped there anymore," and within six months Jess was broke and out of business. Promised Land's successful use of economic boycott preceeded and foreshadowed events of the approaching decade.[23]

The shift in mood at Promised Land was accompanied by an almost imperceptible change in white attitudes toward community residents. Local white merchants had long employed Negroes as janitors and porters, "the real low jobs." As local Negroes acquired "steady employment and a steady income," they more frequently entered the retail stores in Greenwood to buy rather than to look at the goods. Merchants responded to this new purchasing power. One Promised Land youth working as a janitor in the local shoe store was hastily promoted to salesman when "a lot of colored people started coming in the store" with money to spend. He was told by his boss to "take those colored people over in the corner and sell shoes to them."[24] Jim Crow was still a part of life, but the rules were changing a bit.

There were similar changes in other areas of the local economy. In the past Negroes were often denied credit from all but the lien men and merchants who knew them personally. By mid-century, however, the change in their employment status affected their borrowing power. Many Promised Land residents worked for cash wages. These laborers and maids had no need for crop liens; they had no crops. The Home Finance Company, a newly opened local small loan business, discovered that the railroad laborers, textile workers, and women domestics who lived at Promised Land were good credit risks. They borrowed money for furniture, for school clothes, and to meet occasional emergencies; and they repaid the loans on schedule. The people at Promised Land gained a reputation as men and women "who paid their debts and were stable homeowners."[25] The reputation brought a new form of economic independence, consumer credit.

Land and School

From its inception Promised Land found its strength in the land, the churches, and the community school. During the mid-1950's the nature of two, the land and the school, was permanently and radically changed; and the community was altered. Sister Pearl Redd sold the ninety-acre tract of farmland located squarely in the center of the community to a local white entrepreneur, James Boulware. Land owned by members of Sister Redd's family since the 1870's now was passed into white hands. "Sister Redd was an old lady and didn't have no family. They were all dead or gone north. She didn't know what to do with that land."[26] Boulware did know what to do with the land. He intended to subdivide and develop the tract. Like the Home Finance Company loan officers, he realized that "some blacks had got better paying jobs and had some money to buy themselves a little place." Boulware also knew that Promised Land was still "the only place in the county where blacks were allowed to buy land." White folks in Greenwood County were still opposed to Negroes owning land, and the same informal forces that had prevented land acquisition outside Promised Land since Reconstruction were still in effect. In acquiring the largest undivided tract in the community, Boulware established a corner on the Negro land market and with it the potential for a respectable return on his investment.[27]

The first buyers appeared rather soon after Boulware made his purchase. A small group of Negro families were "living down at White Hall on some mill land." The mill sold the property to a timber company, which in turn evicted the families in order to cut the timber for pulpwood. The company, however, permitted the families to purchase the dilapidated homes they had been renting for a nominal sum, with the provision that the homes would be moved off the pulpwood lands. "Eight or ten of them moved up here" to Promised Land, a distance of less than two miles. They bought adjacent lots "back behind Mt. Zion" and joined the community. James Boulware's intuition about the land was correct. There was a market, and there was money to be made. Only his unexpected and premature death in 1955 prevented immediate and full-scale implementation of his scheme.[28]

Shortly after Boulware's death and the store boycott, the county school board responded to the 1954 Supreme Court *Brown* v. *The Topeka Board of Education* decision. It consolidated the county's elementary schools for Negro children. Greenwood County built its newest and most modern elementary school at Promised Land. The old 1880's schoolhouse closed at last, and Lizzie Chiles ended half a century of teaching, retiring at the end of the 1955 term. She moved to Atlanta to live with her step-children.[29]

The 1956 fall school term began with bus after bus of Negro children arriving at the new brick building. They came to the new school "from all around, from Troy, Bradley, Callison, and the Bell Place," the same places that played against the Promised Land baseball team. The children had been to Promised Land before, for ball games, for revivals, and probably for just plain visiting. Now they came for school. There was a room and a teacher for each of the six grades. All of the students were accustomed to one-room schools where everybody crowded in. There was a cafeteria that prepared and served hot lunches, an auditorium, and a fully equipped playground. There were even indoor flush toilets and fountains with cooled water, all without the odious "White" and "Colored" designations. These were all novelties. The facilities seemed a palace to both students and their parents. Greenwood County could not be charged with inferior, "unequal" educational facilities for its Negro children. Now, so long ignored and neglected by the official world, these children had the best the county could afford. They were not expected to demand any more.[30]

The well-equipped and modern consolidated elementary school for rural Negro children did not change the basic ethic at the Promised Land School. Although Lizzie Chiles was gone, the care and concern she gave the children did not leave the community with her. The teachers who came to the new school were equally conscious of the needs of their students. "They instilled a lot of pride in us" as they taught reading, writing, and arithmetic. They taught race pride along with the other basics. "You're black" they told the rooms of children, "but no one else is any better than you, and you're no better than anyone else." The measure of personal worth was still personal achievement, and the route to success was taught in a simple maxim: "Whatever you do, do your best." Despite the influx of new students, there were no discipline problems at Promised Land, not the sort of tensions "you get when you go to mixing" black and white students.[31] Working in concert, teachers emphasized homework, and parents emphasized good behavior.

The buses rolled through Promised Land in both directions now; for, when the county consolidated the rural elementary schools, the school board also made provisions for extending Negro education beyond the eighth grade. The older children went into Greenwood for public secondary education. The county school board acquired the facilities of the old Brewer Normal School and converted them to a secondary school for Negro youths. County response to the 1954 *Brown* decision was swift and thorough. The Brewer facilities were modernized to present a facade of educational adequacy. Measured against its performance of the past, the school board performed a monumental task in a short period of time. Black children finally had educational facilities where they could learn without being cold. Their school term was equivalent to that of white children. They had toilets, bus service, a football team, a homecoming queen, and textbooks. The year was 1956.

When James Boulware's estate was settled, his widow had no use for the ninety acres of land out in Promised Land nor, it appeared, did anyone else, until Jimmy (the Greek) Nicholson heard that it was for sale. Nicholson, a Greek immigrant, found his way to Greenwood as a young boy and over the years accumulated a small fortune buying up, holding, and then selling property that no one else wanted. Nicholson's transactions were extensive and complicated. "There's not a lawyer in Greenwood who understands Jimmy's land deals. There are too many. If you want to know about them, you have to ask Jimmy."[32]

Jimmy, the Greek, bought Sister Redd's ninety acres from the Boulware estate and changed the shape of Promised Land. He shared Boulware's vision of the tract. It could be profitably subdivided and developed; so he went out to Promised Land himself and, with the help of a local surveyor, laid out some roads and marked off the lots. There were two separate areas in Promised Land that Jimmy, the Greek, developed, Promised Land Heights and Nicholson Subdivision. He named them both. He also named the streets, which he personally laid out—Mt. Zion Road ran down past the church; Dandy Street was named for Carrie Dandy, who lived at Promised Land; Nicholson Avenue he named for himself. "When *you're* the developer, you name the streets what you want."

Nicholson set the price of his lots at one hundred dollars. "Not many people had that kind of money"; and he readily accepted ten dollar down payments and a dollar or two a week or, if times were bad, "whatever we could pay when we had it." He never repossessed a lot after he sold it. Instead, he just waited patiently, and the money always came. A relationship of trust emerged between "Mr. Greek" and the people he did business with at Promised Land. Jimmy believed that he would be paid when the money was available. The people who sent him one or two dollar bills sealed in an envelope addressed only to "Mr. Greek, Greenwood, South Carolina" had complete faith that Jimmy would credit their account. The arrangement worked. First one lot, then another was bought up by black families "needing a decent place to live."[33]

The first families who bought Jimmy's new lots were the same people who borrowed money at the Home Finance Company in Greenwood, men and women with small but steady wage incomes. Once again, as it had been in the 1880's and 1890's, some community property was subdivided; and a body of landless Negroes acquired a piece of land they could call their own. The majority of the earliest purchasers in the 1950's were long-time community residents. They were tied to other local residents by extensive kinship bonds and were active members of one of the churches and avid supporters of the local life-style. Now they, too, were bound to the land.

After they bought the land these families needed a house to live in. The Promised Land carpenters had work again, and housing starts at Promised Land during the late 1950's equaled those in Greenwood. Electrical contractor Robert Evans had more business than he could manage; and his brother-in-law Lonnie Norman, the baby who came to Promised Land from Lincolnton, Georgia perched on a pillow in a mule-drawn wagon, worked from early morning to sundown putting up frame houses with less than a thousand square feet of living space. Like Nathan Redd before him, Norman hired his construction crew from Promised Land. The houses they built all had indoor plumbing, still a novelty among rural Negroes. The county ran an electric line out to Promised Land when they built the school, and soon most community residents turned their lights off and on at a wall switch.[34] Everybody kept their kerosene lamps out in the shed, just in case of an emergency.

The prosperity that had so long eluded the folks at Promised Land arrived. In an unprecedented growth spurt the community was transformed as surely and radically as it had been altered in the 1870's, and the changes this time did not pass unheralded. In 1957 Promised Land won the state's Community Development Award for the "most outstanding rural community" in South Carolina. The Extension Service Community Development Club at South Carolina State College in Orangeburg, the state's Negro college, based the award on the judicious use of community resources. The indoor plumbing in the new houses was a major consideration in the award. Equally important were the new street lights, which were recently installed, financed by contributions from community residents. The Community Development Club was also impressed by the number of home freezers at Promised Land, another technological innovation only recently available to the community. The gardens were still there; and the food was still preserved, now in a thoroughly modern way. A final consideration was the success of a community-wide beautification program. Everyone decorated their mail box. The old, agrarian, isolated, and technologically primitive Promised Land was disappearing.[35]

The year after Promised Land received the Community Development Award, Mt. Zion's Board of Stewards decided to replace the old church building erected in the 1880's. Lulu Hackett, one of the most active members of the Stewardess' Board, perpetuated a century-long tradition when she got involved in the project. Her sons worked for A. M. Tuck, a white contractor in Greenwood County. Mrs. Hackett walked down the road to have a talk with Mr. Tuck one day; and, by the time she left his house, the man had "donated the whole top of the new church" (the lumber, the tar paper, the shingles, and the nails) to the Negroes who were his employees and his neighbors. "White mens give the materials, and we do the work." The new Mt. Zion went up slowly but steadily. Every Saturday the men went over after work and built the church, just as their grandfathers had built old Mt. Zion. "The ladies cook them dinner and carried it to the church yard" so that the work could proceed without interruption.[36]

The Fourth of July was still a major holiday at Promised Land, continuing yet another community tradition. The men still "stayed up all night to cook the bar-b-que over hickory coals," and the annual baseball contest between Bradley and the Black Sox from Promised Land had become a "classic rivalry." The lemonade, once described by W. L. Bradley as "made in the shade and stirred with a spade," cooled an otherwise scorching day for the crowds who came to Promised Land "from Coronaca, Piney Grove, Hodges, Bradley, Plum Branch, Damascus, and all around" Greenwood, Abbeville, and McCormick Counties. "Everybody bought a new outfit for Fourth of July," and the cars were parked "for a mile in each direction from the crossroads on both sides of the road." As it had for a century, Promised Land opened its doors to the region's Negro population.[37]

The third generation residents reconstructed their community in ways remarkably similar to the strategies their grandparents employed when they established permanent residence on Dr. Marshall's farm. They used the governmental resources from the New Deal to restore economic vigor to their homes. The AAA, the FCA, parity payments, and soil conservation programs during the 1930's offered the first hope for relief from a stagnating cotton-based economy which had stifled community life during the first three decades of the twentieth century. World War II and the civil rights efforts, which were taking place in distant cities and austere courtrooms, opened new job opportunities for community residents; and they did not hesitate to take advantage of them. A tradition of perseverance, hard work, pride, and initiative were important forces in the transformation. A new school, electricity, consumer credit, and new residents all played a part in changing Promised Land from an isolated collection of indigent Negroes into a rural community with a thoroughly modernized ideology and a firm grasp on its heritage.

ELEVEN

On Coming Home

*I didn't dislike the South. I just didn't like the way I had to come
up. The houses down there—they had to plaster the walls with
newspaper, make up the paste with flour. The mattresses was
made of straw. One time I turned the mattress, and a big old snake
rolled out. Things is better down there now.*
Sarah Price Robinson
Baltimore, Maryland

The unpleasant memories of southern childhoods were balanced for
most migrants by other kind of experiences, piano lessons from Sister
Pearl Redd, "picnics and ball games out in the church yard," courting
up and down White Hall Road, and sleeping on summer nights in the
cotton piled on the front porch. Even though, for many who left
Promised Land, "four or five days back down there is enough for me";
most made an annual pilgrimage back home in August, a special
time at Promised Land.[1]

August is the month for revival and Homecoming, as it has been
since the 1890's. When Promised Land was dominated by the cotton
cycle, August was the month when the crop was "laid by" and left to
ripen. Farm families, weary from months of intensive field work
which began the previous March, looked forward to a time of rest and
rejuvination before cotton picking. The hot dry summer weather in
the South Carolina Piedmont was an ideal time to sit under shade
trees or on front porches, escaping the heat and passing the time. It
was also an ideal time for visiting, and the folks who had gone north
came home for a rest then. Even after farming diminished and most
families had only a garden to tend, August remained the time for
revival and Homecoming. Old friends and family members, separated by time and distance, were drawn together again each August
in a spiritual collective which endured all human trials. At Mt. Zion,
Crossroads, and Jacob's Chapel people knew their churches would be

filled with those from the North, drawn back home by a powerful web of family and community. "That was the time to come home."[2]

Revival week began with Homecoming Sunday and a dinner in the church yard of fried chicken, macaroni, sweet potato pies, iced tea, and lemonade. Mt. Zion borrowed tables from Crossroads and Jacob's Chapel, and Crossroads and Jacob's Chapel borrowed them back for their Homecoming. At mid-century annual family treks reversed the routes to the north. Isaac and Theresa Moragne drove home from New York City. Floyd Reynolds came every year a more and more successful businessman. Herman and Tim Marshall and their sisters made the trip together from Baltimore.

The visit home provided migrants an opportunity to renew old friendships and catch up on the news, to establish once again the spiritual connections of their childhoods. The time served, as well, as an opportunity for community residents to observe first-hand the effects of going north; but the perspective they gained was a biased one. Those who came home every August were generally the more successful, the survivors. Everyone at Promised Land implicitly understood that "after some folks leave you don't never hear from them again." Personal failures, those who did not succeed economically or socially or emotionally in the North, rarely participated in homecoming.[3]

There were enough success stories, however, to fill the houses and churches. Cars bearing northern license plates crowded the yards. Brothers in their forties and fifties sat under shade trees and talked about their boyhoods, which were alike, and their manhoods, which had taken different paths. Cousins in Promised Land took cousins from New York over to the ball field and then to Thomas' Store at the crossroads for a cold drink. Breakfasts were major social events; and during revival week evening meals were extravagent banquets, cooked in three or four separate kitchens to prepare enough food for temporarily reunited kinship circles.

Homecoming was largely symbolic of the community bonds between those who stayed and those who left. The material ties were much deeper. Folks who had moved to the North returned to Promised Land during times of illness and personal crisis; for funerals, births, and weddings; and to attend to family business. They sent money home to help pay taxes and to finance the purchase of new farm machinery. The exchanges were not one-sided. The folks at Promised Land took smoked hams and canned tomatoes with them when they went to the North. They brought unemployed youths back from the cities, housed them, fed them, and found them steady work.

These events rarely conformed to the cotton cycle or the revival schedule, but they were of even greater importance than the August visits because they were instigated by more than ritual. They signified the depths of the intimate and affective ties and responsibilities maintained within families.

The Moragnes

When Isaac Moragne "went on up to Uncle Josh" Richie in New York City, he left his wife and children behind temporarily.[4] The couple "didn't have no fight" over Isaac's decision to go north or over the details of the move. Both knew the separation was temporary and born out of necessity rather than choice. They had no place to live, and Isaac had neither a job nor the financial resources to support his wife and children while he found work. Theresa and the children stayed at Promised Land with her mother.

Josh Richie took Isaac down to the garment district where he had worked for twenty-five years and helped Isaac get a job making ladies' belts. That problem solved, Isaac looked for an apartment and finally found one in Harlem, "which wasn't easy in those days." He bought a few pieces of furniture, and only when he felt secure in his work and settled in a place to live did he send for his family. Moragne's old boyhood friends John Cole and Tom White, also living in New York, were going home to Promised Land for a funeral. Moragne made arrangements with the men for Theresa and his daughters to ride North with them after the funeral.

The couple had been separated almost a year by then, and Theresa was "ready and willing" to join her husband. She planned for her own departure, deciding to leave their two young daughters in Promised Land with her mother until she, too, was able to get a job and otherwise "get settled up here." She gave notice to her white employers, a family in Verdery where she did domestic work making "top wages of $3.25 a week." In her mind, it was a good job. "Some didn't make no more than a dollar a week." Theresa had been with the family throughout Isaac's years in the Army and felt free to borrow from them the thirty dollars she needed for traveling money, promising that she "would pay it back when [she] found work."

In the South Theresa had been a well paid and successful domestic worker. She encountered no difficulty securing similar work in New York City and found immediately that "the pay was better and the work easier." In the South Theresa, like most Negro domestics, was expected to clean, cook, wash, and iron. There was little specialization in housework. In New York "all you have to do is clean." Domestic work suited Theresa Moragne. The hours were flexible, and the pay was good—"thirty or forty dollars [a week]." Theresa was able to balance the demands of her work against her domestic responsibilities, "to be home when the kids got home from school or be here when they get sick." The "honest dollar" she made this way adequately supplemented Isaac's steady income, and there was no reason for her to seek work which paid more.[5]

Isaac and Theresa Moragne found New York City an improvement over Promised Land in many ways. The schools were far better for their children than the little one-room schoolhouse back home. Life was more exciting and faster paced. There were more things to see and do, and the discrimination that was a way of life in the South was less apparent and overt in the North. "That was the biggest part" of the improvement both noticed. When Theresa gave birth to their third child, she discovered yet another advantage of city life, hospitals. Unlike the midwife back home, city hospitals "give you something when you go to having those pains."

The Moragnes entered enthusiastically into community life. They attended the PTA meetings, and they joined a neighborhood African Methodist Church. Isaac sang in the choir, just as he had in Promised Land. They visited regularly with friends and family who were also living in the city, including Josh Richie's white stepson Bill. Even after Rose Richie's death, Bill remained in constant contact with his stepfather and the Moragnes. His Negro nephew and white stepson arranged Richie's funeral together, burying him beside Rose in a New York cemetery.

For Isaac and Theresa Moragne life in New York City held possibilities they never dreamed of at Promised Land. Perhaps because they emigrated to a city where friends and relatives were already established, perhaps because they were trained from childhood to an ethic of self-sufficiency and believed in the dignity of honest labor, they had little difficulty adjusting to their new environment. Their sense of disorganization during the transitional moving period was mitigated by the strategy they employed in the move. It was a gradual one, each phase carefully planned in advance. It was probably through this cautious and systematic approach to migration that the Moragnes avoided many of the difficulties other Negroes experienced during their initial period of adaption to urban life.

Annual family visits back to Promised Land began that first year, and with each trip home their satisfaction and prosperity were increasingly apparent to the friends and relatives down south. Isaac's younger brother Al was among the most attentive when they came home for their vacation. Throughout his childhood Al had watched Uncle Josh take his brothers and sisters and cousins back to New York. Some stayed permanently; others only briefly, to attend school for a year or two; but all came home with exciting stories about New York City and life in the North. As he listened and dreamed Al, too, "just wanted to get away so bad." He waited until he was eighteen and then "one night told my mother that I wanted to go. She naturally didn't want me to go, but she told me to talk to my father." Fred Moragne made the final decision in this matter, as he did in all family affairs. His approval was essential.

The elder Moragne was a landowner and a subsistence farmer who "didn't have much contact with whites." Because of his isolation, he was unable to understand the attraction New York City held for his children. Born in the nineteenth century, Moragne was "a proud man who worked only for himself" and knew remarkably little about life beyond the tightly knit community. The economic independence he valued so highly resulted in a naiveté that was difficult for his children to overcome. The logic of their dissatisfaction escaped him. "He didn't know about the back of the bus because he didn't know about the bus." That discrimination which he could not avoid "was a fact he just accepted" as an immutable part of life. Although he had once traveled to the North briefly as a young man, Moragne viewed Promised Land as an ideal place to raise his family. He assumed it would be so for his children and their children. He neither understood nor accepted the younger generation's insistent drive to leave Promised Land.

When Al approached his father with his request to go north, Fred Moragne objected, just as he had with each of the older children. He wanted Al "to stay [at Promised Land] and work on the farm" and created one reason after another why Al should not go to New York City. Like the others, however, Al was persistent. He met each objection with a counterargument. Moragne's attempts to keep Al in Promised Land were as futile as they had been years before with Isaac, and eventually he capitulated. Al went north to join the others in 1954. Soon after he arrived, he was drafted into the Army and did a hitch in the hills of Korea. When he was discharged, he went directly back to Isaac in New York.

Only after he left Promised Land did Al fully realize the extent of his isolation "out in the hills" of the South Carolina Piedmont. The contrast of New York City to home was startling. In the city "things was so different. You have the opportunity to do what you never did before" as well as the freedom to exercise that opportunity. The discrimination his father passively accepted as a part of life in the South was absent. "Here you don't have to go in the back to get your water." Buying food and riding the bus were equally thrilling, and at first Al was overwhelmed with "just the *idea* of not having to" step automatically to the rear of the bus or buy food through a back door. "You can get on the bus just like everybody else and ride where ever you want. You don't even have to be going anyplace. Nobody asks you." Like many southern Negroes, Al shed "his inferiority complex" and gained a new sense of pride and self-confidence as he adjusted to city life.

In one respect the city was liberating. "You go where you want and do what you want, and nobody says anything." But the city was also terrifying. Its size intimidated Al Moragne. After he was discharged from the Army, he lived with his older brother Clarence; and, although Clarence tried to help him through an initial period of loneliness, for a time Al was "even afraid to go down to the corner" alone. Immobilized by a fear of the city—"things was so big"—and without friends of his own, Al "some days sat and sat" alone in their apartment in Harlem, waiting for Clarence to return at the end of the day.

When Clarence first moved to New York, he lived with Josh and Rose Richie and established a certain domestic stability during his period of transition by participating in their regular household activities. "Clarence was very religious" and enjoyed going with Rose when she went out to preach. When Isaac migrated he, too, stayed with his aunt and uncle and then established his own domestic unit as quickly as possible, bringing Theresa to join him as soon as he found a suitable job and housing for them. Al lacked the settling influences of a domestic routine, which his two older brothers had enjoyed, and as a consequence experienced a somewhat more intense and protracted period of adjustment. For him the turning point came one evening when Clarence "was going over to Yonkers to see his girlfriend." Al had nothing to do, and Clarence invited him along. As the evening wore on Al "got tired of just sitting there watching them," and he asked for directions back to Harlem. Clarence willingly provided them, and Al struck out alone. Traversing the city by subway and bus, he found his way home. "After that [he] wasn't afraid to go out alone."

Al's final adjustment to city life came when he found steady work as a cook. With a reliable income came a new form of freedom, a car. Al lived the life of a carefree bachelor, "running here and there all over the place"; but it was a style which troubled his older, more serious brother. Isaac thought Al needed to get married. Isaac was concerned that Al "used to get very sincere with the girls," but as soon as they responded with equal sincerity he moved on. Al lived a loose life, going "from day to day, spend here, spend there." He lacked the focus and direction that family responsibilities brought; and Isaac, Theresa, and their teenage daughters all "kept insisting that [he] should get married."

For both Isaac and Theresa marriage was an integral component of adulthood. Their own marriage reflected this view, and the dynamics of their relationship were shaped by a childhood and young adulthood in Promised Land. There marriage established the basis for economic, as well as emotional, independence. Al's bachelor life was not appropriate to his adult station. The adult enterprise was a cooperative one. Isaac, Theresa, and their daughters introduced Al to one young woman after another; and eventually the family pressures had a cumulative effect. Al's family introduced him to his wife, a young woman named Mary from Mississippi. She, like Al, came to New York City to escape the South. Their courtship was brief; and, as Isaac and Theresa hoped, "everything turned around" when they married. Al had order in his life.

Mary and Al both had steady jobs when they married, and both believed that a solid marriage was built on economic stability. This value they shared with Isaac and Theresa. Mary worked until their first baby was born. The birth of the baby was a significant moment in Al's life, for "then [he] became responsible." The new parents "had a bad experience" with a babysitter; and, when they were not able to arrange suitable childcare, Mary quit her job. The family's economic well-being rested squarely on Al's shoulders; and the birth of two more children removed Mary from the work force for quite some time, until all three were in school.

From the beginning Al's marriage was different from both his parents' and Isaac and Theresa's. Al's mother Lettie Moragne never worked outside her home and never had her own money, a common practice among Promised Land's subsistence farmers. Still, her work was defined in terms of her family's needs, and Lettie worked in the fields like most of the women of her generation. Isaac and Theresa followed a similar arrangement, with Theresa's work supplementing and complementing Isaac's. Both Lettie and Theresa balanced child care with economic obligations, adhering to a long-standing pattern among Promised Land women. Al and Mary diverged from this pattern when Al assumed sole responsibility for the family's financial stability and Mary for the care of the children.

Despite Mary's temporary retirement from paid employment, the younger Moragne marriage was "more equal" in other ways than Fred and Lettie's. In the elder Moragne's marriage the interpersonal balance of power was decidedly unequal, and to Al it was clear that, "as far as what my father did, it was alright with my mother." Isaac and Theresa followed a similar pattern in their relationship. The decision to move to the North was primarily Isaac's; once made, it was a decision which Theresa supported. Both Fred and Lettie and Isaac and Theresa adhered to a long-standing community precept that "in the family the man is the head" and the woman his cooperative and supportive partner. Even after they moved to New York City they followed this pattern, which was evident in Theresa's balance of financial and maternal obligations. Her labors were needed in both spheres of family life, and she was expected to devise a formula by which both needs could be satisfactorily met. Al and Mary did not follow this pattern, and theirs was a marriage in which "one hand watched the other."

The shift from the more traditional arrangements of his parents and his older brother was not an unwelcome one for Al. He held a certain progressive spirit about women's work and was undisturbed by the possibility "that with industries and other kinds of jobs [than domestic service] a woman can make more money than a man." The values Al learned as a child at Promised Land were basically unchanged, but he and Mary implemented these values in their own marriage in a style refined to suit the conditions of their urban environment. The children were her primary responsibility. In the absence of an older generation who would have helped the couple with their child care under other circumstances, the couple made an initial adjustment in their division of labor. Nevertheless, both believed that a working wife "makes it easier. That gives the opportunity for the woman to carry her weight and the man to carry his."

Although Theresa Moragne and Mary Moragne met their maternal obligations in different ways, both women were attentive and strict in their childrearing. The two families emphasized the traditional values and behaviors they had known as children, school and church, respect for parents, and following the rules set forth by propriety. All the children were told that "when they got grown the mistakes they made now was their own." There was no tolerance for misbehavior in New York any more than similar misbehavior would have been accepted at Promised Land. The premise was set forth in blunt and simple terms when Theresa told her children "I'm a busy person. I don't have time to go running to no jail." She spoke for all the adults, and the children listened.

Both New York City Moragne households went home to Promised Land regularly for annual visits. Their week in the South was always filled with visiting here and there, talking, joking, and going to revival. Theresa slipped down for visits more frequently than the others, taking a few days off "whenever [she] needed a rest" from the hectic pace in New York City. Just as regularly friends and family members from Promised Land came up to New York for visits. Community residents, particularly those who were not farming any more, adopted the notion of vacations; and they, too, found the time to travel. Cars, trains, and occasionally airplanes transported friends and family members north and south along the Atlantic coast. Emigration opened a new world for those who left Promised Land, but it also broadened the world of those who stayed there.

The Marshalls

Daymon Marshall, like most parents at Promised Land, raised his children with a strong sense of family unity as well as the other values which dominated and directed folks at Promised Land.[6] Although Marshall worked away from Promised Land during much of their childhood, he was careful to tutor his nine children in their own family heritage when he was at home. In the evenings he gathered the children "to sit by the fire and tell stories about all them folks who were gone" and about the way life used to be at Promised Land. "That's how we learned about all those peoples we didn't know." Daymon's mother Easter lived with the family in her old age, and she occasionally joined Daymon and her grandchildren by the hearth. Born in 1842, Easter recalled for them times even further past, although neither mother nor son kept alive the slavery days for the next generation. Easter Marshall, even in her eighties, remained a tall, slender, handsome woman with skin so fair that "she looked like a white woman." Together mother and son gave to the children a sense of family continuity.

The Marshall children learned two separate lessons from the stories they heard. Many of their aunts and uncles had moved away from Promised Land as young adults. As the children listened to Daymon and Easter's stories about the various relatives who were gone, they learned the importance of kinship bonds and the strength of those bonds, even when individual members of the family were separated by distance. They learned, as well, that life was not limited to Promised Land and that farming was not the only work Negroes could do. Both of Daymon Marshall's sisters moved away from Promised Land when they married. Ora, the oldest of Easter's children, married a blacksmith and moved to Hodges, South Carolina as the wife of a respectable and successful skilled craftsman. Daymon's younger sister Matilda also moved away from the community as a young adult. Her life was less successful; and, while the children heard stories about her childhood, they were told nothing about her adult circumstances. Dickie and Joe, Daymon's brothers, were also gone. Dickie lived in Greenwood. Joe was farming in Waycross, Georgia; and the difficulty of travel between the two rural settings prevented frequent visits. Daymon sorted out the lives of each aunt and uncle for his children, and as the stories unfolded the lives of the Marshalls were intertwined with those of their mother's family, the Martins. Their uncle Uriah Martin lived at Promised Land and farmed, as did their mother's sister Agnes Coleman; but the others were gone. Wayman Martin was in Waycross with Joe Marshall, and their aunt Mary Martin moved to Atlanta after she married Sam Wideman around 1910. As the children matured Daymon helped them implement the life alternatives he taught through his stories, and one by one the Marshall children moved away. Their migration from Promised Land spanned twenty-five years.

Herman and Tim Marshall, Daymon's oldest sons, were established in Baltimore during the 1920's. Both young men married women from Promised Land. Unlike their father, both took their wives north with them when they emigrated and established permanent homes in the city. The brothers then formed an anchor for the subsequent family migration, in much the same way that Josh Richie guided and directed the move to New York City for his nieces and nephews. As each of their sisters moved up to Baltimore, Herman and Tim helped them find work and housing and settle into a new way of life.

Mary Marshall was the first of the daughters to go north. Following her schooling in Atlanta, she returned to Promised Land only briefly. Herman "wrote home to ask how she was doing" and invited her to come to Baltimore. With Daymon's blessing she left the family and moved north. Mary's twin brother Dave was established farming in Abbeville County; and he stayed in the South; but her younger sister Lilly Belle followed Mary north as soon as she, too, finished high school in Atlanta. Neither Mary nor Lilly Belle had any difficulty adapting to life in Baltimore. The time they spent in school in Atlanta prepared them for city life, and they were immediately at home in Baltimore's urban environment. Mary, who remained single, supported herself by domestic work. Lilly Belle met and married a young man recently emigrated from Virginia, and after her marriage she alone among the sisters "just worked when she felt like it." The others enjoyed no such leisure. They "always got the type of husbands that you have to work."

Daymon Marshall's third daughter, Bessie, married a young man from home, James Price. They were childhood sweethearts and the marriage took place before Daymon could send Bessie to Aunt Mary in Atlanta for her turn in high school. Like her sisters, Bessie's route to Baltimore was circuitous. When James and Bessie married in 1934, they "was very, very young." Times were hard, and James went off to the ccc Camp in Augusta. Bessie followed him there, then returned to Promised Land and Daymon Marshall's house for the births of her two children. Unable to find steady work after a year in the camp, James decided to go on up to Baltimore, "for the same reason as everybody else—to make some money." With family already established in the city, Bessie had no objection to the move.

Following a familiar pattern, James Price went alone to Baltimore. Bessie and the children stayed in Promised Land with Daymon while Price found a job and housing for them. Six months passed, and Price "come back to Promised Land in a car" for his family. He and his brother Dave made the trip down together to take several sets of wives and children back north. "Three grown peoples was in the front seat, and two grown peoples and four childrens in the back" for the long drive north. The group "drove all night," carrying food with them and stopping along the way only for gas and sodas. They were all aware that travel through the South required skill and caution. Few places served Negroes, and Dave Price went along on the trip because "he knew where to stop for sodas and things for the childrens."

When they arrived in Baltimore, James Price took his family to their new home, "an apartment in a big old house on Oak Street." Bessie Marshall Price had never seen such a living arrangement. "There was so many peoples in that house. I wasn't used to that." Although she had lived in crowded conditions all her life, the crowd was always family and the setting rural. Like other northern cities, Baltimore was crowded with Negroes emigrating from the South. The ghettoized housing facilities were makeshift and haphazard.

Living conditions were further complicated by social instability. The combinations of people who were living together shifted constantly, and the situation was fraught with large and small personal conflicts. Matters that were private, or at least discrete, at Promised Land became the source of public gossip in the city. Conversations between neighbors focused on "who's going with this one? Who's going with that one?" The shifting alliances and romances served to "keep something going all the time." Bessie found the accommodations less than satisfactory and told James "if you don't find a decent place for me and my children I'm going home to my daddy." The family moved.

Daymon Marshall's wife, Lilly, died in the early 1930's; and he raised the children still at home by himself after her death. His daughter Lilly Belle made frequent trips home to Promised Land to visit and check on things after that, and when Lilly's younger sister Elnora was sixteen Lilly approached Daymon. It was time for Elnora to go north. Daymon was working away from home much of the time; and, with her mother dead, Elnora was left too often by herself. Daymon agreed that the situation was not the best and that Elnora would benefit from the move. Together father and daughter designed Elnora's future. She would return to Baltimore with Lilly Belle and her husband and finish high school there, just as the older girls had in Atlanta. Daymon felt he "could depend on Lilly because she was older," and Aunt Mary in Atlanta was getting too old for another Marshall teenager. Elnora went north with her sister at the end of revival week in 1938 and settled easily into the routines of city life. She enrolled in high school, made friends her own age, fell in love, and married at seventeen.

Like her older sister Bessie, Elnora was unprepared for the conditions of adult life she faced in the urban environment. She, even more than the older children, was raised in a household marked by dignity and serenity, for as he aged her father grew even more stern and serious. Daymon Marshall was a deacon at Mt. Zion, a prominent member of the Masonic Lodge until it collapsed, and a man with a great deal of self-respect. Elnora found herself in a radically different environment after she married. She and her husband were both young and, although married, were still economically as well as emotionally dependent on their elders. They lived with Elnora's mother-in-law. A baby came along within a year, and the young family was crowded into a single room of an already overcrowded house. "It was awful. They were different" from the Marshalls. As Elnora remembered her childhood in Promised Land, Daymon Marshall maintained a quiet but firm control over his household. When he issued orders, they were followed without question or argument. Elnora's married life in Baltimore contrasted sharply to her childhood. There were three adult children living at home; and "they used to talk back" to her mother-in-law with frightening regularity, behavior totally alien to Elnora. Arguments and quarrels between mother and children and between brothers horrified her. She "just wasn't used to that" and escaped the constant bickering only when she retreated to the small single room she shared with her husband and baby daughter. There she "closed the door" to shut out the angry noise and found a brief moment of tranquility.

At Elnora's insistence the young family moved to their own apartment. Her husband worked irregularly, however; and Elnora was forced to seek work herself to help support this marginal independence she valued. She turned to domestic service, and Lilly kept the baby. The marriage was never a solid one and eventually disintegrated under the stress of divergent backgrounds and contradictory values coupled with poverty and youth. The money Elnora earned from her domestic work was barely enough to pay her rent. Her sisters Lilly and Mary "just bought little things for the baby" and helped her as much as they could without encroaching on Elnora's already tenuous independence.

Elnora's dependence on her older sisters increased quite naturally under these circumstances, and more and more frequently she turned to Lilly for help and guidance. The maternal nature of the relationship between the older and the younger sister was one that evolved through a series of circumstances. Now their adult relationship was forged by the responsibility they shared for Elnora's daughter. Elnora left the baby with Lilly each morning and would "go get her at night" when she finished work. During that first winter of Elnora's forced independence, the baby had one cold and runny nose after another. Lilly said it was because the little girl was taken outside early in the morning and again after supper in the evening. Finally, in exasperation, Lilly proposed a new child care arrangement. She told Elnora: "Don't take this child away from here at night. You come and get her on the weekend." Elnora's dependence on Lilly included complete faith in her older sister's judgement. Although it was not what she wanted, Elnora agreed.

With the baby staying at Lilly's during the week, Elnora's life revolved around her work schedule. "Look like every job" she found required that she rise early in the morning and return home late at night. The realities of her life did not fit her private goals. She wanted the baby with her and missed the little girl. Nevertheless, she "had to go to work," and her daughter was in a far better situation at Lilly's house than she would have been with her mother. The weekend arrangement worked for a time, but soon Lilly once again raised objections with Elnora. The apartment was drafty, and Elnora failed to keep the baby on the feeding schedule Lilly maintained during the week. The child had two mothers.

When the war industries opened to Negroes, Elnora secured a steady job with good pay working on the assembly line at the Western Electric factory. As a new worker and a Negro woman, she was assigned to the swing shift; and her work hours became even less predictable than they had been when she did domestic work. Lilly told Elnora that the baby would be better off living in only one place, that she always came back after her weekend with her mother sick with a cold. Elnora was exhausted from working erratic hours and trying to meet her obligations to her daughter. Finally Lilly put her foot down and told Elnora to "just leave the baby here. And this is how the baby started staying with my sister. Lilly didn't have to work," and Elnora did.

When Bessie Marshall Price and her husband moved from the apartment in the old house on Oak Street, they purchased their own home. James "was working for the city at the time," and Bessie in a neighborhood laundry. Every day Bessie faced the same routine. She "came home all tired out and still had lots to do at home." James Price was a manual laborer during the day, but at night his life was more glamorous. He was a musician, a saxophone player in a band. Bessie, with two small children, a full-time job, and her own housework, had little time or energy for the type of fun James sought. Night after night he left the family to "go rehearse down in East Baltimore." Bessie objected and demanded of him "don't you have something to do in your own house besides running down to East Baltimore?" The attraction James found was more than a band. He had a girlfriend. The marriage which began with a wedding in Promised Land on Daymon Marshall's front porch exploded in the urban ghetto, and James "got his divorce over [Bessie's] head." Among the Marshall sisters, only Lilly's marriage withstood the stress of the city.

Herman and Tim did what they could to help their sisters. All of the Marshall children "lived in the same neighborhood, one of the finest" open to Negroes at the time; and the family gathered regularly for social events. The entire kinship circle occasionally piled into Herman's and Tim's cars and drove out to Sparrow's Point for a day of picnicking. The men got together to play cards from time to time, and the sisters met every Sunday morning for breakfast at Bessie's house before they went to church. All the Marshalls at Promised Land attended Mt. Zion. Each of Daymon Marshall's children was baptized there when they were infants. Now, after breakfast they attended church together in Baltimore, walking in good weather and riding in cars during the winter to the "little [A.M.E.] church over on Oak Street. Everybody there in that church was from Promised Land. Some Fraziers, some Carters, and some Moragnes was all members of that church." Despite troubled marriages and a myriad of economic and social problems endemic to Negro migration and urban life, family and church remained vital sources of personal comfort and support for Daymon Marshall's children.

Daymon Marshall died in 1939 at Promised Land, where he had been born fifty-seven years earlier. The children in Baltimore knew he was ill. Their younger sister Bertha was still at home, married to one of the Glover boys and farming. Bertha took care of her father, cooked for him and nursed him, and kept everyone in Baltimore informed of his condition throughout his illness. Without telephones, however, the details were outdated by the time Bertha's letters arrived. It was a frustrating situation for Marshall's children, and after much discussion the six brothers and sisters agreed that they must go home. All of them crowded into Herman's car and headed south to Promised Land, "just to check on our father's health."

All agreed that the trip would be a short one, for none except Lilly could afford to lose time from work. This, combined with the racial problems inherent in a drive across the South, dictated that they would drive straight through from Baltimore to Promised Land. It was winter, and "there wasn't no heat in the car." They "dressed up good and warm" and wrapped themselves in blankets. Still, the winter cold chilled all of them "down to our bones," and the trip was a miserable one. Perhaps they would have stopped for the night had there been a place which accommodated Negro travelers. In 1939 there were no such public facilities in the South, and the family drove on. Although they did not know it yet, their father was dead. "He died while we were driving home."

During the early morning hours they stopped somewhere in North Carolina for gas, chilled and exhausted. Their condition was immediately apparent to the white man who sold them gas, and he invited them into his store to warm themselves by the wood stove. They accepted the invitation, and while they savored the heat the man's wife "went and made us coffee." It was a small kindness, but one rarely extended by whites to Negroes. "Some white folks was just like that," but not many.

After Daymon Marshall died the only family member still living at Promised Land was Bertha. She had cared for her father throughout his illness and now, although married and herself the mother of a large family, wanted to be near her brothers and sisters. She was not in good health, worn-out from childbearing and farming. Two of her children died tragically: one from pneumonia following burns from the family's open wood stove while Bertha and her husband were out in the fields; and the other from a birth defect. The death of her father combined with those of her children and her own poor health made Baltimore seem an attractive and timely new beginning. Bertha Marshall Glover and her husband made their plans to move north systematically and thoughtfully. First they canned "enough food for a year, 'til we could get on our feet" and packed it in barrels for shipping on the train. They sent their household goods to Baltimore the same way, and the family followed their worldly goods in the old car. Once in Baltimore Bertha's husband found a job as a railroad yard hand, and they rented a house near the other Marshalls. More children were born; the house was too small; and they moved again, purchasing this home and settling into the routines of city life.

None of the Marshall children acquired great wealth after their move to Baltimore. Most struggled to merely "get by," to meet their bills, keep food on their tables, and prepare a future for their own children in turn. After Daymon's death they went "home for revival" less and less frequently; but, even in the late 1950's on their occasional trips down south, they traveled as they had for twenty years, packing enough food "to stop by the side of the road for dinner" and avoiding places they knew to be unfriendly. Herman, the oldest of the children, assumed responsibility for the taxes on his father's seven-acre tract of land and eventually gained title to it. When he died in 1957 his sisters "took him home to Promised Land on the train." He was buried there with the other members of his wife's family in the Crossroads cemetery; and, when his estate was settled, Daymon Marshall's land passed to Herman's widow. She sold the seven-acre tract without consulting any of the surviving Marshall children. After the land was gone "there just wasn't much reason to go back" to Promised Land any more.

The Urban Children

The families who moved north during the third generation, like those who went north before them, took few material resources. In this sense they were not greatly different from the hundreds of thousands of other impoverished and disheartened Negroes who escaped the rural South between 1930 and 1960. Their memories of the southland, a study in contradiction, were the heritage they carried north. From their life within the community they recalled the warmth and security of expansive and encompassing kinship systems. They also recalled the times they and their friends were forced from the sidewalks in Greenwood and endured stinging racial insults from white children their own age or even younger. A sense of impotence and anger blended with their memories of family, church, and community.

When they moved to the North, these members of Promised Land's third generation discovered a world which was, in a relative sense, far better than the one they left. Perhaps because many of them moved into transplanted and functioning kinship systems, they avoided the dislocations associated with the migration of atomized individuals or nuclear families. Even in the urban environments where they settled, they retained and restructured the social networks begun in Promised Land in the 1870's and rebuilt the community along city streets. The advent of widely available public and private transportation made frequent trips home possible. The availability of steady work and vacations with pay made the trips economically feasible. They were never thoroughly urbanized themselves; but they were satisfied in their new environment with the advantages, opportunities, and freedoms of city life. Most agreed that with the changes in the South Promised Land was not such a bad place and dreamed that "if I had plenty of money, could just sit down and do nothing, I would go back and build a home there." But for most, the closest reality to that dream was Homecoming every August.[7]

By the late 1950's the Marshall and Moragne grandchildren, some born down in the South and others in New York City and Baltimore, approached maturity, the first thoroughly urbanized generation in the Promised Land families. Their parents survived life in the cities as unskilled laborers and domestic servants. These urban children faced a destiny quite different from their parents' but influenced nonetheless by the traditional values of the Promised Land community. As much as their parents and grandparents, these youth were driven to "better their condition"; and all viewed education as the means to achieve that goal.

Isaac and Theresa Moragne's children went to college and entered the professions and white-collar management. Bessie Marshall Price's daughter married a soldier, lived for a time in Europe, and attended the University of Maryland's military extension there. Elnora Marshall Williams' daughter, raised by both her aunt and her mother, also went to college, became a grade school teacher, and married a man who owned his own successful business. Bertha Marshall Glover's children were also upwardly mobile—school teachers, nurses, correctional officers, and independent truck drivers. The others prospered in a similar manner. The children stayed in the city; and some eventually moved out to the suburbs. They visited Promised Land and found "everybody down there real friendly" if somewhat quaint.[8] Although they perpetuated the annual pilgrimages instigated by their parents, for most of these urban-born children, Promised Land was a distant memory of their childhoods or a phantom, talked about by an older generation in terms of extraordinary hardships and backbreaking manual labor. It was, in the end, a world of the past about which they knew little.

Epilogue

Me and her raised a heap of children. I thank the Lord now that I
seen them grown. I got thirty grans and a bunch of great grans.
Not all of them live around here, but they don't live too far. I have
two grandsons preaching, and I'm so proud. I thank you Jesus.
Augustus White, Sr. and Pearl Wideman White
Promised Land, South Carolina

The 1960's began more quietly at Promised Land than elsewhere in
the nation. The sit-ins and jail-ins, the freedom rides, demonstrations, and riots that marked the onset of the civil rights movement
were far removed from life "out there in that little colored community." Although the 1964 Civil Rights Act assured equality in voting,
education, and access to public facilities, it was several years before
the Promised Land community realized the benefits of the legislation. Martin Luther King was awarded a Nobel Prize in 1964. His
fame in Promised Land rested on his accomplishments closer to
home, the integrated bus system in Montgomery and the Selma
march. Malcolm X and Mrs. Viola Luizzo were assassinated in 1965.
The people at Promised Land remembered B. J. Glover's encounter
with the Klan of almost thirty years before more vividly.

Watts exploded in the summer heat of 1965 and the United States
Senate confirmed Thurgood Marshall's nomination as United States
solicitor general. There was also a demonstration in Greenwood
sponsored by the NAACP. When they went to Brewer High, the Promised Land teenagers all joined the organization, one of the appropriate things to do in the 1960's. Now they went into town and marched
around the square with the other demonstrators. Some white people
marched and others watched. The police attended, but after a time
the demonstration ended without fanfare, and everyone went home.
While riots and demonstrations continued through 1966 and 1967
and the demand for civil rights grew more strident, at Promised Land

"parents never taught us to be militant" and life proceeded at a more routine level. The community's centennial passed without public recognition but was marked by two events which recalled the past for the older folks: in 1967 the men and women registered to vote; and in 1970 the Greenwood County School Board closed the Promised Land School. The first event was a return to a proud tradition established during Reconstruction by the freedmen who settled the community. The second brought to a close a heritage inherent to community residence.[1]

Voting, Back to Verdery

When the first Promised Land residents walked together the three miles to the Verdery Post Office and cast their ballots during Reconstruction, they did so with a great deal of pride and not a little fear.[2] Over the years, although most were disfranchised, a few men from Promised Land continued to vote; and this heritage of Reconstruction was never entirely lost. The 1964 Civil Rights Act mandated voter registration of Negroes without discrimination or intimidation, but Greenwood County did not rush to comply. Like officials throughout the South, those in Greenwood County procrastinated as long as possible. The state, at that time, held a re-registration drive every ten years; and in 1967 there was a special emphasis on the registration of Negro voters.

That was also the year that Joe T. Ligon, Jr., the former Verdery postmaster, was appointed registrar for the Verdery precinct. In theory that precinct included Promised Land. Ligon was already known in the community. His family had owned some of the slaves who settled Promised Land in the 1870's. They had later employed various residents as sharecroppers and domestic servants, and Ligon himself had extensive contact with the community during his years as postmaster. Now he was charged with their registration. Joe Ligon felt a strong bond with Promised Land; and, in the tradition of the southern rural aristocracy, he also felt a responsibility for the welfare of the people who lived there. It was limited by his own perspective, but it was honest and forthright. The people at Promised Land were "backward, and they needed help" in his estimation. He intended to provide that help. Ligon went over to Promised Land and met with the community leaders. He "explained that it was necessary that they register [to vote] in order to become qualified American citizens." He explained the process of registration and urged them to come to Verdery the following week and register.

The people at the Greenwood County Courthouse were amazed that Ligon intended to take the voter registration books "out to that little colored community." Even the women assigned to assist him in the task protested that "we'll just be wasting time!" Ligon, however, was certain that they would not be wasting time. On a bright fall day in October 1967, he and the two women took the books to Henderson's Store in Verdery. Ligon sat on a bench on the porch so the folks from Promised Land could see him when they drove up. "The little town here was just covered with cars" from Promised Land. "Over a hundred came to register that day. We didn't even bring enough certificates," and some had to be turned away with the promise that Ligon would complete their registration as quickly as possible. He kept his word.

In South Carolina voter registration is nonpartisan and does not require a declaration of party affiliation. That aspect of political participation is accomplished through the Democrat and Republican Club meetings in February of each general election year. Ligon followed up his nonpartisan registration duties several months later, once again calling various leaders at Promised Land during January 1968. He advised them of the approaching club meetings. "I am a Democrat, and I contacted them with reference to the Democrat Club and told them they were welcome. I also made it plain to them that, if any were Republicans, they should contact the [local] Republican leaders about that meeting."

Roosevelt, Martin Luther King, and John F. Kennedy were all Democrats. Joe Ligon was also a Democrat. And most of the registered voters at Promised Land turned out for the 1968 meeting of the Democrat Club in their voting precinct. "They took it as a very important thing." At the first meeting in 1968, Promised Land rediscovered partisan politics and entered into it enthusiastically.

Ligon continued in his role as community benefactor, using as a vehicle his authority in the political system. It was his responsibility to appoint box managers for the voting precinct shared by the black people at Promised Land and the white people at Verdery. He appointed representatives from both communities to watch the ballot boxes and count the votes. At the general election in 1968, a century after their ancestors entered partisan politics, the people at Promised Land once again cast their votes at a racially integrated polling place. A century of violence against Negroes who attempted to exer-

cise their franchise made some from Promised Land uneasy that
year, and "Rev. Glover stood at the door so we know everything be
alright."[3] Two features distinguished election day in 1968 from earlier times: the voters at Promised Land cast their ballots for Democratic candidates rather than Republicans; and there was no violence.

After 1968 the voters from Promised Land were actively involved
in the local Democrat Club. In fact, they brought to the club meetings
a century-old community tradition, probably to the chagrin of some of
the white club members. At Promised Land every public gathering,
regardless of its purpose, begins in a formulary way, with a prayer
asking for God's guidance and blessing, a scripture reading appropriate to the purpose, and some songs. By 1970 the Verdery precinct
Democrat Club meeting opened with a prayer, a scripture reading,
and some spirituals, led by the Negroes from Promised Land. The
white club members prayed and sang with them.

A decade after the civil rights movement began the people at
Promised Land reflected on the events of the 1960's, admitting that
they "didn't know too much about civil rights." They added, however,
that the protests led by Martin Luther King, Jr. and the promises
made by the Kennedy brothers "wasn't no big secret either. Everybody who was connected with civil rights, they was knowing what
they was talking about." Voting was only one small part of a bigger
issue in the minds of the folk at Promised Land. From their own
historical perspective, they realized that "in World War II we learned
an overall lesson. You got to have an education" as a foundation for
other kinds of advancement. Many still remembered working for
"fifty cent a day, sun to sun," and knew that a decent job with a living
wage was equally as important as the franchise. "After civil rights a
man could start his own little business and not be attacked or beaten
for it." Most folk at Promised Land listened to Martin Luther King,
Jr.; and they "agreed when he said, 'You can kill the dreamer but you
can't kill the dream.' That's *right*." For a good many people at Promised Land that dream was being realized.[4]

Promised Land School v. The County School Board

The 1954 *Brown* decision affected education at Promised Land.[5] The
children got a new school. Mrs. Claretta Donaldson was appointed
principal, and she assumed the standard Lizzie Chiles bore before
her. For the local children some things were unchanged. They still

walked to school, and the rules which had governed student manners and demeanor for a century were still in effect. "The teachers knew the parents. If you were bad, the teacher gave you a spanking. If you told your mother, you got another one."

A major advantage of the community school was the close relationship it fostered between teachers and parents. Still, parents were forced to explain an unequal and unfair world to their children. School provided a vehicle for an explanation that the children could understand. "My mother would tell us how fortunate we were to be able to walk" to elementary school, while the white children rode through Promised Land in buses on their way to town every day. "She said the white kids *had* to ride the bus. She would just tell me that white folks don't know any better." The children were oblivious to the inequities—outdated textbooks, nonexistent libraries, overcrowded and understaffed classrooms. The result was a well behaved student body who found themselves woefully behind the white students when the schools were integrated.

The first children from Promised Land to attend integrated schools went "when freedom of choice came along" in the mid-1960's. It was a chance for a better education, and their parents sent them. One of the students recalled an encounter with a white classmate that "amused" her. "I was the only black one in all my classes. A white girl sitting behind me in math said 'Look. She can write!' Like I wasn't supposed to know how to write or anything." The source of her amusement was, not the racial insult, but the fact that the white girl "was so far back," so outmoded, in her ideas. Reflecting on the encounter, the girl from Promised Land observed that "we weren't taught like the black kids in town. They don't like white people." Parents at Promised Land invoked a higher authority in their childrearing, religion. She and her brothers had always been taught that "the Bible says we all are one. If you hate a white person, then you hate God."

School integration became an imposed reality for both black and white students in Greenwood County in 1970. The Supreme Court mandate could no longer be ignored. The Promised Land school doors closed for the last time in June 1970. At first the county intended to use the facilities as an integrated school for the elementary-aged children in that area of the county. "The white people in this vicinity were resentful that integration had become a reality" and declared that they would not sent their children to a school which had formerly "been for colored children and was located in a colored community."

The school board acquiesced to the pressure from the white parents and decided to close the school permanently, only fifteen years after it was built. Some of the other public schools were as much as fifty years old. Claretta Donaldson called on Joe T. Ligon, Jr. and enlisted his cooperation in an appeal to the board. She wanted the school kept open. Ligon agreed with the aim and joined her in the campaign. When their initial petition failed, the board began deliberations on the final disposition of the Promised Land physical plant. "It was suggested that [the school building] be used as a reform school for juvenile delinquents." The proposition horrified Mrs. Donaldson, Mr. Ligon, and everybody at Promised Land. "We got that stopped and even worse happened. It was suggested that the building be sold to some man who wanted to open a chicken farm." The school seemed, for a time, to be fated to become a chicken house. Everybody mobilized once again, and "we got that stopped too." The board was frustrated. They confronted the Promised Land delegation, headed by Donaldson and Ligon, and asked, "What do you want us to use that building for? You object to everything." Ligon explained that all concerned believed "it would be to the advantage of both the Promised Land and Verdery communities to maintain the school building as an educational facility." With that goal in mind a solution was found that pleased everybody. The County Headstart Program moved to the Promised Land school.

All the children at Promised Land boarded school buses and rode into Greenwood to begin the fall 1970 school year in fully integrated classrooms. The first thing they discovered when they began the term was that they were all academically behind their white classmates. One girl realized with a start that "I had never read a book. There were no books at home, and I never even thought about it." Fearing failure, "some kids didn't want to go [to school with the white kids]. They didn't think they could keep up." But, in keeping with established patterns, they helped and encouraged each other through that first year. Some "knew I would come out on top" by putting out the extra effort required to compensate for their deficiencies. "I had to work hard, real hard, but I didn't think I was a dummy." The year passed, and so did the kids from Promised Land. The initial culture shock of integration gave way to long hours of hard study and homework, and several years passed before the students realized the benefits of their extra effort. "By the time I got to Greenwood High I found new ways to do things. I got my point across." Advancement and self-improvement were life goals as potent to the youths of the fourth generation as they had been for their parents and their grandparents, redefined in new ways as circumstances altered and new possibilities for their lives emerged.

God Doesn't Change

Crossroads, Mt. Zion, and Jacob's Chapel were "the center of all the community" in the 1970's in much the same way as they had been for a century. Membership rates for all churches were high. Seventy-eight percent of the families at Promised Land attended church at least several times a month; only 10 percent of the community households claimed no church affiliation; and the other 12 percent of the families indicated membership in one of the three churches but irregular and sporadic participation.[6]

There was little realistic difference between being a Baptist or a Methodist at Promised Land. "It's mostly a matter of where your parents belonged. If they were Methodists, then you would most likely be Methodist; and, if they were Baptists, then you would most likely be a Baptist." Half the families divided their church loyalties between the two denominations, the result of marriages between Baptist and Methodist youths who, like their parents before them, refused to relinquish ties with a church that was second in importance only to their kinship bonds. Children from these households usually attended both churches, alternating weeks. Methodist wives often helped serve dinner at Baptist Homecomings and Baptist husbands were equally visible at Methodist events.[7]

Stewardship in the churches was defined in terms of collectively vested authority. There was general agreement that "the church is the center of the community, and *families* should have power within the church." Individuals drew on the strength of such ties to "spread whatever they want to be done [in the community] through the church. We come here to worship, but then we have to go out into the community for service." Churches, mandated by their congregations "to serve the community as one big family," executed their social responsibilities through the mechanisms established during the nineteenth century.[8]

One of the major vehicles for the fulfillment of this mandate was the Mt. Zion Missionary Society, which drew its membership from the church women. Similar organizations existed at both Crossroads and Jacob's Chapel. The society monitored the welfare of all church members, with particular attention to the old folks, a tradition maintained without interruption since the 1880's. There was still a standing fund, controlled by the society, "which they distributed to the needy"; and, when a family's house burned, as they still did even in the 1960's and 1970's, or when someone suffered a catastrophe, the Society moved immediately, "sponsoring special programs or taking up a collection" to help out and ease the period of crisis.[9]

In addition to emergency relief and assistance, the church also responded collectively to other types of needs, guided by the long-standing bonds between church and school at Promised Land. At various times in the community's history, the churches provided support for community-based education; and all made regular contributions to the Baptist and Methodist higher education funds. Now youths from Promised Land were going on to college in unprecedented numbers. Few of the older folk even completed the eighth grade, and the connection between education and decent work was clearly evident to everyone. As a consequence, postsecondary education was highly valued; and youths who continued their schooling after high school graduation evoked an intense pride within the entire community. This shared pride led to shared responsibility for a financial burden few families could afford. The church put on "programs for all the college students. The programs raise money. Then the church divides the money between all the students."[10]

All of the churches enjoyed a prosperity which reflected the general increase in community well-being. Regular church contributions averaged five hundred and fifty-seven dollars per family annually, almost 6 percent of the median family income of $9700. All three churches implemented building programs during the early years of the fourth generation, yet another indication of the extent to which the people at Promised Land were enjoying a resurgence of economic bounty. Crossroads began its expansion in 1962, intending to remodel the old log church which had served the community's Baptists for eighty-two years. The Willing Workers Club was charged with devising a plan to finance the project. Despite some advances in credit, Negro churches were still not able to secure commercial financing; and the club schemed and promoted the types of programs and events which traditionally had been used to raise money for community projects. After twenty-seven months of chicken suppers and fish dinners, the club met with the congregation in 1964 to announce that sufficient cash had been raised. A remodeling plan was devised in which the old log structure was completely encased in a solid and imposing new brick church, inextricably joining past to future. King David Baptist Church and Generositee Baptist Church sent their choirs to Promised Land for the Crossroads rededication, and The Little River Association provided the official greeting to the Baptists who came from all around the Piedmont countryside to share the pride of the new church. It was quite an accomplishment. Jacob's Chapel and then Mt. Zion followed with their own remodeling programs, both financed with the same strategy, dollar by dollar and "brick by brick."[11]

Modernization and changing social ideologies did not bypass Promised Land. The general sense of equality that had presided over church organization and activities for a century was tested when the women of Mt. Zion requested a locally popular woman evangelist as the guest preacher for the annual Mother's Day celebration in the mid-1970's. Their request evoked some heated discussion in the church regarding the propriety and effectiveness of women preachers in general. The pastor, taking a traditional position, was opposed to their suggestion. He justified his position by asserting that "I don't think God intended women to preach the gospel." The congregation held a contrary opinion. Men and women alike agreed that in principle sex had nothing to do with faith. One of the younger deacons spoke on behalf of equality of the sexes: "Once you accept Christ as your personal Savior . . . be you man or woman, then you have to use what you can to get the Word across." Some of the older men, holding more traditional views, moderated this notion of absolute equality between the sexes and suggested that "in the church or in the home, regardless of what they do, the women are supposed to be the helpmates to the men." And many of the women agreed with the principle of subordination to their husbands. "We stand back and let our men have their way, and we'll let *them* know whether we agree or not." Still, the traditionalism of separate spheres of authority for men and women, and the subordinate position of women in that separation, was offset by another belief, one shared by both men and women. "The women got to share God's Word. I don't care. Women preach. Men preach." The women invited their evangelist.[12]

Fire Departments, Beauty Contests, and Baseball

A renewed interest in politics was sparked by Joe T. Ligon's voter registration drive and subsequent recruitment of the Promised Land voters into the precinct's Democrat Club. The confrontation and qualified victory of the community over the county school board enhanced their sense of potential power, and residents began to survey their needs at Promised Land with a more critical eye. Some of the men were particularly frustrated with the high mortgage insurance rates they paid because Promised Land had no fire protection. They initiated an ambitious drive for a volunteer fire department in 1976. The Promised Land Community Organization became the vehicle for the project, supported and financed almost entirely by local resources.[13]

For two years people held ham raffles and fish dinners, the profits donated to the fire department. The Miss Promised Land Beauty Contest was designed to contribute to the fire department—the winner was the contestant who raised the greatest amount of money. The entire community organized a carnival. Eventually Greenwood County granted limited financial support for the project, but the bulk of the $50,000 necessary to buy and house equipment was generated directly through the efforts of the community.

The first fire truck the organization acquired was an aged and out of order engine donated by the county Department of Disaster Preparedness. Promised Land remodeled it and painted it and restored it to working condition. The second engine came to Promised Land from Shaw Air Force Base in Sumpter, South Carolina, government surplus bought at a bargain price and in working condition. Once the department was organized, the Greenwood Fire Chief agreed to provide training to the thirty-two volunteer firemen during the spring of 1977. The women organized an auxiliary and trained in disaster preparedness and first aid. They stand ready to follow the men where they might be needed within the ten mile radius that can receive assistance from Promised Land. The Promised Land Volunteer Fire Department is pledged to assist "black and white alike," an estimated two thousand residents. The fire department is activated by calling Thomas' Store at the crossroads. They sound the alarm and mobilize the volunteers.

The Promised Land Community Organization did not fade after the fire department was established. To the contrary, the group divided itself into committees to address other community needs. The Special Needs Committee oversees the elderly in the community, monitoring their health and well-being, intervening when necessary, helping out in other ways. The Special Projects Committee functions as a liaison between Promised Land and the world of county politics. Their central concern is obtaining water and sewage service from the county, a problem of some tenure for community residents. Although the county water and sewage lines run within a few miles of Promised Land, the county commissioners have resisted annual attempts by community residents to have the lines extended to Promised Land. Their second concern is voter registration. Little additional interest has been given to voter registration drives since Joe Ligon took the registration books out to Verdery in 1967. Like the water and sewage services, this local need too is largely ignored by county officials.

Activities within Promised Land promote the same collective spirit fostered by the Union Burrial Aid Society, the Masons, and the Mt. Zion Ladies' Aid. The Promised Land Community Organization leases a part of the Promised Land School from the county school board and maintains it for meetings, family dinners, and other community activities. The baseball field is still the home field of the Promised Land Black Sox, who now participate in the Greenwood County Adult Baseball League as well as their traditional contests with Bradley and other nearby Negro teams. The Scout troops lack neither children nor leaders. The Miss Promised Land Beauty Pageant was so popular and so well attended and supported that it has become a major annual celebration. Residents acknowledge a pressing need for a community center that will "keep the young people here" and an equally pressing need for representation on the Greenwood County Council. The sense of collective responsibility is matched by the ability of Promised Land to formulate and execute collective action. Like other communities, they are limited in scope; but rarely are they limited in vision.[14]

Land and Family

The land forms the basis of community life at Promised Land today as it has for a century, providing both a symbolic and material nucleus for all activities. By the 1960's the gradual changes that had been occurring throughout three generations of community life crystallized. Jimmy, the Greek's, subdivisions replaced the collective of farms, and the new shape of the community was clearly that of a residential suburb. The primary function of the land, to provide homes for Negro families, remains constant. Rows of neatly placed brick veneer homes, lawns seeded with grass, carports that shelter new cars, and streets crowded with tricycles and impromptu ball games stand where cotton fields and cane patches presided fifty years ago.

A "heap of people" once again live in Promised Land, three hundred families in the four-square-mile area. Ninety percent of them are descendents of first and second generation residents. In their own

adulthood they have decided to make Promised Land their permanent home, just as their parents and grandparents had before them.
For many, the considerations involved in reaching this decision are
familiar ones, influenced in part by an old grandmother who invoked
a timeless incentive: "I want to give my land to my grandchildren, *if*
they stay." Other factors also contributed to the complex equation,
because now land is available to Negroes, even in the deep South, if
they have the money. Job opportunities are far greater in the Piedmont than they have ever been, and education for their children is
less problematic than it was even during their own school years.
Many of the conditions which pushed their older relatives away from
Promised Land and into the urban North have moderated, if not
dissipated.[15]

Table 17.
*Distribution of Homes by Age, 1960 and 1970**

Construction Date	% 1960	% 1970
Pre-1900	8	3
1900–1925	9	4
1926–1940	15	6
1941–1950	13	5
1951–1960	55	22
post-1960	—	60
$\bar{X}$ Value of Homes	$4,297	$10,672

*Greenwood County Tax Assessor's Office, Promised Land Section, Greenwood
County, S.C., 1960 and 1970 Tax Assessments.

Twenty percent of these native children had moved away from the
community for a time. They lived either in other sections of the
South, primarily in small towns like Greenwood (population 40,000),
or in the urban North, no longer the Eden it was during the early
years of the twentieth century. When they came home, they bought a
lot from Jimmy, the Greek, or were given an acre or two of family
land. There they have settled down to raise their families in a place
where they are "among people who care and love one another." Only
ten percent of the 1970's community residents are total newcomers.
All of these families moved out of Greenwood. Promised Land is, for
them, "a decent place to live and raise their families."[16]

The households at Promised Land in the 1970's are for the most part quite conventional, a reflection of their nineteenth-century heritage. Eighty-three percent are nuclear families with both husband and wife present. Six percent are aging widows or widowers living alone after the death of their spouse. Many of their marriages spanned half a century. Another 10 percent of the families are multigenerational, always cases in which an adult couple has incorporated a widowed parent into their household, as Gipson Nash did his mother and Nathan Redd his mother-in-law in previous generations. Only 1 percent of the 1970's households at Promised Land are headed by divorced or separated women with dependent children.[17]

Families average 3.48 persons, slightly larger than the national average. Both the men and the women who head those families, either together as husband and wife or alone, are in mid-life. The men, whose average age is forty-five, are slightly older than the women, who average forty-one. Even those persons who live alone or are separated from their spouses are not in fact isolated. Most belong to an extensive kinship system, defined not necessarily in terms of spouse and children but in a way which includes parents, brothers and sisters, cousins, aunts, uncles, nieces, and nephews. There is always a willing ear to listen to a problem; and, "if you can't do something, there's always somebody who can."[18]

The land divisions at the beginning of the fourth generation surpassed those of earlier years. At the community's centennial the land had been divided into three hundred and eighty separately taxed tracts, averaging slightly more than seven acres each. Thirty percent of the tracts, all lots still owned by Jimmy, the Greek, are vacant. There is room for more families; and Jimmy sold a lot "every now and then" for three hundred dollars, triple his 1950's price. A few of Jimmy's lots are owned by people like Theresa Moragne in New York, who bought a little land from Jimmy when she was home visiting one summer, "just in case" she ever wanted to come home.[19]

The houses Lonnie Norman built after 1960 are as modern as any built in Greenwood; and they make a significant contribution to the overall increase in the value of taxable property at Promised Land, which jumped 250 percent between 1960 and 1970. Although the community remains racially homogeneous, as new people build homes it grows more diversified economically and socially. Old folks, 14 percent of the 1970's population, are "retired" and live in houses built at the turn of the century. They exist on tiny pensions, Social Security, and abundant gardens, with occasional help from the food stamp program. Their grandchildren, or sometimes even strangers, live less than one hundred yards away in new homes with fireplaces and built-in kitchens instead of wood stoves. During the winter of 1978 when an ice storm knocked out the community's power supply, most of the people who lived in the new homes with central electric heat moved over to their elderly neighbors' and enjoyed the warmth of the wood stove for a few days.[20]

Sixty percent of the employed adults work at Greenwood Mills, Parke-Davis, and in light manufacturing. They are the younger adults, men and women who matured and entered the labor force after Piedmont manufacturing and textiles employed Negroes in nonjanitorial positions. Some of them are now "boss men," joining a newly emerging rural Negro bourgeoisie. There are a few self-employed people in the community in addition to Lonnie Norman, the contractor, and Robert Evans, the electrician. W. A. Thomas owns and operates the store at the crossroads now; and there are two smaller stores and two night-spots, also owned and operated by community residents. There is a barber, a truck driver, and also a mechanic. One man operates a thriving fresh produce business, relying in part on family land to grow the vegetables he sells. Another 10 percent of the working adults are unskilled and construction workers. About 5 percent are professionals, primarily preachers; and another five percent are employed at clerical jobs, as retail salespersons and clerks; and 3 percent of the adults of working age are unemployed. The nature of work, more than any other aspect of community life, was radically redefined after the mid-1960's. This is as evident among employed women as it is among men. While 80 percent of the adult women are gainfully employed, less than one tenth of them work in traditionally "female" occupations—as secretaries, nurses, domestics, and seamstresses. Promised Land is no longer a farming community, although these grandchildren and children of community farmers have a strong consensus that the community "is a wonderful place to live and garden." Their gardens are abundant, but the mules are gone from the community, replaced by cars; and only families with five or six acres still keep hogs out back.[21]

The community expansion clearly evident at the onset of the fourth generation is balanced by an underlying tie with the past. There are still a few large landowners whose relationship to the land itself is strong and vital, who live in Promised Land "because we are able to farm our *own* land." For most, "the fellowship with our neighbors, closeness to relatives and church" are sufficient reason to stay in the community. It is still the land, however, which binds the generations together in a timelessness that defies the changes of a century. One old woman remembered that "my momma willed *this* land to me, like her daddy did to her, 'cause I stayed here. Now my grandchildren *all* get one acre, two acres. I give it to them." At Promised Land there is no more valuable inheritance. Among a younger generation, who "have always lived here and know most of the people," the tranquility of the countryside and nearness of their families are reason enough to make the community their home.[22]

Notes

Introduction

1. Carter Woodson, *The Rural Negro* (Washington, D.C., 1930), provides an imposing inventory of small rural all-Negro towns, most of them unincorporated residential
areas rather than suburbs or ghettoized attachments to urban areas. Guy B. Johnson,
Folk Culture on St. Helena Island (Chapel Hill, N.C., 1930); Elizabeth Ware Peterson,
ed., *Letters from Port Royal Written at the Time of the Civil War* (Boston, 1906); Willie
Lee Rose, *Rehearsal for Reconstruction* (Indianapolis, Ind., 1964); and T.J. Woofter,
Black Yeomanry (New York, 1930); collectively provide a comprehensive portrait of
the Negro Sea Island communities, establishing the relative cultural as well as
geographical isolation of the island inhabitants. These communities are as apart from
the mainstream of Negro life in the rural South as are George Hesslink's Negro
farmers in *Black Neighbors: Negroes in a Northern Rural Community* (Indianapolis,
1968); and William L. Montell's outlaws and misfits in *The Saga of Coe Ridge* (New
York, 1972).

2. The self-hatred hypothesis, thoroughly set forth in Kurt Lewin, *Resolving Social
Conflicts* (New York, 1948), generated a wave of empirical investigations. Representa-
tive of these researches are: Donald L. Noel, "Group Identification Among Negroes: An
Empirical Analysis," *Journal of Social Issues* 20 (1964): 71–84; R.D. Trent, "The
Relationship Between Expressed Self-Acceptance and Expressed Attitudes Toward
Negroes and Whites Among Negro Children," *Journal of Genetic Psychology* 91 (1957):
25–31; Gerald Engel et al., "An Investigation of Anti-Semitic Feeling in Two Groups of
College Students: Jewish and Non-Jewish," *Journal of Social Psychology* 48 (1958):
75–82; and J. Richard Udry et al., "Skin Color, Status, and Mate Selection," *American
Journal of Sociology* 76 (1971): 722–733. Documentations of the pathological conse-
quences of racial/ethnic oppression, in terms of both personality formation and antiso-
cial behavior, real or perceived through the cultural biases of the researchers, are
legion. See typically : Kenneth B. Clark, *Dark Ghetto* (New York, 1965); John Dollard,
Caste and Class in a Southern Town, 3rd ed. (New Haven, Conn., 1937); Abram
Kardiner and Lionel Ovesy, *The Mark of Oppression* (New York, 1951); Helen V.
McLean, "The Emotional Health of Negroes," *Journal of Negro Education* 18 (1949);
and Daniel P. Moynihan, *The Negro Family: The Case for National Action* (Washington, D.C., 1967). Most research in this area of social life focuses on minority group
responses to racial oppression in terms of pathology or deviation. This study of the
Promised Land community diverges from that tradition and assumes throughout that
the internal community structure, while stimulated by a context of isolation and
oppression by the dominant white society, represents the development of a separate

and parallel Negro social structure, a thesis clearly present in John Hope Franklin, *From Slavery to Freedom*, 4th ed. (New York, 1974), esp. 277–303; and C. Vann Woodward, *Origins of the New South*, rev. ed. (Baton Rouge, La., 1971), esp. 205–234.

3. A comprehensive definition of "community" is a task beyond the scope of this work. Helpful in formulating a perspective suitable to an analysis of Promised Land were: E.T. Hiller, "The Community as a Social Group," *American Sociological Review* 6 (1941); Albert J. Reiss, "The Sociological Study of Communities," *Rural Sociology* 24 (1959); Allison Davis and Burleigh Gardner, *Deep South* (Chicago, 1965); Hortense Powdermaker, *After Freedom* (New York, 1939); and Arthur J. Vidich and Joseph Bensman, *Small Town in Mass Society*, rev. ed. (Princeton, N.J., 1968).

4. See especially: Edward Magdol, *A Right to the Land* (Westport, Conn., 1977); Louis S. Gerteis, *From Contraband to Freedman* (Westport, Conn., 1973); Claude F. Oubre, *Forty Acres and a Mule* (Baton Rouge, La., 1978); and Leo McGee and Robert Boone, eds., *The Black Rural Landowner—Endangered Species* (Greenwood, Conn., 1979).

5. Magdol, *Right to the Land*, p. 70.

6. Ibid., p. 77.

7. Ibid., p. 125; Nashville, Tennessee *Daily Press and Times*, 11 August 1866.

8. W.E.B. DuBois, *Black Reconstruction in America* (1935; reprint ed., New York, 1973), pp. 392–396.

9. Steven Joseph Ross, "Freed Soil, Freed Labor, Freed Men: John Eaton and the Davis Bend Experiment," *Journal of Southern History* 44 (1978): 221; Magdol, *Right to the Land*, pp. 145–148.

10. Magdol, *Right to the Land*, p. 73. Some caution must be used in interpreting the overall effects of the contraband camps on long-range economic prospects and patterns for the Negro agricultural enterprise. These camps devised a strategy that predated the sharecropping arrangements commonly attributed to the southern post-1865 agricultural milieu. Freedmen received seed, fertilizer, and equipment from government sources at the beginning of the planting season and repaid their debt with a share of their crops at harvest. Thus the Army, not the southern planters, initiated the first sharecropping arrangements.

11. Magdol, *Right to the Land*, p. 93.

12. Norman L. Crockett, *The Black Towns* (Lawrence, Kan., 1979) provides a comparative analysis of several of the western towns. See also: William E. Bittle and Gilbert Geis, "Racial Self-Fulfillment and the Rise of an All-Negro Community in Oklahoma," *Phylon* 18 (Third Quarter 1957): 247–260; Kenneth Hamilton, "The Origin and Early Development of Langston, Oklahoma," *Journal of Negro History* 62 (1977): 270–282; Mozell Hill and Thelma Ackiss, "Social Classes: A Frame of Reference for the Study of Negro Society," *Social Forces* (1943), pp. 93–98; Edgar R. Iles, "Boley: An Exclusively Negro Town in Oklahoma," *Opportunity: The Journal of Negro Life* 3 (1925): 231–235; Daniel F. Littlefield, Jr. and Lonnie E. Underhill, "Black Dreams and the Town of Mound Bayou," *Phylon* 15 (Fourth Quarter 1954): 396–401; William H. Pease and Jane H. Pease, "Organized Negro Communities: A North American Experiment," *Journal of Negro History* 47 (1962): 19–34; Harold M. Rose, "The All-Negro Town: Its Evolution and Function," *Geographic Review* 55 (1955): 362–381.

13. Crockett, *Black Towns*, p. 186.

14. Woodson, *Rural Negro*, p. 127. For an overview of white political ideologies as they affected southern Negro life between 1877 and 1900 see especially Woodward, *Origins of the New South*, pp. 142–174, 321–349.

15. John Hope Franklin, "Mirror for Americans: A Century of Reconstruction History," *American Historical Review* 85 (1980): 1–14, calls for reassessments of

Reconstruction that transcend the "hoary myths" of the period and newly interpret "the regional experiences of freedmen, the freedmen confronting their new status, aspects of educational, religious, or institutional development, or phases of economic adjustment" (pp. 10–11). In complement, Ira Berlin, "Time, Space, and the Evolution of Afro-American Society on British Mainland North America," *American Historical Review* 85 (1980): 44–78, cautions against the development of meaningless generalizations of "Afro-American culture" that disregard the influence of specific geographical settings and time-specific historical conditions. Urban and rural, northern and southern stand as central and essential considerations in any examination of "the diverse development of Afro-American culture," which is as varied in development and configuration as white American culture. Without a consideration of these variations, studies of Negro life "are limited to the extent that they provide a static and singular vision of a dynamic and complex society" (pp. 77–78).

16. The rather loosely constructed stratification system which characterized Promised Land was evident as well at Boley, Oklahoma. Hill and Ackiss, in "Social Classes," explain the phenomenon, in the case of Boley, in terms of an "underlying egalitarian ideology" based on a common focus of whites as a homogeneous group. "The absence of whites provides . . . a sense of security which in turn facilitates social and general intercourse between the classes" within the community (p. 96). Interdependence, in turn, fosters a widely embraced sense of community pride.

17. Nineteenth-century Negro migration, and particularly the exodus of 1879, is well treated by Nell Irvin Painter, *The Exodusters* (New York, 1976). And Negro migration within a somewhat broader context is examined by George B. Tindall, *The Emergence of the New South* (Baton Rouge, La., 1976); and Carter G. Woodson, *A Century of Negro Migration* (New York, 1969). Early twentieth-century migration is variously examined by St. Clair Drake and Horace R. Cayton, *Black Metropolis*, rev. ed. (New York, 1970); Florette Henri, *Black Migration, Movement North, 1900–1920* (Garden City, N.Y., 1975); Louise V. Kennedy, *The Negro Peasant Turns Cityward* (New York, 1930); Clyde V. Kiser, *Sea Island to City* (New York, 1932); Emmett J. Scott, *Negro Migration* (New York, 1920); Nell Irvin Painter, *Hosea Hudson* (Cambridge, Mass., 1979); and Allan H. Spear, *Black Chicago* (Chicago, 1967). For a particularly clear statistical summary see Lionel C. Florant, "Negro Migration, 1860–1940," Carnegie-Myrdal Manuscripts, Schomberg Collection, New York Public Library.

18. C. Vann Woodward, *The Burden of Southern History*, rev. ed. (Baton Rouge, La., 1974), esp. 213–233. Also see Robert Browne, "Black Land Loss: The Plight of Black Ownership," *Southern Exposure* 2 (1974): 115.

Chapter 1

1. Abbeville, South Carolina *Press*, 6 July 1866 (hereinafter cited as *AP*). *Press* editor Hugh Wilson had no affection or toleration for things northern. He consistently wrote editorials which decried Negro suffrage, charged that the Union League was dominated by "artful and designing demagogues" (*Press*, 19 April 1867), and dismissed Negroes who affiliated with the Republicans and/or the League as "ignorant and deluded." The political polarization was clearly and concisely illustrated by one banner headline in the *Press* which declared: "THIS IS A WHITE MAN'S COUNTRY AND MUST BE RULED BY WHITE MEN," 17 April 1868. Despite *AP* claims to white rule, however, less than 60 percent of the registered white electorate cast a ballot in the 1867 election. They were overwhelmed by an 85 percent participation rate among the state's 81,000 registered

Negro voters. Joel Williamson, *After Slavery, The Negro in South Carolina During Reconstruction, 1861–1877* (Chapel Hill, N.C., 1965), p. 343, summarized Negro political participation between 1868 and 1878 by noting that "the overwhelming majority of adult, male Negroes exercised their suffrage in the Republican direction at every opportunity." Negro and Republican domination of the state's political machinery persisted until the 1876 general elections; and throughout the period of Republican rule there was violent, militant, and persistent objection to the regime by native white Democrats.

2. Fairfield, South Carolina *Herald*, 29 April 1868; W.E.B. DuBois, *Black Reconstruction in America* (1935; reprint ed., New York, 1973), p. 429. Francis B. Simpkins and Robert H. Woody, *South Carolina During Reconstruction* (Chapel Hill, N.C., 1932), pp. 93–94, judged the 1868 constitution, in retrospect, as "embodying some of the best legal principles of the age . . . as good as any other constitution the state has ever had, or as most American states had at that time." Despite the prevailing white belief that the constitutional convention was dominated by unlettered Negroes, many Negro representatives to the convention were involved in the teaching profession through their participation in the Freedman's Bureau schools throughout the state, and an equal number were ministers by profession. Williamson, *After Slavery*, p. 365 ff provides a detailed analysis of the convention's composition. See also Emily Bellinger Reynolds and Joan Reynolds Faunt, *Biographical Directory of the Senate of the State of South Carolina, 1776–1964* (Columbia, S.C., 1964), for additional information.

3. Wilson Nash and his family were enumerated in the 1880 Household Census Manuscripts, Smithville Enumeration District, Abbeville County, S.C. His political activities and involvements were reported in the *AP*, 11 September 1868. The attack was described in Bureau of Refugees, Freedmen, and Abandoned Lands, Letters Received (hereafter cited as Bureau Letters), vol. 6–8, DeKnight to Headquarters, 30 October 1868, South Carolina Department of Archives and History (hereafter cited as SCDAH).

4. See especially Bureau Letters, DeKnight to Headquarters, 5, 7, 8, 12, 16, 19, and 21 September and 2 and 7 October 1868. The frustration and anger accumulated since emancipation erupted in a series of violent interracial attacks in Abbeville during the fall 1868. Freedman David Jones was shot. Freedman Manfield Calhoun was lynched. Justice of the Peace J. S. Chipley, a white Democrat, refused to act on either incident and was removed from office. Wyatt Aiken, a white planter and prominent county Democrat, delivered a speech in the Abbeville city square "calculated to incite the crowd and create a disturbance in general" according to DeKnight. Freedmen George Matthews and Jeff Buchannan were shot in separate incidents, and two other Negroes were beaten in the city square. In his reports to district headquarters DeKnight declared that the condition of the county's freedmen was "worse than bondage . . . crimes are increasing daily. The freedmen are safe nowhere." As the local situation worsened and violence prevailed DeKnight wrote with increasing frustration, asking his superiors "Is there no help or protection for the freedpeople?" Indeed, there was little of either in Abbeville in the 1860's.

5. The Union League was first organized in Pekin, Illinois on 25 June 1862 as a grass roots home militia. At the close of the war the League, with extensive lodges already established throughout the North, moved south and served as the propaganda machine for the Republican party. It organized newly enfranchised Negroes into viable voting blocs. Meetings were cloaked in a web of secrecy, and members were frequently supplied with arms and drilled as militia units. By 1866 the League was well established in South Carolina and by 1867 had captured the majority of the Negro vote in that state. It was this organization that evoked the Ku Klux Klan attacks during

Reconstruction, although by 1870 the League's political potency was greatly diminished. See Austin Marcus Drumm, "The Union League in the Carolinas (Ph.D. diss., University of North Carolina at Chapel Hill, 1955). A recounting of the attack on Willis Smith is contained in U.S., Congress, House, *Report of the Joint Committee to Inquire into the Condition of Affairs of the Late Insurrectionary States*, H. Rep. 22, 42 Cong., 2d sess., 1871–1872, vol. V, pp. 1564–1566.

6. Bureau of Refugees, Freedmen, and Abandoned Lands, Reports, Orders and Circulars, DeKnight to Headquarters, 8 November 1868, SCDAH. One Negro was killed in the incident and four others injured. The politicization of freedmen during Reconstruction elicited violence and strained race relations throughout the South. Charles Nesbitt, "Rural Acreage in Promise Land, Tennessee," in Leo McGee and Robert Boone, eds., *The Black Rural Landowner—Endangered Species* (Greenwood, Conn., 1979), pp. 67–81, reported similar interracial tensions resulting from local freedmen's political involvement for the same period. In the Tennessee community Negro voters refused to approach polling places unarmed or alone.

7. For an excellent history of the commission's operations see: Carol R. Bleser, *The Promised Land, A History of the South Carolina Land Commission* (Columbia, S.C., 1969).

8. The death of the family patriarch, Samuel Marshall, prompted several attempts to dispose of the property. Neither of Marshall's sons was interested in farming. One was a physician in the village of Greenwood, the other a merchant in Abbeville. The first advertisement for the land appeared in the *AP*, 10 November 1865. A second notice appeared 30 October 1868. At that time the family sought to rent the property. The final attempt to dispose of the land publicly was made through the 12 November 1869 advertisement. The Marshall family was typical of many white landowners in their response to the post-1865 economic and social conditions. Faced with the dissolution of their traditional labor force, some planters simply abandoned agriculture and attempted to sell their land. For most the attempt was ineffective. Economic conditions precluded advantageous land transactions for sellers; land prices plunged as a function of oversupply. By 1868, however, the Freedman's Bureau was established in the up-country; and the Marshall family's attempt to rent their land was consistent with prevailing trends. The Bureau at that time was supervising a number of "gang-type" labor arrangements in the county, one indication that large-scale cultivation of entire plantations had resumed. See: Bureau of Refugees, Freedmen, and Abandoned Lands, Labor Contracts for Abbeville County, 1865–1868, SCDAH. One disadvantage the Marshall family faced in utilizing such labor was that their land was only partially cleared; and, with the established pattern of wages paid not in cash but in crop shares, generally one-third, most freedmen were probably reluctant to work the Marshall land. Additionally, the family lacked a supervisor. Thus, although the Marshalls faced typical problems with regard to their land, the solution derived was atypical; and the disposition of the land followed an unusual route. See especially Joel Williamson, *After Slavery*, pp. 99 ff, for a cogent discussion of the state's labor problems during Reconstruction.

9. J. Hollinshead to Governor Robert K. Scott, 3 November 1869, Governor Scott's Papers, SCDAH. It was the conflict between sound economic policy and political expediency that finally led to the corruption of the land redistribution program. In his 1871 Governor's Message Scott urged that the Land Commission pursue the business of subdivision and resale as speedily as possible and that the prices be established at a fixed rate. Only a few months later the fraudulent nature of the commission's operations was exposed to an enraged white public. See *AP*, 3 January 1872, for one example of press coverage of the "outrageous and enormous swindle" in which "hundreds of

thousands of dollars of the public funds have been wasted with no other result than to enrich a number of rapacious plunderers at the expense of the Public Treasury." Of course, the article failed to note that, while there was certainly fraudulent manipulation of public monies, there was also one positive aspect of the program, the advancement of Negro landownership.

10. A distinction is made here between "old" Abbeville County, a geographical and political unit which disappeared after 1897, and the contemporary county lines. In 1897 portions of Abbeville, Laurens, and Edgefield counties were partitioned to create Greenwood County. In that partitioning a portion of the Abbeville-Greenwood county line was drawn directly through the Promised Land community in such as way that the Negro population there was distributed rather evenly between two voting precincts, an obvious instance of nineteenth-century gerrymandering.

11. There is not complete agreement among former and present Promised Land residents regarding the boundaries of the community. Some prefer to exclude Moragne Town in their discussions and ascribe to that area an independent identity. Others disagree as to the southern boundary and do not generally recognize portions of the landholdings south of the east-west road, which merged into the White Hall area during the nineteenth century. This is an important point in the status differences which emerged during the years following settlement, and residents often described one or another of the families in terms of both the location of their homes—"not *really* in Promiseland"—and in terms of their church attendance—"but they went to Mt. Zion." Interview with James Evert Turner, 27 September 1979, Chicago, Ill. I have taken a broader view and defined Promised Land as all land encompassed by the original Marshall Tract and owned by Negroes. In this view Moragne Town is a subset of the community rather than an independent entity and is discussed in terms of status rather than geographical distinctions.

12. Interview with Cora Frazier Hall, 15 February 1978, Promised Land, S.C.; and Isaac Moragne, 14 September 1979, New York, N.Y.

13. Interview with Cleora Wilson Turner, 5 June 1978, Greenwood, S.C. On the matter of immediate postemancipation Negro mobility Samuel A. Stouffer and Lyonel C. Florant, with Eleanor C. Isabell and Rowena Wyant, "Negro Population Movements, 1860–1940," Preliminary Draft of a Memorandum Prepared for the Carnegie-Myrdal Manuscripts, n.d., Schomburg Collection, New York Public Library, note that migration from the South prior to 1910 was minimal, although there was a moderate degree of intraregional movement among the newly emancipated Negroes, typically a rural to urban drift. David H. Donald, *Liberty and Union* (Boston, 1978), is more emphatic in his summary of the immediate post-1865 population shifts, stating that "thousands of former slaves flocked to Southern cities where the Freedman's Bureau was issuing rations." Social services provided by the bureau combined with personal concerns as former bondsmen "set about to find husbands, wives, or children from whom they had been forcibly separated during slavery" (p. 186). Migration, in any case, was purposeful rather than random wandering. The role of kinship in Negro migration is an issue with broad implications, which extend over the whole of Afro-American history. See especially Carol B. Stack, *All Our Kin* (New York, 1974); and Herbert G. Gutman, *The Black Family in Slavery and in Freedom* (New York, 1976), esp. pp. 185–229; for discussions of the interplay between kinship bonds and motives for migration. The behavior of future settlers at Promised Land was wholly consistent with those patterns noted, for they were tied to the region through a complex network of kinship bonds and their own heritage as slaves.

14. Statutes at Large for the State of South Carolina, 1869, Act No. 186, 27 March 1869 set forth the legal stipulations for buyers of Land Commission farms.

15. Interview with John Hall, 1 December 1978, Promised Land, S.C. The names of the original purchasers are listed in: Secretary of State, Duplicate Titles A, pp. 249–277, SCDAH. Agricultural data are derived from : U.S. Bureau of the Census, 1870 Agricultural Census Manuscripts, Smithville and White Hall Enumeration Districts, Abbeville County, S.C. Family relationships were provided by George L. Wilson, Lettie Richie Moragne, Cora Frazier Hall, Elese Morton Smith, Benetta Morton Williams, Lilly Wimms Evans, Cleora Wilson Turner, and Balus Glover, all of Promised Land, S.C.

Farm production for these earliest settlers on the Marshall Tract farms during the 1870 census year revealed a distinct disinterest in cotton cultivation. Crops were equally divided between cotton, corn, and oats. The average ($\bar{X}$) corn yield was 47.8 bushels per household, and the cotton crop averaged ($\bar{X}$) 1.1 bales. Average ($\bar{X}$) value of farms was listed at $404, farm machinery at $6.20, and personal/household property at $282.11. Agricultural resources were minimal and counted as much in terms of human labor as in material assets. Half of these households owned draft animals, 78 percent owned at least one milk cow and/or hog. A pattern of subsistence farming, clearly evident in these data, was to be a persistent and dominant pattern of economic behavior for the entire community in the coming years.

16. C. Vann Woodward, *Origins of the New South*, rev. ed. (Baton Rouge, La., 1971), pp. 182 ff., provides an excellent overview of the difficulties small farmers faced during the 1870's and 1880's, particularly with regard to crop diversification.

17. Register of Signatures of Depositors in Branches of the Freedman's Savings and Trust Company, 1865–1874, Augusta, Georgia Branch, 23 November 1870–19 June 1874, showed savings accounts for Amanda Williams, her adult son Henry Williams, Charles Jackson, and the Redd family, all future purchasers of farms at Promised Land. Although the immediate postemancipation experiences of the first Promised Land settlers are largely a matter of speculation, these data suggest gainful employment away from agriculture for some. Others, like Wilson Nash, were probably surviving for the period between their emancipation and their move to Promised Land on rented farms or by even more direct labor-subsistence exchanges with white employers; a few of the original settlers obtained work for cash wages sufficient to begin minimal savings programs. Of equal importance is the indication from these savings patterns that there was among the first community residents an ideology of futurism and an ability to direct their behavior in such a way as to empirically realize personal goals and plans. These fundamental personality traits came to characterize much of the community's collective behavior as well as individual actions and in part account for the longevity of the Promised Land community.

18. Interviews with Cora Frazier Hall, 15 February 1978, Promised Land, S.C.; John Cole, 19 August 1978, Mt. Vernon, N.Y.; Ada Letman Wilson, 27 September 1979, Chicago, Ill.

19. Teachers' Monthly Reports, 1870, State Superintendent of Education, SCDAH; W. O. B. Hoitt to Governor R. K. Scott, 12 May 1869, Governor Scott's Papers, SCDAH; and *AP*, 13 and 14 May and 3 June 1870. White attitudes toward public education were varied and shifted from year to year. In general, there was opposition to racial mixing within the educational system; and the possibility of integrated schools was the focus of most of the white opposition to the education of Negro children. See especially, Mary Catherine Davis, "Ten O'Clock Scholars, Black Education in Abbeville County, 1865–

1870" (Paper, Department of History, University of South Carolina, 1978), for a cogent survey from the first Freedman's Bureau schools to the implementation of a common school system.

20. Reports and Resolutions of the State of South Carolina, 1869–1870, pp. 1061–1064.

21. *AP*, 20 January 1871. Hollinshead, a carpetbagger from Ohio, came to South Carolina as an Internal Revenue Service agent during Reconstruction. He also served for a time as the local agent for the Land Commission and was probably well known among the county's freedmen. He was elected to the state senate from Abbeville in 1870 and served one term.

22. Drumm, "The Union League," p. 186. Whether or not Henry Nash and Wilson Nash of Promised Land were related is not clear. Both were involved with the Republicans in county politics, both were Negroes, and both lived in the county. There is also a question as to whether either of these men were related to Beverly Nash, a prominent Negro legislator from Columbia during Reconstruction. There was some probability of a link between the three Nash men and Promised Land, however; for the property James Fields owned in Columbia was less than two blocks away from a lumber yard owned and successfully operated by Beverly Nash during Reconstruction.

23. *AP*, 23 February 1871.

24. Interviews with Rufus Nash, 27 May 1978, Promised Land, S.C.; Cleora Wilson Turner, 30 May 1978, Greenwood, S.C.; Cora Frazier Hall, 15 February 1978, Promised Land, S.C. There are few surviving details of the first community settlers among contemporary residents. Rarely does family or community oral history at Promised Land extend beyond three generations, and for the most part aspects of the third generation back are recalled only in hazy terms and with few details. Generally community residents emphasize the future rather than the past. This is in part a function of local childrearing practices which drew sharp distinctions between generations and limited communication between parents and children to instructional rather than narrative forms. None of the contemporary residents reported interactions with their parents at the informal level. Intergenerational exchanged focused on order and commands issued by the parents and obeyed by the children.

25. Interview with Cora Frazier Hall, 15 February 1978, Promised Land, S.C. This information was relayed as gossip to the interviewer. Land management strategies and financial matters are held as private family concerns at Promised Land and are generally not open to scrutiny by others in the community.

26. *AP*, 7 August 1872.

27. *AP*, 25 September 1872, 8 October 1873, and 8 April and 13 May 1874.

28. Interview with John Turner and Cleora Wilson Turner, 30 May 1978, Greenwood, S.C. The trend toward subsistence farming was a common one during the 1870's, explained by DuBois, *Black Reconstruction*, p. 75, in more global terms: "emancipation had enlarged the Negro's purchasing power, but instead of producing solely for export, he was producing to consume. His standard of living was rising." Although agricultural statistics for Reconstruction indicate an overall decline in production in the South, these data neglect the increase in subsistence production among freedmen like the Promised Land farmers. It was this subsistence production, as DuBois suggested, that offset the decline in cash crop production.

29. Interview with Cora Frazier Hall, 1 December 1978, Promised Land, S.C.

30. Secretary of State, Duplicate Titles B, n.p., SCDAH. The average ($\bar{X}$) size of the farms on the Marshall Tract was 48.14 acres. Final purchase prices averaged ($\bar{X}$) $3.24 per acre, a significant decline in price from the original $9.20 per acre contract costs. The Land Commission paid $10.00 per acre for the land and thus absorbed a loss in

excess of $18,000 on this single transaction. It was this pattern of fiscal mismanagement which led ultimately to the bankruptcy of the commission.

31. Interviews with Cora Frazier Hall, 1 December 1978, Promised Land, S.C.; John Turner and Cleora Wilson Turner, 30 May 1978, Greenwood, S.C.

32. *AP*, 17 June 1870. Both mills were renovations, not new structures. Cole's establishment was upstream of the Evans Mill, and the latter was more central to most Promised Land farmers.

33. Interview with George L. Wilson, 7 November 1977, Promised Land, S.C.

34. Direct Index to Deeds, Abbeville County Courthouse, Abbeville, S.C. This information had been lost to contemporary community residents, who commonly date the beginning of Mt. Zion from the erection of the first church building during the 1880's. The donor of the land, James Fields, was not known until the land records were examined.

35. Comments by Amos Wells, Sr., at Jacob's Chapel Baptist Church Meeting, 16 July 1978.

36. Interview with Cora Frazier Hall, 1 December 1978, Promised Land, S.C. The Red Shirts were active white Wade Hampton supporters. The Phoenix community was fraught with racial tensions, which erupted in a riot there on 8 November 1898. See Bruce Lee Kleinschmidt, "The Phoenix Riot," *Furman Review* 5 (Spring 1971): 27–31, for a discussion of the local conditions in the Phoenix community and details of the riot. The aborted invasion of Promised Land by this same group during the same period indicates the extent to which racial tension pervaded and dominated black-white interchanges in Abbeville County during the 1880's and 1890's. That the Promised Land community was able to insulate itself to some extent from these tensions is one indicator of community solidarity. Isolated Negroes in the county were considerably more vulnerable to attack.

37. Interviews with George L. Wilson, 30 March 1978; Balus Glover, 1 April 1978, both at Promised Land, S.C. The pattern of private education at Promised Land was consistent with other educational efforts among the freedmen. See especially: Bureau Letters, Farrow to Headquarters, 6 March and 15 May 1867, for two early cases in the district in which groups of freedmen generated cash and labor for independent educational facilities; ibid., Freedpeople to Headquarters, 8 August 1867, in which a group of freedmen from Due West, S.C. requested funds from the Bureau to supplement the small wages of a teacher they had employed for their children; ibid., Allen to Headquarters, 4 December 1867, containing a request for $200 to support another independent school in the county. Martin Abbott, *The Freedman's Bureau in South Carolina, 1865–1872* (Chapel Hill, N.C., 1967), p. 91, noted that these early educational efforts, whether supported in part by the Bureau or instigated and maintained independently by freedmen, were "concerned with substance and content, with moral maxims, and with promoting mental and social discipline . . . and often alien to the needs of children so recently come from bondage." Abbott's criticism that the schools lacked practical application and an orientation toward vocationalism seems to ignore the fact that this was largely learned by most Negro children through apprenticeship and the fact that the few months children spent in the schoolhouse until as late at the 1940's were a precious time for them. That was the only opportunity most would have for intellectual pursuits. By the age of twelve Negro children assumed adult labor responsibilities in the fields alongside their parents. Negro parents understood this fact in a way neglected by scholars, and their initiative in establishing and supporting schools for their children bears witness to the value placed on education by nineteenth-century Negroes.

38. U.S. Bureau of Census, 1880 Household and Agricultural Manuscripts, Smith-

ville and White Hall Enumeration Districts, Abbeville County, S.C. All subsequent demographic, agricultural, and household data are derived from these sources unless otherwise noted. Interview with Isaac H. Moragne, 14 September 1979, New York, N.Y.

Chapter 2

1. Interviews with Cora Frazier Hall, 1 Decmeber 1978; George L. Wilson, 30 March 1978, both at Promised Land, S.C. Statistical analysis of the 1880 agricultural census manuscripts established a strong relationship (r = +.70) between the number of laborers in a household and overall agricultural production. When agricultural production was correlated with available draft animals the statistical relationship fell to r = +.61, and based on the dollar value assigned by the census taker, the relationship between farm production and farm machinery was r = +.31. All three correlations were statistically significant (N = 40, p < .01). The real value of the correlation coefficient, however, lies not in statistical significance alone, for that figure is only an index of the reproducability, or reliability, or a relationship between variables. In the present case, it is equally important to examine the magnitude or strength of the relationship. This is most easily accomplished by the use of r², which represents the total variance in a dependent variable—agricultural production in this case—explained by independent variables: household laborers, draft animals, and farm machinery. The number of laborers in a household at Promised Land accounted for 49 percent of the variance in overall farm production, draft animal resources for 37 percent, and machinery for only 9 percent. Household laborers, then stand as the single best predictor, or criterion variable in this data set. Taken alone, however, household laborers still account for less than half of the total variance in farm production from one household to another within the Promised Land community in 1880. Analysis of these same laborers by age and sex might further increase the explanatory power of the variable, but the sample was far too small for reliable breakdown of these details.

2. Interview with John Hall, 17 March, 1978, Promised Land, S.C.

3. Interview with Sarah Price Robinson, 14 October 1979, Baltimore, Md. Ms. Robinson's observation is well documented and supported within the literature which addressed the plight of landless Negro farmers in the South. See especially: Theodore Rosengarten, *All God's Dangers* (New York, 1974), for an unusually graphic description of the situation. Sharecropper Nate Shaw aptly depicted the situation: "That white man gettin all he looking for, all he put out in the spring, gettin it all back in the fall. But what am I gettin for my labor? I aint gettin nothin." E.A. Schuler, "Social Status and Farm Tenure—Attitudes and Social Conditions of Corn Belt and Cotton Belt Farmers," USDA Farm Security Administration Social Research Report No. 4 (Washington, D.C. 1938); and H.A. Turner, "A Graphic Summary of Farm Tenure," USDA Miscellaneous Publication No. 261 (Washington, D.C. 1936); both provide empirical descriptions of early twentieth-century sharecropping. Judging from their data, there was little change in the circumstances of Cotton Belt tenants and sharecroppers for half a century. All illustrate the extent to which the sharecropping system was an entrenched aspect of southern agriculture, and one which maintained a static caste system in the rural South for more than two generations after emancipation.

4. Interview with Ada Letman Wilson, 27 September 1979, Chicago, Ill.

5. The household labor patterns at Promised Land were typical of the peasant strategy described by Louise Tilly and Joan Scott, *Women, Work, and Family* (New York, 1978), p. 47, as a "household mode of production." The entire household worked

together to sustain the family's equilibrium. Although a division of labor based on sex and age of available workers created relatively complex types of domestic social organization, at Promised Land as well as in Tilly and Scott's French and English families, "the family economy depended upon the labor of both husband and wife." The tendency for children to replace their mothers in the domestic labor force was a prevailing pattern in the Tilly and Scott cases as it was at Promised Land. See Tilly and Scott, pp. 134–136 for comparative European data.

6. A regression analysis of landowners and tenants living in Promised Land in 1880 yielded a simple linear relationship between number of acres cultivated by a household and number of laborers living in that household. Based on this regression the following table provides a model of cultivation potential based per size of household labor force:

Size of Labor Force	Tilled Acres per Household
1	10.60
2	16.68
3	22.76
4	28.84
5	34.92
6	41.00
7	47.08
8	53.16
9	59.24

These figures represent only the amount of land cultivated by human labor. Farmers able to combine the human resources at their disposal with draft animals and farm machinery were, of course, able to exceed these parameters. There was no effort to determine the extent to which various combinations of human, animal, and machine power affected overall cultivation. Manning Marable, "The Land Question in Historical Perspective," Leo McGee and Robert Boone, eds., *The Black Rural Landowner— Endangered Species* (Westport, Conn., 1979), pp. 8–9, estimated a somewhat lower worker-cultivated acres ratio of 7.5 acres per person for Negro farmers, 12.4 acres per person for white farmers, which fails to match the Promised Land model. Possibly the Promised Land farmers were somewhat better off than the "average" Negro farmer in 1880 but still less well equipped than the "average" white farmer.

7. Primus Letman and Cyrus Lites were selected systematically from the total population because they were typical of the two general types of land tenure. Data on their households were extracted from : U.S. Bureau of Census, 1880 Household and Agricultural Manuscripts, Smithville Enumeration District, Abbeville County, S.C.

8. Interview with John Hall, 17 March 1978, Promised Land, S.C.

9. Interview with Rev. B.J. Glover, 11 June 1978, Columbia, S.C.; and Ada Letman Wilson, 27 September 1979, Chicago, Ill.

10. Interview with Cora Frazier Hall, 1 December 1978, Promised Land, S.C.

11. The farmers at Promised Land, like other Negro farmers in the 1880's and 1890's, planted about half their tilled acres in cotton. Tenants and sharecroppers in the community replicated owner-operator cultivation patterns, a definite divergence from Marabel's data. He indicated that cotton crops constituted 60 percent of the total tilled land among landless Negro farmers. It is unlikely that the Promised Land tenants and sharecroppers were immune to the economic forces which fostered crop concentration in cotton. More likely, those pressures were overshadowed by the examples set for them by their landowning neighbors and kin.

12. Charles H. Wesley, *Negro Labor in the United States, 1850–1925* (New York, 1927), p. 228, notes that Negro agricultural laborers in South Carolina were the lowest

paid farm workers in the United States throughout the nineteenth century, averaging less than ten dollars a month in wages, without board. This impoverished condition was probably offset among the Promised Land farm laborers only by their youth and the possibility most had for some degree of upward mobility.

13. For landowners and tenants combined, the average ($\bar{X}$) cultivated acreage per person was 5.26 for all households. The Chileses' average of 3.5 acres per person was well below average and provides an index of the depth of their poverty. Subsistence acreage was not proportionate, however, to persons in a given household, as illustrated below:

Household Size	Subsistence Acres
3	20.39
4	21.97
5	23.55
6	25.13
7	26.71
8	28.29
9	29.87
10	31.45
15	39.35

These figures do not take into account the age of household members. It is assumed that this variation is distributed randomly within households and therefore accommodated in the regression.

14. These data were derived by subtracting the size of farms purchased from the Land Commission, as described in: Secretary of State, Duplicate Titles A & B, SCDAH, from the amount of acreage each landowner reported as "total acreage" in the 1880 Agricultural Census Manuscripts, allowing an arbitrary five acre plus/minus standard error. None had purchased additional land (Direct and Indirect Indices to Deeds, Abbeville County, S.C., Abbeville County Courthouse).

Chapter 3

1. All land exchanges in Promised Land prior to 1900 were extracted from the Direct and Indirect Index to Deeds, 1770–1905, Abbeville County Courthouse, Abbeville, S.C. Unless otherwise noted the following discussion of land transfers was documented through this source.

2. Landownership was a status which generated remarkable degrees of pride among former bondsmen and even small amounts of land gave rise to community-oriented land-use strategies. Charles Nesbitt, "Rural Acreage in Promise Land, Tennessee: A Case Study," Leo McGee and Robert Boone, eds., *The Black Rural Landowner— Endangered Species* (Westport, Conn., 1979), pp. 67–82, documented a similar type of community-centered philanthropy among a population of Tennessee Negro freeholders.

3. During the 1881 to 1890 decade, sales between kin dominated total land sales at Promised Land. In the following decade the pattern of sales changed in three ways. First, the size of tracts exchanged between kin increased dramatically, although the number of those sales decreased in proportion to total sales. The size of the tracts sold to nonkin also decreased; but the number of them, in proportion to the total sales, increased. Finally, the size of the tracts sold to nonkin was significantly smaller than other types (t>2.05, df=infinity, p<.01). The landowning class in the community

expanded rapidly during these two decades primarily because of the increase in small home lots, the result of the many nonkin and small kin-to-kin sales.

Type of Land Sales, 1881–1890	N	Size in Acres
Sales to Organizations	4	0.62
Sales Between Kin	6	9.70
Sales Between Nonkin	9	24.93
Sales by Whites to Negroes	2	21.15

Type of Land Sales, 1891–1900	N	Size in Acres
Sales to Organizations	0	–
Sales Between Kin	4	73.50
Sales Between Nonkin	23	10.85
Sales by Whites to Negroes	6	55.33

Rates of Land Sales by Type, 1880–1900

Type	1880's	1890's
Sales to Organizations	19%	0%
Sales Between Kin	28%	12%
Sales Between Nonkin	43%	70%
Sales by Whites to Negroes	9%	18%

(Sales to organizations not subjected to statistical analysis. For other sales, in binomial test, $z > 2.44$, $p < .01$.)

4. Estate of Wells Gray, Judge of Probate, Abbeville County Courthouse, Abbeville, S.C.

5. Interview with Ada Letman Wilson, 27 September 1979, Chicago, Ill. Mrs. Wilson, who is Primus Letman's daughter, went on to explain that the younger children did not receive gifts of land at the time of their marriages. There were more children than there was land to go around in the Letman household, and by the time the younger children married the legacy of ownership had disappeared from that family. It was this inheritance pattern which Robert Browne, "Black Land Loss: The Plight of Black Ownership," *Southern Exposure* 2 (Fall 1974): 112–121, suggested was responsible for the decline in Negro-owned farmland in the South. What Browne and others failed to consider was the impracticality of small-scale, family farms, which became less and less economically feasible with the decline of the cotton industry. The Letman land, while it passed out of the family, remained Negro-owned land put to nonagricultural use.

6. Interview with Burnice Evans Norman, 2 November 1979, Promised Land, S.C. This trend was far more common than the practice of transmitting land to elder children at Promised Land; and the reasons are common to agricultural settings dominated by small, family-farming operations. Two independent factors, operating in complement, create conditions favorable to younger heirs. First, children tend to be settled into adult roles sequentially, as they mature. Older children are established in independent economic positions long before fathers are prepared to relinquish control of their farms. At Promised Land these were generally sharecropping or tenancy. Younger children are thus entering adulthood as their parents approach old age and are the most logical ones in the family to assume responsibility for the care of aging parents as well as operation of the farm. In addition to this rather simple matter of chronology, the care of elderly parents often became the responsibility of younger children because they were the ones with the fewest obligations. In other Negro

communities, as observed by Hortense Powdermaker, *After Freedom* (New York, 1939), p. 199, children were often viewed by aging parents as a form of "old age insurance." This same role was ascribed to younger children in an eighteenth-century white agricultural community by Philip Greven, *Four Generations, Population, Land, and Family in Colonial Andover, Massachusetts* (Ithica, N.Y. 1970), pp. 94 ff. Greven explained that to the last child fell the responsibility for the care of aged parents. As a consequence, younger children tended to inherit the parental homestead and with it the responsibility for the surviving parent. This pattern, rather than Primus Letman's land partition or traditional primogeniture, dominated intergenerational land transmission at Promised Land.

7. The tendency at Promised Land to assist new residents in land acquisition was similar to a pattern of accommodation in colonial Andover where "townsmen were prepared to provide house lots and . . . land to newcomers who proved acceptable and wished to settle." Andover differed from Promised Land in one important way. There was not an artificially induced land scarcity. Nonetheless, the original land grants were carefully controlled; and this external limitation established conditions sufficiently similar for a comparison of the two communities on the matter of population control exercised by the residents themselves. See especially Greven, pp. 48 ff., for discussions of the variations in land utilization which emanate from different forms of land-granting in the establishment of communities. See also: Charles S. Grant, *Democracy in the Connecticut Frontier Town of Kent* (New York, 1961); and Richard L. Bushman, *From Puritan to Yankee: Character and Social Order in Connecticut, 1680–1765* (Cambridge, Mass., 1976); for contrasting land grant conditions and their effect on social structure. In Promised Land, as in Andover, the transmission of land to newcomers and to the second generation created multiple ties between households, extending the bonds of kinship and amplifying those relationships through a subtle network of economic interdependence.

8. Interview with Amos Wells, Jr., 1 July 1980, Anderson, S.C.

9. See especially: Norman L. Crockett, *The Black Towns* (Lawrence, Kan., 1979); John Hart, "A Rural Retreat for Northern Negroes," *Geographical Review* 50 (1960): 147–168; George Hesslink, *Black Neighbors* (Indianapolis, Ind., 1967); and Greven, *Four Generations*; for discussions of spatial and ecological aspects of town development.

10. Donald M. Scott, "The Popular Lecture and the Creation of a Public in Mid-Nineteenth-Century America," *The Journal of American History* 66 (1980): 791–809, noted that nineteenth-century Americans were "untiring inventors of cultural and educational institutions." The Americans who established homes at Promised Land appear to be no exception to Scott's generalization; and, as their community institutions became further refined, they incorporated many of the principles which Scott attributed to the Lyceum.

11. Interview with Rosalie Wilson Williams, 27 September 1979, Chicago, Ill. The occupational diversification at Promised Land mirrored a similar process which occurred throughout the larger Negro population. Charles H. Wesley, *Negro Labor in the United States, 1850–1925* (New York, 1927), described the entrance of a small portion of Negroes in all geographic areas into semi-skilled and skilled occupations and a concomitant decline in the proportion of the total Negro labor force employed in agriculture. Notably, carpentry, barbering, mining, and domestic service were the areas of greatest initial increase in this late nineteenth-century shift. Still, at Promised Land as elsewhere, Negroes who left agriculture for other work rarely advanced beyond service to other Negroes. Fortune Wilson and the men who served as mailmen were exceptions.

12. Interviews with Cora Frazier Hall, 15 February 1978; Elese Morton Smith, 5 November 1977; Benetta Morton Williams, 14 November 1977, all at Promised Land, S.C.; and Cleora Wilson Turner, 5 June 1978, Greenwood, S.C. Exactly how Fisher and Reynolds were able to retain their appointive positions at the post office in the face of a mounting lily-white movement within the southern Republican party and increasing alliances between white Democrats and Republicans based on their mutual goal of Negro disfranchisement is something of a mystery.

13. C. Vann Woodward, *Origins of the New South*, rev. ed. (Baton Rouge, La., 1971), p. 292. See also William Herman Patterson, "Through the Heart of the South, A History of the Seaboard Air Line Railroad Company, 1832–1950" (Ph.D. diss., University of South Carolina 1951), for a discussion of the economic considerations inherent to late nineteenth-century railroad expansion in the South. Woodward, pp. 379–384, summaried late nineteenth- and early twentieth-century political considerations of southern railroad expansion.

14. Woodward, *Origins of the New South*, p. 299; Interview with: Isaac H. Moragne, 14 September 1979, New York, N.Y. According to Roger Ransom and Richard Sutch, *One Kind of Freedom: The Economic Consequences of Emancipation* (New York, 1977), p. 196, approximately 79,000 Negroes migrated north from the Black Belt between 1880 and 1910, well before the onset of the Great Migration. Young Josh Richie was among them.

15. U.S. Bureau of Census, 1880 Household Manuscripts, Smithville and White Hall Enumeration Districts, Abbeville County, S.C. Interviews with: Cleora Wilson Turner, 5 June 1978, Greenwood, S.C.; Elese Morton Smith and Bessie Marshall Price, 15 October 1979, Baltimore, Md.

16. Mt. Zion Records, III (held by George L. Wilson, Promised Land, S.C.). Interviews with: Mattie Strong, 27 September 1979, Chicago, Ill.; Cora Frazier Hall, 15 February 1978, Promised Land, S.C.

17. Woodward, *Origins of the New South*, p. 365, asserted that "one of the most important developments in Negro history, not to say the history of the South, was the rise of a whole separate system of society and economy on the other side of the color line." The shape of this separate social order, complete with "churches, schools, banks, theaters, professions, services, and other institutions," was largely constructed at Promised Land within the first two decades of the community's existence. Interviews with: Cora Frazier Hall, 15 February 1978; and George L. Wilson, 30 March 1978, both at Promised Land, S.C.; Elese Morton Smith, 15 October 1979, Baltimore, Md.; and Ada Letman Wilson and Mattie Strong, 27 September 1979, Chicago, Ill.

Chapter 4

1. In Abbeville one of the earliest schools for Negro children was taught by Hattie and Sallie Ransom. These two sisters had no affiliation with northern benevolent societies and taught without pay from 1866 to 1868. Their efforts were soon supplemented by schools which the freedmen generated through their own resources. At Greenwood, Mt. Carmel, Due West, and the Abbeville Courthouse, schools were built, put into operation, and supported by unpredictable combinations of resources. In most of these cases at least half of the operating capital and all of the construction labor for the schools was supplied by the freedmen whose children attended them. Next to landownership education was almost universally regarded as an essential part of freedom. Optimistic beginnings, however, were frequently frustrated by the realities of poverty and the lack of qualified teachers, often only barely more literate than their

students during the 1860's and 1870's. Educational efforts were further inhibited during Reconstruction by the heavy labor demands families placed on their children, who worked beside their parents in the cotton fields more often than they attended school. Doors to the schoolhouses opened erratically, terms were brief, and material resources wholly absent from the classrooms where Negro children learned their letters and numbers. For conditions in Abbeville County see: Bureau Letters, vols. 1–4, Becker to Headquarters, 3 July 1866; Farrows to Headquarters, 6 March & 15 May 1867; Ransom to Headquarters, 12 April 1867; Freedpeople to Headquarters, 8 August 1867; Allen to Headquarters, 4 December 1867; Superintendent of Education, Teachers' Back Payment Claims, 1867–1868, Abbeville County, File #3–12; all SCDAH; *AP*, 2 August 1867, 28 January 1868. See Joel Williamson, *After Slavery, The Negro in South Carolina During Reconstruction, 1861–1877* (Chapel Hill, N.C., 1965), pp. 209–239, for a discussion of Negro education on a state-wide basis. Education, like organized religion, was first established among the Sea Island freedmen during the mid-1860's and then diffused toward the Piedmont during the following three to five years. The majority of the integrated schools were in Charleston; from the beginning of Reconstruction school facilities in the rural regions of the state were *de facto* segregated. See also: Henry L. Swint, *The Northern Teacher in the South, 1862–1870* (Nashville, Tenn., 1941); Sandra E. Small, "The Yankee Schoolmarm in Freedman's Schools: An Analysis of Attitudes," *Journal of Southern History* 45 (1979); Willie Lee Rose, *Rehearsal for Reconstruction: The Port Royal Experiment* (Indianapolis, Ind., 1964).

2. The Abbeville County superintendent of schools wrote to the state superintendent that the county had unpaid drafts in the amount of $5969: "In consequence of this, teachers are selling their claims at a heavy discount as they are compelled to live, . . . [and] the school interests in this county" are severely jeopardized. The discount was 40¢ on the dollar. (Superintendent of Education, Letters Received, Box 2, J. F. C. DuPré to J. K. Jillson, 20 November 1871.) Teacher Maggie Willson, a Northern import, was particularly angry with the situation and wrote bluntly to Jillson that "perhaps I am not entitled to a small pittance of the public school money as some lazy negro who is now teaching without a (certificate) . . . and if I had made out an account for negro children I would have got it all and perhaps more than I had applied for" (Superintendent of Education, Letters Received, Box 1, Maggie Willson to J. K. Jillson, 14 September 1869). Willson's racial slurs were not justified. Hattie and Sallie Ransom were teaching at the same time without pay, and their students were exclusively Negro children. The problem at this point in the Reconstruction education system was one of implementation. The first three years of the common school system in South Carolina were fiscally chaotic.

3. Teachers' Monthly School Reports, 1870, State Superintendent of Education; W.O.B. Hoitt to Governor R.K. Scott, 12 May 1869, Governor Scott's Papers, SCDAH; Mary Katherine Davis, "Ten O'Clock Scholars" (Paper, Dept. of History, University of South Carolina, 1978).

4. Abstracted from: U.S. Bureau of Census, 1880 Household Manuscripts, Smithville and White Hall Enumeration Districts, Abbeville County, S.C.

5. Interviews with George L. Wilson, 7 November 1977; Elese Morton Smith, 5 November 1977; Benetta Morton Williams, 14 November 1977, all of Promised Land, S.C.; and Cleora Wilson Turner, 30 May 1978, Greenwood, S.C. The underlying educational philosophy at Promised Land reflected no overt concern for industrial education, a fashionable and publicly acceptable approach to Negro education popularized first at Hampton Institute in the 1870's and then by Booker T. Washington at

Tuskegee Normal and Industrial Institute beginning in the 1880's. Perhaps because community education was initiated under both formal and informal church sponsorship rather than through the influence of northern philanthropic societies and perhaps because the first teachers in Promised Land were also community residents who apparently received their education as slaves on antebellum plantations, education at Promised Land reflected an orientation more commonly associated with the white elite. Although diluted by limited resources, the classroom emphasis nevertheless remained "academic." Industrial/vocational training came soon enough, usually in the local cotton fields. For a brief but incisive analysis of the emergence of the industrial education philosophy and its relationship to economic conditions of Reconstruction see Charles H. Wesley, *Negro Labor in the United States, 1850–1925,* (New York, 1927), pp. 192–223. Booker T. Washington popularized industrial education, and his educational philosophy is clearly set forth in his autobiography, *Up From Slavery* (Garden City, N.J., 1900).

6. Interviews with: Lettie Richie Moragne, 29 April 1978; and Mattie Brown Morton, 2 April 1978, both of Promised Land, S.C.

7. Interview with Cora Frazier Hall, 5 June 1978, Promised Land, S.C.

8. Miscellaneous Records, County Superintendent of Schools, 1898–1899, General Accounting Ledger, 1899–1900, Greenwood County Superintendent of Schools, Greenwood County Courthouse, Greenwood, S.C. Interview with Ada Letman Wilson, 27 September 1979, Chicago, Ill. Abbeville County was unable to locate any educational records for the Promised Land community.

9. Cash Book, School Funds Expenditures, Greenwood County, 1897–1950, Greenwood County Courthouse, Greenwood, S.C.

10. Interview with Elese Morton Smith, 5 November 1977, Promised Land, S.C.

11. Mt. Zion A.M.E. Church Records, vol. I, n.d. (held by George L. Wilson, Promised Land, S.C. (Hereafter cited as Mt. Zion Records). Wilson received the cloth-bound ledger book from his mother, Annie Wilson. The records for Crossroads Baptist Church were destroyed in 1948 when W.A. Turner's house at Promised Land burned. Turner was the church clerk at Crossroads. Throughout this discussion it is assumed that the Mt. Zion Records reflect general religious activities and processes within the community.

12. Jonathan P. Thomas to Judge of Probate, 26 December 1891, James Fields Probate File, Abbeville County Courthouse, Abbeville, S.C. See Joel Williamson, *After Slavery,* pp. 180–208, for a discussion of the establishment of organized religion among the freedmen in South Carolina. Segregation in this aspect of social life was interpreted by Williamson as a withdrawal by the freedmen from white institutions, an assertion supported by the extensive support among the state's Negro population for African Methodism. At Promised Land, as elsewhere, the establishment of churches designed exclusively for Negroes was one of the first visible steps taken by emancipated Negroes toward the establishment of an independent and overtly separate cultural system.

13. For interesting and readable histories of African Methodism see: Daniel Alexander Payne, *History of the A.M.E. Church* (Nashville, Tenn., 1891); George A. Singleton, *The Romance of African Methodism* (New York, 1952); Charles Spencer Smith, *A History of the A.M.E. Church* (1922; reprint ed., New York, 1968); and for a biography of the A.M.E. church's first bishop see Charles H. Wesley, *Richard Allen, Apostle of Freedom* (Washington, D.C., 1935). The A.M.E. church maintained its long tradition of political involvement in its Reconstruction activities in Abbeville. See especially *AP,* 2 October 1868, in which A.M.E. minister N. E. Edwards published an open letter arguing

that the ultimate salvation for the county's freedmen lay in their affiliation with radical Republicanism and urged their support for Wilson Nash's candidacy for public office.

14. Joel Williamson, *After Slavery*, p. 369.

15. Instances of ecological centralization of effective Negro churches in urban areas clearly illustrate the importance of propinquity in the solidification of church leadership roles within the Negro community or residential setting. See John T. O'Brien, "Factory, Church, and Community: Blacks in Antebellum Richmond," *Journal of Southern History* 44 (1978): 509–536, for an analysis of the use of church-based relationships for the implementation of political power within a Negro community. See also the *Atlanta Constitution*, 13 January, 26 February, 13 April, and 3 December 1882, for a recounting of church relocations into the geographical center of Negro residential areas and the subsequent power gains accomplished by church bodies in local politics. For the urban churches ghettoization strengthened and solidified church power and influence within the community. The same principle explained the power role of the church organizations at Promised Land.

16. Augustus White, Sr. at the Mt. Zion Meeting, 6 June 1978; interview with John Hall and Cora Frazier Hall, 5 June 1978, Promised Land, S.C.

17. There are a number of versions of the church division in the community's oral tradition, most of them rather vague. The membership of each church claims primacy. The only records which document the schism are the land sales by Fields and Gray. The matter of doctrinal disagreement was recounted by James Evert Turner, 20 August 1978, Chicago, Ill. His story, as told to him by his father, aptly fits with the land transfer records and is selected here as the more accurate of the several versions. All information on the founding of Crossroads Baptist Church was extracted from notes of Cynthia Nash (deceased), Promised Land, S.C. Crossroads Baptist Church Rededication Service (printed church program), 22 November 1964; "Cross Roads Baptist Church at Promised Land Rededicated," Greenwood, S.C. *Index-Journal*, n.d. All of this material was provided by Rufus Nash, Promised Land, S.C.; and he holds the original copies. Interview with Mattie Brown Morton, 5 November 1977, Promise Land, S.C.

18. Interview with Ada Letman Wilson, 27 September 1979, Chicago, Ill.

19. Interview with Azzalie Moragne Jones, 10 April 1979, Atlanta, Ga.

20. Mt. Zion Records, I, 17 September 1889, 1 October 1889.

21. Anonymous Interview, Promised Land, S.C.

22. Mt. Zion Records, I, 18 and 25 May 1980.

23. Mt. Zion Records, I, 22 January 1890. When the new Mt. Zion building was erected in the 1950's, the benches were replaced by standard commercially manufactured pews. Some of the old benches were removed to Crossroads where they were used in the recreation hall for additional seating. Others found their way into private homes. The construction plans were sound, for the benches have been in continual use now for almost a century.

24. Mt. Zion Records, I, n.d.

25. These topics are clear in the general ideology they address, incorporating elements of morality, self-discipline, individual enterprise and upward mobility. Although the yeomen at Promised Land were not capitalists in the sense employed by Max Weber, *The Protestant Ethic and the Spirit of Capitalism* (New York, 1958), they adhered to many of the tenets of the Protestant ethic. They lacked the resources and opportunity to expand their farming enterprises or to reinvest that capital which they did accumulate; and many chose, alternatively, to invest in their community instead through support of churches and schools. The "talks, essays, and orations" which

marked special church events were a form of public oratory popular in other nineteenth-century social contexts and can be viewed as a grass roots version of the public lecture. See especially Donald M. Scott, "The Popular Lecture and the Creation of a Public in Mid-Nineteenth Century America," *Journal of American History* 66 (1980): 791–809.

26. Mt. Zion Records, I, n.d.

27. Interview with Ada Letman Wilson, 27 September 1979, Chicago, Ill.

28. Ibid. Interview with Rosalie Wilson Williams, 27 September 1979, Chicago, Illinois.

29. Interviews with John Hall, 5 June 1978; Lilly Wims Evans, 17 August 1978; and Burnice Evans Norman, 2 November 1979, all of Promised Land, S.C.

30. A variety of sources detail the political potential of the Negro and the decline of that potential. See especially: C. Vann Woodward, *Reunion and Reaction: The Compromise of 1877 and the End of Reconstruction* (Boston, 1951); and William A. Mabry, *Studies in the Disfranchisement of the Negro in the South* (Durham, N.C., 1933), for overviews. From the Negro perspective see August Meier, *Negro Thought in America, 1880–1915* (Ann Arbor, Mich., 1963). And for an analysis unusual for its economic emphasis see T. Thomas Fortune, *Black and White: Land, Labor, and Politics in the South* (New York, 1884). The literature of Reconstruction generally deals with the decline of the Negro's position, which is also discussed in several state studies. See: Vernon Wharton, *The Negro in Mississippi* (Chapel Hill, N.C., 1947); Albert D. Kirwan, *Revolt of the Rednecks: Mississippi Politics, 1876–1925* (Lexington, Ky., 1951); Helen G. Edmonds, *The Negro and Fusion Politics in North Carolina* (Chapel Hill, N.C., 1951); Frenise A. Logan, *The Negro in North Carolina, 1876–1894* (Chapel Hill, N.C., 1964); George Brown Tindall, *South Carolina Negroes, 1877–1900* (Columbia, S.C., 1952); and Robert E. Martin, *Negro Disfranchisement in Virginia* (Washington, D.C., 1938).

31. Interview with Cora Frazier Hall, 5 June 1978, Promised Land, S.C. Voter Registration Lists, Smithville Township, Abbeville County, S.C., 1897 showed thirteen Promised Land men, all landowners, still active on the voter rolls.

Chapter 5

1. Particularly useful is C. Vann Woodward, *The Strange Career of Jim Crow*, 3rd ed. rev. (New York, 1974), which demythologizes the tradition of segregation. See Hugh Davis Graham and Ted Robert Gurr, *Violence in America* (New York, 1969), for a comprehensive analysis of interracial violence; and Arthur Raper, *The Tragedy of Lynching* (Chapel Hill, N.C., 1933), for specific analysis of lynching as an extralegal mechanism of social control.

2. Various aspects of Negro economic activity are discussed by: Charles S. Wesley, *Negro Labor in the United States, 1850–1925* (New York, 1927); and W.E.B. DuBois, *The Negro in Business* (Atlanta, Ga., 1899), provides a detailed analysis of Negro business at the turn of the century. Banking and insurance within the independent Negro economy are detailed in: Abraham L. Harris, *The Negro as Capitalist* (Philadelphia, Pa., 1936); and William J. Trent, *Development of Negro Life Insurance Enterprises* (Philadelphia, Pa., 1922).

3. Studies representative of early twentieth-century southern Negro culture include: Allison Davis and Burleigh Gardner, *Deep South* (Chicago, 1965); Allison Davis and John Dollard, *Children of Bondage* (Washington, D.C., 1940); Charles S. Johnson, *Growing Up in the Black Belt, Negro Youth in the Rural South* (Washington, D.C.,

1941); Hortense Powermaker, *After Freedom* (New York, 1939); and Arthur Raper and Ira De A. Reid, *Sharecroppers All* (Chapel Hill, N.C., 1941). In addition to these general overviews two of the Atlanta University Studies directed and edited by W.E.B. DuBois are useful in detailing the charitable and self-help aspects of Negro culture for the period: *The Negro Common School* (Atlanta, Ga., 1901); and *Some Efforts of American Negroes for Their Own Social Betterment* (Atlanta, Ga., 1898). Carter Woodson, *A History of the Negro Church* (Washington, D.C., 1945); and E.N. Palmer, "The Development of Negro Lodges in the United States," Carnegie-Myrdal Manuscripts, n.d., Schomberg Collection, New York Public Library.

4. For various treatments of southern agricultural economics and Negro farmers see: Charles S. Johnson, "The Economic Status of Negroes," Summary and analysis of materials presented at the Conference on the Economic Status of the Negro, Washington, D.C., 11–13 May 1933, under the sponsorship of the Julius Rosenwald Fund (Nashville, Tenn., Fisk Univeristy Press, 1933); Leo McGee and Robert Boone, eds., *The Black Rural Landowner—Endangered Species* (Westport, Conn., 1979); and H.A. Turner, "A Graphic Summary of Farm Tenure," USDA Miscellaneous Publication No. 261 (Washington, D.C., 1936). E.A. Schuler, "Social Status and Farm Tenure—Attitudes and Social Conditions of Corn and Cotton Belt Farmers," USDA Farm Security Administration Social Research Report No. 4 (Washington, D.C., 1938), provides a straightforward analysis of rural social life.

5. The Great Migration has been extensively examined. For representative work see: Florette Henri, *Black Migration, Movement North, 1900–1920* (Garden City, N.J., 1975); Louise V. Kennedy, *The Negro Peasant Turns Cityward* (New York, 1930); Clyde V. Kiser, *Sea Island to City* (New York, 1931); and Carter Woodson, *A Century of Negro Migration* (New York, 1970).

6. Charles Mangum, *The Legal Status of the Negro* (Chapel Hill, N.C., 1940); and Bernard Nelson, *The Negro and the Fourteenth Amendment Since 1920* (Washington, D.C., 1946), provide discussion of the legal struggles for equity. See Wesley, *Negro Labor*; and Raymond Wolters, *Negroes and the Great Depression* (Greenwood, S.C., 1970), for discussions of economic conditions in the 1920's and the impact of those circumstances on Negroes.

7. Philip J. Greven, Jr., *Four Generations, Population, Land, and Family in Colonial Andover, Massachusetts* (Ithaca, N.Y., 1970), p. 177, suggested that a population density of fifty persons per square mile constituted "crowded" conditions in a farming community. He further argued that the demographic history of a community provides one index of the degree to which that setting is "more favorable to life and fecundity" than comparable settings. The Promised Land population more than tripled between 1880–1897, an increase in resident households far greater than might be expected by the natural process of maturation of first generation children. Probably 50 percent of the new households were immigrant families, further supporting Greven's favorability of life hypothesis. Charles Nisbett, "Rural Acreage in Promise Land, Tennessee: A Case Study," in Leo McGee and Robert Boone, eds., *The Black Rural Landowner*, p. 64, documented similar population growth in a Tennessee Negro community. He attributed that growth to a combination of two factors: the prestige of landownership and occupational opportunities. Rates of landownership increased more rapidly in Nisbett's Tennessee population than at Promised Land, perhaps as a function of greater opportunities for wage labor among that Negro population and hence more capital to use for land purchases. Although comparison of the two communities has an obvious element of speculation, availability of employment was clearly a powerful attraction to Negroes among all the generations after Emancipation and may in part account for the pockets of Negro population increase, such as the steady if gradual proportionate

increase of Negroes in urban areas. Still, the cumulative nature of the variables, in the case of Nisbett's population and the Promised Land community, suggests that land acquisition was held in greater relative importance than wage-producing employment.

8. This and later references to twentieth-century land transfers in the community were abstracted from the Grantor-Grantee Land Sales Indices, 1897–1930, Greenwood and Abbeville Counties, S.C. Only the owners of tracts larger than twenty acres were included in these data, that size constituting the minimum subsistence farm (See chap. 2, n. 12). Whether the tracts were sold intact or partitioned was secondary to prevailing kinship bonds between buyer and seller.

9. Interview with John Hall, 5 June 1978, Promised Land, S.C.

10. Interview with George L. Wilson, 7 November 1977, Promised Land, S.C.

11. By the turn of the century the westward migration subsided; and, from 1890 through the early 1900's, the greatest Negro population movement occurred intraregionally, from rural to urban areas within the South. See U.S. Bureau of Census, *Historical Statistics of the United States, Colonial Times to 1957* (Washington, D.C., 1960); Dean Dutcher, *The Negro in Modern Industrial Society: An Analysis of Changes in the Occupations of Negro Workers, 1910–1920* (Lancaster, Pa., 1930); Wesley, *Negro Labor*; Samuel Stouffer and Lionel Florant, "Negro Population Movements, 1860–1920," Carnegie-Myrdal Manuscripts, n.d., Schomberg Collection, New York Public Library; and Louis Ferman, Joyce L. Kornbluh and J.A. Miller, eds., *Negroes and Jobs* (Ann Arbor, Mich., 1968), especially pp. 53–65, for economic interpretations of this population change. Kiser, *Sea Island to City*, provides an excellent case study of the interplay between social conditions and Negro migration trends. Scholars of Negro migration have tended to de-emphasize the problem of land scarcity in favor of more overt factors. See Greven, *Four Generations*, for an analysis of the important role which land and the lack of land plays in intergenerational migration patterns from another land-based community. In many ways the Promised Land freeholders more closely resemble Greven's white colonial landowning population than they do landless Negroes.

12. Tax Auditor's Duplicate Books, 1897–1942, Greenwood County Courthouse, Greenwood, S.C. Land rarely lay completely idle, and there were a number of informal uses to which it was put. A friend or relative was often given permission to use a specific plot of land for farming or pasturage and with that privilege incurred responsibility for upkeep of the taxes. Such "abandoned" land was not rented out for profit. The exchanges were quite equitable and derived through mutual need.

As an additional note, although there were no formal mechanisms within the Tax Auditor's Office for indicating absenteeism, the auditor made handwritten notes to the side of each entry in the ledger. In cases where a landowner was not living in the community the notation was usually "gone" or "away." When available to him, the auditor included additional information: "Baltimore," "Philadelphia," "Washington,"—and a few times, even a secondary mailing address where the tax notice was to be sent. These were generally "c/o" a current community resident. A detailed examination of the Auditor's Duplicate Records revealed no systematic notation system, however; and for that reason no attempt was made to further interpret these informal notes.

13. Jacob and Harriet Burton, and Washington Perrin Estates, Judge of Probate, Abbeville County, S.C. Willis Smith Estate. Judge of Probate, Greenwood County, S.C. There were no probate records for the Wilson Estate. The Wilson land was surveyed and partitioned in 1910 although some of Joshuway Wilson's children, particularly his eldest son Fortune, were in possession of their tract well before the turn of the century.

The 1910 action was recorded in Plat Book 1, pp. 181–182 and 184, Tax Assessor's Office, Greenwood County, S.C. The original surveyor's drawings by Thomas C. Anderson are filed in the law offices of Ayres and Anderson, Greenwood, S.C. James C. Anderson's kind assistance in providing access to his grandfather's surveyor files is gratefully acknowledged.

14. At the turn of the century an estimated one-third of all Negro agriculturalists were sharecroppers, and the plight these young couples faced was not at all unusual. See U.S. Bureau of Census, *Historical Statistics*, pp. 11–12, 278–279. C. Vann Woodward, *The Origins of the New South*, rev. ed. (Baton Rouge, La., 1971), pp. 318–320, provides illustrative per capita wealth statistics which aptly place these people at the lowest strata regionally as well as nationally. George B. Tindall, *The Emergence of the New South* (Baton Rouge, La., 1967), pp. 391–432, provides further contextual analysis of the prevalance of tenancy in the Cotton Belt. It was a condition of life for some three million Negroes and five and one-half million whites, in all 25 percent of the southern population.

15. Interview with George L. Wilson, 7 November 1977, Promised Land, S.C. This phrase is used throughout conversations with contemporary community residents to denote families with whom there is no current contact. It is an important clue to a broader world view prevalent at Promised Land. Families are not necessarily lost when they move away; but, for those who do dissolve into distant urban centers, there is no active attempt to recover them nor is there a negative connotation attributed to the loss of contact. It is accepted as inevitable for some and is most common among people who did not thrive and prosper after they left the community. There is no gossip about such failures.

16. The fate of the Wilson family after the death of Joshuway Wilson was compiled from a variety of sources: U.S. Bureau of Census, 1900 Household Manuscripts, Smithville Enumeration District, Greenwood County, S.C.; interviews with George L. Wilson, 7 November 1977, Promised Land, S.C.; and Cleora Wilson Turner, 30 May 1978, Greenwood, S.C.

17. Mary Burt Estate, Judge of Probate, Greenwood County, S.C. The resale of the farm by Henderson to Carter was traced through the county land transfer records.

18. Calvin Moragne Estate, Judges of Probate, Abbeville and Greenwood Counties, S.C. In some cases lands which originally lay within the boundary of Abbeville County were intersected by the 1897 Abbeville-Greenwood county line, or landowners held tracts in both counties. In either case, the records of the estate probate were filed in both counties. Moragne's son William (Will) Moragne established a permanent home in Honea Path, S.C., a small village approximately ten miles northeast of Promised Land. There he and his wife Lela, both schoolteachers, were active members of the Baptist Church. They retained contact with Promised Land through Will's mother Amelia and by their affiliation with the Little River Association. Lela Moragne was the organist. The couple were probably models of the effect which education and secure nonagricultural employment afforded those who chose to remain in the South. Will and Lela Moragne drove a bright red roadster, which was the envy of every youngster at Promised Land. Lottie Belle Brown, 11 September 1979, New York, N.Y.

19. Elias Harris Estate, Judge of Probate, Abbeville County, S.C.

20. Beverly White Estate, Judge of Probate, Greenwood County, S.C.

21. Marshall Morton Estate, Judge of Probate, Greenwood County, S.C.

22. Because both Wilson and Moriah Nash divested themselves of their land holdings prior to their separate deaths, there are no records probating their estates. The land transfers between husband and wife as well as between mother and children are in the Direct and Indirect Index to Deeds, Clerk of Court, Abbeville County, S.C.

23. William Moragne's land transactions are recorded in the Clerk of Court, Abbeville County, S.C.

24. W.A. Turner's land acquisitions are recorded in the Clerk of Court, Abbeville County, S.C.

25. The notion that wives survived their husbands, while true nationally, did not apply to the Promised Land population. Based on the cemetery markers, which indicated date of death, and crosstabulating with dates of birth as listed in the 1880 manuscript census, shows that those persons who survived childhood, whether male or female, had unusually long lives. There were no significant differences between male and female life spans with the exception of those born between 1881 and 1900. For that group men did live significantly longer than women (t = 1.91, p < .01). Those born before 1865, however, were the cohort transmitting property during this period; and for that group both men and women had unusual longevity. There are no reliable data on Negro life expectancies prior to 1900. Data for the twentieth century reveal a much higher life expectancy for the Promised Land population than for either Negroes or whites on a nationwide basis. U.S. Department of Commerce, *Bicentennial Statistics* (Washington, D.C., 1976), p. 379.

Promised Land Life Tables, 1864-1930

	pre–1865	1865–1880	1881–1900	1900–1930
Male				
N	17	10	20	17
X̄	73.0	63.9	64.1	48.0
s	24.9	22.8	21.4	13.5
Female				
N	12	11	16	12
X̄	72.5	64.0	50.7	51.0
s	13.3	11.9	20.3	18.7

26. Interview with Agnes Martin Coleman, 4 December 1978, Greenwood, S.C. Credit, like land transmission, is generally considered to be a private matter at Promised Land. One's finances are guarded information and not often open to public examination. There are no surviving records for any of the community stores, and apparently what bookeeping existed there was quite informal.

27. An interpretation of the Cotton Reduction Act and its impact on the South Carolina cotton industry can be found in: *Eleventh Annual Report of the Commission of Agriculture, Commerce, and Industry of the State of South Carolina* (Columbia, S.C., 1914), pp. 141 ff.

28. *Eleventh Annual Report of the Commission*, pp. 117 ff. See also George B. Tindall, *Emergence of the New South*, pp. 33–40, for a discussion of the 1914 Cotton Crisis in a regional and national context.

29. Interview with Cora Frazier Hall, 5 June 1978, Promised Land, S.C.

30. Ibid. *The Crisis* 13 (1914): 67. Cora Hall recalled the Crawford lynching in great detail. Her mother, Mary Frazier, was in Abbeville on the day Crawford was lynched and reported the details to her children when she returned to Promised Land. Doubtless, Mary Frazier told the other adults in the community as well. The story was later verified in the *Crisis* lynching reports. (Interestingly, Cora Hall's recollections of the period did not include a community celebration for the 1913 Year of Jubilee, the 50th anniversary of emancipation, an event celebrated in other Negro communities.) In *The Crisis* report of the incident Crawford was described as a farmer "reputed to be worth $20,000" and owning "427 acres of the best cotton land" in Abbeville County. He was

significantly more prosperous than anyone at Promised Land. Of particular importance is Mrs. Hall's assertion that it was violence rather than economic incentive which stimulated Negro migration from Abbeville County after 1915. See: St. Clair Drake and Horace Cayton, *Black Metropolis* (New York, 1945); and Allan H. Spear, *Black Chicago* (Chicago, 1967), for discussions of the urban "pull" which complemented the variously defined rural "push." For a specific examination of the period see: U.S. Department of Labor, *Negro Migration in 1916–17* (Washington, D.C., 1919); *The Crisis*, vol. 13–14; Henri, *Black Migration*, pp. 49–80.

31. Interview with Cora Frazier Hall, 5 June 1978, Promise Land, S.C.

32. Crawford's assailants were later tried in the Abbeville Court. Susan Page Garris, "The Decline of Lynching in South Carolina, 1915–1947" (M.A. thesis, University of South Carolina, 1973), p. 104, noted that the Abbeville *Scimitar*, "a rabidly Bleasite sheet, was in the minority in demanding an acquittal for those charged with the death of Anthony Crawford."

33. For discussions of the fluctuation in cotton prices and the impact of that on Negro farmers see: Charles S. Johnson, Edwin R. Embree and W. W. Alexander, *The Collapse of Cotton Tenancy* (Chapel Hill, N.C., 1935). For specific year by year discussions of the cotton industry in South Carolina see: *Annual Report of the Commissioner on Agriculture, Commerce, and Industry of the State of South Carolina* (Columbia, S.C., 1904–1932). Although cotton prices varied by region and by type, the list below reflects trends in the prices of up-country cotton. For national statistics by decade see *Bicentennial Statistics*, p. 390. National cotton prices were consistently several cents per pound greater than prices paid for cotton in the South Carolina Piedmont. The farmers at Promised Land sold their cotton locally, and their economic fate rose and fell with the up-country prices.

Up-County South Carolina Cotton Prices, 1898–1926

Year	Price per lb. (cents)	Year	Price per lb. (cents)
1898	4.9	1914	12.0
1902	8.2	1915	
1903	12.2	1916	24.6
1904	8.6	1917	31.0
1905	10.9	1918	32.9
1906	10.1	1919	25.6
1907	11.5	1920	17.2
1908	9.2	1921	21.0
1909	14.3	1922	21.0
1910	14.7	1923	26.7
1911	8.8	1924	23.1
1912	12.2	1925	22.1
1913	13.4	1926	13.9

34. Tindall, *Emergence of the New South*, pp. 60–61.

35. Interview with John Hall, 5 June 1978, Promise Land, S.C.

36. Ibid. Interview with Bessie Marshall Price and Elese Morton Smith, 15 October 1979, Baltimore, Md. Picking cracked cotton was a common activity in the late fall practiced by landowning households as well as tenants and sharecroppers. It was a task relegated to women and children. Because of the poor quality of this cotton it had little value and could be converted to cash only with intensive labor. Cleaning was slow and time consuming, and the job was usually assigned to the children.

37. Tindall, *Emergence of the New South*, pp. 60–61.

38. Interviews with Cora Frazier Hall, 5 June 1978, Promise Land, S.C.; and Pearl White Riley, 27 September 1979, Chicago, Ill. The 371st was led by white southern officers. It joined the 186 Brigade of the 93rd Infantry Division which was reluctantly loaned to the French fighting forces with an official admonition from the United States government to the French military commanders. They were to restrict and control fraternization between Negro troops and French women. The men of the 371st participated in the 1918 fall offensive against Germany, but the unit was recalled from German territory following a barrage of German racist propaganda. None of the 124 men in the regiment awarded the Distinguished Service Cross or the Croix de guerre were from Promised Land. Discharged in 1919, the men from Promised Land returned to civilian life along with the other Negro soldiers with a meager two month discharge bonus of $60. For a general analysis of Negro soldiers' participation in World War I see Arthur E. Barbeau and Florette Henri, *The Unknown Soldiers* (Philadelphia, Pa., 1974), especially pp. 111–136, for a discussion of the 93rd Division's French tour. See also: Percy E. Deckard, *List of Officers of the 371st Regiment* (Allegany, N.Y., 1929); Chester Heywood, *Negro Combat Troops in the World War* (Worcester, Mass., 1928); Monroe Mason and Arthur Furr, *The American Negro with the Red Hand of France* (Boston, 1920); Emmett J. Scott, *Official History of the American Negro in the World War* (1919; reprint ed., New York, 1969); and W. Allison Sweeney, *History of the American Negro in the Great World War* (Chicago, 1919).

39. Interviews with John Turner, 30 May 1978, Greenwood, S.C.; and Mattie Strong, 27 September 1979, Chicago, Ill. Mattie Strong insisted that all the Moragne men were skilled in some type of work other than farming. Their grandfather, Abbeville planter Pierre Moragne, insisted on this. "The Moragnes were carpenters, bricklayers, and stone-layers—those three trades. The old man saw to that." Among the second generation Moragnes there were an unusually large number of professionals as well, teachers and preachers.

40. Interviews with John Turner, 30 May 1978, Greenwood, S.C.; and Mattie Strong, 27 September 1979, Chicago, Ill.

41. Interviews with Cleora Wilson Turner, 5 June 1978, Greenwood, S.C.; and Jim White, 24 August 1978, New York, N.Y. U.S. Bureau of Census, 1900 Household Manuscripts, Smithville and White Hall Enumeration Districts, Greenwood, S.C.

42. Interview with Lilly Wims Evans and Burnice Evans Norman, 17 August 1978, Promised Land, S.C.

43. Interviews with John Turner, 30 May 1978, Greenwood, S.C.; and Lizzie Wims Nash, 27 May 1978, Promised Land, S.C. The boll weevil invaded Texas in 1892 and then began a steady progression eastward across the Cotton Belt. The weevil first penetrated South Carolina in 1917 and by 1921 had reached the Sea Islands. The attendant crop destruction was particularly devestating for small farmers. See: Rupert Vance, *Human Factors in Cotton Culture* (Chapel Hill, N.C., 1929); Arthur Raper, *Preface to Peasantry: A Tale of Two Black Counties* (Chapel Hill, N.C., 1936); and T.J. Woofter, *Black Yeomanry* (New York, 1930).

44. Interview with John Turner, 30 May 1978, Greenwood, S.C. Tax Auditor's Duplicate Books, 1897–1932, Greenwood County, S.C.

45. Interviews with Lilly Wims Evans, 27 May 1978, Promise Land, S.C., Jim White, 24 August 1978, New York, N.Y.; and John Turner, 30 May 1978, Greenwood, S.C.

46. John Turner, 30 May 1978, Greenwood, S.C.

47. Cora Frazier Hall, 5 June 1978, Promise Land, S.C.

48. Cleora Wilson Turner, 5 June 1978, Greenwood, S.C.

49. Interviews with Azzalie Moragne Jones, 10 April 1979, Atlanta, Ga.; Elese Morton Smith and Benetta Morton Williams, 14 November 1977, Promised Land, S.C.;

Balus Glover, 6 November 1978, Promised Land, S.C. "Loaning children" or transferring the responsibilities of childcare from one adult to another was a relatively
common practice among early twentieth-century Negroes and was not limited to
Promised Land residents. See also Kiser, *Sea Island to City*, p. 154 for, a similar
description of the practice. The extent to which this is an extension or modification of
earlier fictive kin adaptions common during slavery is an unexplored issue. The
similarities are striking. See especially Herbert G. Gutman, *The Black Family in
Slavery and in Freedom* (New York, 1976), pp. 154, 197, 216–227, for various descriptions of slavery-related fictive kin behaviors. Both strategies blurred the lines of
kinship and established overlapping and reciprocal rights and obligations between
generations. Both were responses to human needs challenged by economic exigencies.

Chapter 6

1. All references to 1900 household and occupational structure were derived from
U.S. Bureau of Census, Household Manuscripts, Smithville and White Hall Enumeration Districts, Greenwood County, S.C. and Smithville Enumeration District, Abbeville County, S.C.
2. Household size, like other aspects of household composition, was dependent upon
whether the household was a nuclear family, one headed by a single adult rather than
a married couple, and whether or not it incorporated additional relatives or nonkin
into the structure. Size differences between landowners and the nonlanded that were
readily apparent in 1880, like other aspects of household composition, now failed to
distinguish between the land tenure groups. The increased similarity in household

Household Size, 1900

	Heads of Household		
Family Type	Husband/Wife	Female Only	Male Only
Two Generation	$\overline{X}$ = 5.46	$\overline{X}$ = 4.62	$\overline{X}$ = 4.50
	s = 2.85	s = 2.45	s = 2.40
Extended	$\overline{X}$ = 6.51	$\overline{X}$ = 4.55	$\overline{X}$ = 4.00
	s = 2.89	s = 2.77	s = 1.85
Nonkin	$\overline{X}$ = 5.55	$\overline{X}$ = 2.50	$\overline{X}$ = 2.77
	s = 0.88	s = 0.70	s = 1.30

(Two generation households headed by a husband and wife were significantly larger than other two generation households. Extended,
husband-wife headed households were significantly larger than all
other household types. Husband-wife headed households which incorporated nonkin were significantly larger than all other households
which incorporated nonkin.)

Analysis of Variance Summary

Source	Sum of Squares	df	Mean Square	F
Total	2,957.57	381		
Heads of Household	135.97	2	67.98	9.85*
Family Type	32.24	2	6.12	2.33
Interaction	215.34	4	53.83	7.80*
Error	2,574.02	373	6.90	

*p < .01

composition was a function of several factors. A general decrease in the average size of the land tracts was one. Another, equally important by the turn of the century, was the way in which the elderly were accommodated within families. As farms were transmitted to a younger generation, the elderly often took up residence with their adult children. Moriah Nash, for example, lived with her adult son Gipson and his family; and Hannah Fields, also a landowning widow, lived with her granddaughter Emily, who married Nathan Redd. Both of these women retained control over relatively large parcels of land for quite some time before deeding the property to their children and grandchildren, and their control of farm lands sufficiently large to support sizable extended family households was probably one of the major factors which influenced their residence patterns. (See chap. 3, n. 6 for a discussion of the dynamics of land transfer as they developed among the first generation settlers.)

Average size for all households through the nation in 1900 was 4.76 persons, only slightly smaller than most Promised Land households. See U.S. Department of Commerce, *Bicentennial Statistics* (Washington, D.C., 1976), table 378; and U.S. Bureau of Census, *Historical Statistics of the United States, Colonial Times to 1970*, table 640.

3. See especially chap. 2 for a discussion of cooperative male farming during the first generation.

4. Demographic data for Promised Land indicate a preponderance of single women, either never married or divorced, widowed or separated from their husbands, who were engaged in domestic work. David M. Katzman, *Seven Days a Week* (New York, 1978), pp. 201–204 indicates that domestic service in the nineteenth-century South was dominated by married Negro women with husbands and children present in the household. The apparent discrepancy between the Promised Land population and Katzman's generalization is understandable when examined in terms of the relationship between household structure and work roles within the community. Role expectations were formed on the assumption that households engaged as total units in subsistence agriculture. Husbands, wives, and children labored cooperatively toward this goal, maintaining whenever possible a domestically centered and self-contained family economy. When this model was rendered ineffective by land scarcity and male migration, adult women turned to domestic work to meet their economic obligations. Katzman's data are based on domestic service in urban areas, and for that reason fail to account for the differential factors which influenced and shaped economic behavior in rural settings.

5. Interview with James Evert Turner, 27 September 1979, Chicago, Ill. Turner asserted that this pattern of migration from Promised Land prevailed throughout his childhood. It was a strategy confined to those exiting agricultural work and seeking urban employment, as also noted by Clyde V. Kiser, *Sea Island to City* (1932; reprint ed., New York, 1969), pp. 151 ff., as characteristic of landowning families or families otherwise tied by various types of social bonds to a community setting. At Promised Land, as in the Sea Islands, economic motives were mediated by domestic responsibilities and social bonds. The Promised Land migrants probably ranged somewhat further on their initial moves than the Sea Islanders for want of nearby opportunities for work. Charleston, Savannah, and the phosphate industry, all provided employment opportunities to migrating Sea Islanders. Promised Land residents were isolated in the sparsely populated up-country and largely excluded from employment in the textile industry by social convention. The nearest large center for industrial employment was Atlanta. Once the pipeline north was established, the Washington-Baltimore-Philadelphia area, accessible by rail, proved a convenient site for cash-wage employment.

6. Interview with Rev. B.J. Glover, 16 March 1979, Columbia, S.C.

7. The domestic strategies devised by the Promised Land families during this period conform to the family wage economy model, Louise Tilly and Joan Scott, *Women, Work, and Family* (New York, 1978), pp. 104–145. Two separate conditions stimulated the shift from a production to wage economy at Promised Land. First, the emigration of a significant number of adult men eroded the labor balance within households essential to small-scale subsistence farming. Second, a general decline in the agricultural industry of the Cotton Belt weakened the traditional division of labor in intact households. In both cases, women whose labor and productivity were still central to the family's economic survival sought work that had the least conflict with their domestic obligations. Domestic service, taking in laundry, and nursing all served as adaptive strategies for these changed circumstances. At Promised Land as elsewhere in the rural South, the specific types of change which prompted the shift from household production to a wage economy among Negro families differed from those specified by Tilly and Scott for their European cases. Nevertheless, the consequences were the same in terms of impact on family organization.

8. Interview with Rev. B. J. Glover, 16 March 1979, Columbia, S.C. Glover asserted that the primary circumstances underlying the rate of illegitimacy among rural Negroes during the first quarter of the twentieth century was the imbalance in the sex ratio that resulted from the migration pattern in which men preceded women to the cities. Glover's explanation of the conditions at Promised Land and his generalizations to other rural Negro settings are open to challenge. The matter seems to defy a general explanation. See: Herbert G. Gutman, "Persistent Myths About the Afro-American Family," *Journal of Interdisciplinary History* 6 (1975): 181–210; and Elizabeth Hafkin Pleck, *Black Migration and Poverty* (New York, 1979), pp. 162–196.

9. C. Vann Woodward, *Origins of the New South*, rev. ed. (Baton Rouge, 1971), p. 55.

10. Ibid., p. 398.

11. Biographical and educational information on Anna E. Chiles was obtained from Register of Negro Teachers for Greenwood County, n.d., Greenwood County Courthouse, S.C. Interviews with Benetta Morton Williams and Elese Morton Smith, 14 November 1977, Promised Land, S.C.; Ada Letman Wilson, 27 September 1979, Chicago, Ill. Lizzie Chiles' two sons continued their residence with their paternal grandparents after her marriage to J.D. Chiles and later moved to Baltimore with their father. She was apparently estranged from them, for in her old age she lived for a time with one of Chiles' daughters in Atlanta rather than with her own children and then returned to live at Promised Land until her death in 1964.

12. Interview with Joe T. Ligon, Jr., 4 November 1977, Verdery, S.C. Lizzie Chiles was an active and vocal member of the Mt. Zion Sunday School Executive Board throughout the first quarter of the twentieth century. Mt. Zion Records, ii–v.

13. Miscellaneous Records, County Superintendent of Education, 1897–1928, Greenwood County Courthouse, S.C. Interview with George L. Wilson, 7 November 1977, Promised Land, S.C.

14. Interview with George L. Wilson, 7 November 1977, Promised Land, S.C.

15. Ibid. Interview with Balus Glover, 6 November 1978, Promised Land, S.C.

16. U.S. Bureau of Census, 1900 Household Manuscripts, Smithville and White Hall Enumeration Districts, Greenwood County, S.C. and Smithville Enumeration District, Abbeville County, S.C.

17. Miscellaneous Records, Receipts and Settlements for School Taxes, 1900–1922, Greenwood County School District, Greenwood County Courthouse, S.C.

18. Interview with Benetta Morton Williams, 14 November 1977, Promise Land, S.C.

19. Interview with George L. Wilson, 7 November 1978, Promise Land, S.C.

20. Ibid. Interview with Balus Glover, 6 November 1978, Promise Land, S.C.

21. Interview with Benetta Morton Williams and Elese Morton Smith, 14 November 1977, Promise Land, S.C.

22. Interview with George L. Wilson, 7 November 1978, Promise Land, S.C.

23. Ibid. Interview with Balus Glover, 6 November 1978, Promise Land, S.C.

24. Interviews with Cora Wideman White, 14 November 1977, Promised Land, S.C.; Cora Frazier Hall, 1 December 1978, Promised Land, S.C.; Balus Glover, 6 November 1978, Promised Land, S.C.

25. Interview with Balus Glover, 6 November 1978, Promise Land, S.C.

26. Ibid. Interview with Rev. B. J. Glover, 16 March 1979, Columbia, S.C. Woodward, *Origins of the New South,* p. 398, describes the rural schools as "wretchedly taught," a reality which the Glover men, in their adulthood, recognize through personal experience.

27. Interview with Rev. B. J. Glover, 16 March 1979, Columbia, S.C. The Promised Land High School was typical rather than unusual and extraordinary. Isolated from many types of societal resources and social services, Negroes consistently established and supported a wide variety of self-help and benevolent institutions during the first quarter of the twentieth century, including hospitals, orphanages, and mutual aid societies, as well as schools. See especially John Hope Franklin, *From Slavery to Freedom,* 4th ed. (New York, 1974), pp. 277–303, for a discussion of this aspect of Negro culture. Although I. A. Newby, *Black Carolinians, A History of Blacks in South Carolina from 1895–1968* (Columbia, S.C., 1973), described the first quarter of the twentieth century as marked by powerlessness for the state's Negro population, he failed to consider the strategies Negroes employed to counter prevailing political and economic isolation within individual communities. The Promised Land High School was one such incidence of creative adaptation.

28. Interviews with John Turner, 30 May 1978, Greenwood, S.C.; Rev. B. J. Glover, 16 March 1979, Columbia, S.C.

29. The tradition of vocational education established in South Carolina during Reconstruction, most prominently on the Sea Islands, and promoted during the early twentieth century by prominent state Negro leaders like Rev. Richard Carroll, a Baptist minister from Columbia, had little impact on education at Promised Land. See Newby, *Black Carolinians,* pp. 162–169, for a discussion of attitudes toward vocational education. Perhaps because vocational education was far too expensive an enterprise to be supported by such a small community, perhaps because of the influence of Lizzie Chiles, or perhaps because of the influence of the original settlers, dominated by literate and unusually well-educated men and women, the parents in the second generation did not choose vocational education for their children even when they sent them to school outside Promised Land.

30. Interview with Balus Glover, 16 March 1979, Columbia, S.C. Glover explained that he was able, more than half a century later, to recall this particular problem because Lizzie Chiles gave it out to the children every year, in some variation, and he worked on it for more than a week before he got the right answer.

31. Interview with Benetta Morton Williams, 14 November 1977, Promised Land, S.C.

32. Interviews with Ada Letman Wilson, 27 September 1979, Chicago, Ill.; Lilly Wims Evans, 17 August 1978, Promised Land, S.C. Mrs. Evans and her daughters, Burnice Evans Norman and Annie Mae Evans Norman, were particularly helpful in sorting out the various social activities within Promised Land during this time, carefully explaining the relationship between church and social life in several rather confusing cases. I gratefully acknowledge their assistance and their patience.

33. Jacob's Chapel Baptist Church Community Meeting, 16 July 1978, Greenwood County, S.C.; interview with Amos Wells, 13 July 1978, Promised Land, S.C.

34. All information on the Mt. Zion leadership structure was abstracted from the Mt. Zion Records, II–V (held by George L. Wilson, Promised Land, S.C. and Cleora Wilson Turner, Greenwood, S.C.).

35. Interviews with Mattie Strong, 27 September 1979, Chicago, Ill.; Agnes Martin Coleman, 4 December 1978, Greenwood, S.C.; Ada Letman Wilson, 27 September 1979, Chicago, Ill. Records of the Promised Land Union Burrial Aid Society are contained within the Mt. Zion Records. Although the society was primarily a Baptist organization, minutes in all organizations were generally kept by the most literate member. This occasionally necessitated suspending other kinds of social conventions, such as the denominational boundaries which otherwise separated the memberships of the society, the Masons, and the Ladies' Aid. The secretary of the society was also the secretary of the Mt. Zion Sunday School Board and apparently kept both sets of minutes in the same book.

36. The Little River Association Minutes, 1900–1925, are also held by George L. Wilson. Although Mr. Wilson is a Methodist and was given the Mt. Zion Records by his mother, Annie Wilson, he is also the unofficial Promised Land archivist and keeps almost everything in print or writing pertaining to the community. He does not recall how or from whom he obtained the Little River records.

37. Hilliard's appeal for financial support of the Negro hospital in Greenwood provides yet another instance of the extensive nature of the self-help/mutual aid ideology that pervaded all aspects of social life for rural Negroes. Through a wide variety of organizations at Promised Land—the High School, the Masonic Lodge, the burial aid society, and the Little River Association—pride and cooperation were fostered among the relatively isolated and impoverished enclaves of Negro farmers in the Piedmont. All were examples in miniature of the extent to which parallel and segregated Negro institutions mediated the impact of political and economic repression.

Chapter 7

1. For children born at Promised Land before 1880, the survival rate from birth through adolescence was .62. For those born between 1880 and 1890, the probability of survival increased to .81; and, for those born between 1895 and 1900, the rate increased to .93. Like other vital statistics describing the community population, these figures were derived from self-reported live births and surviving children (U.S. Bureau of Census, 1900 Household Manuscripts, Smithville and White Hall Enumeration Districts, Greenwood County, S.C. Infants born at Promised Land had a far greater probability of survival to adolescence than most Negro babies. See Harold F. Dorn, "The Health of the Negro," Carnegie-Myrdal Manuscripts, n.d., Schomberg Collection, New York Public Library, for a comprehensive discussion of Negro health problems, including data for infant mortality.

2. Information on childbirth was derived from interviews with Cora Frazier Hall, Lettie Richie Moragne, Elese Morton Smith, and Hazel Moragne Whitecloud. Naming patterns were described by these same individuals and also by George L. Wilson and verified through the 1900 household census manuscripts. Naming patterns among the Promised Land families closely followed a network of affective bonds similar to those described by Herbert G. Gutman, *The Black Family in Slavery and Freedom* (New

York, 1976), pp. 185–229. As Gutman has demonstrated, naming practices are one index of kinship solidarity and prevailing social obligations.

3. Childhood and adolescence were described by: John Cole, Cora Frazier Hall, Willie Mae Wims Byrd, Azzalie Moragne Jones, Lettie Richie Moragne, Theresa Morton Moragne, Elese Morton Smith, James Evert Turner, Pearl Wideman White, Augustus White, Sr., Benetta Morton Williams, Rosalie Wilson Williams, George L. Wilson, Ada Letman Wilson. The four common and recurring themes of socialization at Promised Land—early weaning, repression of sexuality, control of aggression, and severe negative reinforcement—are characteristic of both lower-class and rural socialization. For a specific discussion see Allison Davis and John Dollard, *Children of Bondage* (Washington, D.C., 1940), pp. 263–278. The children at Promised Land were clearly passive agents in their socialization. Sexual repression, control of aggression, and the extent of physical punishment that typified childhood resulted in an adult personality marked by ambivalence, inhibition, and sublimation of drive behavior. Guilt, dependence, and conformity were enhanced personality traits; and achievement striving, creativity, initiative, and spontaneity were all minimized in the socialization process. Despite the protection from the negative effects of caste awareness the Promised Land children enjoyed, their early socialization experiences formed personalities which generally conformed to prevailing racial stereotypes. See especially Arthur Bandura et al., "Transmission of Aggression Through Imitation of Aggressive Models," *Journal of Abnormal and Social Psychology* 63 (1961); John Dollard and Leonard Doob et al., *Frustration and Aggression* (New Haven, Conn., 1939); R.R. Sears, Eleanor Maccoby, and H. Levine, *Patterns of Childrearing* (Evanston, Ill., 1957), for learning theory analyses of this socialization strategy. Ruth S. Cavan, "Subcultural Variations and Mobility," in H.T. Christense, ed., *Handbook of Marriage and the Family* (Chicago, 1964), pp. 535–581; and B.C. Rosen, "The Achievement Syndrome: A Psycho-Cultural Dimension of Social Stratification," *American Sociological Review* 21 (1956); and idem., "Social Class and the Child's Perception of the Parent," Child Development 35 (1964), provide cogent general discussions of the impact of class position on socialization patterns. For alternative theoretic stances on socialization see Edward Zigler and Irvin Child, "Socialization," in Gardner Lindzey and Elliot Aronson, eds., *Handbook of Social Psychology*, 2nd ed., vol. 3 (Reading, Mass., 1969). The role of children within the family economy, and the relationship between this economic prerequisite and socialization is discussed for comparative European cases in Louise A. Tilly and Joan W. Scott, *Women, Work, and Family* (New York, 1978), pp. 56–60. Generally, under economic conditions that required child labor as an integral component of the family's total economic resources, the period of infant nurturance was abbreviated, and children's needs were rarely considered apart from total family needs.

4. Courtship and marriage were described by: anonymous; John Cole; Agnes Martin Coleman; Lilly Wims Evans; Balus Glover; B. J. Glover; Azzalie Moragne Jones; Cora Frazier Hall; John Hall; Theresa Morton Moragne; Lettie Richie Moragne; Bessie Marshall Price; James Evert Turner; and Amos Wells, Sr.

5. Adulthood was described by: Lilly Wims Evans, John Cole, Cora Frazier Hall, John Hall, Agnes Martin Coleman, James Evert Turner, and the Mt. Zion Community Meeting.

6. Community social life was described by: John Cole, Isaac H. Moragne, Burnice Evans Norman, Elese Morton Smith, Balus Glover, George L. Wilson, Ada Letman Wilson, and Azzalie Moragne Jones.

7. Mid-life and community affairs were described by: James Evert Turner; Augustus White, Sr.; B. J. Glover; Agnes Martin Coleman; Elese Morton Smith; Mattie Brown

Morton; Tax Auditor's Duplicate Books, Greenwood County, S.C., 1897–1930; and Mt. Zion Records. The dissolution of the community's Masonic Lodge, the Promised Land High School, and the Promised Land Union Burrial Aid Society coincided in time with the more general collapse of the larger Negro economy. See especially Florette Henri, *Black Migration* (Garden City, N.J., 1975), pp. 306–343; and Raymond Wolters, *Negroes and the Great Depression* (Westport, Conn., 1970), pp. 3–73, for discussions of the collapse of both the economic and cultural systems. The changes at Promised Land were reflections of changes in much wider arenas.

8. The rituals of death were described by Cleora Wilson Turner, Elese Morton Smith, and Agnes Martin Coleman.

9. Greenwood, S.C. *Index-Journal*, 10 February 1923, provided by Catherine Davis Cann. Elestine Smith Norman filled in the details of Aunt Huldy Green that the newspaper neglected, interviewing several older residents at Promised Land to piece together a more complete version of her death.

Chapter 8

1. Nell Irvin Painter, *Exodusters, Black Migration to Kansas after Reconstruction* (New York, 1976); and Elizabeth Hafkin Pleck, *Black Migration and Poverty* (New York, 1979), provide excellent analyses of two distinctive forms of nineteenth-century Negro migration. For an overview of Negro social geography see Richard L. Morrill and O. Fred Donaldson, "Geographical Perspectives on the History of Black America," in Robert T. Ernst and Lawrence Hugg, eds., *Black America, Geographical Perspectives* (Garden City, N.J., 1976), pp. 9–33.

2. In 1910, 90 percent of the nation's Negro population still lived in the South, more than 75 percent in rural settings such as Promised Land. Charles H. Wesley, *Negro Labor in the United States* (New York, 1927), p. 231, notes that by 1910 there were 440,500 southern-born Negroes living in the North, the result of a small but continuous emigration which began in the final quarter of the nineteenth century. See also pp. 284–5 for a comparison of Negro emigration statistics between various southern states. By 1920, 34 percent of the Negro population lived in urban areas; and by 1930, 44 percent. The "economic incentives" commonly cited as the major impetus for this shift were unquestionably present. However, the tendency to overlook the conditions and factors through which economic motives were translated into concrete behavior can be avoided by examining the mass movement in smaller analytic units. The economic factors which "pushed" Negroes from the South prior to 1915 were not the same as the attractions which "pulled" them toward the North. They were not even correlaries. Although Arnold Rose, *The Negro's Morale* (Minneapolis, Minn., 1949), pp. 37–8, suggests that the minimal Negro migration prior to 1915 is explained by an absence of job opportunities in the North and a lack of social contacts to ease the transition from farm to city, his explanation begs the question. It offers no insight into the motives of the earliest twentieth-century migrants. To suggest that migration during the later decades of the century was stimulated solely by economic incentives, as argued by Donald R. Matthews and James W. Prothro, *Negroes and the New Southern Politics* (New York, 1966), pp. 449–55, ignores, as well, the problems posed by Rose. Negro migration occurred in a series of waves, and each new group of emigrants between 1900 and 1930 confronted their circumstances in the urban North in a different way. The first group, those who left the rural South roughly between 1900 and 1915, were pioneers to the city in many ways. Although they were certainly not the only Negroes living in urban environments, it was their presence which established an

identifiable link between country and city. The group which followed, between 1915 and 1920, left the rural South for quite different reasons; and, when they arrived in the cities, they were able to tap into the resources of friends and family already established there. Both of these groups were "pushed" more than they were "pulled," but only those migrants who left the South after 1920 felt the urban "pull" as defined through economic motives, and that pull was interpreted for them by those already established. The interplay between landownership and the lure of the urban setting for early twentieth-century Negroes is alluded to by Robert Browne, "Black Land Loss: The Plight of Black Ownership," *Southern Exposure* 2 (Fall 1974): 112–121, but even Browne largely ignores the connections which exist between the separate waves of immigrants. For specific discussion of emigration from South Carolina see I.A. Newby, *Black Carolinians* (Columbia, S.C., 1973), pp. 193–228; and Susan Page Garris, "The Decline of Lynching in South Carolina" (M.A. thesis, University of South Carolina, 1973).

3. Manning Marable, "The Land Question in Historical Perspective: The Economics of Poverty in the Blackbelt South, 1865–1920," in Leo McGee and Robert Boone, eds., *The Rural Black Landowner—Endangered Species* (Westport, Conn., 1979), p. 19.

4. Interview with James Evert Turner, 27 September 1979, Chicago, Ill. Few of those who emigrated left Promised Land with more than the most marginal material resources. Many emigrants recalled later that they had no more than train fare to Atlanta or Philadelphia and a few additional dollars they had saved up for the trip. Although departures were rarely spontaneous or entered into without planning, it was clear that the belief commonly held by emigrants, that they could "better their condition," was formulated only in the vaguest sense. Few concerned themselves with the details of the self-improvement that they sought by the move.

5. Interviews with Isaac H. Moragne and Al Moragne, 14 September 1979, New York, N.Y.

6. Indirect Index to Deeds, Abbeville County, S.C. Rights-of-way intersected ten community farms; those owned by James Evans, Hannah Fields, Gipson Goodwin, Charles Jackson, W. A. Lomax, Calvin Moragne, Eli Moragne, Wade Moragne, and William Moragne.

7. The Richie household was described in U.S. Bureau of Census, 1900 Household Manuscripts, Smithville Enumeration District, Abbeville County, S.C.

8. Interviews with Ada Letman Wilson and Rosalie Wilson Williams, 27 September 1979, Chicago, Ill.; and George L. Wilson, 7 November 1977, 30 March 1978, Promised Land, S.C.

9. Interview with Ada Ada Letman Wilson, 27 September 1979, Chicago, Ill. Apparently the Exodus of 1879 or the subsequent western drift affected some of the Promised Land families, although in the case of the Reynolds family there is no evidence that the Mississippi branch ever lived at Promised Land. The drift to the west was not limited to the Reynolds. Charlie and Shack Moragne wrote from Overland, Kansas in 1912 to the Judge of Probate, Greenwood, S.C. relinquishing their claims in the settlement of the Mary Burt Estate. There was no further evidence of western migration from Promised Land until the pre-World War II period when the war industries began to accept Negro labor. Even then the movement was insignificant in comparison to the migration northward.

10. Interview with Lettie Richie Moragne, 31 October 1979, Promised Land, S.C. The cream pitcher is preserved and part of the family memorabilia.

11. Interview with Hazel Moragne Roundtree, 31 October 1979, Greenwood, S.C.

12. Interviews with Isaac H. Moragne and Al Moragne, 14 September 1979, New York, N.Y.

13. Ibid.

14. Interview with Hazel Moragne Roundtree, 31 October 1979, Greenwood, S.C.

15. Ibid. Interviews with Isaac H. Moragne and Al Moragne, 14 September 1979, New York, N.Y.

16. Interview with Ada Letman Wilson, 27 September 1979, Chicago, Ill. The Reynolds family's ability to mobilize individuals into a cohesive economic force was consistent with the entire heritage of Promised Land as well as with the "mutual aid society" pattern of domestic/household economics described by St. Clair Drake and Horace R. Cayton, *Black Metropolis* (New York, 1945), p. 581. The capacity and tendency to mobilize and exploit individual economic capacities for the advancement of a family unit is concrete evidence of that adaptation to "changing external circumstances" described by Herbert G. Gutman, *The Black Family in Slavery and Freedom* (New York, 1976), pp. 454–456.

17. Interviews with Pearl White Riley and James Evert Turner, 27 September 1979, Chicago, Ill.

18. James Evert Turner, 27 September 1979, Chicago, Ill.

19. Ibid.

20. Ibid.

21. Pearl White Riley, 26 September 1979, Chicago, Ill.

22. Ibid.

23. Ibid.

24. Ibid. Interview with James Evert Turner, 27 September 1979, Chicago, Ill. Negroes had little impact on the skilled, clerical, or professional categories of the urban labor force in spite of their urbanization rate between 1900 and 1930. For a summary of Negro occupational structure during these three decades see Marion Hays, "A Century of Change: Negroes in the U.S. Economy, 1860–1960," in Louis A. Ferman, Joyce L. Kornbluh, and J.A. Miller, eds., *Negroes and Jobs* (Ann Arbor, Mich., 1968), pp. 53–65. In 1910 there were eight unskilled urban laborers for each skilled worker among the Negro labor force. In 1920 the ratio diminished to 7½ to 1. The gains were insignificantly small, and the employment statistics fail to portray the human dilemma which accompanied this static occupational structure.

25. The concept of networks, frequently employed to examine communication channels in small groups communication processes, is used here within that framework. See Marvin E. Shaw, *Group Dynamics, The Dynamics of Small Group Behavior* (New York, 1971), pp. 137–152; and Harold H. Kelley and John W. Thibaut, "Group Problem Solving," in Gardner Lindzey and Elliot Aronson, eds., *The Handbook of Social Psychology*, 2nd ed. (Reading, Mass., 1969), 4: 119–166, for summaries of network analysis. Here the term is employed with the implicit assumption that the network structure is essential to communication channels between Promised Land and the urban settlements of community migrants. Only after these networks were activated during the 1920's was it possible for community residents to enter urban settings confident of work and housing; and this confidence, in turn, stimulated additional migration. Josh Richie and Martha and Charlie Reynolds served as gatekeepers for those community residents who considered emigration; and through this role the "diffusion effect" described by Everett Rogers and Floyd Shoemaker, *Communication of Innovations* (Glencoe, Ill., 1971), pp. 175–196, further encouraged emigration from Promised Land to a finite "saturation" level. For the Great Migration from the rural South to urban settings, saturation occurred within family or kin groups; and the specific migration pattern of a given family or kin group was predictable given two pieces of information: (1) the destination of the original family representative, or gatekeeper; and (2) the relative success of that initial representative in adapting to the

new environment. Movement within a network was dependent upon the initial (1900 to 1915) behavior of its urban gatekeepers. Certainly those gatekeepers were instrumental in stimulating the 1915 to 1922 wave of emigration from Promised Land, and similar networks doubtless served the same function for the half-million Negroes who left the rural South between 1922 and 1927. See especially U.S. Department of Labor, *Negro Migration in 1916–17* (Washington, D.C., 1919), p. 12, for a discussion of the interface between those who emigrated from the rural South and those who remained. Negroes still down south were "drawn by letters and actual advances of money from Negroes who had already settled in the North." See Charles H. Wesley, *Negro Labor*, pp. 285 ff, for emigration statistics.

26. Josh Richie's marriage to Rose was without a doubt one major factor in his failure to function as an effective gatekeeper for his own kin. Unlike the Reynoldses, who operated within a cohesive common cultural farmework, Richie and Rose lacked the commonality of heritage that facilitated, and at times even demanded, subordination of individual to group.

27. The essentially reciprocal nature of a communication network becomes fully evident only in this phase of migration, the recurrent visiting patterns which urban dwellers established and maintained with Promised Land. These visits "home" were a form of the feedback loop, providing regular opportunities for face-to-face communication between otherwise distant members of networks. Perhaps equally important, the visits to Promised Land provided a period of cultural realignment with their rural heritage for urban dwellers. The annual visits, timed in harmony with the rural calendar, afforded a prolonged period of reassessment for community residents and migrants of each other and the common values and bonds that connected them.

Chapter 9

1. The classic studies of rural Negro life during the period ably portray the depths of Negro rural poverty. See especially David Eugene Conrad, *The Forgotten Farmers* (Urbana, Ill., 1965); Arthur Raper and Ira De A. Reid, *Sharecroppers All* (Chapel Hill, N.C., 1941); and T.J. Woofter, *Black Yeomanry* (New York, 1930). For detailed economic analyses see Charles S. Johnson, *The Economic Status of Negroes* (Washington, D.C., 1933); and Arthur M. Ford, *The Political Economics of Rural Poverty in the South* (Cambridge, Mass., 1973). For agricultural information specifically related to South Carolina, the *Annual Reports of the Commission of Agriculture, Commerce, and Industry of the State of South Carolina* provide good empirical summaries of the state's farm conditions, although commentary and explanations have a decided racial bias.

2. Interview with George L. Wilson, 30 March 1978, Promised Land. S.C.

3. The agricultural problems addressed by the New Deal programs were concerned primarily with overproduction. The Agricultural Adjustment Act of 1933 implemented a crop destruction program designed to limit crops and thereby artificially inflate prices while at the same time providing parity payments to farmers for the loss of their crops. The program was of no benefit initially to landless farmers, because payments were made directly to landowners, who were expected to distribute shares of money to their tenants and sharecroppers. Few did so. Only when the program was modified in 1935 to provide direct parity payments to tenants and sharecroppers as well as landowners was the full potential of the program realized within the Promised Land community. For an especially sympathetic interpretation of the Agricultural Act see Conrad, *Forgotten Farmers*. Comprehensive examination of the impact of New Deal programs on Negroes' economic condition, rural and urban, are available in

Bernard Sternsher, ed., *The Negro in Depression and War* (Chicago, 1969); Raymond Wolters, *Negroes and the Great Depression* (Westport, Conn., 1970); Charles S. Johnson et al., *The Collapse of Cotton Tenancy* (Chapel Hill, N.C., 1935); Carl C. Taylor, Helen W. Wheeler and E.L. Kirkpatrick, *Disadvantaged Classes in American Agriculture* (Washington, D.C., 1938); and H.A. Turner, *A Graphic Summary of Farm Tenure*, U.S.D.A. Miscellaneous Publication No. 261 (Washington, D.C., 1936).

4. Interview with Janie Morris, 1 December 1978, Promised Land, S.C.

5. Sheriff's Tax Execution Book, School District 21, 1920–1937, Greenwood County, S.C., Greenwood County Courthouse. The tax collectors noted the disposition of each tax delinquent in a final column of the ledger, indicating that taxes had been paid, voided, or that the individuals were dead or gone. The conditions in the community conform to those described by George B. Tindall, *The Emergence of the New South* (Baton Rouge, La., 1967), pp. 473–504. There Tindall noted that during the Great Depression "the safety valve of out-migration almost ceased to function." Unemployment for Negroes was far greater in urban than rural areas, particularly in the South, where various New Deal programs had relatively less impact than in the cities and industrialized North.

6. Taylor et al., *Disadvantaged Classes*, estimated that during the 1930's an annual farm income of $1000 was required for a family to live above the poverty level. Annual incomes for Negroes in the Black Belt ranged between a minimum of $180 and a maximum of $417 for the decade. The Promised Land population, even with its landowning advantage, was undistinguishable from other Black Belt Negroes.

7. Interview with Ada Letman Wilson, 27 September 1979, Chicago, Ill.

8. Tax Auditor's Duplicate Books, 1930–1942, Smithville and White Hall Townships, Greenwood County, S.C. Interview with Elnora Marshall Williams, 17 October 1979, Baltimore, Md.

9. Interview with Elese Morton Smith and Bessie Marshall Price, 14 October 1979, Baltimore, Md. This response to threatened land loss revealed the continued symbolic importance of landownership within the Negro population. Lester M. Salamon, "The Future of Black Land in the South," in Leo McGee and Robert Boone, eds., *The Rural Black Landowner—Endangered Species* (Westport, Conn., 1979), pp. 169–172, found similar tenacious attitudes toward their land among Negroes who participated in the New Deal resettlement projects between 1934 and 1943. Salamon was told by one of the project participants that "land is the single most important thing a man can get for himself and his family." Whether at Promised Land or elsewhere, once acquired, land was not willingly relinquished.

10. Interview with Elese Morton Smith and Bessie Marshall Price, 14 October 1979, Baltimore, Md. The Civilian Conservation Corps, created in 1933, was designed to provide work for unmarried young men. The corps was active into the early 1940's and based on voluntary "enlistments" of a one year duration. Some of the men from Promised Land who enlisted apparently fudged on their marital status. For an analysis of the program see Charles P. Harper, *The Administration of the Civilian Conservation Corps* (Clarksburg, W. Va., 1939); Marian T. Wright, "Negro Youth and the Federal Emergency Programs: CCC and NYA," *Journal of Negro Education* (July 1940). Additionally, both *Crisis* and *Opportunity* provide running criticism and analytic commentary on specific New Deal programs throughout the 1930's and 1940's.

11. Interview with Elese Morton Smith and Bessie Marshall Price, 14 October 1979, Baltimore, Md.

12. Interview with Fox Hackett, 20 March 1978, Promised Land, S.C.

13. Interview with Donald Robinson, 9 June 1978, Greenwood, S.C.

14. The estimate of 20 percent may be somewhat inflated. It was derived from an examination of: Tax Auditor's Duplicate Books, 1897–1942, Smithville and White Hall Townships, Greenwood County, S.C.; and Miscellaneous Tax Records, School District 21, 1920–1944, Greenwood County, S.C. Both in the Greenwood County Courthouse.

15. Henry Ford manufactured the Model T unchanged from 1909 to 1927. In all probability both the Glover and Marshall automobiles were purchased some time after 1924 when the purchase price of the Model T was reduced from $950 to $250. Glover bought his car new.

16. Edward Magdol, *A Right to the Land* (Westport, Conn., 1977), pp. 211 ff, stated that Negro landownership peaked between 1910 and 1920 at 15 million acres, divided among 220,000 proprietors. Ownership of tracts which averaged sixty-eight acres, significantly smaller than white-owned farms, was still a major source of status and prestige within the rural Negro population. See especially Charles S. Johnson, *Growing Up in the Black Belt, Negro Youth in the Rural South* (Washington, D.C., 1941), pp. 73 ff; and Hortense Powdermaker, *After Freedom* (New York, 1939), pp. 95–106.

17. Interview with Rev. B. J. Glover, 16 March 1979, Columbia, S.C.

18. This and all subsequent information on agricultural activities at Promised Land for the period are abstracted from Crop Liens and Chattel Mortgages, 1935–1945, Greenwood County, S.C., Greenwood County Courthouse. Equivalent records for those community residents who lived in Abbeville County were either destroyed or not available at the author's inquiry.

19. See chap. 8.

20. Interview with Rev. B. J. Glover, 16 March 1979, Columbia, S.C. This important function lies well within the traditional framework of Negro leadership. The ability to intercede with whites and to convey the results of such intercessions to other Negroes was central to Booker T. Washington's leadership style. Walter White of the NAACP; Robert Abbot, editor of the Chicago *Defender*; and even labor leader A. Philip Randolph all incorporated a strategy of intercession into their leadership styles. At Promised Land this role fell quite naturally to the preachers and teachers, and during the 1930's and 1940's also to Henry Robinson, the undertaker. Reading or retelling the week's news, with emphasis on items deemed particularly important or significant, was a major responsibility of men like C. G. Glover and W. A. Turner. They were the only source of such information for many local residents.

21. This and all subsequent information on the Marshall family was obtained from interviews with Bessie Marshall Price, Elnora Marshall Williams, Junior Price, and Vernice Price Campbell, 14–18 October 1979, Baltimore, Md.

22. Greenwood County School Ledger, School District 21, 1931–38. Greenwood County Courthouse, S.C. Until 1937 Lizzie Chiles was paid $45 a month for her efforts at Promised Land during the five month term. As it had been since Reconstruction, white teachers received almost twice as much ($75 per month) for a longer term. In 1937 Chiles' salary and those of the county's other Negro teachers was increased to $50 per month. The equivalent increase for white teachers brought their salary to $90 per month. In its physical condition and financial arrangements the school was representative of Negro elementary schools across the state. The State Superintendent of Public Schools, *Annual Report of the State Superintendent of Education of the State of South Carolina* (Columbia, S.C., 1920), p. 135, described the status of Negro education thus: "The furnishings of the school buildings for the colored children . . . could not be worse. There is hardly a colored school building in the state that has enough desks to properly seat the children . . . [who] are required to sit on benches without backs and their feet are unable to reach the floor. . . . Maps and globes are things almost

unknown." Still, the general belief among white administrators and politicians was that additional education of Negroes would create crime problems in the state. Over-educated Negroes developed overambitious notions of life. This mythic belief, more than available financing, was responsible for the incredibly retarded nature of the state's public education system. See Kewis K. McMillan, *Negro Higher Education in the State of South Carolina* (n.p., 1952); and C.J. Martin, *History and Development of Negro Education in South Carolina* (Columbia, S.C., 1949), for elaboration of the state's official educational philosophy as it was applied to Negro children. See Robert Burke Everett, "Race Relations in South Carolina, 1900–1932" (Ph.D. diss., University of Georgia 1969), pp. 26–64, for a detailed account of the strategies white superintendents and administrators used to misappropriate the meager school funds intended for Negro schools, channeling them instead into the white schools.

23. South Carolina was rather slow to implement a secondary school system for either white or Negro children, apparently not seeing a need for such advanced learning among the popular classes. Even after the secondary school system for whites was implemented, however, the state delayed a parallel system for Negroes, fearing that the ultimate outcome of such action would be increased demands for "social equality." The first secondary diplomas were awarded to Negro students in 1929; and there were only three Negro high schools in the state then, in Columbia, Union, and Darlington. See especially Louis R. Harlan, *Separate and Unequal, Public School Campaigns and Racism in the Southern Seaboard States* (Chapel Hill, N.C., 1958), for a detailed discussion. The reality of the educational system stood in sharp contrast to the ideals contained within the state's Negro leadership. Thomas E. Miller, president of the Negro State College at Orangeburg, captured the essence of enthusiasm and optimism in an Emancipation Day speech delivered in 1908, telling his audience that the acquisition of "knowledge will make you a full, useful man . . . knowledge that will enable you to break down every barrier that may be constructed against human rights." (Cited by Everett, "Race Relations," pp. 80–81.) It was this same sense of triumph and equality through education and knowledge that guided Daymon Marshall and Rev. C. G. Glover in the plans they devised for their children's post-Promised Land education.

24. Rev. B. J. Glover's ministerial work was closely aligned with the aims and tactics of the Southern Negro Youth Congress, a program which attacked with only limited success the various housing, educational, and public facility Jim Crow practices that circumscribed Negro existence. The following description of Glover's experiences is taken from two interviews with him on 16 March and 11 June 1979, Columbia, S.C.

Chapter 10

1. Interview with Rev. B. J. Glover, 11 June 1978, Columbia, S.C.

2. Clayborn Reynolds Probate File, Judge of Probate, Greenwood County Courthouse, Greenwood, S.C.

3. Interview with Elese Morton Smith and Bessie Marshall Price, 14 October 1979, Baltimore, Md.

4. Interviews with Floyd Reynolds, 17 August 1978, Promised Land, S.C. and 16 September 1979, South Ozone Park, N.Y.

5. Ibid. Reynolds' Brooklyn business was a huge success. Over the years he expanded, bought more trucks, and has since retired and turned the management of the company over to his daughter and son-in-law.

6. Charles S. Johnson, *Growing Up in the Black Belt, Negro Youth in the Rural South* (Washington, D.C., 1941), extensively analyzed the development of occupational aspirations and life goals among Negro youth. He concluded that adolescents with a heritage of landownership and/or stable community identity fit less easily into the traditional patterns of rural society than youths who grew up in more impoverished circumstances. Their goals tended to be more concrete and realistic than youths without a background of either landownership or community identity. Further, those goals were accompanied by realistic plans for implementation. When blocked by conditions beyond their control, such youths tended to move north.

7. Interview with Al Moragne, Isaac Moragne, and John Cole, 14 September 1979, New York, N.Y.

8. Ibid.

9. Ibid. Lester A. Salamon, "The Future of Black Land in the South," in Leo McGee and Robert Boone, eds., *The Black Rural Landowner—Endangered Species* (Westport, Conn., 1979), pp. 155–196, argued that land today constitutes the largest single equity base within the Negro population. In South Carolina slightly more than 8 percent of the commercial farmland is owned by Negroes. The potential power which this resource afforded was well understood at Promised Land, but the meaning was cast in social and psychological terms more than in a specifically economic context. Land provided independence and self-sufficiency, but not necessarily income or livelihood.

10. Interview with John Cole, 14 September 1979, New York, N.Y.

11. Interview with Al Moragne, Isaac Moragne, and John Cole, 14 September 1979, New York, N.Y.; and U.S.S. LSM60 Post-War Ship's Newsletter, n.a., mimeo, c. 1945 (held by Robert Evans, Promised Land, S.C.). The most complete description of enlistment and training practices in the early 1940's is Ulysses Lee, *The Employment of Negro Troops, The United States Army in World War II: Special Studies* (Washington, D.C. 1966). Seymour J. Schoenfeld, *The Negro in the Armed Forces* (Washington, D.C., 1945), discusses military operations; and Neil Wynn, *The Afro-American and the Second World War* (New York, 1975), provides an excellent overview of the effect of the war on various sectors of Negro life, not limited to military conditions. *Crisis* and the *Chicago Defender* both provide contemporary commentary on military inequities. The *Journal of Negro Education* devoted its Summer 1943 edition, "The American Negro in World War I and World War II," entirely to the subject of Afro-Americans and war.

12. Interview with John Cole, 14 September 1979, New York, N.Y.

13. Interview with Al Moragne, Isaac Moragne, and John Cole, 14 September 1979, New York, N.Y.

14. Ibid.

15. Ibid. The following description of Isaac H. Moragne's postwar unemployment, experience with the Greenwood VA office, and decision to leave Promised Land derived from this source. His experience and frustrations were not uncommon. Wynn, *The Afro-American and the Second World War* provides a brief discussion of the postwar Negro occupational problems.

16. Interview with John Cole, 14 September 1979, New York, N.Y.

17. Interviews with Lilly Wims Evans, 22 July 1978, Promised Land, S.C.; and Peggy Evans, 13 December 1978, Greenwood, S.C.

18. Tax Auditor's Duplicate Books, 1897–1950, Smithville and White Hall Townships, Greenwood County, S.C., Greenwood County Courthouse.

19. Interview with Al Moragne, 14 September 1979, New York, N.Y.

20. Interview with Joe T. Ligon, Jr., 4 November 1977, Verdery, S.C.; anonymous interview, Promised Land, S.C.

21. Interview with Theresa Morton Moragne, 11 September 1979, New York, N.Y. David M. Katzman, *Seven Days a Week* (New York, 1978), p. 216, notes that sexual exploitation of Negro domestics by white employers "was one of the major abuses of the southern caste system." There was, furthermore, no recourse for women so exploited other than the skillful exercise of their own wits. Katzman, p. 217, vividly illustrated the problem, describing the fate of one Negro husband who filed a formal legal complaint against his wife's employer for sexual harassment. "Her husband was arrested and fined twenty-five dollars" for the insult he issued against the white man. See also Mary Anderson, "The Plight of Negro Domestic Labor," *Journal of Negro Education* (January 1936); and George O. Butler, "The Black Worker in Industry, Agriculture, Domestic and Personal Service," *Journal of Negro Education* (July 1939), for discussions of the labor-related problems and economic exploitation faced by Negro women in domestic service.

22. Interviews with Benetta Morton Williams and Elese Morton Smith, 14 November 1977, Promised Land, S.C.; and Amos Wells, Jr., 2 July 1980, Anderson, S.C.

23. Interview with Amos Wells, Jr., 2 July 1980, Anderson, S.C.

24. Interview with Al Moragne, Isaac Moragne, and John Cole, 14 September 1979, New York, N.Y.

25. Interview with Steve Byrd, 4 December 1978, Greenwood, S.C. Byrd was the manager of the Home Finance Company during the 1950's; and, although he was not able to provide access to the company's loan records, he summarized in general terms the relationship that emerged between the Promised Land residents and Home Finance. Salamon, "The Future of Black Land," pp. 176–177 found similar access to consumer credit among FSA landowners. He noted that "land placed these [owners] on a far more equal footing than would otherwise have existed, and consequently enabled them to establish workable business relationships with local white enterprises and credit sources in ways that contributed significantly to a sense of pride and independence."

26. Interview with George L. Wilson, 30 March 1977, Promised Land, S.C. Pearl Redd's ambivalence was unusual for Promised Land freeholders. It was, however, more widespread than might be initially thought. Charles Nesbitt, "Rural Acreage in Promise Land, Tennessee: A Case Study," in Leo McGee and Robert Boone, eds., *The Black Rural Landowner*, pp. 75–79, attributed second and third generation decline of a land-based Negro community in Tennessee to the loss of affinity for lands acquired during the first generation. Fragmented kinship systems and vulnerability to "a coercive system of legal and illegal manipulations" erroded the Tennessee community's land base. The Promised Land community's protection against similar deterioration was probably a function of a well-developed communication network between local residents and distant kin who shared ownership of heir lands. The nature of the community's relationship with influential whites and a tradition of selling to other Negroes when land was sold both helped keep the Promised Land acreage in Negro hands.

27. Interview with Bettie R. Horne, 20 September 1977, Greenwood, S.C.

28. Interviews with Janie Morris, 16 February 1978, Promised Land, S.C.; and Benetta Morton Williams and Elese Morton Smith, 14 November 1977, Promised Land, S.C.

29. The Greenwood, S.C. *Index-Journal*, 5 April 1955, clipping provided by Fox Hackett, Promised Land, S.C. Benetta Morton Williams and Elese Morton Smith, 14 November 1977, Promised Land, S.C. The *Brown* decision was the culmination of a long legal struggle for equity. The legal strategies and various Supreme Court decisions leading up to the *Brown* case are ably reviewed by Raymond Pace Alexander,

"The Upgrading of the Negro's Status by Supreme Court Decisions," *Journal of Negro History* (April 1945); Charles S. Mangum, *The Legal Status of the Negro* (Chapel Hill, N.C., 1940); Thurgood Marshall, "An Evaluation of Recent Efforts to Achieve Racial Integration Through Resort to the Courts," *Journal of Negro Education* (Summer 1952); Loren E. Miller, *The Petitioners: The Story of the United States Supreme Court and the Negro* (New York, 1966); Bernard Nelson, *The Fourteenth Amendment and the Negro Since 1920* (Washington, D.C., 1946); idem, "The Negro Before the Supreme Court," *Phylon* (First Quarter 1947); and Joseph Tussman, ed., *The Supreme Court on Racial Discrimination* (New York, 1963).

30. Interview with Willie Neal Norman and Elestine Smith Norman, 31 October 1979, Promised Land, S.C.

31. Ibid.

32. Interview with Jimmy Nicholson, 10 October 1978, Greenwood, S.C. C. Rauch Wise, a Greenwood attorney, gave me this bit of advice one day when I was attempting to trace Nicholson's land deals through the Greenwood County Index to Deeds. Wise was correct in his judgement.

33. Ibid. Nicholson's records are all kept in aged and worn ledger books in the basement of his corner grocery store in Greenwood. An examination of those records revealed that he charged no interest to the purchasers of the Promised Land lots.

34. Interview with Lonnie Norman, 2 November 1979, Promised Land, S.C. Tax Assessor Valuations, 1950–1960, Greenwood County Courthouse. Commissioner of Public Works, Greenwood County, S.C.

35. Interview with Amos Wells, Jr., 2 July 1980, Anderson, S.C.

36. Interview with Burnice Evans Norman, 2 November 1979, Promised Land, S.C.; Mt. Zion Community Meeting, 6 June 1978; and interview with Amos Wells, Jr., 2 July 1980, Anderson, S.C. See chap. 4 for a description of the erection of the old Mt. Zion. The strategy of cooperative community effort was unchanged.

37. Amos Wells, Jr., 2 July 1980, Anderson, S.C.

Chapter 11

1. Interview with Sarah Price Robinson, 15 October 1979, Baltimore, Md.

2. Ada Letman Wilson, 27 September 1979, Chicago, Ill.

3. Interview with Bessie Marshall Price and Elese Morton Smith, 14 October 1979, Baltimore, Md.

4. The information about the New York City Moragnes was reconstructed through a series of interviews with Isaac H. Moragne, Theresa Morton Moragne, Al Moragne, Mary Lois Moragne, Imogene Moragne, Diane Moragne, Cynthia Moragne, and Gregory Moragne, 12–15 September 1979, New York, N.Y.

5. Louise A. Tilly and Joan W. Scott, *Women, Work, and Family* (New York, 1978), p. 232, concluded that "values, behavior, and strategies shaped under one mode of production continued to influence behavior as the economy changed. The older practices were slowly adapted to the new circumstances." Indeed, in the case of Isaac and Theresa Moragne, and most likely in many other Negro migrant families as well, the values and strategies indigenous to the southern Negro sociocultural system persisted well after families emigrated to urban environments; and it was this condition as much as lack of opportunity for employment in other spheres of the economy that perpetuated the tendency for married Negro women to dominate the domestic service labor force. Unlike other migrant groups, particularly European ethnics, primarily women who entered domestic service on a temporary basis when they were young and unmar-

ried, Theresa Moragne and thousands of other Negro women viewed domestic service as a permanent and respectable occupation, attractive because it permitted a balance between reproductive activity/responsibility and the demands of a chronically marginal household economy.

6. The dynamics of the urban Marshall family were reconstructed through a series of interviews with Bessie Marshall Price, Elnora Marshall Williams, Vernice Price Campbell, Junior Price, and Brenda Williams Davenport, 12–15 October 1979, Baltimore, Md.; and Balus Glover, 1 April and 6 November 1978, Promised Land, S.C. The Marshall family kinship system illustrated once again the fallacies inherent to the disorganization-breakdown thesis popularized by Daniel P. Moynihan, *The Negro Family: The Case for National Action* (Washington, D.C., 1967). While the impact of urban proletarian conditions on individuals within the kin group was at times conducive to interpretation through the Moynihan thesis, the holistic picture that emerges when the kinship system is examined as a total unit across generations lends itself to the opposite interpretation. The couples who formed stable nuclear family groups within the kin system played a pivotal role, enhancing and promoting stability for the individuals less capable of coping effectively with the changed circumstances. These data further reinforce the perspective already well documented by Herbert G. Gutman, *The Black Family in Slavery and Freedom* (New York, 1976); Joyce Ladner, *Tomorrow's Tomorrow: The Black Woman* (Garden City, N.J., 1972); and Carol B. Stack, *All Our Kin* (New York, 1974).

7. Interview with Sarah Price Robinson, 15 October 1979, Baltimore, Md.

8. Interview with Kevin Davenport, 16 October 1979, Baltimore, Md.

Epilogue

1. Interviews with Peggy Evans and Brenda Norman, 13 December 1978, Greenwood, S.C.; and W. Neal Norman, Jr. and Elestine Smith Norman, 31 October 1979, Promised Land, S.C.

2. The 1967 voter registration was described by Joe T. Ligon, Jr., 4 November 1977, Verdery, S.C.; and this recounting follows his description unless otherwise noted.

3. Interview with Elese Morton Smith, 5 November 1977, Promised Land, S.C.

4. Interviews with Amos Wells, Sr., 14 July 1978, Promised Land, S.C.; and Amos Wells, Jr., 1 July 1980, Anderson, S.C.

5. Interviews with Claretta Donaldson, 10 June 1978, Promised Land, S.C.; Peggy Evans and Brenda Norman, 13 December 1978, Greenwood, S.C.; Joe T. Ligon, Jr., 4 November 1977, Verdery, S.C.; and W. Neal Norman, Jr. and Elestine Smith Norman, 31 October 1979, Promised Land, S.C. The Greenwood County School District was not willing to discuss this event or to make their records available for documentation.

6. All post-1970 demographic data for Promised Land were gathered in a random sample household survey conducted during 1978 as a part of this research project (hereafter cited as 1978 Survey).

7. Author's observations, 1977–1980.

8. W. Neal Norman, Jr. at Mt. Zion Meeting, 6 June 1978, Promised Land, S.C.

9. Burnice Evans Norman and Lilly Wims Evans at Mt. Zion Meeting, 6 June 1978, Promised Land, S.C.

10. Burnice Evans Norman at Mt. Zion Meeting, 6 June 1978, Promise Land, S.C.

11. Greenwood, S.C. *Index-Journal*, 23 November 1964, clipping provided by Rufus Nash, Promised Land, S.C. The Mt. Zion remodeling project was initiated during the course of this research and, while near completion now, has posed several financial

crises between 1978 and 1980. The church was unable to obtain financing from any of the local banks and has been forced to solicit cash contributions on a regular and ongoing basis just to purchase materials. While the majority of the money was raised within the Mt. Zion congregation, there has been a cash flow from the North, sent home by former residents.

12. W. Neal Norman, Jr., Balus Glover, Burnice Evans Norman, and Augustus White, Sr. at Mt. Zion Meeting, 6 June 1978, Promised Land, S.C.

13. W. Neal Norman, Jr. and Elestine Smith Norman, 31 October 1979, Promised Land, S.C.; and Wilbert Lewis, "The Promise Land Community, A Survey of Contemporary Community Needs" (Paper, Department of Social Work, University of South Carolina, 1977).

14. Wilbert Lewis, "The Promise Land Community"; and 1978 Survey.

15. Interview with Cora Frazier Hall, 17 March 1978, Promised Land, S.C.; and 1978 Survey.

16. Interview with Jimmy Nicholson, 4 December 1978, Greenwood, S.C.; and 1978 Survey.

17. 1978 Survey.

18. Peggy Evans and Brenda Norman, 13 December 1978, Greenwood, S.C.; and 1978 Survey.

19. Interview with Theresa Morton Moragne, 29 July 1978, Promised Land, S.C.; and 1978 Survey.

20. 1978 Survey.

21. Ibid.; Wilbert Lewis, "The Promise Land Community."

22. 1978 Survey; and interview with Cora Frazier Hall, 17 March 1978, Promise Land, S.C.

Essay on Sources and Methodology

The Promised Land community represents a corner of American life relatively unexplored by the social sciences. The reasons for this neglect of rural southern Negro history and culture are tied in part to a belief that there are not sufficient data available to warrant objective scholarly inquiry into the topic. In the case of Promised Land, this belief proved unfounded. While scattered and fragmented, information on the community was rich and abundant, more than sufficient to document the history of the community and its residents. Some sources were those that provide the conventional data for both historical and sociological research: government documents; state and local tax and school records; probate files; census manuscripts; church records; and financial accounts—all standard indices of institutional structures and functions. This body of material established the framework and context of life at Promised Land and provided an objective picture of the ways in which that setting changed over time.

A second body of data, drawn from less conventional sources, were the reflections and memories of community residents. Variously labeled oral history, openended interviews, and ethnography, this material probed more intimate and private aspects of community life. Transcending cultural mythology and idiosyncratic narrative, this material interpreted and explained the community's institutional framework. It established the cultural meaning of kinship bonds, the relationships between parents and their children, the courtship patterns and religious rituals that wove daily routines into coherent and enduring sociocultural patterns. In so doing, it guided and enriched a perspective otherwise impoverished by objectivity.

Sources

The origins of the Promised Land community were squarely centered in the events and conditions of the Reconstruction South. E. Merton Coulter, *The South During Reconstruction*, provides a sweeping account of the period and the region; and his work is complemented by a number of excellent monographs detailing conditions in South Carolina during Reconstruction: Martin Abbott, *The Freedman's Bureau in South Carolina*; Willie Lee Rose, *Rehearsal for Reconstruction, The Port Royal Experiment*; Francis B. Simpkins and R. H. Woody, *South Carolina During Reconstruction*; A. A. Taylor, *The Negro in South Carolina During Reconstruction*; and Joel Williamson, *After Slavery*. Although none of these mentions the Promised Land community specifically, together they establish a comprehensive description of conditions in the state during the years of Reconstruction and explain the ways in which those conditions affected the state's Negro population.

Carol R. Bleser, *The Promised Land, The History of the South Carolina Land Commission*, locates the specific origins of the community in her analysis of the Land Commission and its role in South Carolina's attempt to implement a land redistribution program. The importance of the community is clearly vested in its beginnings as a body of landowning freedpeople, putting down their roots on soil once owned by white planters and cultivated by slaves. The original fifty contiguous farms represent the fulfillment of a dream held by hundreds of thousands of freedpeople but denied to most. The intensity of this dream, its origins, and its destruction, a more common outcome for freedpeople, are surveyed by: Louis S. Gerteis, *From Contraband to Freedman*; Edward Magdol, *A Right to the Land*; and Claude F. Oubre, *Forty Acres and a Mule.*

Within the framework of Reconstruction politics, the records of the South Carolina Land Commission and the state superintendent of education detail the early ties between Promised Land and the government bureaucracy that gave birth to it. The inherent dangers faced by freedpeople there, as elsewhere in the South, are apparent in the records of the Bureau of Freedmen, Refugees, and Abandoned Lands. Weekly and sometimes daily reports from the Abbeville bureau office to district headquarters recount by name the Negro victims of various attacks and outrages and detail the specific circumstances surrounding each violent incident. These records implicitly clarify the links between Reconstruction politics and land acquisition for Promised Land settlers. Among the bureau records are letters from various groups of freedpeople requesting aid for the establishment of churches and schools, the major institutional centers of many emerging Negro communities. Promised Land residents duly filed their requests for assistance and for protection against racial violence along with other freedpeople.

The structure of family life and the internal economic activities of community residents are made clear in the manuscripts of the agricultural and household censuses. County records, particularly those of the offices of the clerk of court and the judge of probate, yield additional details of the dynamics within the community. Often written by community residents, the land descriptions, wills, petitions, and affidavits contained within these records document the routines of land exchange and inheritance and also provide valuable insights into literacy levels and the relationships of friendship and kinship that surrounded the transmissions of property. The county records are particularly valuable in a study such as this because they provide a consistent record of activities and events over the life of the community and, unlike the federal census manuscripts, remain a part of the public record into the present.

Local newspapers typically provide substantial data for community studies. In the case of Promised Land the local newspapers were less important than other data sources. Owned and edited by white men, and dependent on a white readership, the papers reported few activities within the Negro community. The Abbeville *Press* and later the Greenwood *Index-Journal*, however, regularly carried lists of tax delinquents, candidates for public office, local political appointees to positions such as precinct manager, persons charged locally with crimes, and jurors for county and district court sessions. By their nature these lists were biracial and provided occasional information about the activities of Promised Land residents.

The community supplied two important sources of data for the period: the records of the Mt. Zion African Methodist Episcopal Church that included minutes of Sunday School Board meetings, Sunday School rosters, and financial accounts; and the memories and interpretations of events that swirled around the little community. Both were fragmented, but were vital parts of a completed picture of life in Promised Land during the years immediately following its establishment. The church records provided an index of internal social organization, community philanthropy and morality, and techniques of social control. The memories of those early days, as the original settlers conveyed them to their children and grandchildren, assessed the quality of life at Promised Land, revealing the nature of what was good and what was bad, what was important and what was not particularly relevant to the freedpeople who forged the community. These data complement and enrich the documentary sources. They both humanize and personalize the setting.

During the final quarter of the nineteenth century, the years of Democratic Redemption in the South, Promised Land residents struggled along, coping collectively with oppressive political and social conditions and economic hardships that confronted all rural southern Negroes. The economic and political foundations of the situation are well explained in C. Vann Woodward, *The Origins of the New South*; and the direct effect on South Carolina Negroes is clarified in George B. Tindall, *South Carolina Negroes, 1877–1900*. The details of the final years of the century at Promised Land are readily obtainable in county records and the federal manuscript censuses. Oral descriptions for the period fail to reinforce the general sense of powerlessness and hopelessness portrayed as typical of the late nineteenth-century Negro experience. Instead, the oral accounts reflect a cohesive and well-defined community of farmers. Promised Land residents, clustered as families and kin groups, focused their attention on an internal community structure, on work, family, church, and school. Certainly the removal of wider options and opportunities explained this increased innerdirectedness of community life, but without the oral accounts there would be no basis for knowing or understanding the specific adaptive strategies community residents chose as a collective response to these conditions.

These adaptive strategies continued into the early years of the twentieth century and explain, in part, the strength of much internal social organization in the community. Domestic life, religious organization, community philanthropy, and economic circumstances described in church and county records were all shaped in part by nineteenth-century adaptive behaviors. The similarities between life at Promised Land and the cultural patterns of a broader Negro population are apparent through the detailed data of *The Atlanta University Studies* edited by W.E.B. DuBois. The DuBois surveys and reports demonstrate direct institutional parallels to life at Promised Land as reflected in the Mt. Zion documents, the minutes of the Promised Land Union Burrial Aid Society, and the Little River Association. Promised Land was a microcosm of rural Negro life and culture. The social, religious, and economic features of the community; the relative importance of school and church; the centrality of family and kinship; and the hardships of farming first framed by the documentary sources are reinforced in oral descriptions by the men and women who lived their day-to-day routines within the community. These data convey the tenor of community life in a manner not possible through the use of documents alone.

Promised Land, like the entire region, anticipated by two decades the overriding theme of early twentieth-century Negro history, emigration from the South. The origins of this great movement of peoples are described in Carter G. Woodson, *A Century of Negro Migration*, and Nell Irvin Painter, *The Exodusters, Black Migration to Kansas After Reconstruction*. Those same conditions are reflected in the tax and land records at Promised Land. They are sustained by memories of aunts and uncles who moved away from the community to both the North and the West. That those memories have survived for more than half a century, transmitted to a second and then a third generation of community residents, is an important comment on the nature of community life. They are one index of the vital and enduring bonds of kinship documented by Herbert G. Gutman, *The Black Family in Slavery and Freedom*, as a central feature of Negro culture.

Poverty and the constant threat of violence dominated all aspects of life for southern Negroes throughout the early years of the twentieth century. *The Crisis* and the Chicago *Defender* document this insidious crime. The conditions surrounding the near epidemic nature of interracial violence during the period are examined in Arthur Raper, *The Tragedy of Lynching*; and the immediate impact of these circumstances on community life and social organization at Promised Land is related through the descriptions of the men and women who lived under those conditions. The practical responses of a people under constant threat of attack and assault, but intent upon survival, is not apparent in conventional sources. That insight remains imbedded in oral accounts.

Poverty compounded the problems imposed by violence on southern Negroes, and migration from the South escalated. The men and women of Promised Land participated in the mass exodus and their motives did not differ substantially from those described in Clyde Kiser, *Sea Island to City*; Louise V. Kennedy, *The Negro Peasant Turns Cityward*; and Florette Henri, *Black Migration, Movement North, 1900–1920*. Life in the urban North as these migrants confronted it is well described in Allan H. Spear, *Black Chicago*; St. Clair Drake and Horace Cayton, *Black Metropolis*; Claude McKay, *Home to Harlem*; T.J. Woofter, *Negro Problems in Cities*; Gilbert Osofsky, *Harlem: The Making of a Ghetto*; and Elliot Redwick, *From Plantation to Ghetto*.

The pathology of Negro urban life is a theme that dominates much of this literature. The personal and social trauma of migration is moderated for Promised Land migrants, and probably for many other Southern Negroes as well, by an ongoing but relatively undocumented reciprocity between country and city. The extension of kinship and friendship recounted by both the migrants and those who stayed at Promised Land are data not reflected in more objective documentary sources, yet they are central to an understanding of the experiences of Promised Land natives living in both the North and the South during this period. Like other adaptive strategies, they are subtle and delicate variations masked by documentary sources that often distort and objectify the intrinsic qualities of the human experience.

World War I, the Great Depression, the New Deal, and World War II are great divides in the life of the region and the nation—events skillfully detailed and explained in George B. Tindall, *The Emergence of the New South*. The distinctions between these periods, however, are blurred at Promised Land; and comparison of the perspectives established by conventional data sources and oral accounts of community residents illustrates that contrast. Young men from Promised Land were drafted into the Army, trained, and sent into active duty under conditions similar to those described by Arthur E. Barbeau and Florette Henri, *The Unknown Soldiers*; Monroe Mason and Arthur Furr, *The American Negro with the Red Hand of France*; and Emmett J. Scott, *Scott's Official History of the American Negro in the World War*. Yet, oral accounts of the war years indicate that the absence of these young soldiers from the community was perceived by residents no differently than if they had migrated north. The Great War was of little consequence to a people preoccupied with local conditions. Without radios and with only limited access to a national press, Promised Land residents generally failed to realize the relationship between their own increased opportunities for work and the global conflict.

The prosperity of the war years was short lived for all Americans, and even more abbreviated for Negro farmers, who generally did not benefit from the decade of postwar affluence. The conditions that circumscribed life for rural Negroes were more protracted than the conditions surrounding the Great Depression, although the depression heightened and exaggerated their poverty. These conditions and subsequent New Deal programs aimed at rectifying them have been discussed and analyzed from many perspectives. Among those most relevant to life at Promised Land are David Conrad, *The Forgotten Farmers*; Charles S. Johnson, *Growing Up in the Black Belt, Negro Youth in the Rural South*; Charles S. Johnson, Edwin R. Embree and W. W. Alexander, *The Collapse of Cotton Tenancy*; Hortense Powdermaker, *After Freedom*; Arthur Raper and Ira De A. Ried, *Sharecroppers All*; Raymond Wolter, *Negroes and the Great Depression*; and T.J. Woofter, *Black Yeomanry*. Additional details of the economic conditions that persisted among southern Negroes in rural areas were issued by a variety of government agencies, particularly the United States Department of Agriculture and, more specifically local, by the South Carolina Board of Agriculture and the state Commission of Agriculture, Commerce and Industry. All portray a level of extreme poverty evident at Promised Land and reflected in local tax and land transfer records, church account books, and the county school board expenditure records. Yet, those aspects of life that retained primary importance for community residents were only indirectly tied to their poverty. The important and sustaining elements of community life were the immediate products of the community's own creation: its churches and schools; the circles of kinship that gave meaning and security to an otherwise marginal economic existence. Birth and death, courtship and marriage, baseball games and church turn-outs mitigated poverty at Promised Land.

The end of the Great Depression coincided at Promised Land, as it did elsewhere in the nation, with the onset of World War II. Again, as it had more than two decades earlier, the Army siphoned young men away from the community. Their military experiences were broadening ones as described in Ulysses Lee, *The Employment of Negro Troops, The United States Army in World War II: Special Studies*; Seymour J. Schoenfeld, *The Negro in the Armed Forces*; and Neil Wynn, *The Afro-American and the Second World War*. This time the war seemed more immediate to community residents. Local documents attested to a certain upbeat tempo of life at Promised Land. Land transfers and school expenditures increased, and the financial affairs of Mt. Zion also were marked by a new prosperity. Often the dollars that financed each of these arrived in the community by mail, sent by soldiers to their families back home.

Oral accounts recall changes in the community environment as well as an awareness of the war that was absent from recollections of the World War I period. Work opportunities and patterns were viewed as directly linked to national and international events. Travel between Promised Land and the North intensified in both directions. Oral accounts of life during the 1940's and 1950's show that, while the values of previous generations were constant, community residents were deeply affected in other ways by the altered circumstances of their times. Their outlook on life and their expectations for themselves and their children were shaped now by the influences of northern kin and by the experiences of discharged soldiers. Both groups returned to Promised Land with a new kind of sophistication and heightened demands for racial equality, for better schools, work that paid a living wage, equity and dignity in their personal lives.

The postwar years at Promised Land continued the economic trends begun during the war years. Local records, tax assessments, land sales, church financial accounts, and oral histories after the mid-1940's generally reinforce this aspect of community life. Oral accounts, however, reveal a dimension of life at Promised Land not apparent in the documentary sources, an increasing dissatisfaction with the conditions shaped by a century or more of racism. Emancipation and the events of the 1870's fulfilled only in part the promises of freedom, and community residents moved during the 1960's to seize and reclaim as their own that larger definition of equality. While less than militant in their changing perspective, the men and women of Promised Land abandoned the superficial obsequiousness that had shielded them in previous decades. Their own words provide the only vehicle for conveying the depth and power of this change.

Methodology

Data, whatever their source, are rendered useful to the research enterprise through analysis and orderly interpretation. The strategies by which these steps proceed are governed only in part by the nature of the data at hand, for this is a condition subject to some degree of manipulation. They are shaped as well by the design of the research and by the questions posed within that design. Historical research assumes a comparison over time of a set of comparable and sometimes continuous variables. Quantification and statistical description of those variables holds three fundamental advantages in the tasks of analysis and interpretation. It imposes precision, specificity, and uniformity on the data.

The basic requirements of statistical analysis, however, require a certain rigor of method that often discourages those engaged in historical research. These requirements, particularly as applied to the use of parametric statistical procedures, are viewed as insurmountable obstacles by those confronted with missing data sets, lack of control over samples, and irregularity of measurement indices. Each of these conditions challenges the validity of statistical analysis. Nevertheless, statistical description and analysis remain the single best approach toward fulfillment of the basic aims of historical research: establishing a valid and reliable basis for objective consideration of information; generalization of that information from a limited group to a broader population; and comparison over time.

Meaningful statistical analysis begins early in the research enterprise, as data are gathered from various sources. One of the central assumptions of statistical analysis, randomization, is established in part by the sampling procedures employed to extract orderly data sets. This poses a major methodological problem for historians, whose task is often hampered by a lack of control over sources. Representativeness and sampling bias are major issues under these conditions; and these issues existed with respect to much of the documentary data used in this study, particularly with the manuscript census data, local tax and school records, and the Mt. Zion records.

The tax records were relatively complete over time and because of this were the least problematic of the documentary sources. They were randomly sampled by year; and, because there were no racial designations for individual taxpayers, a 10 percent population pool was randomly selected within the Promised Land tax district. There were relatively few white families living in the area (less than 5 percent of the total district population), and randomization was the only appropriate strategy for selection of a taxpaying sample of community residents. Although there is probably some statistical inflation as a result of a small but unidentified white group in this sample, it was used to establish the basic demographic profile of community financial and economic structures as well as the landowning-nonlandowning contrasts.

The census manuscripts were less problematic than the tax records in some ways, more so in others. They provided racial designations that eliminated white households from the sample. Organized by enumeration districts, which were somewhat larger in population size than county-designated tax districts, the manuscripts contained no inherent criteria for determining the community population limits. With only a list of landowners, any limitation of community size was to some degree arbitrary and was aided in part by cross-referencing the census manuscripts with the tax records. Land-owning households were located in the manuscripts and they, along with all the listings of nonlandowning households interspersed among them, the five households immediately preceding the appearance of the first landowner on the listing, and the five immediately following the last listed landowner in the sequence, were defined a priori as the parameters of community residents. A similar strategy was applied to the examination. Random sampling within this predefined population provided the basis for all statistical analysis of economic conditions and household structures in the community during the nineteenth century.

Another type of sampling problem accompanied the use of the Mt. Zion records. Those data were fragmented, often with as much as a decade of records missing from the data set. Here random sampling was conducted within available time periods. A statistical correlate to the church data was derived from the more constant tax records and regressions used to estimate missing data. This proved an effective strategy for solving a common dilemma of historical research and was particularly important in the case of Promised Land. There the churches provided the only index of internal economic activities. There were no records or accounts of any sort for the various small community businesses, and the link between internal economics and conditions in a larger social setting could be established only through patterns of church contributions and financial expenditures.

Randomization is but one step in a larger process by which the data extracted from documentary sources are rendered analyzable through statistical methods. Those data must meet other assumptions with regard to distribution and independence of samples. These assumptions are easily verified through preliminary statistical procedures; standard checks for skewness and kurtosis as well as Bartlett's test for homogeneity of variance established the usability of samples. Intervality of data was assumed whenever possible because of the greater flexibility such a data level afforded in statistical analysis. While it was not necessary in these data, intervality can sometimes be forced by logarithmic transformations when data fail to meet the assumptions of normal distributions. In the Promised Land data Z tests were employed for checks of statistical significance more often than t-tests to assure flexibility when violations of assumptions seemed likely or when checks against a hypothetical standard error were not feasible.

The nature of these assumptions and cogent guidance in statistical decision-making is discussed in a variety of sources. Among the most useful are Hubert M. Blalock, *Social Statistics*; William Cochran, *Sampling Techniques*; George A. Ferguson, *Statistical Analysis in Psychology and Education*; John H. Mueller, Karl F. Schuessler and Herbert L. Costner, *Statistical Reasoning in Sociology*; and Quinn McNemar, *Psychological Statistics*. In cases where violation of assumptions prevents the use of parametric statistics, alternative approaches are offered and clearly explained in both Eugene S. Edgington, *Statistical Inference: The Distribution-Free Approach*, and Sidney Siegel, *Nonparametric Statistics for the Behavioral Sciences*. The flexibility and variety of statistical applications in historical study is well illustrated in Gennett Dyke and Jean Walters MacCluer, *Computer Simulation in Human Population Studies*, and Kenneth W. Wachter, Eugene A. Hammel and Peter Laslett, *Statistical Studies of Historical Social Structure*.

Oral sources pose methodological problems that differ only in substance from those associated with the use of documentary sources. Central among these are issues related to content analysis, transcription and editorial procedures, and sampling. These, like the methodological problems associated with quantification and statistical analysis, are resolved by establishing a priori standards and procedural criteria by which the material will be ordered and analyzed.

Content analysis provides a number of useful strategies that have direct application to the exploitation of oral sources in historical research. Although interviewing rarely progresses in an orderly fashion, most oral accounts, particularly when gathered from within a single population such as the Promised Land community, address a uniform set of topics. Once identified, the topical consistencies provide the structure within which oral accounts are transcribed and compared. Consistencies, contrasts, areas of agreement and disagreement emerge establishing an analytic framework that is only in part imposed by external constraints. Particularly helpful in shaping interview strategies toward this end are Louis Gottschalk, Clude Kluckhohn and Robert Angell, *The Use of Personal Documents in History, Anthropology and Sociology*; Robert K. Merton, Marjorie Fiske and Patricia L. Kendall, *The Focused Interview*; and S.A. Richardson et al., *Interviewing*. Paul F. Lazarsfeld, Bernard Berelson and Hazel Gaudet, *The People's Choice: How the Voter Makes up His Mind in a Presidential Campaign*, and William H. Chafe, *Civilities and Civil Rights*, provide excellent examples of the relationship between interviewing strategies and social research; and Ithia de Sola Pool, *Trends in Content Analysis*, surveys the basic problems and strategies designed to solve those problems in content analytic research.

Cultural anthropologists and ethnographers have long recognized the utility of oral sources in describing and explaining the social environments of groups which have few or no written records. The particular applicability of this approach to Afro-American studies, long written from a decidedly white bias, is made clear in both Theodore Rosengarten, *All God's Dangers*, and Nell Irvin Painter, *The Narrative of Hosea Hudson*. Both provided focus for the narratives of Promised Land residents and guidance in shaping those narratives into usable data. Particularly important within this process was the editorial treatment of the language structures of informants. Following these precedents, no attempt was made to replicate dialect in the transcription of the Promised Land interviews although grammatical structures were retained intact.

The extent to which any set of interview data are representative of a population is always open to question, although the matter can be largely resolved by seeking an understanding of the interplay between cultural patterns and individual behavior within the research design. Strategies for the pursuit of this end are discussed in Harold Garfinkel, *Studies in Ethnomethodology*; E.J. Webb et al., *Unobstusive Measures*; and Arthur J. Vidich, Joseph Bensman and Maurice R. Stein, *Reflections on Community Studies*. The biography of a community, like the biography of an individual, must explore social and demographic frameworks, culturally prescribed behaviors and expectations, and the realities of day-to-day routines. At Promised Land the nexus between these elements of social life were illuminated by the oral sources, and herein lies the value of their contribution to a larger research enterprise.

Index

Abortion, 157
Adolescence: apprenticeship during, 151; migration during, 113; pregnancy during, 157; social life during, 155–56
Agriculture. *See* Farming; Land
Aiken, Osburn, 63
Atlanta, migration to, 91, 103, 173, 177, 183–84
Atlanta Life Insurance Company, 96
Baltimore, migration to, 210–12, 247–54
Baptist Educational Society and Union, 62
Birth Control, techniques of, 156
Bradley: Harriet, 57, 58; W.L., 68, 69, 77, 210, 236
Brewer Normal School, 135, 213, 234
Brown, Joe, 113
Bulow, Samuel, 28, 53, 55, 57, 58
Burt: Adeline, 55; James, 55, 67; Joe Lee, 194; Mary, 103; Samuel, 28, 65, 67, 103; Sarah, 146, 161
Burton: Jacob, 57, 79, 102; Moses, 166
Campbell, Vernice Price, xv, xvi
Carter: Marion, 36; North, 36, 70, 79, 103, 109, 165, 221
Chappell: Amy Wilson, 106; Edd, 106, 165; White, 65, 68
Chicago, migration to, 179–80, 183–87
Child Birth, conditions of, 146, 161, 241
Child Labor. *See* Work
Children: attitudes toward school, 131, 134; discipline of, 116–17, 130, 148–49, 245–46; infant mortality, 145, 302 n. 1; isolation from adults, 149;

naming patterns, 147; upward mobility of urban born, 254–55
Chiles: Dave, 126; Harris, 57; Henderson, 57; Iverson, 57; J.D., 129; John, 53, 57; Lizzie, xii, 128, 129, 131, 134–36, 212–14, 223, 233, 260; Lucy, 53
Churches: and revivals, 238; as communication networks, 143–44; as social control, 81; as sponsors of social activities, 137; establishment at Promised Land, 37, 62, 137; leadership patterns in, 138–41; role in secular education, 86; schism between African Methodists and Baptists, 79. *See also* Homecoming; Social Life
Cole: Harrison, 36, 185; John, 224, 225, 227, 240
Coleman, Agnes Martin, 247
Consumer Credit, effects of, 232, 235
Cotton: Cotton Reduction Act of 1911, 109; description of growing cycle, 111–12; price trends, n. 33, 296 n. 33. *See also* Farming
Courtship, patterns of, 154–55, 159
Crossroads School for Colored, 39, 68, 75, 76
Devlin, Sarah, 68
Domestic Service: absence of in 1880, 46; as alternative to farm labor, 124–25; attitudes toward among urban migrants, 116, 184, 250; household structure of workers in 1900, 126–27; sexual exploitation in, 230; socialization of daughters into, 151
Donnelly: Carson, 27; Will, 27, 58